Noble's Party Venues Guide
First Edition

©Copyright 2000
The Noble Publishing Company
Pavillon (Publishing) Limited
The Old Corn Store
Hawkhurst
Kent TN18 5EU
Tel: 01580 752404
Fax: 01580 752604
Email: NoblePublishing@aol.com

All rights reserved.
No part of this publication may be copied, reproduced,
stored in a retrieval system or transmitted in any form
or by any means electronic, mechanic, photocopy, recording
or otherwise, without the prior permission of the publishers.

Editor: Janet Simpson

The publishers have made every effort to ensure that the information
contained in this book is correct at the time of going to press.
They cannot, however, accept any responsibility for any
errors or inaccuracies contained herein.

ISBN: 0 9528 144 47

Written and designed by Pavillon (Publishing) Ltd
Front cover illustration by Kate Chitham
Printed in the UK

FOREWORD

Noble's Guides
Impartial information for the independently minded.

Welcome to the 1st edition of Noble's Party Venues Guide, the sister publication to Noble's Wedding Venues Guide, which is now in its 5th edition. With this publication we continue our philosophy of providing impartial, factual information for our readers, while facilitating direct contact to the venues you are interested in. None of the venues in this Guide has paid for a written entry, so we have therefore been able to include a broad selection of properties, including more unusual venues and privately owned houses.

Everyone's idea of a party is slightly different, which is why it has been hard to select the right venues to include in this book. Essentially we are aiming to show you a wide selection of venues in England, Scotland, Ireland and Wales, which are suitable, and geared up for, a gathering of 10 or more people, whether it is for a wedding reception, significant anniversary or birthday celebration, or a group of friends or family looking for somewhere to celebrate Christmas, New Year, Easter, or any other special occasion.

We hope that this book will not only help you find the right venue at the right price for an event that you are already planning, but may perhaps also inspire you to organise a party or a weekend away with friends simply because there are some fantastic places to go! By bringing these venues together in one publication, we are simplifying and speeding up the task of finding the good places to go. We have spent 18 months planning and researching this publication, so we know how long it takes to get the information you need.

Our thanks go to all those venues that have completed our lengthy questionnaires or have taken the time to talk to us. We haven't included all the venues on our database and research continues as an on-going process. So, if you know of somewhere that we may not have found yet, then let us know.

Meanwhile, look out for our new publications due out in 2001 including: Noble's Big Holiday Houses; Noble's Romantic Places to Stay; and Noble's Garden Hotels, as well as our soon-to-be-launched Web site at www.NoblesGuides.com.

Enjoy!   *Janet Simpson, Editor*

HOW TO USE THIS GUIDE

FINDING YOUR REGION

Venues in England have been listed alphabetically by name within their region. Those in Scotland, Ireland and Wales have been listed alphabetically within their country section. Alongside the venue name we have included a location identifiier - postcodes in London, nearest place name in the rest of England, Scotland and Wales, and County in Ireland. If you are seeking venues in a particular county within England, see the Contents pages, where the county names are grouped into their regions.

THE INFORMATION PROVIDED

In order to include more venues, we have not included full postal addresses, although we have included all other contact information, such as telephone and fax numbers, and Email and Website addresses where appropriate.

Where possible, we have included the name the most appropriate person to deal with your enquiry. We have made every effort to make sure that this information is accurate, but inevitably people change jobs, and there will undoubtedly be changes throughout the lifetime of this book. Generally you will find that the person you need to speak to is a Functions or Events Manager/Coordinator, or the Conference and Banqueting Manager.

The Facilities and Services mentioned with each entry are those to be found **on site**, or **provided by the venue itself**. Many venues are also situated near to such facilities, or can recommend others to provide services, so we suggest that readers ask if they have any particular requirements.

Price guides are always just that, and are provided in order to give you some idea of the costs involved. They will always be subject to change and usually increase marginally each year.

We have included several properties in this Guide that are marketed by agencies (self-catering in particular), or are serviced by contract caterers. Both of these are valuable sources for further information on other venues that may not be included in this book. We have therefore provided a selective listing overleaf.

Finally, this Guide is intended as a first stop for those organising parties and events, providing sufficient, well researched information to help you shortlist possible venues for your event. We recommend that venues are contacted directly for more detailed information and, of course, availability. If possible, venues should also be visited prior to booking •

LISTINGS

AGENCIES

The Big House
T: 01823 662673
F: 01823 663558
E: party@thebighouseco.com
W: www.thebighouseco.com

Brecon Beacons Holiday Cottages
T: 01874 676 446
F: 01874 676416
E: enquiries@breconcottages.com
W: Breconcottages.com

Finlayson Hughes (Scotland)
T: 01463 226990/224707
F: 01463 716723
E: holidays@ckdfh.co.uk
W: www.ckdfh.co.uk

Large Holiday Houses (Scotland)
T: 01381 610496
F: 01381 610481
E: largeholidayhouses@cali.co.uk

CONTRACT CATERERS

Gastronomes
T: 0208 305 6800
F: 0208 305 6801

Party Ingredients
T: 0207 627 3800
F: 0207 720 6249

Searcy's
T: 0207 585 0505
F: 0207 350 1748
W: www.searcys.co.uk

Mustard Catering
T: 0207 840 5900
F: 0207 840 5929

Table Talk
T: 0207 401 3200
F: 0207 401 9500

Milburn's
T: 0208 858 7090
F: 0208 858 6395

USEFUL CONTACTS

Everyman Corporate Events
Mallory Park Racing Circuit
Kirkby Mallory
Leicestershire LE9 7QE
T: 0870 789 0888
E: everyman@pipemedia.co.uk
W: www.corporateevents.com

Redcliffe Event Management
T: 0121 454 5432

CONTENTS

Foreword 3
How To Use This Guide 5
Listings 6
Contents 7

LONDON 9

SOUTH EAST ENGLAND 28
East Sussex
Kent
Surrey
West Sussex

SOUTH OF ENGLAND 45
Berkshire
Buckinghamshire
Hampshire
Isle of Wight
Oxfordshire

WEST COUNTRY 58
Bath & North East Somerset
Bristol
Cornwall
Devon
Dorset
Isles of Scilly
Somerset
Wiltshire

EAST OF ENGLAND 76
Bedfordshire
Cambridgeshire
Essex
Hertfordshire
Lincolnshire
Norfolk
Suffolk

HEART OF ENGLAND 92
Derbyshire
Gloucestershire
Herefordshire
Leicestershire
Northamptonshire

Nottinghamshire
Rutland
Shropshire
Staffordshire
Warwickshire
West Midlands
Worcestershire

NORTH WEST 114
Cheshire
Manchester
Lancashire
Merseyside

YORKSHIRE 126
East Riding of Yorkshire
North Yorkshire
South Yorkshire
West Yorkshire

CUMBRIA 136

NORTHUMBRIA 141
Co. Durham
Northumberland
Tees Valley
Tyne & Wear

WALES 147

SCOTLAND 156

IRELAND 163

INDEX 164

NOBLE'S PARTY VENUES GUIDE 1ST EDITION

LONDON

41 Portland Place, W1
T: 020 7636 9456 or 0207 283 5057 (Caterers)
F: 020 7436 2840
W: www.novartisfound.org.uk
Contact: Functions organiser
Party Max: 120

41 Portland Place offers 5 attractive rooms for private meetings, lunches and dinners. The building is owned by the Novartis Foundation, a scientific and education charity. All of the rooms are decorated and furnished to complement the original 18th Century architecture of the building. The rooms range from the Committee Room which seats 10 up to the Reception Room which will seat 60 for a lunch or dinner, or 120 for a reception. The house is available for hire 7 days a week. Catering here is by Everson Hewett, with menus created by top chef Pierre Koffman.
Catering: In house

Price Guide: Facility hire is from £95 (1/2 day) to £350 (full day), but this is waived if a catering package is chosen. Special rates for medically related organisations.
Catering (sit down): Packages (including drinks) £26.25pp - £33.25pp + vat

Alexandra Palace, N22
T: 020 8365 2121   **F:** 020 8883 3889
Contact: Debbie Dudley, Sales Co-ordinator
Party Max: 6500 (marquee: unlimited)

This impressive Victorian Palace can accommodate even the largest of functions in style. Facilities are available in several rooms including The Palm Court (with seating for 170), The Palace Restaurant (seating 300), The West Hall (seating 2,000) and The Great Hall (seating 5,500 or accommodating 6,500 for a buffet style reception). A marquee of unlimited capacity can be sited in nearby parkland.
Catering: In house

SERVICES:
- Marriage Licence

Price Guide: Prices on application.
Catering (sit down): from £30.50pp

Amadeus Centre, W9
T: 020 7286 1686   **F:** 020 7266 1225
E: amadeus@amadeuscentre.co.uk
W: www.amadeuscentre.co.uk
Contact: Raynler Platings, General Manager
Party Max: 250

The Amadeus Centre, described as an enchanting building with great individuality, is a former Victorian chapel. The Upper Hall is an elegant room for parties, while the Lower Hall, featuring a fine vaulted ceiling, is a suitable setting for pre-dinner drinks or as a late night dance area. While there is an experienced in-house catering team here, outside caterers are also welcome. An in-house decoration and theming service is also available.
Catering: In house/Contract (any)

SERVICES:
- Exclusive Use   • Flowers   • Disco/Dance
- Live Music   • Entertainers   • Performance Area

Price Guide: £1000
Catering (sit down): from £29.50pp
Catering (buffet): from £20pp

Apsley House, W1
T: 020 7499 5676   **F:** 020 7493 6576
Contact: Banqueting & Event Manager
Party Max: 200

Apsley House was designed by Robert Adam in 1771-8 and subsequently enlarged by the Duke of Wellington in 1817. The house is now The Wellington Musuem and home to old masters by Velazquez, Goya, Rubens and de Hooch amongst others, as well as collections of sculpture, silver, furniture and memorabilia.
Catering: Contract approved list

Price Guide: Prices on application.

Armourers' & Brasiers' Hall, EC2
T: 020 7256 5335   **F:** 020 7606 7481
Contact: John Barrett, Comptroller
Party Max: 125

Armourers' Hall is one of the few buildings that escaped the Great Fire of 1666. In 1795 the Hall was enlarged, and in 1839 the building was rebuilt completely. Rooms within the building that are available for hire include The Livery Hall, The Drawing Room and the Court Room. Original features of this, now Grade II listed, building include an 18th Century chandelier, complete with candles, which can be used for candlelit dinners.
Catering: Contract approved list

SERVICES:
- Exclusive Use   • Flowers   • Toastmaster

Price Guide: Room hire starts at £80 room hire for the Livery Dining room to £850 for the evening hire of the Hall.
Catering (sit down): POA
Catering (buffet): POA

BAFTA, W1
T: 020 7292 5800   **F:** 020 7734 1009
E: amyn@bafta.org
W: www.bafta.org
Contact: Amy Minyard, Corporate Events Coordinator
Party Max: 200

BAFTA is housed in a Grade II listed building called The Institute of Painters in Watercolours. It is centrally located in London on Piccadilly. It has 2 theatres and a dining room with a Member's Club bar and food facilities. Contract caterers here are Roux Fine Dining.
Catering: In house

FACILITIES:
- Theatres

SERVICES:
- Exclusive Use   • Marriage Licence   • Piped Music
- Performance Area

Price Guide: Hire rates on application.
Catering (sit down): from £23.50pp
Catering (buffet): from £14pp

LONDON

Bank of England Sports Centre, SW15
T: 020 7585 0505   **F:** 020 7350 1748
W: www.searcys.co.uk
Contact: Banqueting Manager
Party Max: 200

Situated in 42 acres of sporting fields and woodland, the Bank of England Sports Centre has a luxury health centre, swimming pool, conference centre, and banqueting facilities. Catering here is by Searcy's.
Catering: Contract approved list

Price Guide: Approximately £500

Banqueting House, SW1
T: 0207 839 3787 – 020 7839 7569   **F:** 020 7930 8268
Contact: Fiona Thompson
Party Max: 500

The Banqueting House is the only remaining complete building of Whitehall Palace. Designed by Inigo Jones for James I and completed in 1622, the Banqueting House was originally built for occasions of state, plays and masques. The Banqueting House later became the scene of Charles I's execution. Today the Banqueting House is a popular visitor attraction and one of the finest banqueting venues in London, playing host to many royal and society occasions.
Catering: In house/Contract approved list

Price Guide: Prices on application.
Catering (sit down): POA

Barbican Arts & Conference Centre, EC2
T: 020 7382 7246   **F:** 020 7382 7247
Contact: Clare Sbiti, Sales Manager
Party Max: 500

This well known arts centre in the City of London offers several rooms for private or corporate entertaining including an art gallery, and a wonderful conservatory, which is home to finches, quails, exotic fish and over 2,000 species of tropical plants and trees.
Catering: Contract approved list/In house

FACILITIES:
- Theatres
- Cinemas
- Art Gallery

SERVICES:
- Marriage Licence
- Performance Area

Price Guide: £650 - £3000
Catering (sit down): from £30pp
Catering (buffet): from £20pp

Barn Hotel, HA4
T: 01895 636057   **F:** 01895 638379
Contact: Mr Serrano, General Manager
Party Max: 500 (marquee: 500)   Bedrooms: 250

The Barn Hotel is a 17th Century listed building set in 2 acres of landscaped rose gardens. The hotel offers a honeymoon suite with double sunken whirlpool bath, as well as four poster suites with Jacuzzis.
Catering: In house

SERVICES:
- Marriage Licence

Price Guide: Prices on application
Catering (sit down): from £22.95pp
Catering (buffet): from £9.50pp

Belvedere Restaurant, W8
T: 020 7602 1238/020 7734 7333   **F:** 020 7610 4382
Contact: Catherine Cyzer, Function Co-ordinator/Manager
Party Max: 250 (marquee: 200)

The Belvedere Restaurant and orangery is housed in a listed building in the grounds of Holland Park. This has been the venue for many society weddings and events, all held in the strictest confidence. A late night drinking licence can be applied for if required. Other services can be organised by this venue, such as themes, fireworks and transport.
Catering: In house

SERVICES:
- Marriage Licence
- Fireworks
- Themeing

Price Guide: Prices on application
Catering (sit down): from £35pp

Berkeley Hotel, SW1
T: 020 7235 6000   **F:** 020 7823 1743
Contact: Yola Drage, Banqueting
Party Max: 450   Bedrooms: 156

Three rooms are available for functions at this central London hotel: the Waterloo Room, which seats 20, the Belgravia Room (40) and the Ballroom (250).
Catering: In house

SERVICES:
- Marriage Licence

Price Guide: Prices on application.
Catering (sit down): £42.50pp

Blackheath Halls, SE3
T: 020 8318 9758   **F:** 020 8852 5154
E: mail@blackheathhalls.com   **W:** www.blackheathhalls.com
Contact: Jenni Darwin, Operations Manager
Party Max: 1000

These concert halls are housed in a Grade II listed building near the centre of Blackheath. Three function rooms are available for receptions, from the intimate Cafe Bar to the Grand Hall. The venue can offer in-house catering for smaller parties and has a list of recommended caterers for more formal events. You may also use your own caterers.
Catering: Contract (any)/Self catering

SERVICES:
- Marriage Licence

Price Guide: Prices on application.
Catering (sit down): from £25pp
Catering (buffet): from £20pp

Bramah Museum of Tea & Coffee, SE1
T: 020 7378 0222   **Contact:** Mr Bramah
Party Max: 200

LONDON

This modern Museum of unusual tea and coffee pots is housed in a converted 1930's warehouse. This venue is only available between 6.30pm and 10.30pm for cocktail and buffet functions.
Catering: In house

Price Guide: £500 - £1000

The Brewery, EC1
T: 020 7638 8811 **F:** 020 7638 5713
E: parties@chiswellstreet.com
W: www.thebrewery.chiswellstreet.com
Contact: Chris Lynn, Regional Sales Manager
Party Max: 900 (marquee: 150)

The Brewery offers an inimitable blend of history, tradition and contemporary hospitality in the heart of the City of London. It is an unique and prestigious venue for large or small events, with a choice of 9 versatile, well-equipped rooms.
Catering: Contract approved list

SERVICES:
• Exclusive Use
Price Guide: Prices range from £1250 to £6200.
Catering (sit down): from £39.50pp
Catering (buffet): from £39.50pp

British Museum, WC1
T: 020 7323 8128/8136
Contact: Cathy Brannon or Sarah Wray
Party Max: 800

This majestic building, refurbished in 2000 and now featuring a splendid glass dome over a former courtyard, is perfect for prestigious occasions. The museum offers a selection of galleries for functions.
Catering: Contract approved list

Price Guide: from £5000

Burgh House, NW3
T: 020 7431 0144
F: 020 7435 8817
E: burghhouse@talk21.com
Contact: Helen Wilson, General Manager
Party Max: 90

This is a Queen Anne Grade I listed building, erected in 1703 and extended in the 1720s. It is located in the heart of Old Hampstead. Features include original panelling, fine 'barley sugar' staircase ballusters and a Music Room with panelling from the adjacent Weatherall House (now demolished) The house also contains an art gallery while the first floor is Hampstead's local history museum.
Catering: In house

FACILITIES:
• Art Gallery
SERVICES:
• Exclusive Use   • Marriage Licence   • Performance Area
Price Guide: £250 - £700
Catering (sit down): POA
Catering (buffet): POA

Café de Paris, W1
T: 020 7734 7700 **F:** 020 7287 4861
E: parties@cafedeparis.com **W:** www.cafedeparis.com
Contact: Michelle 020 7935 5534, Events
Party Max: 500

Sited near Leicester Square, the exclusive Café de Paris is glamorously decorated in the style of the SS Lucitania. The restaurant is situated on the balcony and features a VIP table where diners are apparently presented with a minimum bill of £1,000.
Catering: In house

SERVICES:
• Marriage Licence
Price Guide: Prices on application.
Catering (sit down): POA
Catering (buffet): POA

Cambridge Cottage, TW9
T: 020 8332 5641 **F:** 020 8332 5632
E: K.Innes@rbgkew.org.uk
Contact: Karen Innes, Events Manager
Party Max: 80

Cambridge Cottage, a Grade II listed 18th century building, is set in over 300 acres of the famous Kew Gardens. The Gallery at Cambridge Cottage can house receptions of up to 80 for a seated dinner and 120 for a buffet. The venue has a list of approved caterers. Guests can enjoy an intimate reception here surrounded by an exhibition of fine botanical paintings.
Catering: Contract approved list

SERVICES:
• Marriage Licence
Price Guide: Prices on application.
Catering (sit down): POA
Catering (buffet): POA

Canning House, SW1
T: 020 7235 2303
Contact: Mrs Bianca Farrant
Party Max: 150

Canning House offers a large, high ceilinged, L-shaped reception room on the the first floor of this Georgian building.
Catering: Self catering

Price Guide: £550 - £800

Cannizaro House, SW19
T: 020 8879 1464 **F:** 020 8879 7338
Contact: Katy Whitby, Banqueting
Party Max: 110   *Bedrooms: 45*

Cannizaro House, a Georgian mansion on the edge of Wimbledon Common, claims to be London's first country house hotel. Receptions can be held in the elegant drawing room, which overlooks the terrace and Cannizaro Park. Drinks can be served outside if weather permits. Alternatively, a choice of private dining rooms is available. These can seat up to 100 guests for waited service, or 110 for a buffet reception. Smaller rooms, for around 40 guests, can also be hired. Award winning in-house chefs provide catering.

LONDON

Catering: In house

SERVICES:
- Marriage Licence

Price Guide: Prices on application.
Catering (sit down): from £28pp

Canonbury Academy, N1
T: 020 7359 6888
Contact: Bookings Manager
Party Max: 120

This is a refurbished 16th Century Benedictine Priory standing in its own gardens. Each room has antique furniture and all overlook the gardens. Only corporate training and seminar style events can take place here.
Catering: Contract approved list

Price Guide: £500 maximum
Catering (sit down): POA

Chelsea Old Town Hall, SW3
T: 020 7361 2220   **F:** 020 7361 3442
E: hall-let@rbkc.gov.uk   **W:** www.rbkc.gov.uk
Contact: Maxine Howitt, Conference Sales Executive
Party Max: 250

Located on the famous King's Road in one of the most fashionable parts of London, Chelsea Old Town Hall's prestigious heritage is apparent from the moment you walk through the marbled entrance hall. A classic example of late Victorian design and elegance, the listed building has easy access between 2 halls (which can be hired separately or combined), in addition to a dedicated bar and catering area. Although the Old Town Hall still houses the well known register office, both halls here are also licensed for civil marriage ceremonies.
Catering: Contract approved list

SERVICES:
- Exclusive Use
- Marriage Licence
- Cashiers
- Security Staff

Price Guide: Hire fees start at £465.

Chiswick House, W4
T: 020 8742 1978   **F:** 020 8742 3104
E: marion.doherty@english-heritage.org.uk
Contact: Marion Doherty, Hospitality Manager
Party Max: 80 (marquee: 400)

Receptions, dinners and dances are available in the house and/or marquee. The beautiful gardens surrounding the house provide a tranquil setting for any occasion. Wedding ceremonies here must take place after 4pm. This venue is not suitable for children. Meetings and conferences held here are restricted to Nov-Apr, Mondays and Tuesdays only.
Catering: In-house / Contract / Contract Approved / Self-Catering

SERVICES:
- Exclusive Use
- Marriage Licence

Price Guide: Hire fee £3000 for the evening (6.30 - 11.30pm, with wedding ceremonies at 4pm).
Catering (sit down): from £50-100pp

Churchill Intercontinental Hotel, W1
T: 020 7486 5800   **F:** 020 7299 2200
E: Churchill@interconti.com   **W:** www.interconti.com
Contact: George Brown, Conference & Banqueting Manager
Party Max: 240 (marquee: 400)   *Bedrooms: 435*

The hotel offers a choice of eight well-appointed banqueting suites, allowing it to accommodate everything from an intimate celebration for 10 or a wedding banquet for 240. The hotel also has access to the private gardens of Portman Square, ideal for a summer reception. The Churchill boasts chef Idris Caldora heading its team. Perhaps one of the most unusual events which has taken place here was the indoor Fun Fair, which included Velcro-suited human flying men, bucking Broncos and side shows.
Catering: In house

SERVICES:
- Marriage Licence
- Themeing

Price Guide: Prices on application.
Catering (sit down): POA
Catering (buffet): POA

City of London Club, EC2
T: 020 7588 8558   **F:** 020 7374 2020
E: cityclub@dial.pipex.com
Contact: Lisa Hasler, Functions Administrator
Party Max: 600

The City of London Club, housed in a listed building, dates back to 1832 and boasts members such as the Duke of Wellington and Winston Churchill. It is steeped in history and offers traditional and modern function suites for a variety of events, including wedding ceremonies, as well as an outdoor area for gatherings in warmer months. The location of this venue is central, with car parking and hotels nearby.
Catering: In house

SERVICES:
- Exclusive Use
- Marriage Licence
- Flowers
- Cake
- Toastmaster
- Disco/Dance
- Live Music
- Entertainers
- Photography
- Piped Music

Price Guide: Evening hire (from 5pm) ranges from £125 - £3000
Catering (sit down): from £25pp
Catering (buffet): from £12.50pp

Claridge's Hotel, W1
T: 020 7629 8860   **F:** 020 7872 8092
Contact: Sarah Porteous, Banqueting Manager
Party Max: 400   *Bedrooms: 75*

One of London's most famous hotels, Claridge's banqueting rooms are: the Royal Suite (250), the Ballroom (125), the Drawing Room (100), The French Salon (75) and The Mirror Room (75). They all boast superb interiors, some with original Art Deco from the 1930s. Catering is in-house, but Claridge's use contract caterers to provide for special requirements.
Catering: In house / Contract approved list
SERVICES:
- Marriage Licence

Price Guide: Prices on application.

Catering (sit down): from £38pp
Catering (buffet): from £23pp

Commonwealth Institute, W8
T: 020 7603 4535
Contact: Functions and Events
Party Max: 1500

At this venue three floors of circular galleries overlook a marble central podium, which may be used as a dance floor. Interactive displays to entertain guests include a simulated helicopter ride.
Catering: Contract approved list

Price Guide: Prices on application

Cotton's Atrium, SE1
T: 020 7940 7700   **F:** 020 7940 7711
E: marketing@samaprop.co.uk
Contact: Rochelle Kleyn, Marketing Coordinator
Party Max: 250

Cottons Central Atrium is like a vast glazed conservatory within this office building which is centrally palce tranquil, with exotic plants and trees reflected in the glass. There are views across the River Thames from this venue, which is adjacent to London Bridge City Pier. This pier can also be booked and used to transport guests. Numerous professional caterers can be recommended.
Catering: Self catering/Contract (any)

SERVICES:
• Exclusive Use
Price Guide: £1500 (exempt from VAT)

Courtauld Gallery, WC2
T: 020 7848 2549   **F:** 020 7848 2589
E: galleryinfo@courtauld.ac.uk **W:** www.courtauld.ac.uk
Contact: Fiona Moorhead, Public Affairs Administrator
Party Max: 400

This venue houses a world-famous collection of old masters; Impressionists and Post-Impressionist paintings, in a Grade I listed 18th Century building. The Gallery is a perfect setting for receptions for up to 400 guests, or for intimate, elegant dinners for a maximum of 50 guests. For obvious reasons, no smoking is permitted on the premises.
Catering: Contract approved list

SERVICES:
• Exclusive Use   • Flowers   • Live Music
Price Guide: Day rates start at £4000.
Catering (sit down): POA
Catering (buffet): POA

Dartmouth House, W1
T: 020 7493 3328   **F:** 020 7495 1886
Contact: Charlotte Berry, Sales Manager
Party Max: 150

Situated in the heart of Mayfair, Dartmouth House, home to The English-Speaking Union, offers several rooms for functions including The Ballroom (100), with Louis XIV walnut panelling, the Long Drawing Room (120), with a magnificent Adams fireplace, and the chateau-styled courtyard (80). The smallest room accommodates 20 and two rooms can be joined to accommodate 150 for dinner. Catering here is provided by Leith's, a division of the Compass group.
Catering: In house

SERVICES:
• Exclusive Use
Price Guide: Room hire rates start at £170. Whole house rental (not including the Courtyard is £200 for a Saturday or Sunday. The Courtyard prices start at £400.
Catering (sit down): from £35.95pp + vat
Catering (buffet): from £19.95pp + vat

The Design Museum, SE1
T: 020 7403 6933   **F:** 020 7378 6540
W: www.designmuseum.org
Contact: Tamasine Henderson or Neil Ormondroyde, Events Managers
Party Max: 250 (marquee: 120)

Once a 1950's warehouse, the Design Museum is just one of the many stylish warehouse renovations concentrated along the Thames. The Museum's clean modern space, marble floors and sources of natural light create a perfect ambience for a variety of events. Floor to ceiling windows open out onto the riverside walkway where guests can enjoy stunning views of Tower Bridge.
Catering: Contract approved list

SERVICES:
• Exclusive Use
Price Guide: Prices range from £400 for a half day hire of the Arthur Andersen Room to £2750 for a weekend evening's hire of the Entrance Hall and Galleries.
Catering (sit down): POA
Catering (buffet): POA

Dickens House Museum, WC1
T: 020 7405 2127   **F:** 020 7831 5175
E: dhmuseum@rmplc.co.uk   **W:** dickensmuseum.com
Contact: Mr Andrew Xavier, Curator
Party Max: 60

The Dickens House Museum was first opened to the public in 1925. It houses the world's largest collection of Dickens-related material including manuscripts, paintings by well-known 19th Century artists, furniture, personal items and memorabilia. The Georgian terraced house was Dickens' home between 1837 and 1839 and is his only London residence still standing today.
Catering: Contract (any)

SERVICES:
• Exclusive Use
Price Guide: Hire fees range from £250 - £500.

Dorchester Hotel, W1
T: 020 7629 8888   **F:** 020 7317 6363
Contact: Anke Starr, Banqueting
Party Max: 600   Bedrooms: 248

Built in 1931, the hotel's accolades include Egon Ronay 'Hotel of the Year'. Seven rooms are licensed for wedding ceremonies

LONDON

including the Orchid room, the Ballroom and the Pavilion. The hotel features in-house catering although contract caterers may be brought in providing they are from an approved list.
Catering: In house/Contract approved list

SERVICES:
- Marriage Licence

Price Guide: Prices on application.
Catering (sit down): from £38pp

Duke of York's Headquarters, SW3
T: 020 7414 5513 **F:** 020 7414 5513
E: secretary@reserve-forces-london.org.uk
Contact: Susan Stuart
Party Max: 240

This venue offers a variety of rooms and halls, all with natural daylight. Other facilities inludes a selection of dining/reception suites, which vary in size and style.
Catering: Contract (any)

SERVICES:
- Exclusive Use
- Performance Area

Price Guide: £150 - £1300 per day.
Catering (sit down): POA
Catering (buffet): POA

Duke's Hotel, SW1
T: 020 7491 4840
F: 020 7493 1264
Contact: Connie Scott, Private Dining Coordinator
Party Max: 60   Bedrooms: 64

Duke's Hotel, almost adjacent to St James's Palace, is a traditional London hotel. It has recently undergone extensive restoration and now offers its Marlborough Suite for wedding ceremonies.
Catering: In house

SERVICES:
- Marriage Licence

Price Guide: price comment
Catering (sit down): from £30.00pp

Dulwich College, SE21
T: 020 8299 9284
F: 020 8693 6319
E: enterprise@dulwich.org.uk
Contact: Julia Field, Enterprise Manager
Party Max: 500 (marquee: unlimited)

Dulwich College, a well known school, was built in 1866. Today, it offers an elegant combination of classical, medieval and contemporary architecture, with spacious grounds. A number of rooms are available for wedding receptions, including the Great Hall, the Lower Hall, the Pavilion Salle, the Cloisters and the Christison Hall which seats a maximum of 300 guests. The majority of catering is undertaken by the in-house team.
Catering: In house

SERVICES:
- Marriage Licence

Price Guide: Wedding ceremony prices start at £190
Catering (sit down): £9.00 - 35.00pp

Eltham Palace, SE9
T: 0208 294 2577 **F:** 0208 294 2621
E: amanda.dadd@englsih-heritage.org.uk
Contact: Amanda Dadd, Hospitality Manager
Party Max: 250

This English Heritage site claims a unique combination of Art Deco and Medieval styles. The moated Palace is on the site of the boyhood home of Henry VIII, although much of the original was destroyed. Most of the present day Palace is the restored Art Deco house built in 1936. Two rooms are licensed for civil wedding ceremonies; the smaller seating up to 100 guests. This venue is not suitable for children.
Catering: In house/Contract approved list

SERVICES:
- Exclusive Use
- Marriage Licence

Price Guide: Hire fee is £4000 for the evening (6.30pm - 11.30pm). Other prices start at £100.
Catering (sit down): £50 - £100+

Fairfield Halls, CR9
T: 020 8681 0821 **F:** 020 8760 0835
E: dbarr@fairfield.co.uk
Contact: Gary Barnes
Party Max: 500 (marquee: 200)

Fairfield Halls in Croydon offers four rooms including The Concert Hall, complete with balcony, tiered seating and oak panelling (up to 1800). Smaller rooms are The Maple Room, (120), and The Arnhem Suite (500). Hirers may use their own caterers here for a fee of £2765 + vat (Sundays only).
Catering: In house/Contract (any)/Self catering

SERVICES:
- Marriage Licence

Price Guide: Prices on application.
Catering (sit down): from £10.00pp

Foreign Press Association, SW1
T: 0207 930 0445 **F:** 0207 925 0469
Contact: Laura Hazlerigg, Events Manager
Party Max: 200

Set in a Nash Terrace, the Foreign Press Club once belonged to Gladstone and featuresa sweeping double staircase and an elegant Music Room. The building provides a good central location for many types of event, from wedding receptions to dinners, cocktail parties and business meetings, with several rooms, or the whole house available.
Catering: Contract (any)

SERVICES:
- Disco/Dance

Price Guide: Prices range from £75 for the Committee Room for 4 hours, to £900 for the whole house.

Four Seasons Hotel, W1
T: 020 7499 0888
F: 020 7499 5572
Contact: Sarah English, Banqueting Manager
Party Max: 350   Bedrooms: 220

LONDON

The Four Seasons offers a choice of four rooms for events: the Pine Room with its painted ceiling, the Oak Room, the Garden Room (which opens onto the private garden) and the Ballroom for up to 400 seated or 750 standing. In-house catering is provided by executive chef Eric Deblonde.
Catering: In house

SERVICES:
- Marriage Licence

Price Guide: Prices on application.
Catering (sit down): POA
Catering (buffet): POA

Fredericks Restaurant, N1
T: 020 7359 2888 **F:** 020 7359 5173
E: eat@fredericks.co.uk **W:** fredericks.co.uk
Contact: Hannah Triggs, Party Organiser
Party Max: 300

Established for 30 years this fine dining restaurant, set in a listed building in the heart of Islington, features a large colonial style garden room overlooking a garden patio area. The restaurant has two private rooms for parties and corporate meetings. It also has a licence for civil wedding ceremonies.
Catering: In house

SERVICES:
- Exclusive Use
- Marriage Licence

Price Guide: £40 - £200
Catering (sit down): From £30pp
Catering (buffet): From £25pp

Fulham House, SW6
T: 020 7414 5513 **F:** 020 7414 5513
E: secretary@reserve-forces-london.org.uk
Contact: Ms Susan Stuart, Marketing & Events Manager
Party Max: 200

Fulham House is a restored Georgian building (Grade II listed) and is 2 minutes walk from Putney Bridge Station. It comprises a Hall, which can cater for up to 160 for a seated dinner, and also has a formal dining room with 2 ante rooms, with kitchen facilities close to all rooms.
Catering: Contract (any)

SERVICES:
- Performance Area

Price Guide: £300 - £1000
Catering (sit down): POA
Catering (buffet): POA

Fulham Town Hall, SW6
T: 020 8576 5008 **F:** 020 8576 5459
Contact: Dee Little, Civic Facilities Manager
Party Max: 300

Fulham Town Hall is a late Victorian, early Edwardian, listed building, which has recently been completely refurbished. Internally the building is highly decorative with stained glass panels and marble painted columns. There is no wheelchair access to Fulham Town Hall.
Catering: In house

SERVICES:
- Marriage Licence

Price Guide: Prices on application.
Catering (sit down): from £12.50pp
Catering (buffet): from £4pp

Gilbert Collection, WC2
T: 020 7240 5782 **F:** 020 7240 8704
E: info@gilbert-collection.org.uk
W: www.gilbert-collection.org.uk
Contact: Suzy Denbigh
Party Max: 350

The modern styled Silver Galleries are available as the function area in this Grade I listed building. The rooms, on the first floor, offer stunning views of the Thames, but the whole museum is open for your evening function.
Catering: Contract approved list

Price Guide: £4000 facility fee for a reception. £5000 facility fee for a dinner (6.30pm - 11pm).

Glaziers' Hall, SE1
T: 020 7409 1814 **F:** 020 7407 6036
E: sales@glaziershall.co.uk
W: www.glaziershall.co.uk
Contact: Deborah Dawoon, Marketing & Sales Executive
Party Max: 500

The Glaziers' Hall describes itself as a 'Window over the Thames'. The livery hall is located in central London within easy reach of London Bridge and Monument tube stations.
Catering: Contract (any)

SERVICES:
- Exclusive Use
- Toastmaster
- Disco/Dance
- Performance Area

Price Guide: £240 - £2315
Catering (sit down): POA
Catering (buffet): POA

Golden Hinde Sailing Ship, SE1
T: 08700 118700 **F:** 020 7407 5908
E: info@goldenhinde.co.uk
W: www.goldenhinde.co.uk
Contact: Roddy Coleman, Director
Party Max: 120 (marquee: 300)

Berthed between London Bridge and Shakespeare's Globe, the reconstruction of Sir Francis Drake's 16th Century ship is an unique and memorable location for any event. Smaller events can use the Great Cabin, while larger events can use the whole ship and the dockside. The ship offers themed events (and provide the costumes) with the opportunity to sleep aboard ship. Accommodation is basic; between the cannons on the gun deck! Murder mysteries, team building and promenade performance can all be arranged here.
Catering: Contract (any)

SERVICES:
- Exclusive Use
- Marriage Licence
- Performance Area

Price Guide: £200 - £2000

LONDON

Goring Hotel, SW1
T: 020 7396 9000 **F:** 020 7834 4393
Contact: David Morgan Hewitt, Hotel Manager
Party Max: 200   Bedrooms: 74

This is one of the best known, and most respected, privately owned and family run hotels in London. The hotel holds many accolades from hotel guides and individuals. Set in central London, the hotel enjoys a peaceful location with its own gardens. The Goring offers traditional British cuisine, and holds a Michelin Red Turret.
Catering: In house
SERVICES:
- Marriage Licence

Price Guide: Prices on application.
Catering (sit down): from £30pp

Great Conservatory, TW8
T: 020 8758 1888
F: 020 8568 0936
W: www.syonpark.co.uk
Contact: Lucy Hampton, Wedding & Events Manager
Party Max: 160

Situated halfway between Central London and Heathrow Airport is Syon Park, the London home of the Dukes of Northumberland. Set within the Capability Brown landscaped gardens is Charles Fowler's Great Conservatory with its spectacular central dome. Built during the 1820s, its glass doors open onto lawns leading to the Mercury Pond. Used as an inspiration for Crystal Palace, this splendid building is ideal for summer evening parties, corporate events and wedding receptions.
Catering: Contract approved list

SERVICES:
- Exclusive Use
- Marriage Licence

Price Guide: Standard day rate is £2500 - £2700
Catering (sit down): POA
Catering (buffet): POA

Grosvenor House Hotel, W1
T: 020 7499 6363   **F:** 020 7493 3341
Contact: Hugh Harris
Party Max: 1500   Bedrooms: 454

This is one of the oldest and largest hotels on Park Lane. Numerous function rooms are available and hold ceremony licences allowing for wedding for 10 to 1500 people.
Catering: In house

Price Guide: Prices on application.
Catering (sit down): from £30.00pp

Ham House, TW10
T: 020 8332 6244
Contact: Gill Sims, Events Manager
Party Max: 300

Ham House, owned by the National Trust, is located on the banks of the River Thames. This Stuart house retains much of its architectural fabric of the 1670s, as well as many furnishings from the period.
Catering: Contract approved list

SERVICES:
- Exclusive Use
- Marriage Licence

Price Guide: from £3000.
Catering (sit down): POA
Catering (buffet): POA

Hammersmith Town Hall, W6
T: 020 8576 5008   **F:** 020 8576 5459
Contact: Helen Pinnington, Civic Facilities Manager
Party Max: 400

Hammersmith Town Hall dates from the 1930s and is a listed building. The Hall's Assembly Hall is claimed to be one of the largest halls in west London and features a Canadian sprung dance floor which has been meticulously maintained.
Catering: In house

SERVICES:
- Marriage Licence

Price Guide: Prices on application.
Catering (sit down): from £12.50pp
Catering (buffet): from £4pp

Hayes Galleria, SE1
T: 020 7940 7700
F: 020 7940 7711
E: marketing@samaprop.co.uk
Contact: Rochelle Kleyn, Marketing Coordinator
Party Max: 250

Hayes Galleria is a sister venue to Cottons Atrium. Formerly Hay's Wharf, the Galleria has undergone a complete restoration behind the original brick facade. The original dock, where tea clippers once morred, has beeen sealed and bridged over at ground level to create the galleria, which is covered by a glass and steel barrel-vaulted roof. The Galleria contains a mix of shops, restaurants and bars, and is therefore only available for hire on Saturday evenings from 7pm to midnight. Numerous professional caterers can be recommended.
Catering: Self catering/Contract (any)

SERVICES:
- Exclusive Use

Price Guide: £2500 (exempt from VAT)

Hendon Hall Hotel, NW4
T: 020 8203 3341
F: 020 8203 9709
Contact: Alexandra Gold, Conference & Banqueting Manager
Party Max: 180   Bedrooms: 58

Hendon Hall dates from the 1500s and has its own gardens. All function rooms are licensed for civil wedding ceremonies and are available on any day of the year. The hotel has its own catering, but couples can also appoint their own caterers.
Catering: In house/Contract (any)

SERVICES:
- Marriage Licence

Price Guide: Prices on application.
Catering (sit down): from £25pp
Catering (buffet): from £16.50pp

LONDON

Highgate School, N6
T: 020 8342 8323 **F:** 020 8342 8225
E: office@highgateschool.org.uk
Contact: Bob Jones, Lettings Manager
Party Max: 6500 (marquee: unlimited)

This public school is housed in listed buildings. Ceremonies take place in the Undercroft (featuring vaulted ceilings and gothic pillars), or the The Central Hall, a galleried room complete with hammer beam ceiling. The Big School (oak panelled and beamed, with stage at one end), and the School Dining Room, are also used for functions. Wheelchair access is limited. The latter two rooms would require the services of an outside caterer.
Catering: Contract approved list
FACILITIES:
• Indoor Pool   • Gym   • Tennis
Price Guide: Hire charges are £300 - £1400 + 10% on Bank Holidays.

Hilton St Ermins Hotel, SW1
T: 020 7222 7888 **F:** 020 7222 6914
Contact: Functions Manager
Party Max: 170   Bedrooms: 290

This Grade II listed hotel is located between the Houses of Parliament and Buckingham Palace in a quiet corner of Westminster. The Ballroom, which is late Victorian style with a central chandelier, has a balcony surrounding the entire room and is ideal for functions of between 120 and 150 guests. Wedding ceremonies are held in The Balcony Room.
Catering: In house

SERVICES:
• Marriage Licence
Price Guide: Prices on application.
Catering (sit down): from £26.00pp

The Howard, WC2
T: 020 7836 3555 **F:** 020 7379 4547
E: sales@thehowardlondon.com
W: www.thehowardlondon.com
Contact: Mr Steven Malarkey, Conference & Banqueting Manager
Party Max: 120   Bedrooms: 135

Situated in the heart of the West End, The Howard Hotel is stylishly decorated with pillars of Italian marble and glittering chandeliers, and boasts panoramic views of the River Thames.
Catering: In house

SERVICES:
• Marriage Licence
Price Guide: Prices on application.
Catering (sit down): from £27.50pp
Catering (buffet): from £25pp

Hurlingham Club, SW6
T: 0207 731 0839
Contact: Banqueting & Event Manager
Party Max: 650 (marquee: 1000)

Hurlingham is a charming Georgian house featuring a columned rear facade from which the grounds roll down to the River Thames. The house is set in 40 acres of landscaed gardens with lake, croquet lawns and a cricket ground. 650 can be catered for in the building itself.
Catering: In house/Contract approved list

Price Guide: £1000 - £1500

Hyatt Carlton Tower, SW1
T: 020 7858 7200 **F:** 020 7858 7085
Contact: Michael Crisp
Party Max: 670 (marquee: 670)   Bedrooms: 224

The Hyatt Carlton Tower, a five star hotel in the centre of Knightsbridge, offers its Garden Room and Water Garden and Ballroom for wedding ceremonies. The Garden Room, which seats 50 theatre style, offers excellent views of the gardens. The Ballroom is more suitable for large functions and can host up to 400 guests.
Catering: In house

SERVICES:
• Marriage Licence
Price Guide: Prices on application.
Catering (sit down): from £40.00pp

Imperial War Museum, SE1
T: 020 7416 5394 **F:** 020 7416 5396
E: swilliams@iwm.org.uk **W:** www.iwm.org.uk
Contact: Sarah Williams, Corporate Hospitality Officer
Party Max: 800 (marquee: 1000)

From James Bond to the Beatles, the Imperial War Museum has played host to a veritable banquet of celebrity events, film premieres and fashion shows. With 5 full-sized suspended aeroplanes, a Polaris missile and a WWI German Mast Periscope, the main atrium is a perfect and unusual venue for Christmas parties, drinks receptions, themed events and gala evenings. As night falls the dramatic and spacious atrium is transformed under an aquamarine glass ceiling itno a magical and fascinating place.
Catering: Contract (any)

FACILITIES:
• Helipad
SERVICES:
• Exclusive Use
Price Guide: Various areas are available including the cinema and the atrium. Daytime hire ranges from £250 and hour to £800 an hour, with evening hire ranging from £3000 to £5000. The cinema, for 200, costs £250 an hour to hire. Special events inclued the Trench Experience at £250 an hour and the Blitz Experience (inlcuding actor) at £350 an hour.
Catering (sit down): POA
Catering (buffet): POA

Institute of Directors, SW1
T: 020 7451 3107 **F:** 020 7930 9060
E: 116@compass-group.co.uk
Contact: Deborah Kandel, Sales Coordinator
Party Max: 400

NOBLE'S PARTY VENUES GUIDE 1ST EDITION

LONDON

116 Pall Mall is a Grade I listed building and home to the Institute of Directors. It was designed by architect John Nash and boasts chandeliers and a feature staircase. Letherby & Christopher are the contract caterers for 116 Pall Mall and offer a comprehensive selection of set menus.
Catering: Contract approved list

Price Guide: Prices on application.
Catering (sit down): from £29.75pp
Catering (buffet): from £21.75pp

Ironmongers' Hall, EC2
T: 020 7606 2726   **F:** 020 7600 3519
E: beadle@ironhall.co.uk   **W:** www.ironhall.co.uk
Contact: Michael E Pearson, Hall Manager
Party Max: 250

This Tudor style hall, sited in the heart of the City of London, has traditions dating back to the 13th Century. The Hall offers 4 very different function rooms suitable for events such as dinners, conferences, exhibitions and weddings. 2 NCP car parks are adjacent and 3 tube stations are nearby.
Catering: Contract approved list

SERVICES:
- Flowers
- Toastmaster
- Performance Area

Price Guide: £440 - £995
Catering (sit down): POA
Catering (buffet): POA

Kensington Palace, W8
T: 020 7376 2452   **F:** 020 7376 0198
Contact: Charlotte Baker, Business Development & Operations Manager
Party Max: 200

A royal residence for over 300 years, Kensington Palace is now avilable for exclusive functions. Situated in the heart of West London, the Palce can offer an unique selection of rooms for corporate and charity formal dinners and receptions. Use of The Orangery or The Victorian Gardens Rooms offers an inimitable evening for your guests. With the opportunity to enjoy a private view of the State Apartments and the Royal Ceremonial Dress Collection, This venue offers an insight into the history and intrigue of life at this Royal Palace from 1689 to the present day.
Catering: Contract approved list

SERVICES:
- Exclusive Use

Price Guide: Facility fee from £5000 - £15,000 + vat
Catering (sit down): POA
Catering (buffet): POA

Kensington Town Hall, W8
T: 020 7361 2220   **F:** 020 7361 3442
E: hall-let@rbkc.gov.uk   **W:** www.rbkc.gov.uk
Contact: Maxine Howitt, Sales Conference Executive
Party Max: 800

Set within a series of courtyards and gardens, Kensington Town Hall boasts a dedicated reception area in addition to offering separate access to the 2 main halls (which can be combined). Foyers leading to the Great and Small Hall include dedicated cloakrooms, toilets, bar and catering areas. Extensive dressing room facilities can be accessed below the Great Hall Stage.
Catering: Contract approved list

SERVICES:
- Exclusive Use
- Marriage Licence

Price Guide: from £400

Kenwood House, NW3
T: 0207 973 3507   **F:** 0207 973 3891
Contact: Rod Wilson, Hospitality Manager
Party Max: 150

Internationally renowned for its priceless collection of old masters and stunning setting beside Hampstead Heath, London's neo-classical villa, Kenwood House, is now available for sophisticated dinners and concerts. Many of Kenwood's sumptuous Robert Adam interiors, originally designed to impress the cream of 18th Century society, have been recently represented to enhance the art collection, including paintings by Gainsborough, Rembrandt, Vermeer and Turner. The rooms open out onto the terrace where guests can enjoy glorious views of landscaped grounds and the capital beyond.
Catering: Contract approved list / In house FB

SERVICES:
- Exclusive Use

Price Guide: £1000 - £8000
Catering (sit down): £60 - £150pp

Kingswood House Centre, SE21
T: 020 8761 7239   **F:** 020 8766 7339
Contact: Facility Manager
Party Max: 250 (marquee: unlimited)

This English Heritage Centre is Grade II listed and set in enclosed grounds. The nucleus of the house was built in the 18th Century, while the greater part of the building dates from the 19th Century. You may choose your own caterer at this venue.
Catering: Contract (any)

SERVICES:
- Marriage Licence

Price Guide: Prices on application.

Landmark London Hotel, NW1
T: 020 7631 8000
F: 020 7630 8097
Contact: Douglas Glen, Conference & Banqueting Manager
Party Max: 500   Bedrooms: 302

Dating from 1899, this Grade II listed Edwardian hotel has many original features including the clock tower. It offers several rooms for functions: The Ballroom (seating 400), The Music Room (330), The Empire Room (200), the Drawing Room (200) and The Tower Suite (30). Small receptions in the 5th floor Tower Room are afforded views of the clock tower through its glass roof.
Catering: In house

LONDON

SERVICES:
- Marriage Licence

Price Guide: Prices on application.
Catering (sit down): from £36.95pp

Lanesborough Hotel, SW1
T: 020 7259 5599   **F:** 020 7259 5606
E: info@lanesborough.co.uk   **W:** www.lanesborough.co.uk
Contact: Director of Private Dining

Party Max: 150   Bedrooms: 95

The Lanesborough, a listed building close to Hyde Park Corner, offers six elegant rooms for functions. The largest of these, The Belgravia, seats 100 (250 standing) and features a fireplace (which can be lit), and the option of division by a set of antique gold leaf screens. Other rooms are The Wilkins, The St George's, The Wellington and The Westminster which seats 40, as well as The Wine Cellar, suitable for an intimate dinner for 12.
Catering: In house

SERVICES:
- Marriage Licence

Price Guide: Prices on application.
Catering (sit down): from £45pp
Catering (buffet): from £25pp

The Langham Hilton, W1
T: 020 7636 1000   **F:** 020 7436 7418
Contact: Conference & Banqueting Department

Party Max: 300   Bedrooms: 429

Opened by the Prince of Wales in 1865, but badly damaged during the war, the hotel was restored by Hilton in the 1990s. From the marble floor and pillars of the lobby upwards, The Langham is once again one of the finest places to dine and stay in the capital.
Catering: In house

SERVICES:
- Marriage Licence

Price Guide: Prices on application.
Catering (sit down): from £38.00pp

Lauderdale House, N6

T: 020 8348 8716   **F:** 020 8442 9099
E: carolyn.naish@hillingwall.co.uk
Contact: Sarah Tresidder, Bookings Manager

Party Max: 180

Built in 1582 and set in the splendour of Waterlow Park, Lauderdale House is a Grade 2 listed building, run as an arts centre, with 2 rooms to choose from for your celebration. Waterlow Park also offers a children's playground and duck ponds, an bonus for family events, and is 5 minutes walk from Highgate Cemetery for Karl Marx fans. The venue can accommodate live music and discos.
Catering: In house

SERVICES:
- Exclusive Use

Price Guide: £95 per hour plus catering
Catering (sit down): from £25pp
Catering (buffet): from £10pp

Le Gothique, SW18
T: 020 8870 6567
Contact: Mark Justin, Proprietor

Party Max: 400 (marquee: 400)

Le Gothique is situated in a Grade II listed building with unique and award winning cloistered gardens. Two distinct areas are available for functions: the 90 seat restaurant (with no hire charge); and the large baronial style Great Hall, which seats 300 (hire fee of £1000). Head chef Jean-Marie Martin will individually design menus for each specific occasion.
Catering: In house

SERVICES:
- Exclusive Use   • Marriage Licence   • Cake
- Toastmaster   • Piped Music   • Performance Area
- Valet Parking

Price Guide: £1000 hire fee for Great Hall only.
Catering (sit down): from £25pp
Catering (buffet): from £25pp

Leith's At London Zoo, NW1
T: 020 7449 6374/81   **F:** 020 7722 0388
E: antoniasargent@compass-group.co.uk
W: www.londonzoo.co.uk
Contact: Antonia Sargent, Sales Manager

Party Max: 240 (marquee: 3000)

The building used for functions at London Zoo has a traditional 19th Century exterior which houses contemporary internal decor with 2 contrasting suites available for any type of event. A private terrace and lawn is also available, as is a selection of the animal houses, some of which are listed buildings.
Catering: In house/Contract approved list

SERVICES:
- Marriage Licence   • Performance Area

Price Guide: Animal houses from £375 + vat
Day hire or evening hire from £800 - £1200 + vat
Catering (sit down): from £25pp + vat
Catering (buffet): from £16.50pp + vat

London Palladium, W1
T: 020 7494 5217   **F:** 020 74341217
E: knew@stoll-moss.com
Contact: Kersti New, Retail Services Manager

Party Max: 250

The London Palladium, the home of variety theatre since 1910, was made famous in the 1950s with Saturday Night at the Palladium. Licensed for civil wedding ceremonies, this Grade I listed building offers four locations for functions in the theatre including the Hall of Fame and the Cinderella Bar.
Catering: In house

SERVICES:
- Exclusive Use   • Marriage Licence   • Flowers
- Cake   • Toastmaster   • Disco/Dance
- Live Music   • Entertainers   • Performance Area

Price Guide: Prices on application
Catering (sit down): from £20pp
Catering (buffet): from £25pp

LONDON

London Planetarium, NW1
T: 020 7487 0224   **F:** 020 7465 0884
E: events@madame-tussauds.com
Contact: Events Department
Party Max: 300

The London Planetarium can arrange all kinds of events from cocktails in the auditorium to dinners in the interactive zones.
Catering: Contract approved list

SERVICES:
- Exclusive Use
- Disco/Dance

Price Guide: Venue hire fee here is £4200
Catering (sit down): from £41.50pp
Catering (buffet): from £26pp

London Scottish Regimental HQ, SW1
T: 020 7414 5513   **F:** 020 7414 5513
E: secretary@reserve-forces-london.org.uk
Contact: Ms Susan Stuart, Marketing & Events Manager
Party Max: 300

Within the Parliamentary Bell area of London, this imposing hall is a spectacular setting for most functions. A variety of small rooms can be used for receptions or dining with modern kitchen facilities available.
Catering: Contract approved list

SERVICES:
- Performance Area

Price Guide: £200 - £1200
Catering (sit down): POA
Catering (buffet): POA

Machin Conservatory, SW11
T: 020 7924 1274
Contact: Banqueting & Event Manager
Party Max: 100

This roof top conservatory with marble floor and exotic plants leads on to an outside terrace.
Catering: Contract approved list

Price Guide: £500

Madame Tussauds, NW1
T: 020 7487 0224   **F:** 020 7465 0884
E: events@madame-tussauds.com
Contact: Events Department
Party Max: 550

Madame Tussauds is available every night for exclusive hire, with events taking place within the exhibition itself.
Catering: In house

SERVICES:
- Exclusive Use
- Disco/Dance

Price Guide: Venue hire fees range from £4500 to £6900.
Catering (sit down): from £41.50pp
Catering (buffet): from £26pp

Mandarin Oriental Hyde Park, SW1
T: 020 7235 2000   **F:** 020 7235 4552
Contact: Tracy Mokes, Conference & Banqueting Sales Manager
Party Max: 650 (marquee: unlimited)   *Bedrooms: 185*

This well known hotel located in the heart of Knightsbridge offers several rooms for functions, including the Ballroom, which overlooks Hyde Park. Most rooms have natural daylight. Not only does the hotel offer all the usual services, it can also provide printing, room themeing, and even baby-sitting.
Catering: In house

SERVICES:
- Marriage Licence
- Themeing
- Baby Sitting

Price Guide: Prices on application.
Catering (sit down): from £35pp

May Fair Inter-Continental London, W1
T: 020 7629 7777   **F:** 020 7629 1459
E: mayfair@interconti-com   **W:** www.interconti.com
Contact: Stephanie Segoura, Conference & Banqueting Manager
Party Max: 350   *Bedrooms: 287*

The May Fair offers an extensive range of facilities including a ballroom with magnificent chandeliers. The building itself dates from 1927 and features 6 function rooms, including The May Fair Theatre (seating 292), The Crystal Room (320), The Danziger Suite (120), The Berkeley Suite (45) and The Curzon Room (40).
Catering: In house

SERVICES:
- Marriage Licence

Price Guide: Prices on application.
Catering (sit down): from £28pp

The Mayfair Club & Restaurant, W1
T: 020 7629 0010   **F:** 020 7499 2566
E: suzi.mayfairclub@virginnet.co.uk
Contact: Suzi Alexson, Events Manager
Party Max: 800

The Mayfair Club, in the heart of London's Mayfair, claims 'dedication to entertaining a host of industries with decadent glamour'. The Club, housed in a listed building that was once home to Queen Victoria's Ladies in Waiting, offers 6 rooms on 3 floors, suitable to meetings of 10 to parties for 800.
Catering: In house

SERVICES:
- Exclusive Use
- Flowers
- Cake
- Disco/Dance
- Entertainers
- Performance Area

Price Guide: Prices vary depending on numbers and space used. Contact the Club for a detailed quotation.
Catering (sit down): from £30pp
Catering (buffet): from £25pp

National Maritime Museum, SE10
T: 020 8312 6644   **F:** 020 8312 6722
E: egoody@nmm.ac.uk   **W:** www.nmm.ac.uk
Contact: Elanor Goody, Events Assistant
Party Max: 1000

Set in the heart of the World Heritage site of Maritime

Greenwich, the National Maritime Museum offers 3 unique venues, The National Maritime Museum Galleries, The Queen's House and The Royal Observatory. After extensive rebuilding, the Museum Galleries reopened in Spring 1999. The raised podium at the heart of the Museum is suitable for large dinners for 500 and receptions for up to 1000. See separate entries for the other venues.
Catering: In house/Contract approved list

SERVICES:
- Exclusive Use

Price Guide: £5000 + vat 6pm - midnight. Additional hours at £1250 + vat

National Portrait Gallery, WC2
T: 0207 306 0055/ 020 7312 2490
Contact: Banqueting & Event Manager
Party Max: 300

The National Portrait Gallery was founded in 1856 to collect likenesses of British men and women. Today the collection is the most comprehensive of its kind in the world, and constitutes a unique record of the men and women who created (and are still creating) the history and culture of the nation. The Portrait Restaurant the new roof-top restaurant and bar located in the Ondaatje Wing- offers some of the finest British food in a spectacular setting; its windows offering views of Nelson's column, the Houses of Parliament and the London Eye. This is available for evening receptions and dinner parties.
Catering: Contract approved list

Price Guide: Prices on application

Natural History Museum, SW7
T: 020 7942 5000   E: functions@nhm.ac.uk
W: www.nhm.ac.uk/functions
Contact: Ian Fraser, Conference & Events Manager
Party Max: 400

The world famous Natural History Museum, housed in a splendid listed building, offers several areas for functions. In the Earth Gallery guests may travel through a revolving globe, experience earthquakes and volcanoes and party in the futuristic Atrium. This seats up to 200 for dinner or 600 for a cocktail party. The Central Hall, renowned for its wonderful dinosaur skeleton, meanwhile, seats up to 600 for a dinner and 1200 for a reception. Two smaller rooms are also available: the John Flett Lecture Theatre which seats 209 and can cater for 150 in an adjoining room; and the Spencer Gallery, which sets 120 theatre style.
Catering: Contract approved list

Price Guide: John Flett Theatre and Spencer Gallery from £1800. Earth Gallery from £5750. Central Hall from £7700.

New Connaught Rooms, WC2
T: 020 7405 7811
Contact: Nikki Dunderdale
Party Max: 1000

This listed building in the centre of Covent Garden was once a Masonic house. The Drawing Room is licensed for civil weddings, and this takes a minimum of 30 guests. A choice of caterer is offered at this venue.
Catering: In house

Price Guide: Prices on application.
Catering (sit down): from £29pp
Catering (buffet): from £26pp

One Great George Street, SW1
T: 020 7665 2323   F: 020 7976 0697
E: simpson_n@ice.org.uk
W: www.onegreatgeorgestreet.co.uk
Contact: Nicola Simpson, Sales & Events Executive
Party Max: 700

One Great George Street is the home of the Institution of Civil Engineers and is just a few steps from Parliament Square. The Edwardian building features a large entrance hall, grand staircase and spacious rooms. Several rooms are available for functions: the smallest seating 20 for dinner; the largest seating 260. Special children's menus are available, with children under 3 years old dining free. A selection of menu packages is available which includes half a bottle of wine per person, plus reception drinks and the services of a toastmaster.
Catering: Contract approved list

SERVICES:
- Marriage Licence   • Performance Area

Price Guide: Prices on application
Catering (sit down): from £36.70pp + vat
Catering (buffet): from £25pp + vat

One Whitehall Place, SW1
T: 020 7839 3344   F: 020 7839 3366
E: whitehallplace@cixcompulink.co.uk
Contact: David Gibbons, Conference & Banqueting Manager
Party Max: 228   Bedrooms: 280

This Victorian building, designed by Alfred Waterhouse for the National Liberal Club, is now Grade I listed. The building boasts Europe's largest unsupported marble staircase. The Reading & Writing Room has a balcony overlooking Whitehall Gardens, which is opposite the Millennium Wheel, with views across to the Thames. Many of the rooms have natural daylight. Charing Cross Pier is very close to this venue.
Catering: In house

SERVICES:
- Marriage Licence

Price Guide: Prices on application.
Catering (sit down): from £45pp
Catering (buffet): from £37.50pp

Osterley Park, TW7
T: 020 8568 7714   F: 020 8568 7714
E: tossms@smtp.ntrust.org.uk
W: www.nationaltrust.org.uk
Contact: Siobhan Scullion, Vistor Services Manager
Party Max: 80

An historic property set in over 100 acres of landscaped parkland, and yet just 8 miles from Piccadilly, Osterley hosts wed-

LONDON

dings, receptions, corporate training days, meetings and hospitality and provides catering and visitor care which is exemplary. Easy access to public transport, Heathrow and major road networks. Daytime functions only.
Catering: In house/Contract approved list

SERVICES:
- Marriage Licence

Price Guide: Standard day rate is £500.
Catering (sit down): £13 - £30pp
Catering (buffet): £7 - £30pp

The Painted Hall, SE10
T: 020 8269 4741/4744   **F:** 020 8269 4759
E: mgodfrey@greenwichfoundation.org.uk
W: www.greenwichfoundation.com
Contact: Mr MC Godfrey, Functions Manager
Party Max: 400

The Painted Hall is a World Heritage site and is located inside the former Royal Naval college. The hire charge for this venue includes staff to set out chairs to your specification. Several rooms are available for functions in the Old Naval College, including several ante rooms and a skittle alley. Capacities range from 100 to 400.
Catering: In house

SERVICES:
- Marriage Licence

Price Guide: Prices on application.
Catering (sit down): from £30pp
Catering (buffet): from £8pp

Park Lane Hotel, W1
T: 020 7499 6321   **F:** 020 7499 1965
Contact: Banqueting Manager
Party Max: 500   Bedrooms: 308

The hotel has several rooms for functions including the Drawing Room, Orchard Room and Tudor Rose Room, which have varying capacities from a minimum of 25 to a maximum of 500 guests. The hotel holds a Kosher licence.
Catering: In house

SERVICES:
- Marriage Licence

Price Guide: Prices on application.
Catering (sit down): from £32.00pp

Pump House Gallery, SW11
T: 020 8871 7572
F: 020 7228 9062
E: pump-house@lineone.net
Contact: Catherine Davies, Events Coordinator
Party Max: 120 (marquee: 120)

This is a Grade II listed Victorian tower on Battersea Park's lakeside, and set in 200 acres of parkland. It is now used as an attractive contemporary art gallery over 4 floors. The building offers excellent natural daylight inside and opens up onto a front terraced area.
Catering: Contract (any)/Self catering

SERVICES:
- Exclusive Use
- Marriage Licence
- Piped Music

Price Guide: Prices on application.

The Queen's House, SE10
T: 020 8312 6644   **F:** 020 8312 6722
E: egoody@nmm.ac.uk
W: www.nmm.ac.uk
Contact: Elanor Goody, Events Assistant
Party Max: 150

Set in the heart of the World Heritage site of Maritime Greenwich, the National Maritime Museum offers 3 unique venues, The National Maritime Museum Galleries, The Queen's House and The Royal Observatory. The Queen's House was England's first purely classical building and was designed by Inigo Jones in 1616 as a palace for Jame's I's Queen, Anne of Denmark. Areas available for functions within the house include The Orangery, with views across Greenwich Park, The Great Hall, with views of the Thames and Old Naval College, and the Undercroft, with its barrel-vaulted ceiling. See separate entries for the other venues.
Catering: In house/Contract approved list

SERVICES:
- Exclusive Use

Price Guide: £4000 + vat 6pm - midnight. Additional hourse £1250 + vat

Ranger's House, SE10
T: 020 8853 0035
Contact: House Manager
Party Max: 100

This red brick villa, located at the top of Greenwich Park, is home to the famous Suffolk painting collection. The New Gallery is claimed to have the 3 best views in the world - overlooking Greenwich Park, Blackheath and the Thames Estuary.
Catering: Contract approved list

Price Guide: £2500 - £3500
Catering (sit down): POA
Catering (buffet): POA

Ravens Ait Island, KT6
T: 0208 390 3354
F: 0208 399 7475
Contact: Keith Hartog, Managing Director
Party Max: 200 (marquee: 200)

This is a beautiful island on the Thames near Kingston and boasts landscaped lawns, patios and Georgian balustrading. The venue is suitable for all types of functions including dinner dances and balls. Each of the 10 rooms overlooks the river or Hampton Court Home Park. Sole use hire is available with access by private boat. A selection of menus is available with all special diets being catered for. DJs and entertainers are available or guests can provide their own. This venue can offer a range of activities, including sailing, canoeing and kayaking courses for one-off 'Splash Days' to residential weekends (there is no accommodation on the island itself).
Catering: In house

LONDON

FACILITIES:
- Watersports
- Sailing
- Canoeing

SERVICES:
- Exclusive Use
- Marriage Licence
- Disco/Dance
- Live Music
- Entertainers
- Piped Music

Price Guide: Function packages range from £32.50 - £39pp + vat.
Catering (sit down): from £29.50 + vat
Catering (buffet): from £29.50 + vat

Regent Banqueting Suite, N3
T: 020 8343 3070
Contact: Susan Damary
Party Max: 400

This banqueting suite was built at the turn of the century, and still retains all its original features including decorative ceilings and chandelier. The Regency Suite is available any day except Saturday and Jewish religious holidays.
Catering: In house

Price Guide: Prices on application.
Catering (sit down): from £55.00pp

Rembrandt Hotel, SW7
T: 020 7589 8100   **F:** 020 7225 3363
E: rembrandt@sarova.co.uk
Contact: Ernie Kane, Banqueting
Party Max: 200   Bedrooms: 195

Built in 1906 as Harrods apartments, this hotel features Georgian architecture and ornate pillars. The hotel has full banqueting facilities.
Catering: In house

SERVICES:
- Marriage Licence

Price Guide: Prices on application.
Catering (sit down): from £25pp

Richmond Gate Hotel, TW10
T: 020 8940 0061   **F:** 020 8332 0354
Contact: The Reservations Office
Party Max: 90   Bedrooms: 63

The hotel is a country house overlooking the Royal Park and is RAC and AA recommended. Catering is in-house and the hotel boasts a speciality of international cuisine and vegetarian dishes. It has recently been awarded two AA Rosettes.
Catering: In house

SERVICES:
- Marriage Licence

Price Guide: Prices on application.
Catering (sit down): from £26.50pp

Richmond Hill Hotel, TW10
T: 020 8940 2247   **F:** 020 8940 5424
Contact: Jane Smeeton, Conference & Banqueting
Party Max: 300   Bedrooms: 138

This Grade II listed building has original Georgian remains forming the central part of the hotel, which dates back to 1726. The Georgian decor and much of the original architecture has been conserved. The hotel's Chef de Cuisine, Jean-Claude Seraille, insists that the finest, freshest foods from around Britain are used in the restaurant.
Catering: In house

SERVICES:
- Marriage Licence

Price Guide: Prices on application.
Catering (sit down): from £40pp

Richmond Theatre, TW9
T: 020 8940 0220
Contact: Kate Littlewood, Theatre Manager
Party Max: 120

The theatre was built in 1899 and restored in 1991. Both the Auditorium (max 850) and the Matcham Room (max 20) are licensed for civil wedding ceremonies. Catering is buffet style.
Catering: In house

Price Guide: Prices on application.
Catering (buffet): from £15pp

Ritz Hotel, W1
T: 020 7493 8181   **F:** 020 7499 7487
Contact: Paul Chamberlain, Banqueting Manager
Party Max: 80   Bedrooms: 130

This famous central London hotel offers several function rooms and suites. Personalised menus are created for each occasion and complimentary cards and place cards are also provided.
Catering: In house

SERVICES:
- Marriage Licence

Price Guide: Prices on application.
Catering (sit down): from £80pp

The Roof Gardens, W8
T: 020 7937 7994   **F:** 020 7938 2774
W: roofgardens.com
Contact: Lucy Baker, Functions Manager
Party Max: 500

The Roof Gardens is situated 100 feet above Kensington High Street and its 1.5 acres of themed gardens are available for parties to hire exclusively. Ideally situated for themes from a winter wonderland to medieval banquets. This venue can arrange themed games, with, for example, the creation of an ice rink.
Catering: In house

SERVICES:
- Exclusive Use
- Marriage Licence
- Flowers
- Disco/Dance
- Fireworks
- Piped Music
- Performance Area
- Valet Parking

Price Guide: £800 - £14000
Catering (sit down): from £35pp
Catering (buffet): from £28.50pp

Royal Academy of Arts, W1
T: 020 7300 5701   **F:** 020 7287 6312
W: www.royalacademy.org.uk

LONDON

Contact: Corporate Events Manager
Party Max: 350
This is a famous art gallery located in the heart of London.
Catering: Contract approved list

Price Guide: from £8,000 + vat
Catering (sit down): POA
Catering (buffet): POA

Royal College of Art, SW7
T: 0207 598 4125   **F:** 0207 590 4124
E: k.willimas@rca.ac.uk   **W:** www.rca.ac.uk
Contact: Kate Williams, Exhibitions & Events Manager
Party Max: 450

The Royal College offers 6 exhibition areas and 3 seminar rooms, all of which are very modern and light featuring rubber studded or wooden floors. A flexible screen system allows for infinite configuration.
Catering: Contract approved list/In house

SERVICES:
• Exclusive Use

Price Guide: £275 - £11400. All parties in the Galleries will incur a standard fee of £900 for security, floor cleaning and the services of an electrician. Prices for hire of the Senior Common room (comprising Dining room, Sitting Room and Bar) are available on application.
Catering (sit down): POA
Catering (buffet): POA

Royal Geographical Society, SW7
T: 0171 591 3090   **E:** info@rgs.org
Contact: Denise Prior, Kate Denny or Nicholas Leevers, House Management Team
Party Max: 120 (marquee: 400)

The home of the Royal Geographical Society is situated next to the Royal Albert Hall and opposite Kensington Gardens. This venue specialises in ethnic cuisine, and will cater for children separately. While there is no accommodation on the premises, a list of local establishments can be provided. Most services can be recommended including fireworks and carriages.
Catering: Contract approved list

Price Guide: Prices on application.
Catering (sit down): POA

Royal Observatory, SE10
T: 020 8312 6644   **F:** 020 8312 6722
E: egoody@nmm.ac.uk   **W:** www.nmm.ac.uk
Contact: Elanor Goody, Events Assistant
Party Max: 100

Set in the heart of the World Heritage site of Maritme Greenwich, the National Maritime Museum offers three unique venues, The National Maritime Museum Galleries, The Queen's House and The Royal Observatory. The Observatory is situated on the hill in Greenwich Park and commands views of the City of London and the Thames. The building was designed by Sir Christopher Wren and is home to Greenwich Mean Time - the Prime Meridian of the world. Three areas are available for functions within this venue, including the cobbled courtyard.

See separate entries for the other venues.
Catering: In house/Contract approved list

SERVICES:
• Exclusive Use

Price Guide: Prices on application.

Royal Opera House, WC2
T: 020 7212 9297   **F:** 020 7212 9172
W: www.royalopera.org.uk
Contact: John Harrison
Party Max: 500

The Royal Opera House opened its doors in December 1999 following extensive reburbishment and rebuilding. Several areas are now available for functions but, during performance times, only the audience is permitted in the building. There are fewer performances during the day time and none on Sundays, so there is more availability and flexibility at these times. The Vilar Floral Hall Balcony (350 for dinner) is said to be the place to gaze on the world and is available for hire at £9000 + vat for the day. Other areas are: the Amphitheatre Restaurant and Bar (200 for dinner) at £1000 + vat; the Linbury Theatre (300 for a conference) £5500 + vat; and the Conservatory (160 for cocktails) £1500 + vat. Catering here is by Searcy's in partnership with Glynn Woodin of Mustard Catering.
Catering: Contract approved list

Price Guide: £1000 - £9000 + vat
Catering (sit down): from £43pp + vat (private dining)
Catering (buffet): from £20pp + vat

Royal Society of Arts, WC2
T: 020 7839 5049
F: 020 7321 0271
E: conference@rsa-u/z.demon.co.uk
W: www.rsa.org.uk/conf/wedding.html
Contact: Nicki Kyle, Conference Administration Manager
Party Max: 250

The house of the RSA (the Royal Society for the Encouragement of Arts, Manufacture & Commerce) was designed in the 1770s by Robert Adam specifically for the Society. After a complex £4.5 million refurbishment programme, the terrace of five 18th Century vaults are now fully equipped for receptions and private dining.
Catering: In house

SERVICES:
• Marriage Licence

Price Guide: Prices on application.
Catering (sit down): from £23pp

Royal United Services Institute, SW1
T: 020 7930 5854
F: 020 7321 0943
E: facilities@rusi.org
W: www.rusi.org
Contact: Melanie Fogg, Facilities Manager
Party Max: 150

The Royal United Services Institute for Defence Studies

(RUSI) occupies a listed Victorian building in Whitehall. The facilities include The Duke of Wellington Hall, The Library, The Reading Room, and the Council Room. The elegant surroundings are suitable for intimate dinners, receptions for up to 200 and meetings for under 10.
Catering: Contract (any)

SERVICES:
- Exclusive Use

Price Guide: Prices on application.
Catering (sit down): POA

Searcy's, SW1
T: 020 7823 9212   **F:** 020 7823 8694
Contact: Paul Jackson, General Manager
Party Max: 200   Bedrooms: 12

30 Pavilion Road was created specifically by Searcy's for the purpose of entertaining, and must be hired on an exclusive basis. The Georgian town house features log fires, antique furniture and chandeliers. Pavilion Road boasts a speciality in French, English and Oriental cuisine and in addition to the usual services, is happy to provide a full event management service. At the top of the house there are 12 bedrooms with en-suite facilities.
Catering: In house

SERVICES:
- Marriage Licence

Price Guide: Prices on application.
Catering (sit down): POA
Catering (buffet): POA

Skinners' Hall, EC4
T: 0207 236 5629
Contact: Hall Manager
Party Max: 300

This is an old oak panelled hall with timber ceiling and medieval paintings. Features include a roof patio and private courtyard.
Catering: Contract approved list

Price Guide: £1000 - £1500

Soho House, W1
T: 020 7734 5788   **F:** 020 7734 1447
E: podge@sohohouse.com
Contact: Podge (Christopher Day), General Manager
Party Max: 450

Soho House is a Grade II listed Georgian building. Within this, Soho 21, a members club, features modern styling. This venue is part of the popular group that also runs Cafe Boheme in London and Oxford.
Catering: In house

SERVICES:
- Marriage Licence

Price Guide: Prices on application.
Catering (sit down): from £25pp
Catering (buffet): from £18.50pp

Spencer House, SW1
T: 020 7514 1964   **F:** 020 7409 2952
Contact: Jane Rick
Party Max: 450

Spencer House is available as one of the most beautiful and stunning settings in London to entertain. Each client has the exclusive use of the House in it's entirety, whatever the size or scale of the occasion. The state rooms have been restored to their former splendour of their late 18th Century appearance and are decorated with distinguished paintings and furniture, providing a magnificent setting for luncheons, dinners, receptions and meetings. The 8 state rooms available for hire provide an elegant backdrop for wedding receptions, musical evenings, lectures and press presentations. Receptions can be held for up to 450 guests, 500 if using the terrace, while seated lunches and dinners can be accommodated for any number from 2-138. Theatre style meetings can also be held, for a maximum of 100 guests.
Catering: In house

Price Guide: Prices on application.

Stationer's Hall, EC4
T: 020 7248 2934   **F:** 020 7489 1975
E: marketing@stationers.org   **W:** www.stationers.org
Contact: Mrs Janet Parry, Marketing Manager
Party Max: 400

Close to St Paul's Cathedral, Stationer's Hall, completed in 1673, comprises a suite of inter-linking rooms and is licensed for civil weddings. The Stock Room has original oak panelling and carving. The walls bear armorial shields of Past Masters of the Company. The Hall has stained glass windows, rich oak panelling, carved oak screen with music gallery above and armorial banners and is renowned for its musical acoustics. The Ante Room also features a stained glass window dipicting the Company's Coat of Arms, while the Court Room has fine plasterwork, rococo ornamentation and an 18th Century carved fireplace.
Catering: Contract approved list

SERVICES:
- Exclusive Use   • Marriage Licence   • Flowers

Price Guide: £545 - £2941
Catering (sit down): from £28pp
Catering (buffet): from £20pp

Sutton House, E9
T: 020 8986 2264
F: 020 8525 9051
E: tshgns@smtp.ntrust.org.uk
Contact: Glen Sillett, Enterprises Manager
Party Max: 100

Built in 1535 by Sir Ralph Sadleir, Principal Secretary of State to Henry VIII, Sutton House is the oldest brick house in East London. Since being restored by the National Trust in the early 199s, Sutton House has gained a reputation for its outstanding hospitality and friendly, professional service. Situated in Hackney, East London, the house is easily accessible by car or public transport. The historic rooms can be hired for celebra-

LONDON

tions and business functions of all kinds, and provides an unique venue for weddings, birthday parties, anniversaries, baby-naming ceremonies, retirement celebrations, and Christmas parties, as well as business meetings, seminars and away-days.
Catering: In house

SERVICES:
- Exclusive Use
- Marriage Licence

Price Guide: £145 - £850
Catering (sit down): from £24pp
Catering (buffet): from £13.50pp

Syon Park, TW8 8JF
T: 020 8758 1888 **F:** 020 8568 0936
Contact: Events Coordinator
Party Max: 200

Syon Park is the London home of the Dukes of Northumberland, and is situated half way between central London and Heathrow Airport. The Great Hall was designed by Adam and modelled on a Roman Basilica. It is furnished with antique statuary, and the venue will provide chairs and lectern. The Great Conservatory is used for receptions and is available on an exclusive basis from 6pm to midnight between April and October. The caterers on site are Payne & Gunter.
Catering: Contract (any)

SERVICES:
- Marriage Licence

Price Guide: £2400 - £4500
Catering (sit down): POA
Catering (buffet): POA

TS Queen Mary, WC2
T: 0207 240 9404 **F:** 0207 497 8910
E: info@queenmary.co.uk **W:** www.queenmary.co.uk
Contact: Karen Wales, General Manager
Party Max: 300

After spending 55 years sailing the Clyde in Scotland, the TS Queen Mary is now located on London's Victoria embankment, between Waterloo Bridge and Cleopatra's Needle. From the ship there are wonderful views of the Thames, as well as Canary Wharf, City Hall, Westminster and Big Ben.
Catering: In house

SERVICES:
- Exclusive Use
- Marriage Licence
- Piped Music
- Performance Area

Price Guide: £450 - £8000
Catering (sit down): from £30pp
Catering (buffet): from £13.50pp

Templeton, SW15
T: 020 8878 1672 **F:** 020 8876 2753
E: froebel.templeton@pop3.hiway.co.uk
W: www.scoot.co.uk/templeton-estates/
Contact: Jill Leney, Functions Secretary
Party Max: 100

Templeton is a Grade II listed mansion on the edge of Richmond Park in Roehampton, and was once home to Sir Winston Churchill. The spacious public rooms on the ground floor are available to hire for a wide range of functions both private and business; the spacious Entrance Hall leads into the Panelled Refectory and Marble Hall, which then lead into two further reception rooms. The gardens include a terrace and portico, lawns, a pond and a fountain.
Catering: Contract approved list

SERVICES:
- Exclusive Use
- Marriage Licence
- Cake
- Disco/Dance

Price Guide: £1500 - £1650 + vat
Catering (sit down): from £26pp
Catering (buffet): from 26pp

Trafalgar Tavern, SE10
T: 020 8858 2437 **F:** 020 8858 2507
E: amanda.seal@trafalgartavern.co.uk
W: www.trafalgartavern.co.uk
Contact: Amanda Seal, Banquet Coordinator
Party Max: 250

The Trafalgar Tavern is situated on the River Thames at Greenwich and is surrounded by one of the most exceptional world heritage sites. There has been a tavern on the site since the mid 1700s. Previously known as the Old George, The Tavern was redesigned and opened its doors as the Trafalgar Tavern in 1837. Dickens dined frequently here and immortalised the Trafalgar in his novel Our Mutual Friend.
Catering: In house

SERVICES:
- Exclusive Use
- Marriage Licence
- Piped Music
- Performance Area

Price Guide: £150 - £1200
Catering (sit down): from £15.75pp
Catering (buffet): from £10pp

Victoria & Albert Museum, SW7
T: 020 7938 8500
Contact: Banqueting & Event Manager
Party Max: 700

This Victorian museum of art and design, reflects every civilisation, style and subject. Areas available include the Pirelli Garden, The Silver Galleries, the Great Dome and the Raphael Gallery.
Catering: Contract approved list

Price Guide: £3500 - £5000

Waldorf Hotel, WC2
T: 020 7836 2400
F: 020 7240 9277
Contact: Simone Shaw, Business Development Manager
Party Max: 600   *Bedrooms: 292*

This famous hotel, set in the heart of London's theatreland, is a traditional five star Edwardian hotel with authentic decor. Guests can arrive and depart by boat as Charing Cross Pier is five minutes walk away.
Catering: In house

LONDON

SERVICES:
- Marriage Licence

Price Guide: Prices on application.
Catering (sit down): from £26pp

Watermen's Hall, EC3

T: 020 7283 2373 **E:** info@watermenshall.org
W: www.watermenshall.org
Contact: Hall Manager

Party Max: 60

The Watermen's Hall claims to be the only Georgian Hall in the City of London. The Hall is located in the heart of the City of London. The Hall dates back to 1780, but was extended in 1983 to include more substantial dining and meeting facilities. Several rooms are available for hire.
Catering: Contract approved list

SERVICES:
- Exclusive Use

Price Guide: Hire prices on application.
Catering (sit down): POA
Catering (buffet): POA

York House, TW1

T: 020 8831 6108
W: www.richmond.gov.uk/leisure/
Contact: Janet Pattenden, Senior Lettings Officer

Party Max: 250

York House, a listed civic building which dates from the 17th Century, sits amid gardens overlooking The Thames. Contract caterers are used, or self-catering facilities are available.
Catering: Contract (any)/Self catering

Price Guide: Prices on application.
Catering (sit down): POA
Catering (buffet): POA

SOUTHEAST ENGLAND

Abbots Barton, Canterbury
T: 01227 760341   F: 01277 785442
Contact: Miss Moore
Party Max: 250 (marquee: unlimited)   Bedrooms: 47
This is a 17th Century gothic house set in two acres.
Catering: In house

SERVICES:
- Marriage Licence

Price Guide: Prices on application.
Catering (sit down): from £12.50pp
Catering (buffet): from £7.00pp

Alexander House Hotel, Turners Hill
T: 01342 714914   F: 01342 717328
Contact: Kate Hargrave
Party Max: 80 (marquee: 150)   Bedrooms: 15
This property was previously owned by the Bysshe family (of the poet Shelley fame), and is set in 135 acres of gardens and parkland.
Catering: In house

SERVICES:
- Marriage Licence

Price Guide: Prices on application.
Catering (sit down): from £28.00pp

Alexandra Suite, Swanley
T: 01322 613900   F: 01322 664739
E: swanleybanqueting@swanley.org.uk
W: www.swanley.org.uk
Contact: Marketing Manager
Party Max: 300
Swanley Banqueting has a number of function rooms located at 3 venues in Swanley of which this is one. They hold regular party nights, including 70s and 80s Nights and Tribute Bands. For private functions Swanley will tailor-make a package which can include a disco or band and sporting facilities.
Catering: In house

SERVICES:
- Exclusive Use   • Marriage Licence   • Disco/Dance
- Performance Area

Price Guide: £113 - £211 per day.
Catering (sit down): from £18.95pp
Catering (buffet): from £7.95pp

Amberley Castle, Nr Arundel
T: 01798 831992   F: 01798 831998
E: info@amberleycastle.co.uk   W: www.amberleycastle.co.uk
Contact: Emma Pearson
Party Max: 45 (marquee: 150)   Bedrooms: 20
Stunning is the only word to describe this Grade I listed 12th Century castle nestling in the lee of the South Downs. Through the portcullis and 60ft thick walls lie ornamental gardens and dramatic medieval architecture, plus an atmosphere of intimacy and privacy. 3 rooms are available for private dining; the smallest seating 12 and the largest 45. Extra services coordinated by the venue can include speciality cakes, photography, horse-drawn carriages, floral design, marquee hire, music consultancy, harpists, string quartets, event management, helicopter flights and fireworks.
Catering: In house

SERVICES:
- Marriage Licence   • Cake   • Photography
- Flowers   • Fireworks   • Live Music
- Entertainers

Price Guide: Prices on application.
Catering (sit down): from £35.00pp

Anne Of Cleves House, Lewes
T: 01273 474610   F: 01273 486990
Contact: Stephen Watts
Party Max: 75
Although it bears her name, this Tudor property was part of Anne of Cleves' estate from which she received rent. It is now a local history museum owned by the Sussex Archaeological Society. Outside caterers would have to be appointed for a reception at the house. Tudor weddings have, not surprisingly, proved popular here.
Catering: Contract (any)

SERVICES:
- Marriage Licence

Price Guide: Prices on application.

Arts Club, Brighton
T: 01273 727371
Contact: Mary Sassi
Party Max: 130
This venue offers a Ballroom which accommodates from 70 to 130 and has a bar, stage, PA system, etc, and a meeting room/theatre for up to 50.
Catering: Self catering/Contract (any)

SERVICES:
- Exclusive Use   • Performance Area

Price Guide: Ballroom £500 Friday or Saturday night hire. Other times £50 per hour.

Ashdown Park Hotel, Forest Row
T: 01342 824866   F: 01342 826206
Contact: Banqueting Department
Party Max: 110   Bedrooms: 95
This impressive Victorian mansion was built in 1867 and restored in the 1990s. It is now a 4-star hotel. The building is set in 186 acres of countryside in the heart of Ashdown Forest, and features open fires, gilt and embossed ceilings and tranquil views. Facilities on site include swimming pool, gym, snooker, tennis courts and an 18 hole golf course.
Catering: In house

FACILITIES:
- Golf   • Indoor Pool   • Gym
- Tennis   • Pool/Snooker

SERVICES:
- Marriage Licence

Price Guide: Double rooms start at £152 per night.

SOUTHEAST ENGLAND

Bailiffscourt Hotel, Littlehampton
T: 01903 723511   F: 01903 723107
E: bailiffscourt@hshotels.co.uk W: www.hshotels.co.uk
Contact: Richard Smith
Party Max: 80 (marquee: 120)   Bedrooms: 32

This listed building is a recreation of a medieval manor house and features oak beams, log fires and four poster beds. It is set in 30 acres adjacent to the sea and has two tennis courts and an outdoor heated swimming pool.
Catering: In house

FACILITIES:
• Tennis   • Outdoor Pool
SERVICES:
• Exclusive Use   • Marriage Licence
Price Guide: Prices on application.
Catering (sit down): from £32.50pp

Barnsgate Manor Vineyard, Nr Uckfield
T: 01825 713366   F: 01825 713543
E: info@barnsgate.co.uk W: www.barnsgate.co.uk
Contact: Keith Johnson
Party Max: 250

Functions can be held at the Manor House Restaurant or the Ashdown Restaurant and Disco Cellar, both of which have patios and views over Ashdown Forest. The vineyard's own wine is available.
Catering: In house

SERVICES:
• Marriage Licence
Price Guide: Prices on application.
Catering (sit down): POA

Beauport Park Hotel, Hastings
T: 01424 851222   F: 01424 852465
Contact: Stephen Bayes
Party Max: 120 (marquee: 250)   Bedrooms: 23

Beauport Park is a Georgian country house (1719) set in 35 acres of woodland and garden, and situated just three miles from Hastings and Battle. Both the hotel's restaurant and its cocktail bar overlook the formal Italian and sunken gardens.
Catering: In house

SERVICES:
• Marriage Licence
Price Guide: Prices on application.
Catering (sit down): from £16.50pp

Bentley Wildfowl & Motor Museum, Lewes
T: 01825 840573   F: 01825 841322
E: barrysutherland@pavilion.co.uk
Contact: Barry Sutherland
Party Max: 150 (marquee: unlimited)

The Motor Museum and Wildfowl Collection are set in the grounds of the Bentley Estate, which covers some 100 acres and includes Bentley House, a farmhouse that has been converted into a Palladian-style mansion. While there is in-house catering, you can also appoint a contract caterer from an approved list. A late night drinking licence can be applied for if required.
Catering: In house/Contract approved list

SERVICES:
• Marriage Licence
Price Guide: Prices on application.
Catering (sit down): from £10.00 - £50.00pp

Bluebell Railway, Uckfield
T: 01825 722008
Contact: Peter Gray, Catering Manager
Party Max: 100

This Golden Arrow Pullman is a train of restored Pullman cars, dating back to 1924. Dinners can be accomodated on board for up to 100 people, while the buffet building, the Birchgrove Suite, can seat 60 people and is licensed for wedding ceremonies. The train is available for exclusive charter all year round, except January, with scheduled services running on Saturday Evening and Sunday lunchtimes. Extra scheduled services are also available in December. Train journeys last 3.5 hours.
Catering: In house

Price Guide: Private charter - £1200 - £1500
Scheduled trips £44- £50pp
Catering (sit down): from £24-35pp
Catering (buffet): POA

Bookham Grange Hotel, Bookham
T: 01372 452742   F: 01372 450080
Contact: Mr Perry
Party Max: 100 (marquee: unlimited)   Bedrooms: 21

The Wedgewood and Eastwick Rooms of this Victorian country house hotel, are available for functions. The hotel is set in 2.5 acres of gardens and says it blends modern with traditional facilities.
Catering: In house

SERVICES:
• Marriage Licence
Price Guide: Prices on application.
Catering (sit down): from £19.75pp

Boughton Monchelsea Place, Nr Maidstone
T: 01622 743120   F: 01622 741168
Contact: Mrs Marice Kendrick, Owner, Events Manager
Party Max: 120 (marquee: 750)

Sited just outside Maidstone, this Elizabethan battlemented manor house sits in 165 acres. It offers spectacular views from formal lawns over unspoilt countryside, and has its own deer park, woods, lake and walled gardens. It also has a 20 acre activity/exhibition site which is available 365 days a year. Described as 'not massive and daunting, but gracious and welcoming' this property is only available on an exclusive use basis. Events can only take place inside the house itself on weekdays, 9am to 8pm, although marriage ceremonies are sometimes permitted on a Saturday morning.

SOUTHEAST ENGLAND

Catering: Contract approved list

FACILITIES:
- Shooting
- Go Karting
- Table Tennis
- Quad Bikes/Off Road

SERVICES:
- Exclusive Use
- Marriage Licence

Price Guide: £150 - £1500
Catering (sit down): from £20pp
Catering (buffet): from £8pp

Bourne Hall, Epsom
T: 020 8393 9571 **F:** 020 8386 7265
Contact: Sandra Dessent
Party Max: 180

Bourne Hall has a variety of different sized halls and rooms for events. The stunning grounds make an ideal backdrop.
Catering: In house

SERVICES:
- Marriage Licence

Price Guide: Prices on application.
Catering (sit down): POA

Brandshatch Place Hotel, Fawkham
T: 01474 872239 **F:** 01474 879652
Contact: Helen Norris
Party Max: 150   *Bedrooms: 41*

A Georgian country house, set in 12 acres, this listed building can play host to events on any day of the week. The Head Chef is Aimé Zbingden who holds two rosettes for his skills in modern English cuisine. Other facilities at the hotel include an indoor heated pool, snooker, beauty centre, gym, and tennis and squash.
Catering: In house

SERVICES:
- Marriage Licence

Price Guide: Prices on application.
Catering (sit down): from £52.00pp (inclusive packages)

Brickwall House, Nr Rye
T: 01797 252001 **F:** 01797 255267
E: post@frewcoll.demon.co.uk
W: www.frewcoll.demon.co.uk
Contact: Peter Mould, Director
Party Max: 65 (marquee: 250)

This independent school is housed in a listed building, with extensive grounds and gardens.
Catering: Contract approved list

FACILITIES:
- Gym
- Tennis
- Outdoor Pool
- Quad Bikes/Off Road
- Table Tennis

SERVICES:
- Exclusive Use
- Marriage Licence
- Flowers

Price Guide: £950 - £1500 per day.
Catering (sit down): from £16.50pp
Catering (buffet): from £16.50pp

The Brighton Dome, Brighton
T: 01273 700747 **F:** 01273 707505
E: info@brighton-dome.org.uk
W: www.brighton-dome.org.uk
Contact: Lisa Wolfe, Marketing Manager
Party Max: 1200

The Brighton Dome, in the grounds of the Royal Pavilion estate, comprises 3 venues; The Dome, The Corn Exchange and the Pavilion theatre. Currently undergoing refurbishment to make it it one of the leading art and conference venues in the south, it will be fully functional in the Autumn of 2001. The Corn Exchange is a versatile space, suitable for all sorts of events, from gigs to banquets, while the Pavilion Theatre, which reopened in May 2000, is suited to more intimate events.
Catering: Contract (any)

Price Guide: Standard rates are: Dome - £2750 to £3500 Corn exchange £1500 to £1750 and Pavilion Theatre £350 to £450. Registered charities can claim a reduced rate.
Catering (sit down): POA
Catering (buffet): POA

Brighton Museum & Art Gallery, Brighton
T: 01273 290900
Contact: Debbie Steel, Functions & Visitor Services Manager
Party Max: 500

Currently undergoing redevelopment, with completion due in Autumn 2001, The Museum houses many fine collections in its galleries including 20th Century Art and Design such as Art Nouveau and Art Deco, fashion from 18th Century to the present day and a collection of fine art.
Catering: Contract (any)

SERVICES:
- Exclusive Use

Price Guide: Prices on application.

Brighton Racecourse, Brighton
T: 01273 603580 **F:** 01273 673267
E: info@brighton-racecourse.co.uk
W: www.brighton-racecourse.co.uk
Contact: Marie Norman
Party Max: 1000 (marquee: 120)

Brighton Racecourse is available for functions on any day of the year, including during racing. Drinks licences can be applied for as required.
Catering: In house

SERVICES:
- Marriage Licence

Price Guide: Prices on application.
Catering (sit down): from £20.00pp
Catering (buffet): from £10.00pp

Broome Park, Canterbury
T: 01227 831701 **F:** 01227 831973
Contact: Gwen Willbye
Party Max: 300 (marquee: 400)   *Bedrooms: 44*

SOUTHEAST ENGLAND

Built in the reign of Charles I, this listed mansion, set in 268 acres, was once the home of Lord Kitchener. It is now a club operated on a time-share basis. The Club has three restaurants including Dizzy's Jazz Bar and Creole Restaurant, and a more formal a la carte restaurant. Other facilities include an 18 hole championship golf course, driving range, tennis courts, squash courts, putting green, outdoor pool and health centre. While accommodation is usually available on site; there are 18 suites in the main building and a further 26 villas in the grounds; availability is variable. The club can recommend numerous services that cannot be offered in-house.
Catering: In house

FACILITIES:
- Golf
- Tennis
- Outdoor Pool
- Health Centre
- Squash

SERVICES:
- Marriage Licence

Price Guide: Prices on application.
Catering (sit down): from £18.00pp

Buxted Park Country House Hotel, Uckfield
T: 01825 732711 **F:** 01825 732770
Contact: Rebecca Ray
Party Max: 120 (marquee: 200) Bedrooms: 43

This is a Georgian mansion, dating from 1725. The hotel is set in 312 acres of parkland featuring exotic plants and lakes. Functions can take place in the hotel's restaurant (for 45) or in its newly renovated Orangery (for 50). Larger parties can be catered for in the Ballroom and Coat of Arms Lounge.
Catering: In house

SERVICES:
- Marriage Licence

Price Guide: Prices on application.
Catering (sit down): from £47.50pp

Chaucer Hotel, Canterbury
T: 0870 400 8106 **F:** 01227 450397
E: HeritageHotels-Canterbury.Chaucer-Hotel@forte-hotels.com
W: www.heritage-hotels.com
Contact: Miss Vicky Leah
Party Max: 150 Bedrooms: 42

The Chaucer belongs to the Forte Heritage collection of hotels and was once the home of the creator of Rupert Bear. The Georgian building stands opposite Canterbury's ancient city walls.
Catering: In house

SERVICES:
- Marriage Licence

Price Guide: Prices on application.
Catering (sit down): from £32.00pp
Catering (buffet): from £8.00pp

Chiddingstone Castle, Nr Edenbridge
T: 01892 870347
Contact: Functions Manager
Party Max: 80 (marquee: 100)

One of the historic houses of Kent, and formerly the home of Denys Eyre Bower, Chiddingstone Castle is now maintained by a private charitable trust. Set in its own grounds, with lake, woods and a cascade, the castle is a particularly tranquil setting. It should be noted that stiletto heels are prohibited since they cause irreparable damage to the floors. Receptions can take place in one of several rooms; either informal buffets or sit down meals. A marquee can be hired and sited on the north hard standing overlooking the lake. The castle has a restaurant licence for drinks, but you may also provide your own drinks and pay corkage.
Catering: In house/Contract approved list

SERVICES:
- Marriage Licence

Price Guide: Prices on application.
Catering (sit down): POA

Chilston Park Hotel, Lenham
T: 01622 859803 **F:** 01622 858352
Contact: Lynsey McCormick
Party Max: 85 (marquee: 250) Bedrooms: 53

This is a Grade I listed mansion house set in parkland.
Catering: In house

SERVICES:
- Marriage Licence

Price Guide: Prices on application.
Catering (sit down): from £38.50pp (3-courses)

Clandon Park, Guildford
T: 01483 225804 **F:** 01483 223176
E: shagen@smtp.ntrust.org.uk
W: nationaltrust.org.uk/southern
Contact: Louise Lawton, Events Coordinator
Party Max: 200 (marquee: 400)

This is a magnificent Palladian mansion, built c1730 by Venetian architect Leoni, is Grade I listed and now National Trust owned. The white marble interior of the 2 storey Marble Hall contrasts with the red brick exterior to provide a stunning venue for functions. A licensed restaurant in the basement provides meals and buffets. Marquees can be put up in the grounds.
Catering: In house

SERVICES:
- Marriage Licence
- Performance Area

Price Guide: Venue hire fee is £275 - £2000
Catering (sit down): POA
Catering (buffet): POA

Cobham Hall, Cooling
T: 01474 823371 **E:** cobhamhall@aol.com
Contact: Mrs Johnson
Party Max: 200 (marquee: unlimited)

This 16th Century mansion, former home of the Earls of Darnley and now a girls' school, is set in 150 acres of landscaped parkland and gardens. The Hall has its own helicopter landing area.

SOUTHEAST ENGLAND

Catering: In house

SERVICES:
- Marriage Licence

Price Guide: Prices on application.
Catering (sit down): from £22.00pp

Cooling Castle Barn, Rochester
T: 01634 222244
F: 01634 222233
E: enquiries@coolingcastlebarn.com
W: www.coolingcastlebarn.com
Contact: Paul & Julir Collins, proprietors
Party Max: 250

This venue comprises 3 barns, each with their own character, historical architecture and beauty. The imposing Great Barn has been sympathetically renovated to provide seating for up to 150. Civil wedding ceremonies can be perfomed in the medieval beamed Fathom Barn, which features a minstrel's gallery. The heritage Barn is the most useful and contemporary barn. This has a light and airy Mediterranean flavour.
Catering: Contract approved list

SERVICES:
- Marriage Licence
- Disco/Dance
- Piped Music
- Performance Area
- Valet Parking

Price Guide: £800 - £1200 per day.
Catering (sit down): from £15pp
Catering (buffet): POA

Court Room, Sandwich
T: 01304 617197   **F:** 01304 620170
Contact: Mrs M E Bull
Party Max: 200

This is an ancient court room dating back to Elizabethan times. A stained glass window in the room depicts the visit of Queen Elizabeth I to Sandwich in 1563. Two rooms are available for functions. The Jury Room seats 80 or takes buffets for up to 90. The Main Hall holds up to 200. Parties can arrange their own caterers, which includes applying for drinks licences or public house to run a bar if required. Receptions can take place from Monday to Saturday.
Catering: Contract (any)

SERVICES:
- Marriage Licence

Price Guide: Prices on application.

Darnley Arms, Cobham
T: 01474 814218
Contact: Beryl Howard
Party Max: 75 (marquee: 100)

The Darnley Arms is a listed building, boasting a beamed hayloft, in a listed village. Live modern music and dancing are not permitted on the premises. This venue can arrange for motor and horse drawn transport if required.
Catering: In house FB

SERVICES:
- Marriage Licence

Price Guide: Prices on application.
Catering (sit down): from £16.50pp
Catering (buffet): from £10.00pp

De La Warr Pavilion, Bexhill on Sea
T: 01424 212023   **F:** 01424 787940
Contact: Tina Styles
Party Max: 400

This 1930's Grade I listed building is a popular film set (Poirrot was filmed here), and is situated on the seafront with views across the channel. Two rooms are available for functions.
Catering: In house

SERVICES:
- Marriage Licence

Price Guide: Prices on application.
Catering (sit down): POA

Duncton Mill, Petworth
T: 01798 342294   **F:** 01798 344122
E: all@dunctonmill.com
W: www.dunctonmill.com
Contact: Sheila, Tom or Richard Bishop
Party Max: 25

Duncton Mill is a small country estate nestling in a secluded valley on the north side of the South Downs. The dozen buildings here cluster around the Georgian farmhouse, mill and mill pond. Activitites here are based on the 8 acres of fly fishing lakes, with self-catering (3 cottages) or b&b accommodation. Corporate entertaining, team building days and other celebratory events have been popular here, with previous fly fishing experience not essential.
Catering: In house/Self catering

FACILITIES:
- Fishing
- Archery

Price Guide: Corporate entertaining from £50 - £150pp. B&B from £26pp per night. Self catering from £180 per week.
Catering (sit down): POA

East Court, East Grinstead
T: 01342 323636
F: 01342 327823
E: egtc@pncl.co.uk/egtc
W: www.egnet.co.uk/egtc
Contact: Mrs Rudin
Party Max: 180

East Court Mansion is an 18th Century Grade II listed manor house to which the Meridian Hall was a fairly recent addition. The Mansion's Cranston Suite (max 40) and the Meridian Hall (max 100) are both available for functions. They offer views over the gardens and the Ashdown Forest. The Meridian Hall also has its own private patio. Organisers may bring in their own caterers for a function at East Court
Catering: Contract (any)

SERVICES:
- Marriage Licence

Price Guide: Prices on application.

SOUTHEAST ENGLAND

Eastwell Manor, Ashford
T: 01233 213000
F: 01233 635530
Contact: Oriel Stratford
Party Max: 200 (marquee: 300+) — Bedrooms: 62

This country house hotel and restaurant offers two function rooms: the Bayeaux Room (max 50) and the Rose Garden Room (max 80); plus a gazebo in the garden.
Catering: In house

SERVICES:
- Marriage Licence

Price Guide: Prices on application.
Catering (sit down): from £33.00pp

Finchcocks, Goudhurst
T: 01580 211702
F: 01580 211007
E: katrina@finchcocks.co.uk
W: www.finchcocks.co.uk
Contact: Mrs Katrina Burnett, Owner
Party Max: 120 (marquee: 150)

Finchcocks is a fine Grade I 18th Century manor, housing a famous collection of musical instruments. It is set in a beautiful garden, surrounded by unspoilt countryside. Wedding ceremonies can take place in the panelled hall, while small receptions can take place in the cellar restaurant. Larger receptions can take place in a marquee on the the brick terrace next to the house.
Catering: In house

SERVICES:
- Exclusive Use
- Marriage Licence
- Flowers
- Live Music
- Performance Area
- Valet Parking

Price Guide: £600 - £1600. Prices depend on timing and whether exclusive use is required.
Catering (sit down): from £25pp
Catering (buffet): from £15- £25pp

Frensham Heights, Farnham
T: 01252 850089
F: 01252 794335
E: headmaster@frensham-heights.org.uk
W: www.demon.co.uk/frensham- heights
Contact: Margaret Grimwood
Party Max: 300 (marquee: unlimited)

This Edwardian, neo-Elizabethan style, country house (now a school) stands in 100 acres with views south towards the Blackdown Hills. Functions can be held in the Ballroom (with minstrel's gallery), Jacobean Hall, Blue Drawing Room or Orangery, together with the terraces and lawns. A la carte catering is by a specialist firm. Up to 150 can be accommodated in the Ballroom or a reception for 300+ using connecting rooms.
Catering: Contract approved list

SERVICES:
- Marriage Licence

Price Guide: Facility fee is £1950.
Catering (sit down): from £18.00pp

Garden Hotel, Faversham
T: 01227 751411 **F:** 01227 751801
Contact: Karen Carr
Party Max: 80 (marquee: 110) — Bedrooms: 10

Set in a village location, The Garden Hotel is a 17th Century listed building converted from an antique shop in 1889.
Catering: In house

SERVICES:
- Marriage Licence

Price Guide: Prices on application.
Catering (sit down): from £18.50pp
Catering (buffet): from £12.50pp

Goodwood House, Chichester
T: 01243 775000 - 755048
F: 01243 775045 - 755005
Contact: Sally Laver, Sales Manager
Party Max: 600 (marquee: 1500+)

Home to the Dukes of Richmond for the last 300 years, Goodwood has long been internationally renowned for its special atmosphere and spectacular setting. Every meticulous detail is arranged and carried out from small, intimate weddings to grand society affairs. Several rooms are available for functions, the largest being The Ballroom (150 for dinner) or, if the whole house is taken for a dinner dance, 310 can be accommodated. Smaller rooms take just 8 or 10 for meetings. The Goodwood estate, which includes the racecourse, produces a beautiful brochure on the house, with leaflets on all details of its facilities. Receptions and lunches prior to race meetings can be arranged at the house.
Catering: In house

FACILITIES:
- Helipad

SERVICES:
- Exclusive Use
- Marriage Licence
- Flowers
- Cake
- Disco/Dance
- Piped Music
- Performance Area

Price Guide: £3000 facility fee, plus event costs starting from £48PP + vat, based on 100 people.
Catering (sit down): from £48.50pp
Catering (buffet): from £48.50pp

Goodwood Racecourse, Chichester
T: 01243 755022 **F:** 01243 755025
E: events@goodwood.co.uk
W: www.goodwood.co.uk
Contact: Sarah Edgar, Events & Leisure
Party Max: 250

Goodwood has been described as the most beautiful racecourse in the world. It is set on top of the spectacular South Downs and has views over the cathedral city of Chichester and the sea beyond. The racecourse holds a licence for civil wedding ceremonies, and can also offer the sweeping green lawns of the members' enclosure for a drinks reception. All facilities and function rooms can be used on race and non-race days, with 11 areas for events offered around the site
Catering: Contract approved list/In house

SOUTHEAST ENGLAND

SERVICES:
- Marriage Licence

Price Guide: Venue hire prices start at £250.
Catering (sit down): from £31pp
Catering (buffet): from £25pp

Grand Hotel, Brighton

T: 01273 224300
F: 01272 202694
W: www.grandbrighton.co.uk
Contact: Claire Richardson

Party Max: 850 Bedrooms: 200

This famous hotel, built in 1865 and a listed building, is situated on Brighton's seafront. The Empress Suite and Regent Room are licensed for wedding ceremonies. The former breaks down into four separate rooms, the smallest of which will seat 40.
Catering: In house

SERVICES:
- Marriage Licence

Price Guide: Prices on application.
Catering (sit down): packages from £50.00pp

Great Ballard School, Nr Chichester

T: 01243 814236
F: 01243 814586
E: GBSchool@breathemail.net
Contact: Mrs S Jay

Party Max: 120 (marquee: unlimited)

This Grade II listed Regency building was modernised by Lutyens. It is set within a conservation area and features an orangery and dovecote within its 30 acres of grounds. The building as been the home of Great Ballard School for the last 40 years. Any special catering requirements can be catered for. Helicopters and hot air balloons may use the grounds.
Catering: In house

FACILITIES:
- Helipad
- Hot Air Balloons

SERVICES:
- Marriage Licence

Price Guide: Prices on application.
Catering (sit down): from £22.00pp
Catering (buffet): from £11.00pp

Great Fosters, Near Virginia Water

T: 01784 433822
F: 01784 437383
W: www.greatfosters.co.uk
Contact: Amanda Berry

Party Max: 180 Bedrooms: 40

The Tithe Barn, Orangery and Anne Boleyn Rooms are available here and range in capacity from 40 to 120.
Catering: In house

SERVICES:
- Marriage Licence

Price Guide: Prices on application.
Catering (sit down): from £34.50pp

Hampton Court Palace, Kingston

T: 020 8781 9500
Contact: Functions Manager

Party Max: 400

This world famous palace on the banks of the Thames, was commissioned by Thomas Wolsey in 1514. The house features magnificent architecture and sumptuous interiors, and reflects the varying tastes of successive monarchs. Numerous rooms are available for functions, the largest being the Grand Hall (400), the smallest taking 60 to 100.
Catering: In house

Price Guide: from £5000
Catering (sit down): POA
Catering (buffet): POA

Herstmonceux Castle, Hailsham

T: 01323 834479 F: 01323 834419
W: www.seetb.org.uk/herstmonceux
Contact: Sally Sutton

Party Max: 180 (marquee: 200) Bedrooms: 160

Herstmonceux is a 15th Century brick moated castle. Features of the Ballroom include wood panelling and a painted Palladian ceiling. It overlooks an Elizabethan walled garden and courtyard. Overnight accommodation is available at Bader Hall on the castle estate.
Catering: In house

SERVICES:
- Marriage Licence

Price Guide: Prices on application.
Catering (sit down): from £35.00pp

The Honeyclub, Brighton

T: 07000 446639 F: 07000 620860
E: info@thehoneyclub.co.uk W: www.thehoneyclub.co.uk
Contact: Joy, Manageress

Party Max: 660

Situated in the picturesque artistes quarter of the lower seafront, this split level venue has just undergone extensive enlargement and modernisation. The largest and most luxurious of the seafront clubs, this venue operates as a cafe bar during the day, complete with its own sun terrace, air-conditioning and state of the art lighting, and as one of Brighton's trendiest clubs open 7 nights a week.
Catering: In house

FACILITIES:
- Theatre

SERVICES:
- Exclusive Use
- Flowers
- Cake
- Disco/Dance
- Live Music
- Fireworks
- Piped Music
- Performance Area

Price Guide: Venue hire is £400 per night.
Catering (sit down): from £12pp
Catering (buffet): from £4pp

Hop Farm Country Park, Nr Paddock Wood

T: 01622 872068 F: 011622 872630 - 872830

SOUTHEAST ENGLAND

E: nigel@thehopfarm.co.uk **W:** www.thehopfarm.co.uk
Contact: Fiona Pollard, Owner
Party Max: 500 (marquee: 2000)

Set in and amongst the largest collection of Victorian oast houses in the world, The Hop Farm is a unique venue with easy access from London and the south East. The venue offers a wide range of meeting and function rooms, plus a 200 acres fully serviced event field.
Catering: In house

FACILITIES:
- Helipad
- Go Karting
- Hot Air Balloons
- Quad Bikes/Off Road

SERVICES:
- Exclusive Use
- Marriage Licence
- Piped Music
- Performance Area

Price Guide: Prices on application.
Catering (sit down): from £12pp
Catering (buffet): from £7.50pp

Horsted Place, Uckfied
T: 01825 750581 **F:** 01825 750240
E: hotel@horstedplace.co.uk **W:** www.horstedplace.co.uk
Contact: Jenny Pinnegar
Party Max: 120 (marquee: 200) Bedrooms: 20

This is a Victorian Gothic mansion. Horsted Place can also arrange car hire if required. A bedroom is usually available on site.
Catering: In house

SERVICES:
- Marriage Licence

Price Guide: Prices on application.
Catering (sit down): POA

Hythe Imperial, Hythe
T: 01303 267441 **F:** 01303 264610
Contact: Jane Burden
Party Max: 300 (marquee: 300) Bedrooms: 100

The Imperial, built in 1880, is sited on the unspoilt seafront at Hythe.
Catering: In house

SERVICES:
- Marriage Licence

Price Guide: Prices on application.
Catering (sit down): from £24.50pp

Inn on the Lake, Godalming
T: 01483 415575 **F:** 01483 860445
Contact: James Ginders
Party Max: 130 Bedrooms: 21

The Inn on the Lake (which claims to be an inn, not a hotel) is a part Tudor building with a listed Georgian frontage. It is set in two acres of landscaped grounds overlooking is own lake. The building has limited wheelchair access. The venue has a lakeside restaurant as well as a bar which features a log fire and real ale.
Catering: In house

SERVICES:
- Marriage Licence

Price Guide: Prices on application.
Catering (sit down): from £32.00pp

Jarvis Great Danes Hotel, Maidstone
T: 01226 31163 **F:** 01622 735290
Contact: Functions Manager
Party Max: 500 (marquee: unlimited) Bedrooms: 126

Originally a manor house, Great Danes has had more recent additions over the years. It is set in 26 acres of landscaped gardens. Great Danes has considerable experience of both Greek and Asian weddings, providing traditional fayre. Other services that can be offered include a free postal service for your invitations, free table fun packs for children, and free cake boxes.
Catering: In house

SERVICES:
- Marriage Licence

Price Guide: Prices on application.
Catering (sit down): from £18.00pp

Knowle Restaurant, Rochester
T: 01474 822262
Contact: Michael Baragwanath
Party Max: 90 (marquee: 120)

Knowle is a Victorian Gothic-style mansion set in three acres of old English gardens. The proprietor will allow you sole use of the premises. Food at Knowle is English and continental style.
Catering: In house

SERVICES:
- Exclusive Use
- Marriage Licence

Price Guide: Prices on application.
Catering (sit down): from £24.00pp

Komedia, Brighton
T: 01273 647101 **F:** 01273 647102
E: info@komedia.co.uk **W:** www.komedia.co.uk
Contact: Amy Cannon, Administrator
Party Max: 200

Komedia is Brighton's celebrated arts and entertainment venue. The building comprises a 210 seat theatre, a theatre bar, a 250 cover cafe-bar (managed by seafood specialists English's of Brighton) and a cabaret bar seating 230.
Catering: In house

SERVICES:
- Toastmaster
- Disco/Dance
- Live Music
- Piped Music
- Performance Area

Price Guide: £120 - £2100
Catering (sit down): from £12pp
Catering (buffet): from £9pp

Langshott Manor, Horley
T: 012393 786680 **F:** 01293 783905
E: admin@langshottmanor.com **W:** www.langshottmanor.com
Contact: Functions Coordinator
Party Max: 60 Bedrooms: 15

SOUTHEAST ENGLAND

Langshott Manor is a restored Elizabethan manor (1580) set amidst an award winnning English garden featuring a listed medieval moat, swans, a rose arbour and traditional herbaceous borders. The Manor, which only became an hotel in the mid 1980s, prides itself on its old fashioned hospitality. The Boardroom and Lounge are licensed for marriages, with only one ceremony permitted per day.
Catering: In house

SERVICES:
- Marriage Licence

Price Guide: Prices on application.
Catering (sit down): from £37.50pp
Catering (buffet): from £35.00pp

Leeds Castle, Maidstone
T: 01622 765400   **F:** 01622 735616
E: enquiries@leeds-castle.com   **W:** www.leeds-castle.co.uk
Contact: Judy Murray, Sales Manager
Party Max: 200   Bedrooms: 15

Leeds Castle is one of the Treasure Houses of England and is now run by the Leeds Castle Foundation. The Castle is surrounded by 500 acres of parkland and gardens and is set in the middle of a natural lake. The castle houses a fine collection of paintings, tapestries and furnishings, while the grounds include the Culpeper Garden, a maze and an underground grotto. If accommodation is taken here, a minimum of 8 rooms must be booked.
Catering: In house

FACILITIES:
- Helipad
- Golf
- Hot Air Balloons

SERVICES:
- Flowers
- Disco/Dance
- Piped Music
- Performance Area

Price Guide: £300 any day of the week
Catering (sit down): from £20pp
Catering (buffet): from £19pp

Little Thakeham, Storrington
T: 01903 744416   **F:** 01903 745022
Contact: Fiona Watson
Party Max: 110 (marquee: 200)   Bedrooms: 9

This Grade I listed house was designed by Edwin Lutyens, as were the five acres of gardens. Little Thakeham is most suited to small dinner party style events in the house itself. A pianist can be arranged, and the grounds are suitable for hot air balloons and helicopters. The house has an outdoor swimming pool and tennis courts, and can arrange a spit roast in the gardens. A horse and carriage is available. The house regrets that facilities for children are limited.
Catering: In house

FACILITIES:
- Helipad
- Hot Air Balloons
- Outdoor Pool
- Tennis

SERVICES:
- Marriage Licence
- Live Music

Price Guide: Prices on application.

Catering (buffet): from £21.50pp

Long Hall, Chiddingfold
T: 01428 654167   **F:** 01428 658345
E: ramster@bigfoot.com   **W:** www.bigfoot.com/ramster
Contact: Mrs M Gunn
Party Max: 200

The Long Hall, located in a privately owned house, is beamed and panelled and dates from 1604. It lies in the seclusion of a private estate and has central heating and inglenook fireplaces which can be used for log fires.
Catering: In house

SERVICES:
- Marriage Licence

Price Guide: Prices on application.

Loseley Park, Guildford
T: 01483 304440   **F:** 01483 302036
E: sally@loseley-park.com   **W:** www.loseley-park.com
Contact: Sally Hallum, Marketing & Events Manager
Party Max: 200 (marquee: 400)

This estate features a 2.5 acre walled garden and an Elizabethan mansion. Three areas are available; The Great Hall (100), The Drawing Room (50) and The Tithe Barn (160).
Catering: In house

FACILITIES:
- Helipad
- Shooting
- Quad Bikes/Off Road

SERVICES:
- Marriage Licence

Price Guide: Prices on application.
Catering (sit down): from £28pp
Catering (buffet): from £26pp

Lythe Hill Hotel, Haslemere
T: 01428 651251   **F:** 01428 644131
E: lythe@lythehill.co.uk   **W:** www.lythehill.co.uk
Contact: K Lorimer
Party Max: 130   Bedrooms: 41

Three rooms are available for functions within this cluster of buildings, the oldest of which dates from 1475. The hotel's 20 acres of grounds includes a lake, a floodlit tennis court, a croquet lawn, games room and even a jogging track. The hotel specialises in traditional English and French cuisine. Children under 10 are charged at half price.
Catering: In house

FACILITIES:
- Tennis
- Croquet
- Games Room
- Jogging Track

SERVICES:
- Marriage Licence

Price Guide: Prices on application.
Catering (sit down): from £64.50pp

Manor Barn, Bexhill
T: 01424 220231
Contact: Booking Services Manager
Party Max: 120

SOUTHEAST ENGLAND

The manor Barn is situated in a small attractive public park, with free car parking. Once the ballroom of the Earl De La Warr, the venue was used for entertaining lords and ladies in the late 19th Century. The Grade II listed building has been converted into function suite, with kitchen reception area and main hall, while outside are the remains of the original old house, as well as a traditional rose garden and lily pond. No party bookings for under 30 year olds is permitted here.
Catering: Self catering

SERVICES:
• Marriage Licence
Price Guide: Hourly hire rate is £30.
Catering (sit down): n/a
Catering (buffet): n/a

The Manor, Guildford
T: 01483 222624 **F:** 01483 211389
Contact: David Hill
Party Max: 200 Bedrooms: 20

The Manor is a country house hotel set in 9 acres of parkland, and within easy reach of Heathrow and Gatwick airports. Three rooms are available for functions; Saturdays are only available in November, January and February.
Catering: In house
SERVICES:
• Marriage Licence
Price Guide: Prices on application.
Catering (sit down): from £23.00pp

Mansion House, Littlehampton
T: 01903 700152 **F:** 01903 245387
Contact: Tracy Cotton
Party Max: 140

The Mansion House, originally owned by the Lyon family, features famous chalk gardens.
Catering: In house

SERVICES:
• Marriage Licence
Price Guide: Prices on application.
Catering (sit down): from £10.30pp

Market House, Kingston upon Thames
T: 020 8547 6418
F: 020 8547 6426
E: pat.jenkins@rbk.kingston.gov.uk
W: www.kingston.gov.uk/libs/misc/hallsforhire.htm
Contact: Mrs Pat Jenkins, Administrative Assistant
Party Max: 60

The Market House was refurbished in 1995 and is sited in the centre of Kingston. Rooms available for hire include the Main Hall and the Ante Chamber. The Tourist Information Centre is located on the ground floor, as is The Cafe Whittard, which can provide refreshments.
Catering: In house/Self catering

SERVICES:
• Exclusive Use   • Marriage Licence

Price Guide: Hire rates are £10 - £50 per hour.
Catering (buffet): from £4.50pp

Marle Place, Burgess Hill
T: 01444 248275 **F:** 01444 871269
Contact: Heather Wright
Party Max: 70 (marquee: 150)

Marle Place is an Edwardian house set in a quiet location near Burgess Hill. Among its prominent features is a sweeping staircase. It also has French doors that lead directly onto the verandah and well-stocked garden.
Catering: In house

SERVICES:
• Marriage Licence
Price Guide: Prices on application.
Catering (buffet): from £6.95pp

Marriott Goodwood Park Hotel, Chichester
T: 01243 775537 **F:** 01243 775537
Contact: Paul Goldthorpe
Party Max: 120 (marquee: unlimited) Bedrooms: 94

The hotel is set in the 12,000 acre Goodwood Estate, ancestral home to the Dukes of Richmond.
Catering: In house

SERVICES:
• Marriage Licence
Price Guide: Prices on application.
Catering (sit down): from £22.50pp
Catering (buffet): from £21.95pp

Mount Ephraim Gardens, Faversham
T: 01227 751496 **F:** 01227 751496
Contact: Mrs Lesley Dawes, Owner
Party Max: 150 (marquee: 450)

This elegant Victorian house is set in 9 acres of landscpaed gardens, which includes a lake, topiary, rose terraces, water gardens and Japanese style rock garden. The house has a grand entrance hall (licensed for wedding ceremonies and suitable for dancing), plus three other reception rooms.
Catering: Contract approved list

FACILITIES:
• Shooting   • Tennis   • Pool/Snooker
• Table Tennis
SERVICES:
• Marriage Licence   • Disco/Dance
Price Guide: £250 - £1700.
Catering (sit down): from £15pp
Catering (buffet): from £7pp

Netherfield Place, Battle
T: 01424 774455 **F:** 01424 774024
Contact: Michael Collier
Party Max: 100 (marquee: 250) Bedrooms: 13

This country house hotel, set in 30 acres, is available every day except Bank Holidays.

SOUTHEAST ENGLAND

Catering: In house

SERVICES:
- Marriage Licence

Price Guide: Prices on application.
Catering (sit down): from £18.00pp
Catering (buffet): from £7.50pp

Newick Park, Newick

T: 01825 723633 **F:** 01825 723969
E: bookings@newickpark.co.uk **W:** www.newickpark.co.uk
Contact: Nick Hughes, Manager

Party Max: 150 (marquee: 250)   Bedrooms: 16

Only 20 minutes from Brighton, this Grade II listed Georgian building is set in over 200 acres of landscaped grounds, featuring Victorian gardens with views of the lake to the South Downs. The oldest part of the house dates from the 16th Century and was an Ironmaster's home. The present owners have recently completed a total renovation and refurbishment of the house, which can be enjoyed on an exclusive basis if required. Newick boasts an award-winning chef.
Catering: In house

FACILITIES:
- Helipad
- Go Karting
- Outdoor Pool
- Shooting
- Tennis
- Quad Bikes/Off Road
- Paint Ball
- Watersports
- Tank Driving

SERVICES:
- Exclusive Use
- Marriage Licence
- Disco/Dance

Price Guide: Accommodation is from £95 per night for a single room to £235 for the premium rooms. Facility fee £4500 - £8000 per day.
Catering (sit down): from £32.50pp
Catering (buffet): from £17.50pp

Nizel's Golf Club, Nr Sevenoaks

T: 01732 833138 **F:** 01732 833764
Contact: Wedding Co-ordinator

Party Max: 200 (marquee: 150)

The recently refurbished Georgian Manor House at Nizel's is adjacent to formal rose gardens and a summer marquee. The house overlooks an 18 hole golf course in the heart of the Kentish Weald.
Catering: In house

SERVICES:
- Marriage Licence

Price Guide: Prices on application.
Catering (sit down): from £27.50pp

Northdown House, Margate

T: 01843 296111 **F:** 01843 295180
Contact: Mr Steven Davis, Operations Manager

Party Max: 130 (marquee: 500)

Northdowns House is situated in park grounds. This was once the country home of a notable local family, but has now been restored by Thanet District Council, to its former splendour. Various rooms and suites are available for hire, with viewing by appointment. A marquee can be erected abutting the rooms.

Catering: In house/Self catering

SERVICES:
- Exclusive Use
- Toastmaster
- Entertainers
- Flowers
- Disco/Dance
- Cake
- Live Music

Price Guide: £25 - £55 for 3 hours.
Catering (sit down): from £12.50pp
Catering (buffet): from £10.50pp

Nutfield Priory, Redhill

T: 01737 824400 **F:** 01737 823321
E: nutfield@arcadianhotels.co.uk **W:** nutfield-priory.com
Contact: John Pearman, Manager

Party Max: 120   Bedrooms: 60

This is a Victorian gothic folly set in 40 acres of grounds, and with its own luxury leisure centre. The mansion, with its crenellated towers, stained glass and pierced stonework, claims outstanding views of Surrey and Sussex from its elevated position. The Priory is now a 4-star hotel and part of the Arcadian group.
Catering: In house

FACILITIES:
- Helipad
- Pool/Snooker
- Steam Room
- Indoor Pool
- Quad Bikes/Off Road
- Sauna
- Gym
- Table Tennis

SERVICES:
- Exclusive Use
- Piped Music
- Hairdressing
- Marriage Licence
- Performance Area
- Creche
- Disco/Dance
- Beauty Treatment

Price Guide: From £80pp dinner b&b. Christmas and New Year, £2012 exclusive use.
Catering (sit down): from £35pp
Catering (buffet): from £35.50pp

Oakwood House Conference Centre, Maidstone

T: 01622 764433 **F:** 01622 763704
E: beu.palmer@kent.gov.uk
Contact: Functions Manager

Party Max: 120 (marquee: 300)   Bedrooms: 41

This Victorian house, run by Kent County Council, is set in mature parkland, and is about a mile from the centre of Maidstone.
Catering: In house

SERVICES:
- Marriage Licence

Price Guide: Prices on application.
Catering (sit down): from £23.75pp

Oatlands Park Hotel, Weybridge

T: 01932 847242 **F:** 01932 821413
Contact: James Addison

Party Max: 300   Bedrooms: 137

Three function rooms are available in this Grade II listed building which is set on the original estate where Henry VIII built a palace for Anne of Cleves. The rooms are The York Suite (120-

SOUTHEAST ENGLAND

220 people), The Broadwater Restaurant (80-160 people), and the Drawing Room & Garden Room (up to 60 people).
Catering: In house

SERVICES:
- Marriage Licence

Price Guide: Prices on application.
Catering (sit down): from £30.00pp

Ockenden Manor, Cuckfield
T: 01444 416111   **F:** 01444 415549
E: ockenden@hshotels.co.uk
W: www.hshotels.co.uk
Contact: Mr Kerry Turner, Manager

Party Max: 70 (marquee: 150)   Bedrooms: 22

Ockenden Manor is set in 9 acres of grounds with views of the countryside towards the South Downs. It features open fireplaces, crystal chandeliers and antique furniture.
Catering: In house

FACILITIES:
- Helipad
- Shooting

SERVICES:
- Exclusive Use
- Marriage Licence

Price Guide: £350 - £7500
Catering (sit down): from £35pp
Catering (buffet): from £29.50pp

Old Market, Hove
T: 01273 736222   **F:** 01273 329636
Contact: Tanya Ashdown, Event Manager

Party Max: 300

This venue was built as the local market for Brunswick Town in 1828. It is now a Grade II listed building and was restored with Lottery funding in 1995 to become a centre for the arts, education and community. Features inlcude an acoustically excellent Hall, a Gallery, Meeting Rooms, a recording suite, and dressing rooms/practice rooms etc for artistes. There is also a bar and cafe.
Catering: Contract (any)

SERVICES:
- Exclusive Use
- Marriage Licence
- Disco/Dance
- Performance Area

Price Guide: £75 - £650.
Catering (sit down): POA
Catering (buffet): POA

Old Ship Hotel, Brighton
T: 01273 329001   **F:** 01273 820718
Contact: Lorissa Bull

Party Max: 300   Bedrooms: 152

The Old Ship is housed in a Regency building (Grade I listed) and claims to be Brighton's oldest hotel. It is situated on Brighton's seafront, opening up interesting opportunities for outdoor photography. Functions can take place in the Paganini Ballroom, or the Regency Suite, or both rooms can be used together. Four smaller rooms are also available for receptions of between 20 and 75 guests.

Catering: In house

SERVICES:
- Marriage Licence

Price Guide: Prices on application.
Catering (sit down): from £20.00pp

The Orangery at the Mill, Maidstone
T: 01622 765511   **F:** 01622 765522
Contact: Maureen Camp, Events Manager

Party Max: 240 (marquee: 200)

Opening on May 5th 2001, The Orangery is a purpose-built wedding/party centre set in 9 acres of parkland and set beside the mill leat. It is within the sound of a tumbling waterfall and has a backdrop of Wellingtonia pines and blue cedar trees, set off by a lake and a boat house.
Catering: Contract approved list

FACILITIES:
- Shooting
- Fishing
- Archery

SERVICES:
- Exclusive Use
- Flowers
- Disco/Dance
- Performance Area

Price Guide: £2000 - £2950 per day.
Catering (sit down): from £20pp
Catering (buffet): from £16pp

Painshill Landscape Garden, Cobham
T: 01932 868113   **F:** 01932 868001
Contact: Mrs Harriet Richards, Events Manager

Party Max: 2000 (marquee: 2000)

Set in 160 acres, Painshill is an 18th Century landscape garden, with two sites offered for marquees: the Ampitheatre site - an oval surrounded by a tiered shrubbery withviews to the North Downs, and the Gothic Temple lawn, next to the lake and looking across to the Chinese bridge and Grotto Island. The buildings here are Grade I listed.
Catering: Contract (any)/Self catering

Price Guide: £8000 - £5000.
Catering (sit down): n/a
Catering (buffet): n/a

Palace Pier, Brighton
T: 01273 609361   **F:** 01273 684289
Contact: Marie Henley

Party Max: 260 (marquee: 300)

This famous pier features Victoria's Bar and Palm Court Restaurant which are available for functions from Monday to Friday, but not during Bank Holidays.
Catering: In house

SERVICES:
- Marriage Licence

Price Guide: Prices on application.
Catering (sit down): from £6.00pp

Pekes Manor House, Hailsham
T: 0207 352 8088   **F:** 0207 352 8125

SOUTHEAST ENGLAND

E: pekes.afa@virgin.net **W:** www.stilwell.co.uk
Contact: Ms E Morris
Party Max: 26

Several properties are available to rent in the grounds of this 16th Century manor house The largest is the Oast (11), with Tudor cottage sleeping 4 to 6.
Catering: Self catering

Price Guide: Short breaks in the Oast start at £575, with a week at £900 - £1205.

Penshurst Place, Tonbridge
T: 01892 870307
F: 01892 870866
E: banqueting@penhurstplace.com
W: penshurstplace.com
Contact: Terri Scott or Bridget Bamford, Banqueting Coordinators
Party Max: 200 (marquee: 750)

Penshurst is an historic family home dating from the 14th Century. Features include the medieval Baron's Hall, with 60ft high chestnut beamed roof and a mixture of paintings, tapestries and furniture from the 15th, 16th and 17th Centuries. The house is available for all kinds of functions including parties, receptions, product launches and even team building and activity days.The gardens, first laid out in the 14th Century, now include an adventure playground, nature trail and toy museum.
Catering: Contract (any)

FACILITIES:
- Helipad
- Go Karting
- Hot Air Balloons
- Quad Bikes/Off Road
- Country Pursuits

SERVICES:
- Marriage Licence
- Flowers
- Cake
- Toastmaster
- Disco/Dance
- Live Music
- Entertainers
- Fireworks
- Photography
- Performance Area

Price Guide: Room hire rates vary from £560 - £3000
Catering (sit down): from £33pp
Catering (buffet): from £28pp

Philpots Manor, Hildenborough
T: 01732 833047 or 0378 658793
Contact: Helen Garvey
Party Max: 40 (marquee: 100)   *Bedrooms: 3*

This 15th Century Grade II listed manor house was affiliated to Anne Boleyn's estate. It features minstrel's galleried landing, oak panelled rooms, log fire and a four poster wedding suite. There is also a decorative orangery suitable for photo sessions. All kinds of cuisine is offered. Tudor costumed and themed weddings have taken place here. Other services can be provided such as string quartets, classic cars, hairdressers and even bridesmaids!
Catering: In house

SERVICES:
- Marriage Licence

Price Guide: Prices on application.
Catering (sit down): from £20.00pp

Powder Mills Hotel, Battle
T: 01424 775511   **F:** 01424 774540
E: powdc@aol.com
W: www.powdermills.co.uk
Contact: Nick Walker
Party Max: 250   *Bedrooms: 35*

The Powder Mills Hotel is housed in a listed building, built 1720, that was originally a famous gunpowder mill; set in 150 acres. The Powder Mills Hotel has a famous chef, and has won awards for its cuisine.
Catering: In house

SERVICES:
- Marriage Licence

Price Guide: Prices on application.
Catering (sit down): from £20.00 - £25.00pp

Queen's Hall, Cuckfield
T: 01444 451610
Contact: Bookings Officer
Party Max: 150

The Queen's Hall, in the centre of the village of Cuckfield, was built to celebrate Queen Victoria's Diamond Jubilee. The building has recently undergone extensive refurbishment.
Catering: Self catering

SERVICES:
- Exclusive Use
- Marriage Licence
- Performance Area

Price Guide: Hire rates are £250 per day, £10.50 - £22 per hour.

Quex House & Gardens, Birchington-on-Sea
T: 01843 842168   **F:** 01843 346661
Contact: Graham Aylott
Party Max: 350 (marquee: unlimited)

This Regency country manor house, with museum adjacent, is set in 250 acres of parkland and gardens.
Catering: In house

SERVICES:
- Marriage Licence

Price Guide: Prices on application.
Catering (sit down): from £16.00pp
Catering (buffet): from £5.95pp

Ravenswood, Sharpthorne
T: 01342 810216
F: 01342 811393
E: theravenswood@compuserve.com
W: www.uk-expo.com/theravenswood
Contact: Stephen McArthur
Party Max: 300   *Bedrooms: 33*

Ravenswood is a manor house dating from the 15th Century, set in 22 acres of grounds and gardens, and overlooking its own lake. Inside, the house has minstrel's galleries and a panelled baronial hall. The house, which is now an hotel and restaurant, offers two rooms for receptions, ranging from the smallest gathering up to to 300. All types of cuisine can be created with past events including full medieval weddings.

SOUTHEAST ENGLAND

Catering: In house

SERVICES:
• Marriage Licence
Price Guide: Prices on application.
Catering (sit down): from £24.50pp
Catering (buffet): from £14.95pp

Read's Restaurant, Faversham
T: 01795 535344 **F:** 01795 591200
Contact: Mrs R C Pitchford
Party Max: 70 (marquee: unlimited)

The restaurant is set in a rural location with gardens and views. Read's is the only Michelin starred restaurant in Kent. Helicopters and hot air balloons may use the grounds.
Catering: In house

FACILITIES:
• Helipad   • Hot Air Balloons
SERVICES:
• Marriage Licence
Price Guide: Prices on application.
Catering (sit down): from £18.00pp

Romney, Hythe & Dymchurch Railway, New Romney
T: 01797 362353   **F:** 01797 363591
E: rhdr@dels.demon.co.uk   **W:** www.rhdr.demon.co.uk
Contact: Derek Smith, Marketing Manager
Party Max: 100

This is a 13.5 mile long unique tourist railway and the world's smallest public railway. It was built as a millionaire's toy in 1927 and now carries over 150,000 passengers a year. Along the line there are 6 stations, two cafes (at New Romney and Dungeness), picnic areas, steam and deisel hauled trains, a toy and model museum and other attractions.
Catering: In house

FACILITIES:
• Steam Driving
SERVICES:
• Exclusive Use
Price Guide: Prices on application.
Catering (sit down): POA

Rowhill Grange, Dartford
T: 01322 615136
F: 01322 615137
E: admin@rowhillgrange.com
Contact: Jane Brown
Party Max: 200   *Bedrooms: 30*

Capable of catering for parties from 12 to 150 guests, Rowhill Grange is an AA/RAC four-star hotel. It is a partly thatched house dating from 1868 set in nine acres of woodland and landscaped gardens with lake. Facilities include 30 individually designed bedrooms, including suites and four-poster rooms. Rowhill Grange is also home to what claims to be "the finest health spa in the South"; the Utopia Health and Leisure Spa.
Catering: In house

FACILITIES:
• Health Spa
SERVICES:
• Marriage Licence
Price Guide: Prices on application.
Catering (sit down): from £29.95pp

Royal Pavilion, Brighton
T: 01273 292815   **F:** 01273 292871
E: visitor.services@brighton-hove.gov.uk
W: royalpavilion.brighton.co.uk
Contact: Melanie Woodland, Events Assistant
Party Max: 50

The Royal Pavilion is the famous seaside residence of King George IV. Originally a simple farmhouse but transformed by John Nash into an Indian style palace with lavish interiors inspired by the Orient. The magnificent state rooms are available to hire for evening receptions, dinners and recitals.
Catering: Contract (any)

SERVICES:
• Exclusive Use   • Marriage Licence
Price Guide: Hire fees range from £400 - £2400.
Catering (sit down): POA
Catering (buffet): POA

Runnymede Hotel & Spa, Egham
T: 01784 436171   **F:** 01784 436340
E: info@runnymedehotel.com
W: www.runnymedehotel.com
Contact: Sue Wolton
Party Max: 300 (marquee: 200)   *Bedrooms: 180*

Runnymede Hotel has a splendid riverside setting with gardens on the banks of the Thames. Guests can arrive or depart from the hotel by boat, and the site is also suitable for helicopters. All catering at Runnymede is in house. Children can be catered for separately and the hotel has 180 rooms to offer plenty of accommodation on site for guests.
Catering: In house

SERVICES:
• Marriage Licence
Price Guide: Prices on application.
Catering (sit down): from £29.00pp
Catering (buffet): from £29.00pp

Salomons, Tunbridge Wells
T: 01892 507601/507645   **F:** 01892 539102
E: enquiries@salomons.org.uk **W:** www.salomons.org.uk
Contact: Julia Welch, Sales Administrator
Party Max: 435 (marquee: 175)   *Bedrooms: 24*

This elegant listed Victorian country mansion is set in 36 acres of landscaped gardens, woodland, parkland and lakes. The venue offers a choice of several function rooms seating 20 to 200 and is available for exclusive use. Summer functions can include a barbecue on the terrace, which offers wonderful rural views. The building also houses a large Victorian theatre. Salomons is part of Canterbury Christ Church University College.

SOUTHEAST ENGLAND

Catering: In house

SERVICES:
- Exclusive Use
- Marriage Licence
- Performance Area

Price Guide: Room hire fees are waived if a 3-course meal for minimum numbers is booked. Otherwise facility fees range from £135 to £900.
Catering (sit down): from £18.95pp
Catering (buffet): from £9.10pp

Sandown Park, Esher
T: 01372 464790   **F:** 01372 465205
E: sandown@rht.net   **W:** www.sandown.co.uk
Contact: Lynn Ingrey, Sales Manager
Party Max: 600 (marquee: 500)   *Bedrooms: 21*

Well known racecourse Sandown Park offers a choice of seven suites in its main building for receptions; and three suites for wedding ceremonies. This venue is currently undergoing a £23 million refurbishment programme which will include a new glass fronted Lawn Complex with a view across the racecourse.
Catering: In house

FACILITIES:
- Helipad
- Gym
- Golf
- Pool/Snooker
- Go Karting

SERVICES:
- Marriage Licence
- Disco/Dance
- Performance Area

Price Guide: From £39pp. Other prices on application
Catering (sit down): from £23pp
Catering (buffet): from £17.50pp

Saville Court, Englefield Green
T: 01784 472000   **F:** 01784 4472200
Contact: Banqueting Manager
Party Max: 800 (marquee: 250)   *Bedrooms: 105*

This hotel and conference centre is housed in a Grade II listed building set in attractive grounds.
Catering: In house

SERVICES:
- Marriage Licence

Price Guide: Prices on application.
Catering (sit down): from £28.00pp

Sharsted Court, Nr Sittingbourne
T: 01795 890343   **F:** 01795 890713
Contact: Mrs Judith Shepley
Party Max: 100 (marquee: unlimited)

This stately home is Grade I and II listed and dates from the 12th Century. It features ornamental brick and flint walls, gazebos, and clipped yew trees (including a maze). Three rooms are available for receptions: the Ballroom, the Billiard Room and the Front Hall. The venue hosted five marquee functions in 1998, but limits these to a maximum of 150 guests. Couples have a complete choice of caterer.
Catering: Contract (any)

SERVICES:
- Marriage Licence

Price Guide: Prices on application.

Catering (sit down): from £20.00pp
Catering (buffet): from £7.50pp

Spread Eagle Hotel, Midhurst
T: 01730 816911
F: 01730 815668
Contact: Karen Edgington
Party Max: 120 (marquee: unlimited)   *Bedrooms: 100*

This is a Grand Heritage Hotel, dating from 1430. Features include Flemish stained glass windows, inglenook fireplaces, tudor bread ovens and four-poster beds.
Catering: In house

SERVICES:
- Marriage Licence

Price Guide: Prices on application.
Catering (sit down): from £21.00pp

Squerryes Court, Westerham
T: 01959 562345/563118   **F:** 01959 565949
E: squerryescourt@pavilion.co.uk
Contact: Mrs Warde, Owner
Party Max: 60

This 17th Century manor house is still lived in the by decendants of John Warde, who purchased the house in 1731. The house features a fine collection of Old Master paintings from the Italian, 17th Century Dutch and 18th Century English schools, as well as furniture, procelain and tapestries. The house is set in attractive gardens with spring bulbs, herbaceous borders and old roses.
Catering: In house

Price Guide: Prices on application.

St Augustines, Westgate-on-Sea
T: 01843 836900   **F:** 01843 836900
E: enq@st-augustines.ision.co.uk
W: www.st-augustines.ision.co.uk
Contact: David Hill
Party Max: 300 (marquee: unlimited)

This Grade II listed building set in 11 acres of grounds, is only one mile from the beach. A chapel for up to 400 guest is also on site, and available for blessings. Some Bank Holidays may not be available.
Catering: In house

SERVICES:
- Marriage Licence

Price Guide: Prices on application.
Catering (sit down): from £34.50pp
Catering (buffet): from £24.50pp

Stanhill Court Hotel, Horley
T: 01293 862166
F: 01293 862773
Contact: Functions Manager
Party Max: 200 (marquee: 700)   *Bedrooms: 13*

This Victorian country house was built in 1881 in the Scottish Baronial style. It is set in 35 acres of ancient wooded country-

SOUTHEAST ENGLAND

side. Its grounds feature an open-air ampitheatre and a walled garden. Stanhill was Hotel of the Year in 1998 and has been voted Most Romantic Hotel of the Year by the AA. This venue can be made available on an exclusive use basis.
Catering: In house

SERVICES:
- Exclusive Use
- Marriage Licence

Price Guide: Prices on application.
Catering (sit down): from £30.00pp

Swallows Oast, Ticehurst
T: 01797 223902
F: 01580 200638
Contact: Mark Vidal

Party Max: 120

Swallows Oast is a listed building dating back to the 1830s and set in the midst of rural Sussex. The Oast claims a Medieval atmosphere and has often hosted medieval and themed banquets. You may also do your own catering at this venue.
Catering: In house/Contract (any)/Self catering

SERVICES:
- Marriage Licence

Price Guide: Prices on application.
Catering (sit down): from £17.00pp
Catering (buffet): from £5.00pp

Swarling Manor, Canterbury
T: 01227 761816   **F:** 01227 700377
Contact: Mrs Nicola Dibley

Party Max: 120 (marquee: unlimited)

This private manor house, dating from 1750, is located in a rural setting with its own 12 self catering cottages. There is also a Kentish barn on this site with open country views and room for a marquee. There are no reception facilities on site, but couples may appoint their own caterer, with the reception in a marquee. Accommodation is available in self-catering cottages.
Catering: Contract (any)/Self catering

SERVICES:
- Marriage Licence

Price Guide: Prices on application.
Catering (sit down): POA

Tenterden Town Hall, Tenterden
T: 01580 762271
F: 01580 765647
E: townhall@tenterden.freeserve.co.uk
Contact: Mrs Angela Patrick, Deputy Town Clerk

Party Max: 140

Tenterden's listed 18th Century town hall, situated on the High Street, offers the plush but intimate Mayor's Parlour Room (licensed for ceremonies), as well as The Assembly Hall.
Catering: Self catering

SERVICES:
- Exclusive Use
- Marriage Licence
- Performance Area

Price Guide: £100 - £300.

Tottington Manor, Henfield
T: 01903 815757   **F:** 01903 879331
E: tottingtonmanor@compuserve.com
W: www.tottingtonmanor.co.uk
Contact: Kate Miller or David, Proprietors

Party Max: 60 (marquee: 100)   Bedrooms: 6

This Grade II listed building is located at the foot of the downs, and now operates as a 4-Diamond hotel. The Chef/Proprietor here was Head Chef at London's Ritz Hotel on Piccadilly.
Catering: In house

FACILITIES:
- Helipad

SERVICES:
- Exclusive Use
- Marriage Licence
- Disco/Dance
- Piped Music

Price Guide: Marquees (May to Sept) £1100 per day. Other rates on application.
Catering (sit down): from £22.25pp
Catering (buffet): from £19.50pp

Turkey Court, Maidstone
T: 01622 765511   **F:** 01622 765522
Contact: Maureen Kemp

Party Max: 250 (marquee: 150)

Turkey Court is a Queen Anne Grade II house with nine acres of gardens and grounds. An Orangery, suitable for receptions, should be completed by May 2001 (see separate entry). Events are booked here on an exclusive basis and guests can wander in the grounds. There is also a site where fireworks can be set off, which can be arranged by the venue. There are no tied caterers here, although they should be chosen from a list of approved caterers. The venue itself does not have a liquor licence and does not charge for couples to supply their own alcohol.
Catering: Contract approved list

SERVICES:
- Marriage Licence

Price Guide: Prices on application.

TuTu L'Auberge, South Godstone
T: 01342 892318   **F:** 01342 893435
E: Tutu@Dial.Pipex.com
Contact: Antoine Jalley, Owner

Party Max: 150 (marquee: 250)

Tutu L'Auberge is an eclectic Edwardian house set in 14 acres of gardens with a lake and pasture land. The house has a main restaurant, conservatory, the Garden Room and the banqueting suite, Le Zazou, are available for functions.
Catering: In house

FACILITIES:
- Helipad
- Hot Air Balloons

SERVICES:
- Exclusive Use
- Marriage Licence
- Disco/Dance
- Entertainers
- Piped Music
- Valet Parking

Price Guide: £185 - £850
Catering (sit down): from £25.50pp
Catering (buffet): from £18.50pp

SOUTHEAST ENGLAND

Waltham Court Hotel, Canterbury
T: 01227 700413 **F:** 01227 700127
E: sgw.chives.waltham@dial.pipex.com
Contact: Steve Weaver

Party Max: 100 (marquee: 180) | Bedrooms: 4

This was originally an 18th Century poor house and is now a Grade II listed building with two acres of gardens, situated in a conservation area. Quality fresh cuisine is boasted by this venue. Helicopters and hot air balloons may use the grounds if required.
Catering: In house

FACILITIES:
- Helipad
- Hot Air Balloons

SERVICES:
- Marriage Licence

Price Guide: Prices on application.
Catering (sit down): from £18.50pp
Catering (buffet): from £14.00pp

Weald & Downland Open Air Museum, Chichester
T: 01243 811363 **F:** 01243 811475
E: wealddown@mistral.co.uk **W:** www.wealddown.co.uk
Contact: Museum Secretary

Party Max: 30

Set in the heart of the South Downs, the Weald and Downland Open Air Museum is one of the country's leading museums of historic buildings and traditional rural life, with over 45 buildings on site. The Museum is available as a venue for children's parties, weddings and meetings, as well as marquee-based events, at designated times.
Catering: In house

SERVICES:
- Marriage Licence

Price Guide: £36 - £400.
Catering (sit down): POA
Catering (buffet): POA

Wentworth Club, Virginia Water
T: 01344 842201
F: 01344 842804
E: banquetsales@wentworthclub.com
W: www.wentworthclub.com
Contact: Karin Bidgood, Conference & Banqueting Promotions Manager

Party Max: 400 | Bedrooms: 12

A rhododendron-lined drive leads to the famous castellated clubhouse of Wentworth (extensively redeveloped in 1993), a famous golfing venue which hosts the annual PGA and World Match Play Championships. The Club offers 4 versatile private function rooms, including the gabled Ballroom, which can accommodate up to 200.
Catering: In house

FACILITIES:
- Golf
- Gym
- Tennis
- Outdoor Pool
- Pool/Snooker

SERVICES:
- Marriage Licence • Flowers • Disco/Dance
- Performance Area

Price Guide: Venue hire ranges from £125 for a part-day meeting in the Members' Lounge, to £1500 for a full-day meeting in the Ballroom. For private hire rates range from £150 to £600.
Catering (sit down): from £28.95pp
Catering (buffet): from £28.95pp

Woodlands Park Hotel, Cobham
T: 01372 843933 **F:** 01372 842704
E: info@woodlandspark.co.uk
W: www.woodlandspark.co.uk
Contact: Judy Watts

Party Max: 200 | Bedrooms: 59

A member of the Arcadian Hotels group, Woodlands Park is a Victorian mansion set in 10 acres of grounds. Its interior features original oak panelling, a minstrel's gallery and a stained glass roof. The bedrooms incude several four-poster beds.
Catering: In house

SERVICES:
- Marriage Licence

Price Guide: Prices on application.
Catering (sit down): from £27.50pp
Catering (buffet): from £29.75pp

SOUTH OF ENGLAND

Alton House Hotel, Alton
T: 01420 80033   **F:** 01420 89222
Contact: Peter Dunbar
Party Max: 180 (marquee: 300)   Bedrooms: 39

Set near the centre of the old market town of Alton, this Victorian built hotel has over two acres of landscaped gardens and an outdoor pool.
Catering: In house

SERVICES:
- Marriage Licence

Price Guide: Prices on application.
Catering (sit down): from £21.50pp

Alverbank Country House Hotel, Gosport
T: 02392 510005   **F:** 02392 520864
E: alverbank@clara.co.uk
Contact: Muir Wilson
Party Max: 200 (marquee: 200)   Bedrooms: 9 + 2

This listed building built in 1842 is set in landscaped grounds and situated just one minute from the beach. Adjacent to the hotel is the newly refurbished cottage, which has two interconnecting bedrooms and two sitting rooms. It is possible for guests to arrive and depart by boat.
Catering: In house

SERVICES:
- Marriage Licence

Price Guide: Prices on application.
Catering (sit down): from £16.00pp
Catering (buffet): from £7.50pp

Aurora Garden Hotel, Windsor
T: 01753 868686   **F:** 01753 831394
E: aurora@auroragarden   **W:** www.auroragarden.co.uk
Contact: Karen Castle
Party Max: 120 (marquee: 200)   Bedrooms: 19

This country house hotel and restaurant is situated in a residential part of the town and set in its own acre of gardens, featuring a landscaped water garden.
Catering: In house

SERVICES:
- Marriage Licence

Price Guide: Prices on application.
Catering (sit down): from £22.95pp (package)

Avington Park, Winchester
T: 01962 779260   **F:** 01962 779864
E: sarah@avingtonpark.co.uk   **W:** www.vingtonpark.co.uk
Contact: Sarah Bullen, Proprietor
Party Max: 120 (marquee: 800)

Avington has an enviable history for entertaining important guests. King Charles II frequently the place and Nell Gwynne enjoyed its unique ambience. Parts of the house date back to Roman times, but it was also mentioned in the Domesday Book, and was once owned by Henry VIII. Now the house is a family home and is available for exclusive hire for corporate and private functions.

Catering: Contract approved list

FACILITIES:
- Hot Air Balloons

SERVICES:
- Exclusive Use
- Marriage Licence
- Performance Area
- Valet Parking

Price Guide: There is a minimum fee of £10 per head.
Catering (sit down): from £25pp
Catering (buffet): from £18pp

Bartley Lodge Hotel, Cadnam
T: 02380 812248   **F:** 02380 812075
Contact: Christine Turner
Party Max: 150 (marquee: 200)   Bedrooms: 31

This Grade II listed hunting lodge, which dates from 1759, is set in eight acres of parkland and walled gardens. Interior features include a minstrel's gallery and a grand oak panelled room.
Catering: In house

SERVICES:
- Marriage Licence

Price Guide: Prices on application.
Catering (sit down): from £18.00pp

Bassetsbury Manor, High Wycombe
T: 01494 421888 or 01494 421883   **F:** 01494 421808
E: russell-page@wycombe.gov.uk
Contact: Sarah Randall, Sports & Facilities Manager
Party Max: 90 (marquee: 180)

Bassetsbury Manor is a Grade II listed manor building situated on the edge of the Rye, a town centre park. The manor is surrounded by grounds including a bowls green, croquet lawn, tennis court, putting green and petanque area. The ground floor of the manor can accommodate parties up to 90 people, but a marquee can be used in the grounds.
Catering: Self catering

FACILITIES:
- Tennis
- Bowls
- Croquet
- Petanque
- Putting

SERVICES:
- Marriage Licence

Price Guide: The top hourly rate for hiring this venue is £370.

Beech House, Chipping Norton
T: 01608 641435   **F:** 01608 641435
Contact: The Owner
Party Max: 19   Bedrooms: 10

This spacious Cotswold farmhouse is situated in an Area of Outstanding Natural Beauty and boasts a beautifully renovated interior, including marble floors and period fireplaces. There are 3 reception rooms and a large modern, fully equipped kitchen/dining room. There are good walks directly from the property.
Catering: Self catering

SERVICES:
- Exclusive Use

Price Guide: From £1500 to £2200 per week

SOUTH OF ENGLAND

Blenheim Palace, Nr Oxford
T: 01993 811091
F: 01993 813527
E: administration@blenheimpalace.com
W: www.blenheimpalace.com
Contact: Stuart MacFarlane, Functions Manager

Party Max: 300 (marquee: 1000)

Blenheim Palace, home of the 11th Duke of Marlborough, and birthplace of Winston Churchill, is probably one of the UK's finest country houses featuring gilded state rooms and the majestic Long Library. The house was built in the baroque style by Sir John Vanbrugh and is considered his masterpiece. Evening functions only are possible in this 18th Century palace.
Catering: Contract approved list

FACILITIES:
- Helipad
- Hot Air Balloons

SERVICES:
- Toastmaster

Price Guide: £7500 - £35000
Catering (sit down): from £85pp
Catering (buffet): from £75pp

Botleigh Grange Hotel, Southampton
T: 01489 787700
F: 01489 788535
Contact: Functions Manager

Party Max: 200 (marquee: 500) | Bedrooms: 43

This 17th century country house is set in parkland with lakes and a sweeping drive.
Catering: In house

SERVICES:
- Marriage Licence

Price Guide: Prices on application.
Catering (sit down): from £21.50pp

Boulters Lock Hotel, Maidenhead
T: 01628 621291   **F:** 01628 626048
Contact: Valerie Chappel

Party Max: 110 | Bedrooms: 18

The hotel, which features in Jerome K Jerome's novel 'Three Men in a Boat', was built in 1726 as a miller's house. Set on Boulters Island, it offers panoramic views of the River Thames. The hotel has its own pontoon.
Catering: In house

SERVICES:
- Marriage Licence

Price Guide: Prices on application.
Catering (sit down): from £25.00pp

Burley Manor Hotel, Ringwood
T: 01425 403522   **F:** 0125 403227
Contact: Andrew Rogers

Party Max: 100 (marquee: 200) | Bedrooms: 30

This RAC/AA 3 star hotel is set in five acres of landscaped grounds with an outdoor pool.
Catering: In house

SERVICES:
- Marriage Licence

Price Guide: Prices on application.
Catering (sit down): from £19.75pp

Burnham Beeches Hotel, Burnham
T: 01628 429955   **F:** 01628 603994
Contact: Cliff Hasler

Party Max: 200 (marquee: 250) | Bedrooms: 75

This Georgian manor is set in over ten acres of grounds on the edge of Burnham Beeches. One of the main function suites opens on to lawns, making it ideal for summer events. The hotel has arranged fireworks for weddings and guests have arrived and left by helicopter.
Catering: In house

FACILITIES:
- Helipad

SERVICES:
- Marriage Licence
- Fireworks

Price Guide: Prices on application.
Catering (sit down): from £65.00pp (packages)

Cantley House Hotel, Wokingham
T: 01189 789912   **F:** 01189 774294
Contact: Robert Frankland

Party Max: 90 (marquee: 200) | Bedrooms: 29

This Victorian country house, set in 59 acres, was formerly the home of the Marquis of Ormonde.
Catering: In house

SERVICES:
- Marriage Licence

Price Guide: Prices on application.
Catering (sit down): from £55.00pp

Careys Manor Hotel, Brockenhurst
T: 01590 623551   **F:** 01590 622799
E: careysmanorhotel@binternet.com
W: www.newforesthotels.co.uk
Contact: Mandy Walker

Party Max: 110 | Bedrooms: 79

Dating from 1888 and built on the site of a royal hunting lodge used by Charles II, Careys Manor is set in landscaped grounds on the edge of the New Forest. The restaurant here offers English and French cuisine. Children under 7 will be charged half price. Also on site is a health club, complete with indoor pool and steam room.
Catering: In house

SERVICES:
- Marriage Licence

Price Guide: Prices on application.
Catering (sit down): from £28.95

Chartridge Conference Centre, Chesham
T: 01494 837484   **F:** 01494 837305
E: mail@chartridge.co.uk
W: www.chartridge.co.uk

SOUTH OF ENGLAND

Contact: Claire Wearne
Party Max: 150 (marquee: unlimited)
This conference centre is housed in a 19th Century building set in 25 acres of gardens and woods.
Catering: In house

SERVICES:
• Marriage Licence
Price Guide: Prices on application.
Catering (sit down): from £32.00pp
Catering (buffet): from £9.00pp

Chewton Glen Hotel, New Milton
T: 01425 275341   **F:** 01425 272310
E: sales@chewtonglen.com
Contact: Thierry Lepinoy
Party Max: 180   Bedrooms: 54
A renowned health and country club with five stars AA and RAC rating, Chewton Glen's catering has earned it one Michelin star. Discos and live music are available upon discussion with the hotel.
Catering: In house

SERVICES:
• Marriage Licence
Price Guide: Prices on application.
Catering (sit down): from £30.00pp

Chilworth Manor, Southampton
T: 023 8076 7333   **F:** 023 8070 1743
E: general@chilworth-manor.co.uk
W: www.chilworth-manor.co.uk
Contact: Jo Tozer, Sales Executive
Party Max: 170 (marquee: 200)   Bedrooms: 95
Chilworth Manor is a traditional Ewardian manor house set in 36 acres of Hampshire parkland. Special features include a galleries hall and a terrace overlooking the gardens and a lake. The Manor is now a conference centre offering 4-star accommodation.
Catering: In house

FACILITIES:
• Gym   • Quad Bikes/Off Road   • Tennis

SERVICES:
• Marriage Licence   • Disco/Dance
Price Guide: Prices on application.
Catering (sit down): from £30pp
Catering (buffet): from £30pp

Cliveden, Maidenhead
T: 01628 668561   **F:** 01628 661837
Contact: Vikki Greenway
Party Max: 60 (marquee: unlimited)   Bedrooms: 38
Once the home of Lady Astor, Cliveden was built in 1851 and is set in 375 acres of landscaped grounds high above the Thames. While entertainment and dancing are allowed, they must not interfere with the normal running of the hotel, or inconvenience other guests, which precludes loud bands or discos. This, of course, does not apply if you take over the whole hotel (190 guests with accommodation for up to 38 couples), plus a band and dinner.
Catering: In house

SERVICES:
• Marriage Licence
Price Guide: Prices on application.
Catering (sit down): POA

Compleat Angler Hotel, Marlow
T: 01628 484444   **F:** 01628 481349
Contact: Alison Smith
Party Max: 140 (marquee: 200)   Bedrooms: 65
This famous country house hotel sits on the banks of the river Thames within walking distance of the centre of Marlow, a short drive to Heathrow, and 30 miles from the centre of London.
Catering: In house

SERVICES:
• Marriage Licence
Price Guide: Prices on application.
Catering (sit down): from £69.00pp (including drinks)

Corn Exchange, Faringdon
T: 01367 240281   **F:** 01367 240303
Contact: June Rennie, Town Clerk
Party Max: 200
The Corn Exchange, managed by Faringdon Town Council, is situated in the heart of this market town and dates from the 1860s. The main hall with its vaulted ceiling is available for events, as well as the first floor council chamber, and the newly refurbished kitchen. Hirers may do their own catering at this venue or use contract caterers of their choice.
Catering: Self catering

SERVICES:
• Marriage Licence
Price Guide: Hire fees are £11 - £17 per hour for functions and £6 - £9 per hour setting up time. A one-off Peforming Rights fee of £7.50 is charged per function, while heating is charged at £1.20 per hour.

The Dairy, Waddesdon Manor, Aylesbury
T: 01296 653230   **F:** 01296 653208
E: twmflm@smtp.ntrust.org.uk   **W:** www.waddesdon.org.uk
Contact: Fiona McGeough, Events Executive
Party Max: 110 (marquee: 300)   Bedrooms: 11
Within the extensive grounds of Waddesdon Manor, the award-winning Dairy is a private building restored in cotemporary style that provides an unique setting for parties, lunches, dinners, wine tastings, receptions, meetings, conferences and weddings. Absolute exclusivity is guaranteed by the Dairy's policy of never accepting more than one client at a time. The Dairy has 4 rooms: the West Hall with roaring log fires; the Wintergarden, which overlooks the lake; the intimate Dieppe Room; and the Buttery. Outside the Pavilions provide cover for al fresco entertaining or relaxing by the lake and restored

SOUTH OF ENGLAND

Victorian water gardens.
Catering: In house FB

FACILITIES:
- Helipad
- Shooting
- Hot Air Balloons

SERVICES:
- Exclusive Use
- Marriage Licence
- Cake
- Disco/Dance
- Piped Music
- Performance Area

Price Guide: Facility fee: Mon - Fri £4000 Sat - Sun £5000
Catering (sit down): from £35pp
Catering (buffet): from £35pp

Dimbola Lodge, Freshwater Bay
T: 01983 756814 **F:** 01983 755578
E: administrator@dimbola.co.uk
W: www.dimbola.co.uk
Contact: Ron Smith, Chairman
Party Max: 40

This is a large Victorian property with galleries exhibiting contemporary photgraphic exhibitions, including a large display of Julia Margaret Cameron's 19th Century photographic work, The house has been tastefully restored and has small conference rooms and a vegetarian restaurant.
Catering: In house

SERVICES:
- Exclusive Use
- Photography
- Piped Music

Price Guide: Prices on application.
Catering (sit down): from £12.50pp
Catering (buffet): from £4pp

Dorney Court, Windsor
T: 01628 604638 **F:** 01628 665772
E: palmer@dorneycourt.co.uk **W:** www.dorneycourt.co.uk
Contact: Mrs Peregrine Palmer, Owner
Party Max: 60 (marquee: 1000)

Country Life magazine once claimed this to be one of the finest Tudor manor houses in England. Grade I listed Dorney Court was built around 1440 and has been in the Palmer family through 13 generations. The house contains a fine collection of English furniture, family portraits and needlework. Adjacent is the 13th Century church of St James which boasts a Norman font and a Tudor tower. In the grounds, a Blooms of Bressingham plant centre and tea room is found in the Victorian walled garden, and PYO is open June to August.
Catering: In house

FACILITIES:
- Helipad
- Go Karting
- Hot Air Balloons
- Tennis
- Outdoor Pool
- Quad Bikes/Off Road
- Table Tennis

SERVICES:
- Flowers

Price Guide: Prices on application.
Catering (sit down): from £45pp
Catering (buffet): from £40pp

Dorton House, Aylesbury
T: 01844 238217 **F:** 01844 23505

Contact: Christine Shaw
Party Max: 80 (marquee: unlimited)

Dorton House is a prep school in a Jacobean mansion set in its own 70 acre estate.
Catering: In house

SERVICES:
- Marriage Licence

Price Guide: Prices on application.
Catering (sit down): from £25.00pp
Catering (buffet): from £6.95pp

Easthampstead Park, Wokingham
T: 0118 978 0686 **F:** 0118 979 3870
E: rita@eastpark.co.uk **W:** www.eastpark.co.uk
Contact: Rita Monney, Conference Manager
Party Max: 200 (marquee: 1000)   Bedrooms: 27

Easthampstead Park is a Victorian country house standing at the end of a half mile tree-lined drive in 60 acres of parkland in the Berkshire countryside. The size and disposition of rooms gives flexibility for all types of functions. In addition, it is host to a themed Christmas party in a marquee in the grounds.
Catering: In house

FACILITIES:
- Helipad
- Paint Ball
- Gym
- Hot Air Balloons
- Tennis
- Pool/Snooker
- Quad Bikes/Off Road
- Table Tennis

SERVICES:
- Marriage Licence
- Disco/Dance
- Performance Area

Price Guide: Prices on application.
Catering (sit down): from £24.50
Catering (buffet): from £17.50

Elmers Court Country Club, Lymington
T: 01590 676011 **F:** 01590 679780
Contact: Catherine Deville, Sales Executive
Party Max: 200 (marquee: 500)   Bedrooms: 42

Elmers Court is situated on the edge of the New Forest with extensive views of the Solent. This Tudor-style manor house, built in 1820, stands in 23 acres of gardens and lawns and features oak panelling and embossed ceilings. Self-catering timeshare apartments, managed by Barratt, are available at this venue.
Catering: Self catering/In house

FACILITIES:
- Helipad
- Golf
- Indoor Pool
- Gym
- Tennis
- Outdoor Pool
- Pool/Snooker
- Table Tennis

SERVICES:
- Marriage Licence
- Flowers
- Cake
- Disco/Dance

Price Guide: Rates on application.
Catering (sit down): from £10pp
Catering (buffet): from £10pp

Esseborne Manor Hotel, Andover
T: 01264 736444 **F:** 01264 736725

SOUTH OF ENGLAND

E: esseborrnemanor@compuserve.com
Contact: I. Hamilton, Proprietor

Party Max: 60 (marquee: 150)   Bedrooms: 15

This is a small 3-star country house hotel set in rich farm lands in an area designated as one of outstanding natural beauty. The 100 year old house is set in 3 acres of landscaped gardens. The Dining Room has open log fires and fabric lined walls. Dishes here use local produce and herbs from the Manor's own garden.
Catering: In house

FACILITIES:
- Helipad
- Tennis

SERVICES:
- Exclusive Use
- Marriage Licence
- Flowers
- Cake
- Toastmaster
- Disco/Dance
- Fireworks
- Piped Music
- Valet Parking

Price Guide: £1500 - £3000 for a day. Weekly rates £10500 - £20000. Christmas and New Year £25000.
Catering (sit down): from £25pp
Catering (buffet): from £20pp

Forest Park Hotel, Brockenhurst
T: 01590 622844   **F:** 01590 623948
Contact: Mrs Clair Mallen

Party Max: 150 (marquee: 200)   Bedrooms: 38

Originally built as a vicarage, this venue became an hotel in 1902. The hotel, set in four acres, boasts a tennis court, outdoor heated pool, and log cabin sauna.
Catering: In house

FACILITIES:
- Tennis
- Outdoor Pool
- Sauna

SERVICES:
- Marriage Licence

Price Guide: Prices on application.
Catering (sit down): from £20.00pp

Fort Brockhurst, Gosport
T: 023 9258 1059
Contact: Pam Braddock, Custodian

Party Max: 3000 (marquee: 3000)

This English Heritage owned 19th Century fort was built to protect Portsmouth. The fort boasts a parade ground, a moated keep and a ghost in Cell No 3! The Fort is open to the public at weekends from April to October.
Catering: Contract (any)

SERVICES:
- Exclusive Use

Price Guide: from £100
Catering (sit down): POA
Catering (buffet): POA

Fountain Court Hotel, Southampton
T: 02380 846310   **F:** 02380 847295
Contact: Mrs V Harris

Party Max: 200 (marquee: 100)   Bedrooms: 24

Built in 1856, the hotel boasts intricate decor, a garden fountain and an undergarden chamber. The hotel offers a wide vegetarian menu, as well as a children's menu, with cuisine ranging from Cajun to oriental, French and American.
Catering: In house

FACILITIES:
- Helipad
- Hot Air Balloons

SERVICES:
- Marriage Licence

Price Guide: Prices on application.
Catering (sit down): from £12.50pp
Catering (buffet): from £5.00pp

Grovefield Hotel, Burnham
T: 01628 603131   **F:** 01628 668078
Contact: Jacqui Bagnall

Party Max: 150 (marquee: 250)   Bedrooms: 40

This is a turn of the century Edwardian house set in eight acres. Several packages are available with special touches including ice carving and bespoke food items.
Catering: In house

SERVICES:
- Marriage Licence
- Ice Carving

Price Guide: Prices on application.
Catering (sit down): from £57.50pp (package)

Guard's Polo Club, Windsor Great Park
T: 01784 434212
Contact: Events Manager

Party Max: 3000 (marquee: 3000)

The Guards' Polo Club, located in the middle of Windsor Great Park, offers a marquee for functions. Searcy's is one of the approved contract caterers here (see Contract Caterers listing).
Catering: Contract approved list

SERVICES:
- Exclusive Use

Price Guide: Prices on application.

Hatton Court Hotel, Hanslope
T: 01908 510044   **F:** 01908 510945
Contact: Trudy or Judy

Party Max: 90 (marquee: 350)   Bedrooms: 20

This country house is set in six acres of private gardens. It is described as 'typical mid-Victorian architecture with gothic mullioned windows and main porchway'. The interior features include an oriental lounge and a conservatory. The sit down meal packages may start at £29.50, but rise to £67.50 per head. The latter includes delicacies such as 'Charentais melon filled with ragout of lobster tail and king scallops with a truffle and hazelnut vinaigrette' - and that's just for starters! Local entertainment is provided by Towcester Racecourse (7 miles), and Silverstone (10 miles).
Catering: In house

SERVICES:
- Marriage Licence

Price Guide: Prices on application.
Catering (sit down): from £29.50pp

SOUTH OF ENGLAND

Catering (buffet): from £7.50pp

Hawkwell House Hotel, Iffley Village
T: 01865 749988   F: 01865 748525
Contact: Jacqueline Lee
Party Max: 300 (marquee: 150)   *Bedrooms: 27*

The hotel was originally a family home dating back to 1856 and features two houses on the same site. The hotel is 1.5 miles from the centre of Oxford and is set in three acres of grounds. 5 rooms are available for functions.
Catering: In house

SERVICES:
• Marriage Licence

Price Guide: Prices on application.
Catering (sit down): from £37.00pp

Highclere Castle, Highclere
T: 01635 253210   F: 016635 810193
Contact: Lindsey Giles
Party Max: 200

Highclere Castle is a listed building and is claimed to be the finest Victorian home still in existence.
Catering: In house

SERVICES:
• Marriage Licence

Price Guide: Prices on application.
Catering (sit down): POA

HMS Warrior, Portsmouth
T: 02392 291379   F: 02392 821283
Contact: Debbie Richards
Party Max: 300

This restored 1860's warship lies within Portsmouth's Historic Dockyard. Smoking is not permitted, and ladies are requested not to wear high heels. Functions may be held on board after the ship is closed to the public. These are held in the Wardroom (20), on the Half Deck (up to 60) or on the Gun Deck for larger numbers. There is a choice of two contract caterers who will obtain the relevant drinks licence.
Catering: Contract approved list

SERVICES:
• Marriage Licence

Price Guide: Prices on application.
Catering (sit down): £10.00 - £25.00pp

Hook House Hotel, Hook
T: 01256 762630   F: 01256 760232
Contact: Mr Tim Bull
Party Max: 50   *Bedrooms: 114*

This is a Grade II listed Georgian house on the edge of the village of Hook. The house is set in two acres of grounds featuring lawns and mature trees and shrubs.
Catering: In house

SERVICES:
• Marriage Licence

Price Guide: Prices on application.
Catering (sit down): from £26.95pp
Catering (buffet): from £17.95pp

The John Rennie Floating Restaurant, Bath
T: 01225 447276   F: 01225 336029
E: enquiries@bath-narrowboats.co.uk
W: www.bath-narrowboats.co.uk
Contact: Richard Clarke or Alex Roberts, Directors
Party Max: 60

The John Rennie is a narrowboat, but still over 12 feet wide, with an open deck at the front. The boat is moored within a 10 minutes walk of the centre of Bath, and cruises the Kennet and Avon Canal through the Limply Stoke Valley as far as Bradford on Avon. On board there is a fully glazed saloon with fully fitted carpets, central heating and a flexible seating layout. All meals are prepared on board from fresh local ingredients. Cruises last from 2 to 4.5 hours, although all programmes are flexible.
Catering: In house

SERVICES:
• Exclusive Use   • Fireworks   • Piped Music
• Performance Area

Price Guide: Charter fee is £100 - £500 depending on length of trip, time of day and season.
Catering (buffet): £3.50 - £18.50pp

Lains Barn at Ardington, Wantage
T: 01235 760991   F: 01235 760991
E: Iainsbarn@wantage.com   W: www.lainsbarn.co.uk
Contact: Annie Hill, Administrator
Party Max: 200

This magnificent historic barn (dating in part from 1750) is located in rural Oxfordshire close to the market town of Wantage. It has a majestic hall and gallery, and its huge barn doors lead to a lawn area - suitable for a barbecue.
Catering: Contract (any)/Self catering

SERVICES:
• Exclusive Use   • Marriage Licence

Price Guide: £70 - £400 +£200 for marriages at the Barn. Charity discounts may apply.
Catering (sit down): POA
Catering (buffet): POA

Lainston House Hotel, Winchester
T: 01962 863588
F: 01962 776248
Contact: Patsie Enright, Sales & Marketing Manager
Party Max: 150 (marquee: 300)   *Bedrooms: 38*

This William and Mary 17th Century country house hotel is set in 63 acres of parkland featuring a lime tree avenue. Several rooms are available for events, including the Dawley Barn, (a 17th Century half-timbered barn). For larger numbers a marquee can be set up on the lawn adjacent to the dining room. Room hire includes a toastmaster.
Catering: In house

SOUTH OF ENGLAND

SERVICES:
- Marriage Licence
- Toastmaster
- Performance Area
- Flowers
- Live Music
- Cake
- Photography

Price Guide: Facility fee from £775.
Catering (sit down): from £28pp

Langrish House Hotel, Petersfield
T: 01730 266941 **F:** 01730 260543
Contact: Robina Talbot-Ponsonby
Party Max: 120   Bedrooms: 14

This hotel and award-winning restaurant is also a family home. Function rooms include The Old Dungeons (35) and the Garden Room (35). The hotel boasts an 'excellent' setting for outdoor photographs.
Catering: In house

SERVICES:
- Marriage Licence

Price Guide: Prices on application.
Catering (sit down): from £23.00pp
Catering (buffet): from £23.00pp

Le Manoir Aux Quat' Saisons, Great Milton
T: 01844 278881 **F:** 01844 278847
Contact: Sarah Carter
Party Max: 24   Bedrooms: 19

Raymond Blanc's 15th Century manor house is a listed building set in 30 acres of grounds with a water garden. The Manoir's famous restaurant (two Michelin stars, five Egon Ronay rosettes and four AA red stars) offers three menu packages: all on a waited service basis, plus a 'Menu Gourmand' with seven courses. A children's menu is also available. Kosher cuisine can also be prepared by the venue's appointed Kosher Licensee, Steven Wolfisz. Buffets are not available.
Catering: In house

SERVICES:
- Marriage Licence

Price Guide: Prices on application.
Catering (sit down): £55.00 - £100.00pp

Lingfield Park Racecourse, Lingfield
T: 01342 831 700
E: fgaunt@lingfieldpark.co.uk
Contact: Laura Nuttall or Frances Court, Sales & Marketing Coordinators
Party Max: 350 (marquee: 80)

Lingfield Park, near East Grinstead, is one of the oldest established premier racecourses in the UK. There are race meets here throughout the year and the site offers a number of specially constructed training facilities and conference rooms, as well as function suites, and even an exhibition space. A number of packages are available for parties of 8 to 350, and include box/suite hire, free car parking, closed circuit TV and members day badge. You can also sponsor a race from £500, and can book a behind the scenes tour.
Catering: In house

FACILITIES:
- Helipad
- Golf

SERVICES:
- Exclusive Use
- Toastmaster
- Entertainers
- Flowers
- Disco/Dance
- Photography
- Cake
- Live Music

Price Guide: Conference tariffs start at £28pp.
Catering (sit down): from £60pp - includes private box
Catering (buffet): from £45pp - includes private box

Long Hall, Godalming
T: 01428 654167 **E:** ramster@bigfoot.com
W: www.bigfoot.com/ramster
Contact: Mrs M Gunn, Proprietor
Party Max: 200

Available on an exclusive use basis, the Long Hall dates from 1604. It features beams and oak panelling throughout its 100 foot length, with a traditional inglenook fireplace, as well as central heating and all modern comforts. The Great Drawing Room adjoining the Hall is licensed for civil marriages and is also available as an additional reception room. You may also have use of the private courtyard garden.
Catering: In house/Contract approved list

SERVICES:
- Disco/Dance

Price Guide: £1600 - £2000 10% discount Mon-Thurs.

Lyndhurst Park Hotel, Lyndhurst
T: 02380 283923
F: 02380 283019
Contact: Alison Mayne
Party Max: 300 (marquee: 200)   Bedrooms: 59

Located on the edge of the New Forest, Lyndhurst Park is set in its own gardens of five acres. Marquee only for daylight hours.
Catering: In house

SERVICES:
- Marriage Licence

Price Guide: Prices on application.
Catering (sit down): from £22.00pp

The Manor House, Aldermaston
T: 01189 819333
F: 01189 819025
Contact: Melanie Perrish
Party Max: 140 (marquee: 200)   Bedrooms: 34

This Grade II Victorian mansion is set in 137 acres. Leisure facilities at the hotel include tennis, putting, croquet and snooker.
Catering: In house

FACILITIES:
- Tennis
- Putting
- Croquet
- Pool/Snooker

SERVICES:
- Marriage Licence

Price Guide: Prices on application.
Catering (sit down): from £33.00pp

SOUTH OF ENGLAND

Marwell Hotel, Winchester
T: 01962 777681   F: 01962 777850
E: info@marwell.macdonald-hotels.co.uk
W: www.macdonaldhotels.co.uk/marwell-hotel/
Contact: Mr R Middlehurst

Party Max: 180   Bedrooms: 68

This Macdonald hotel is sited opposite the Marwell Zoological Park. It is a colonial style 3-star hotel set in woodlands. This perhaps has the prize for hosting the most unusual event – a wedding with all the guests dressed as animals! Unusual themed events obviously present no problem for this venue.
Catering: In house

SERVICES:
- Marriage Licence

Price Guide: Prices on application.
Catering (sit down): Sit down from £15.00pp
Catering (buffet): Buffets from £5.95pp

Mill House Hotel & Restaurant, Reading
T: 01189 883124   F: 01189 885550
E: info@themillhousehotel.co.uk
W: www.themillhousehotel.co.uk
Contact: Kim Pybus

Party Max: 175 (marquee: 175)   Bedrooms: 10

Built in 1823, the Mill House originally formed part of Stratfield Saye estate, home to the 1st Duke of Wellington.
Catering: In house

SERVICES:
- Marriage Licence

Price Guide: Prices on application.
Catering (sit down): from £25.00pp
Catering (buffet): from £8.00pp

Missenden Abbey, Great Missenden
T: 01494 866811   F: 01494 866737
Contact: Sue Newman

Party Max: 150 (marquee: unlimited)   Bedrooms: 56

This restored 12th Century abbey is a management centre from Monday to Friday, but is available for events, with exclusive use, at the weekends, mostly during the Spring and Summer. The Abbey offers a suite of Library, Garden Room, Bar and a choice of three adjoining dining rooms, availably singly or together, to seat up to 100. Exclusive hire of the Abbey costs £2000 + vat.
Catering: In house

SERVICES:
- Marriage Licence

Price Guide: £2000 + vat for exclusive use.
Catering (sit down): from £40.00pp + vat

Monkey Island Hotel, Bray on Thames
T: 01628 623400   F: 01628 784732
E: monkeyisland@btconnect.com
Contact: Simon Nelms, Wedding Coordinator

Party Max: 120   Bedrooms: 26

Monkey Island sits in the River Thames and is the exclusive location for this hotel. The island features a Temple and a Pavilion, both Grade I listed and dating from the early 1800s. The hotel has peaceful landscaped gardens, with informal shrubberies and lightly wooded areas. The hotel itself has a variety of banqueting rooms, catering for 30 to 120.
Catering: In house

FACILITIES:
- Helipad

SERVICES:
- Exclusive Use
- Marriage Licence
- Disco/Dance
- Entertainers
- Piped Music
- Valet Parking

Price Guide: £6000 - £10000 exclusive hire
Catering (sit down): from £35pp
Catering (buffet): from £35pp

Mottisfont Abbey, Romsey
T: 01794 340757   F: 01794 341492
Contact: Penny Curry

Party Max: 60 (marquee: 200)

This National Trust property is set on a tributary to the River Test. Its grounds feature lawns and gardens, (including a collection of old-fashioned roses), while inside the house is a room painted by Whistler. Catering at the Abbey includes fresh local produce such as trout from the River Test and Mottisfont Rose Petal Ice Cream.
Catering: In house

SERVICES:
- Marriage Licence

Price Guide: Prices on application.
Catering (sit down): POA

New Mill Restaurant, Eversley
T: 01189 732105
F: 01189 328780
Contact: Mark Mulrainey

Party Max: 200 (marquee: 400)

This Grade II listed restored watermill can be hired on any day of the year. New Mill is known for its award-winning British cooking. A list of local accommodation can be provided.
Catering: In house

SERVICES:
- Marriage Licence

Price Guide: Prices on application.
Catering (sit down): POA

New Place Management Centre, Southampton
T: 01329 833543
F: 01329 833259
W: www.initialstyle.co.uk
Contact: Sue Conduct

Party Max: 200 (marquee: unlimited)   Bedrooms: 110

This Grade I listed building was designed by Sir Edwin Lutyens and is set in 30 acres of landscaped gardens and woodland. It also has a swimming pool. Cuisine by Laurent Beaunier, ex-Boulestin.
Catering: In house

SOUTH OF ENGLAND

SERVICES:
- Marriage Licence

Price Guide: Venue hire from £2000 + vat.
Catering (sit down): from £25.00pp

Northwood House, Cowes
T: 01983 299752   **F:** 01983 823369
Contact: Mrs Lesley Kenrick
Party Max: 200 (marquee: unlimited)

Northwood House stands in about 27 acres. It was originally built as the seat of the Ward family in 1837, but is now used for local meetings and social functions. In more recent years, the Duke of Edinburgh and other members of the Royal Family have made regular visits during Cowes week. The venue holds a public entertainment licence and a liquor licence can be arranged if one is required.
Catering: In house

SERVICES:
- Marriage Licence

Price Guide: Prices on application.
Catering (sit down): POA

Oakley Court Hotel, Windsor
T: 01753 609988   **F:** 01628 637011
E: oakleyct@atlas.Co.uk
Contact: Functions Manager
Party Max: 180 (marquee: 200)   Bedrooms: 115

This four-star hotel is set in 35 acres of landscaped gardens sweeping down to the River Thames.
Catering: In house

SERVICES:
- Marriage Licence

Price Guide: Prices on application.
Catering (sit down): from £85.00pp (package)

The Old Mill, Aldermaston
T: 0118 971 2365   **F:** 0118 971 2371
Contact: Robin or Diane Arlott
Party Max: 150 (marquee: unlimited)

This Grade II listed building is set in 20 acres alongside the river Kennet. The restaurant, which has been family run for 60 years, offers traditional home cooked food. No accommodation is available on site and a list of local establishments is available. Helicopters or hot air balloons may land on site, and guests may arrive or depart by boat.
Catering: In house

FACILITIES:
- Helipad
- Hot Air Balloons

SERVICES:
- Marriage Licence

Price Guide: Prices on application.
Catering (sit down): from £18.00pp
Catering (buffet): from £10.00pp

Pewsey Vale Charter Cruises, Pewsey
T: 023 8026 6200 Moblie: 07831 807196

Contact: Bill & Hilda Smith, Owners
Party Max: 50

This cruise company offers cruises along the Kennet and Avon Canal from Pewsey Wharf near Marlborough. Other cruises go from Wootton Rivers, passing through the Four Locks and the 502 yard long Brick Tunnel to Crofton Top Lock.
Catering: Self catering/In house

SERVICES:
- Exclusive Use

Price Guide: £200 - £500
Catering (sit down): from £5.75pp
Catering (buffet): from £4.10pp

Phyllis Court Club, Henley on Thames
T: 01491 570500   **F:** 01491 570500
E: phyllisc@globalnet.co.uk   **W:** www.phylliscourt.co.uk
Contact: Roger Best, Banqueting Manager
Party Max: 200   Bedrooms: 9

This club, with its Grade II grandstand pavilion, stands on the banks of the Thames, opposite the winning post of the Royal Regatta. The Club has a long history dating back as far as 1301, and is housed in a listed Georgian building, with extensive function rooms. The landscaped gardens and lawns lead down to the river where the Club has its own landing stage which may be used by guests. Several areas are available for functions at the Club, including the Grandstand Pavilion itself, and several rooms within the Clubhouse.
Catering: In house/Contract approved list

FACILITIES:
- Helipad
- Tennis

SERVICES:
- Marriage Licence
- Flowers
- Performance Area

Price Guide: £150 - £1600
Catering (sit down): from £30.00pp
Catering (buffet): from £29.95pp

Potters Heron Hotel, Nr Romsey
T: 01703 266611   **F:** 01703 251359
Contact: Helen Crawford
Party Max: 130   Bedrooms: 54

This is a thatched building, surrounded by woodland.
Catering: In house

SERVICES:
- Marriage Licence

Price Guide: Prices on application.
Catering (sit down): from £18.00pp

Rhinefield House Hotel, Brockenhurst,
T: 01590 622922   **F:** 01590 622800
E: reservations@virgin.co.uk   **W:** www.arcadianhotels.co.uk
Contact: Lisa Schofield
Party Max: 150   Bedrooms: 34

The hotel, part of Arcadian Hotels, is set in the New Forest. The hotel's award-winning gardens have been restored to the original 1890's design, with maze and formal parterres. Rhinefield features a model of Westminster Hall, as well as an

SOUTH OF ENGLAND

authentic recreation of part of the Alhambra Palace in Granada (these are not marriage rooms). It has three AA and RAC stars as well as one AA Rosette. Accommodation discounts are available.
Catering: In house

SERVICES:
- Marriage Licence

Price Guide: Prices on application.
Catering (sit down): £28.00 - 31.00pp

Royal Armouries, Fareham
T: 01329 233734　　　F: 01329 822092
E: tpridmore@armouries.org.uk.
Contact: Tony Pridmore
Party Max: 100

Fort Nelson is a scheduled ancient monument and is the Royal Armouries Museum of artillery. Smoking is only allowed in designated areas.
Catering: In house

SERVICES:
- Marriage Licence

Price Guide: Prices on application.
Catering (sit down): from £16.50pp
Catering (buffet): from £7.50pp

Royal Berkshire Hotel, Ascot
T: 01344 623322　　　F: 01344 627100
Contact: Helen Moore
Party Max: 100 (marquee: 150)　　Bedrooms: 63

This old manor house, dating from 1705, was originally built for the Churchill family. It is now a Hilton International hotel under the Country Style brand. The hotel is set in 15 acres of landscaped garden, with a sunken garden as a special feature.
Catering: In house

SERVICES:
- Marriage Licence

Price Guide: Prices on application.
Catering (sit down): from £65.00 (packages)

Silchester House, Silchester
T: 0118 970 1901　　　F: 0118 970 0192
E: info@silchesterhouse.com　W: www.yoursexclusively.co.uk
Contact: Carol Johnson, Manager
Party Max: 200 (marquee: 200)　　Bedrooms: 12

This Grade II listed country house, set in extensive grounds with mature trees, is only available on an exclusive use basis, making this suitable for a party weekend if desired. 14 bedrooms with private bathrooms are available here, but the venue also has arrangements with two local hotels, one only 200 yards away, and the other 10 minutes away, for which a minibus can be provided. The venue also has a heated swimming pool (indoor/outdoor) as an added attraction for the 'day after party'. While the venue has no liquor licence, couples may provide their own drinks for which a corkage fee will be charged. Operating company, Exclusively Yours, also owns a large country house in southern France.
Catering: In house/Contract approved list

FACILITIES:
- Helipad
- Gym
- Outdoor Pool
- Indoor Pool
- Tennis
- Table Tennis
- Paint Ball
- Outdoor Pool

SERVICES:
- Exclusive Use
- Disco/Dance
- Valet Parking
- Marriage Licence
- Piped Music
- Toastmaster
- Performance Area

Price Guide: £500 - £1400 per day. Weekend rate from £2800.
Catering (sit down): from £35pp
Catering (buffet): from £20pp

Sir Christopher Wren's House Hotel, Windsor
T: 01753 861354　　　F: 01753 869311
Contact: Nicki Foot
Party Max: 120　　Bedrooms: 57

One of the main features of this hotel is its York stone terrace which overlooks the Thames and Eton Bridge. The location means that guests can arrive and depart by boat. In addition, the hotel can organise leisure and dinner boat cruises. Services that cannot be arranged for you can be recommended, while a late night drinking licence will be applied for as required. Many of the rooms have four-poster beds, while the initiated can ask for one of the suites that are separate from the main building (reached through a 'secret' door). One of these has its own kitchen where the chef will come and cook for you. The chef spent his formative years in Michelin starred restaurants.
Catering: In house

SERVICES:
- Marriage Licence

Price Guide: Prices on application.
Catering (sit down): from £30.00pp
Catering (buffet): from £18.00pp

Solent Hotel, Fareham
T: 01489 880000　　　F: 01489 880007
E: solent@shire-inns.co.uk　W: www.shireinns.co.uk
Contact: Nikki Carpenter
Party Max: 250　　Bedrooms: 111

This purpose-built hotel features log fires, polished stone floors and cherry-wood panelling.
Catering: In house

SERVICES:
- Marriage Licence

Price Guide: Prices on application.
Catering (sit down): £27.50 - 32.50pp
Catering (buffet): from £12.00pp

Somerley, Ringwood
T: 01425 480819　　　F: 01425 478613
E: info@somerley.com　W: www.somerley.com
Contact: Richard Horridge, General Manager
Party Max: 200 (marquee: unlimited)　　Bedrooms: 8

Somerley is the privately owned stately home of the Earl of Normanton. It is situated in 7000 acres of glorious meadows, parkland and forest on the edge of the New Forest and is avail-

SOUTH OF ENGLAND

able for a wide range of events.
Catering: In house

FACILITIES:
- Helipad
- Hot Air Balloons
- Quad Bikes/Off Road
- Shooting
- Tennis
- Table Tennis
- Paint Ball
- Pool/Snooker

SERVICES:
- Exclusive Use
- Toastmaster
- Flowers
- Valet Parking
- Cake

Price Guide: £1500 - £2500
Catering (sit down): from £30pp
Catering (buffet): from £22pp

Stansted Park, Rowlands Castle
T: 023 9263 1223
F: 023 9263 1355
E: weddings@stansted.co.uk or p.b.robinson@btinternet.com
W: www.stanstedpark.co.uk
Contact: Danielle Jennings, Event Manager
Party Max: 150 (marquee: 4000)

Set in an historic parkland setting, Stansted is considered one of the most beautiful stately homes in the south and is said to still retain the charm of a much-loved home. The Grade II listed house and 'below stairs' (with 17th Century crypt) are available for corporate and private parties, while the grounds can accommodate large numbers in marquees. Murder Mystery dinners and casino evenings are popular here.
Catering: In house

FACILITIES:
- Helipad
- Hot Air Balloons
- Shooting
- Quad Bikes/Off Road
- Outdoor Pool
- Falconry

SERVICES:
- Exclusive Use
- Marriage Licence
- Performance Area

Price Guide: from £750 - £1750 +
Catering (buffet): from £10pp

Stanwell House Hotel, Lymington
T: 01590 677123   **F:** 01590 677756
E: sales@stanwellhousehotel.co.uk
W: www.stanwellhousehotel.co.uk
Contact: Annette Oldfield, Functions Manager
Party Max: 80   Bedrooms: 31

This renovated Georgian building is now a 3-star hotel boasting sumptuous public areas. The hotel was winner of the Southern Hampshire Tourism Awards in 1999. A cottage is also available for rent here.
Catering: In house

SERVICES:
- Exclusive Use
- Marriage Licence
- Piped Music

Price Guide: Prices on application.
Catering (sit down): from £25pp
Catering (buffet): from £20pp

Stoke Park Club, Stoke Poges
T: 01753 717171   **F:** 01753 717181
E: info@stokeparkclub.com   **W:** stokeparkclub.com

Contact: Joanne Scott, Sales Manager
Party Max: 110 (marquee: 500)   Bedrooms: 20

The Grade I Palladian mansion is set in historic gardens and has recently undergone a £20 million refurbishment, including that of its 20 bedrooms.
Catering: In house

FACILITIES:
- Helipad
- Pool/Snooker
- Golf
- Tennis

SERVICES:
- Exclusive Use
- Toastmaster
- Piped Music
- Marriage Licence
- Disco/Dance
- Flowers
- Fireworks

Price Guide: £250 - £15000
Catering (sit down): from £39pp
Catering (buffet): from £39pp

Stonor Arms Hotel, Nr Henley-on-Thames
T: 01491 638866   **F:** 01491 638863
E: stonorarms.hotel@virgin.net   **W:** www.stonor-arms.co.uk
Contact: Sophia Williams
Party Max: 90 (marquee: 100)   Bedrooms: 10

The 18th Century Stonor Arms is a privately owned country hotel and award winning restaurant, set in the countryside and featuring its own walled garden. The restaurant has won various culinary awards and claims an 'industry-respected chef'.
Catering: In house

SERVICES:
- Marriage Licence

Price Guide: Prices on application.
Catering (sit down): from £25.00pp
Catering (buffet): from £15.00pp

Stowe House, Buckingham
T: 01280 818282   **F:** 01280 818186
E: sses@stowe.co.uk   **W:** www.stoweschoolorg
Contact: Ms Chris Shaw
Party Max: 560

Stowe School is an attractive period building set in extensive grounds. State rooms and extensive leisure facilities make this a suitable venue for conferences, balls, weddings and hospitality days.
Catering: In house

FACILITIES:
- Golf
- Indoor Pool
- Tennis

SERVICES:
- Exclusive Use
- Cake
- Marriage Licence
- Performance Area
- Flowers

Price Guide: £500 - £6000
Catering (sit down): from £28pp
Catering (buffet): from £28pp

Studley Priory Hotel, Horton-cum-Studley
T: 01865 351203   **F:** 01865 351613
E: res@studley-priory.co.uk or cw@studley-priory.co.uk
W: www.studley-priory.co.uk

SOUTH OF ENGLAND

Contact: Chrissie Wright
Party Max: 100 (marquee: 200)   Bedrooms: 18

This Elizabethan manor house was converted from a 12th Century nunnery, and is situated in 13 acres of wooded grounds with views, to the West, of the Cotswolds and, to the East, along the line of the Chilterns. The hotel has been awarded three AA stars and is ETB four crown highly commended with Silver Award for excellence.
Catering: In house

SERVICES:
- Marriage Licence

Price Guide: Prices on application.
Catering (sit down): from £30.00pp

Sudbury House Hotel, Faringdon
T: 01367 241272   **F:** 01367 242346
W: www.sudburyhouse.co.uk
Contact: Donna O'Sullivan
Party Max: 250 (marquee: unlimited)   Bedrooms: 49

This listed Regency building offers several function rooms, all of which are available on any day of the year. These include The Terrace Lounge, which has a balcony overlooking the grounds, and the Garden Room, which opens directly onto the croquet lawn.
Catering: In house

FACILITIES:
- Croquet

SERVICES:
- Marriage Licence

Price Guide: Prices on application.
Catering (sit down): from £32.85pp
Catering (buffet): from £9.50pp

Swainston Manor Hotel, Newport
T: 01983 521121   **F:** 01983 521406
Contact: Mr Woodward
Party Max: 120 (marquee: 500)   Bedrooms: 19

This Grade II listed building is set in 32 acres of grounds and has three rooms available to hold functions with varying capacities from 12 to 120.
Catering: In house

SERVICES:
- Marriage Licence

Price Guide: Prices on application.
Catering (sit down): from £12.00pp

Tylney Hall, Hook
T: 01256 764881   **F:** 01256 768141
Contact: Carol Harriss
Party Max: 100   Bedrooms: 110

Victorian Tylney Hall is set amidst 66 acres of parkland, gardens and lakes. The Hall has RAC 4 Red Stars and Gold Ribbon, AA 4 Red Stars, RAC 3 Ribbon dining award and AA 2 Red Rosettes. The Oak Room restaurant is said to offer excellent cuisine. Accommodation includes two lakeside honeymoon suites, plus other rooms with 4-poster beds.

Catering: In house

SERVICES:
- Marriage Licence

Price Guide: Prices on application.
Catering (sit down): from £35.00pp
Catering (buffet): from £35.00pp

Tyrells Ford Hotel, Nr Christchurch
T: 01425 672646   **F:** 01425 672262
Contact: Collette Tuddenham
Party Max: 130   Bedrooms: 16

This 18th Century family owned manor house is set in ten acres of grounds on the edge of the New Forest. The Lounge (with minstrel's gallery) is available for functions.
Catering: In house

SERVICES:
- Marriage Licence

Price Guide: Prices on application.
Catering (sit down): from £22.00pp

Tythrop Park, Aylesbury
T: 01844 291310   **F:** 01844 291102
Contact: Medina or Jonathan Marks
Party Max: 200 (marquee: unlimited)

This Carolean house is set in 60 acres of mature grounds. Small events are catered for in house.
Catering: In house

SERVICES:
- Marriage Licence

Price Guide: Prices on application.
Catering (sit down): from £27.00pp
Catering (buffet): from £21.00pp

Villiers Hotel, Buckingham
T: 01280 822444   **F:** 01280 822113
Contact: Jean Rush
Party Max: 250 (marquee: 200)   Bedrooms: 46

This Grade II listed 400-year old coaching inn, formerly known as the Swan & Castle Inn, is set around an original cobbled courtyard, where Cromwell billeted his troops in 1643. The chef, who holds two rosettes, offers elegant English-style cuisine.
Catering: In house

SERVICES:
- Marriage Licence

Price Guide: Prices on application.
Catering (sit down): from £25.00pp
Catering (buffet): from £20.00pp

The Vineyard at Stockcross, Newbury
T: 01635 528770   **F:** 01635 528398
E: general@thevineyard.Co.uk **W:** www.the-vineyard.co.uk
Contact: Kathy Kernutt
Party Max: 70   Bedrooms: 33

The Music Room and Morning Room are available at this hotel and restaurant on any day of the week.

SOUTH OF ENGLAND

Catering: In house

SERVICES:
• Marriage Licence
Price Guide: Prices on application.
Catering (sit down): from £45.00pp

Westover Hall, Milford on Sea
T: 01590 643044 **F:** 01590 644490
E: westoverhallhotel@barclays.net **W:** www.westoverhallhotel.com
Contact: Stewart Mechem or Nicola Musetti, Joint Proprietors
Party Max: 100 (marquee: 120)   Bedrooms: 14

This Grade II listed Arts & Crafts Victorian mansion overlooks Christchurch Bay to The Needles rocks. The house, now a 3-star hotel, features extensive oak panelling, stained glass windows, minstrel's gallery, carved stone fireplaces by William de Morgan and antique furniture.
Catering: In house

FACILITIES:
• Outdoor Pool
SERVICES:
• Marriage Licence • Disco/Dance • Piped Music
• Performance Area
Price Guide: £110 - £5000+ per day. Weekend rate £10000. Weekly rate from £16000.
Catering (sit down): from £29pp
Catering (buffet): from £18pp

Whately Hall Hotel, Banbury
T: 0870 4008104 **F:** 01295 271736
W: www.heritage-hotels.com
Contact: Graham Evans
Party Max: 150 (marquee: 150)   Bedrooms: 68

Whately Hall is a Forte Heritage hotel, with its own resident, authenticated ghost (whatever that means). Cuisine at the Hall has a strong Italian influence. Dinner on the beach has been arranged here for one romantic couple.
Catering: In house

SERVICES:
• Marriage Licence
Price Guide: Prices on application.
Catering (sit down): from £22.00pp

Winchester Guildhall, Winchester
T: 01962 840820
F: 01962 878458
E: guildhall@winchester.gov.uk
W: www.winchester.gov.uk
Contact: Clare Churcher, Sales & Events Manager
Party Max: 300

Situated in the heart of Winchester, the Guildhall is a busy conference and banqueting venue with a choice of 11 function rooms, all furnished to a high standard, and each offering unique features and ambience. Self-catering is possible in the Saxon Suite at this venue.
Catering: Contract (any)/Self catering

SERVICES:
• Marriage Licence • Piped Music
Price Guide: £150 - £650
Catering (sit down): from £19.90pp
Catering (buffet): from £9.40pp

Woodstock Town Hall, Woodstock
T: 01993 811216 **F:** 01993 811216
Contact: Mrs Marian Moxon, Town Clerk
Party Max: 60

Woodstock Town Hall is a Grade II listed building built by William Chambers in 1766. It commands one of the finest views over the historic market place and town of Woodstock and is adjacent to Blenheim Palace and estate. The ground floor Council Chamber is used for wedding ceremonies, while the Assembly Room, with adjacent kitchen, is available for functions.
Catering: Contract (any)/Self catering

SERVICES:
• Marriage Licence
Price Guide: £130 for wedding ceremony. £28 per hour for functions/receptions.
Catering (sit down): from £15pp
Catering (buffet): from £8pp

Wroxton House, Banbury
T: 01295 730777 **F:** 01295 730800
E: wroxtonhse@aol.com
Contact: Helen Wilson
Party Max: 70   Bedrooms: 32

The hotel is a thatched, country house, dating back to the 17th Century. Catering is in-house with a speciality in modern French and English cuisine. A list of local accommodation with preferential rates is available.
Catering: In house

SERVICES:
• Marriage Licence
Price Guide: Prices on application.
Catering (sit down): from £37.00pp (package)

Wycombe Swan, High Wycombe
T: 01494 537777 **F:** 01494 473705
E: enquiries@wycombeswan.co.uk
Contact: Liz Carden, Catering Manager
Party Max: 400

The Wycombe Swan is located in the centre of High Wycombe, and has a 1000 seater theatre and 2 banqueting suites. The Oak room is a listed room.
Catering: In house

FACILITIES:
• Theatre
SERVICES:
• Marriage Licence • Piped Music • Performance Area
Price Guide: Hire fees are £250 - £1000.
Catering (sit down): from £16pp
Catering (buffet): from £7pp

WEST COUNTRY

Alverton Manor, Truro,
T: 01872 276633 F: 01872 222989
Contact: Michael Warren, Conference Coordinator
Party Max: 200   Bedrooms: 33

Grade II listed Alverton Manor is close to the heart of the cathedral city of Truro, yet within reach of Cornwall's spectacular cliff's beaches and countryside. The historic building, now a 3-star hotel, has a hillside setting and features fine sandstone walls and mullioned windows. Several rooms are available for functions, including The Great Hall (with splendid vaulted ceiling) and The Library. Plans are afoot for a leisure centre to be built here, which will include an indoor pool and fitness centre. Contact the Manor for an update.
Catering: In house

FACILITIES:
• Pool/Snooker
SERVICES:
• Marriage Licence   • Disco/Dance   • Piped Music
• Performance Area
Price Guide: £70- £500
Catering (sit down): from £15.25
Catering (buffet): from £8.95

The Arched House, Lyme Regis
T: 01297 445158 F: 01297 445158
Contact: Pearl Winsborough
Party Max: 18   Bedrooms: 8

The Arched House arches over the River Lym and is only 150m from the sea. It offers spacious accommodation on 3 floors with a 10m by 5m sitting/dining room, sauna, gym and split level garden.
Catering: Self catering

FACILITIES:
• Gym   • Sauna
SERVICES:
• Exclusive Use
Price Guide: Short breaks are from £200 per night (min 3 nights), with Christmas and New Year week at £2200.

Ashton Court Mansion, Bristol
T: 0117 963 3438 F: 0117 953 0650
E: chris-wood@msn.com   W: www.bristol-city.gov.uk/acm
Contact: Christopher Wood, Operations Manager
Party Max: 750

With over 900 years of fascinating history, Ashton Court Mansion, which is run by Bristol City Council, stands in beautiful gardens at the heart of glorious rolling parkland including delightful deer park, just two miles from Bristol. Offering a distinctive setting for weddings, conferences, banquets and training seminars, this imposing mansion offers a highly experienced team who will cater for the most sumptuous occasion.
Catering: Contract approved list/In house

FACILITIES:
• Hot Air Balloons
SERVICES:
• Exclusive Use   • Marriage Licence   • Piped Music

• Performance Area
Price Guide: £206 - £1480
Catering (sit down): from £22pp + vat
Catering (buffet): from £6.55pp + vat

Assembly Rooms & Museum of Costume, Bath
T: 01225 477782 F: 01225 477476
E: historic-venuehire@bathnes.gov.uk
W: www.museumofcostume.co.uk
Contact: Sharon Stewart or Anne Harris
Party Max: 500

On their completion is 1771 the Assembly Rooms were described as 'the most noble and elegant of any in the Kingdom'. Within the rooms hang the original crystal chandeliers and paintings by Gainsborough and Hoare. The two larger rooms, the Tea Room and the Ball Room, are linked by the Great Octogan. These rooms together can accommodate up to 500 for a buffet and dancing. The Ballroom alone seats up to 270 people for a dinner dance. This venue regrets that it cannot accept bookings for 18th or 21st birthday parties.
Catering: Contract approved list

SERVICES:
• Exclusive Use   • Marriage Licence   • Disco/Dance
• Performance Area
Price Guide: £91 - £269 per hour
Catering (sit down): from £26pp
Catering (buffet): from £15pp

Barton Hall, Torquay
T: 01273 648761 F: 01273 676290
E: lmildiner@3d-education.co.uk
Contact: Laura Mildiner, Marketing Manager
Party Max: 700   Bedrooms: 300

Barton Hall is a large old house which was originally built in the 1830s and is set in 50 acres of attractive gardens. The house itself has 89 rooms which range from single to large family rooms. Additional accommodation is provided in chalets in the grounds. This venue can provide a wide range of leisure and entertainment facilities.
Catering: In house

FACILITIES:
• Tennis   • Outdoor Pool   • Pool/Snooker
• Quad Bikes/Off Road   • Table Tennis
SERVICES:
• Exclusive Use   • Marriage Licence   • Disco/Dance
• Live Music   • Entertainers   • Performance Area
Price Guide: £50 - £150
Catering (sit down): from £13pp
Catering (buffet): from £7pp

Bath Guildhall, Bath
T: 01225 477782 - 477786 F: 01225 477476
E: historic-venuehire@bathnes.gov.uk
W: www.romanbaths.co.uk
Contact: Sharon Stewart or Anne Harris
Party Max: 200

WEST COUNTRY

The Grade I listed Guildhall, located in the centre of the city, is a magnificent 18th Century building. The ornate plasterwork and gilding of the banqueting rooms epitomise the finest of the Georgian era The Banqueting Room seats up to 180 for a dinner dance, and an adjoining room, the Aix-en-Provence is included within the hire. Those who book the Guildhall for a function are free to choose their own caterers. This venue regrets that it does not accept bookings for 18th or 21st birthdays.
Catering: Contract (any)

SERVICES:
- Exclusive Use
- Marriage Licence
- Disco/Dance
- Performance Area

Price Guide: £1200 - £120 per hour. Set up/dismantle time is charged at half the hourly rate.

Bath Spa Hotel, Bath
T: 0870 400 8222 **F:** 01225 444006
E: fivestar@bathspa.u-net.com
W: www.bathspahotel.com
Contact: Carole Devonshire
Party Max: 110   Bedrooms: 98

This is a Grade I listed Georgian mansion set in 7 acres of formal gardens featuring a temple and a grotto.
Catering: In house

SERVICES:
- Marriage Licence

Price Guide: Prices on application.
Catering (sit down): from £43.00pp

The Beeches, Bristol
T: 0117 972 8778 **F:** 0117 971 1968
Contact: Sharon Barr
Party Max: 150 (marquee: unlimited)   Bedrooms: yes

This Victorian mansion, set in 22 acres, is now a conference and training centre.
Catering: In house

SERVICES:
- Marriage Licence

Price Guide: Prices on application.
Catering (sit down): from £17.50pp
Catering (buffet): from £5.90pp

Bindon Country House Hotel, Wellington
T: 01823 400070
F: 01823 400071
Contact: Simon D'Offay
Party Max: 80 (marquee: 150)   Bedrooms: 12

Bindon is a Grade II listed Baroque style building with an orangery. It is set in seven acres of woodlands and gardens.
Catering: In house

SERVICES:
- Marriage Licence

Price Guide: Prices on application.
Catering (sit down): from £35.00pp

Bishopstrow House, Warminster
T: 01985 212312 **F:** 01985 216769
Contact: David Dowden
Party Max: 100 (marquee: 150)   Bedrooms: 31

This Grade II listed Georgian house with temple dates from 1770 and is located by the River Wylye.
Catering: In house

SERVICES:
- Marriage Licence

Price Guide: Prices on application.
Catering (sit down): from £26.95pp
Catering (buffet): from £19.50pp

Bitton House, Teignmouth
T: 01626 775030
Contact: Mr Lambert
Party Max: 100 (marquee: unlimited)

Bitton House is set in its own grounds and has a gun deck with cannons and balustrading.
Catering: In house

SERVICES:
- Marriage Licence

Price Guide: Prices on application.
Catering (sit down): from £7.50pp
Catering (buffet): from £3.50pp

Boringdon Hall Hotel, Colebrook
T: 01752 344455 **F:** 01752 346578
Contact: Nicole Williams
Party Max: 150 (marquee: 400)   Bedrooms: 40

This Grade I listed mansion sits in its own grounds on the edge of Dartmoor. Interior features include a Great Hall with minstrel's gallery.
Catering: In house

SERVICES:
- Marriage Licence

Price Guide: Prices on application.
Catering (sit down): from £17.50pp

Bosinver Farmhouse, St Austell
T: 01726 72128 **F:** 01726 72128
E: bosinver@holidays2000.freeserve.co.uk
W: www.bosinver.co.uk
Contact: Mrs Pat Smith, Owner
Party Max: 50 (marquee: 90)   Bedrooms: 6

Bosinver Farmhouse is the largest of 18 properties at Bosinver Farm that are available for rent. The 30 acre farm, which guests are free to roam, is tucked away in the countryside, with the coast and attractions such as the Lost Gardens of Heligan less than 5 miles away. The farm is also within walking distance of the local pub. If all the properties were taken, 90 people could be accommodated in a total of 47 bedrooms.
The thatched, Grade II listed, Farmhouse is over 400 years old and features a 38ft long oak beamed living room with wood burning stove, as well as a smaller living room with a glass door leading to a private garden and patio. The kitchen has an Aga

WEST COUNTRY

as well as conventional oven and hob. Murder Mystery weekend breaks can be arranged at this venue. Weddings are also a speciality here.
Catering: Contract (any)/Self catering

SERVICES:
- Exclusive Use
- Murder Mystery

Price Guide: Farmhouse £400 - £1250 per week. Other prices on application.
Catering (sit down): from £15pp
Catering (buffet): from £10pp

Bowood Golf & Country Club, Calne
T: 01249 822228 F: 01249 822218
E: enquiries@bowood-estate.co.uk
W: www.bowood-estate.co.uk
Contact: Gill Elliot
Party Max: 250 (marquee: 200)   Bedrooms: 4

This Grade I listed building is part of the Bowood Estate, which covers 2,000 acres in total. The park itself was designed by Capability Brown.
Catering: In house

SERVICES:
- Marriage Licence

Price Guide: Prices on application.
Catering (sit down): from £20.50pp

Braddon Cottages, Beaworthy
T: 01409 211350 F: 01409 211350
W: www.braddoncottages.co.uk
Contact: George Ridge, Owner
Party Max: 50

Braddon Cottages is 6 large self-catering cottages (4-key commended), all claiming spectacular views south to Dartmoor. The houses are positioned together with mature lawns and gardens on a 150 acre estate with 3 acre fishing lake, meadowland and forest. Special arrangements can be made for parties (max 50+), taking several cottages for a week to eat together in one room.
Catering: Self catering

FACILITIES:
- Tennis
- Pool/Snooker
- Table Tennis

SERVICES:
- Exclusive Use

Price Guide: £1700 - £3800 per week.

Bridge House Hotel, Nr Ferndown
T: 01202 578828 F: 01202 572620
Contact: Emma Chisholm
Party Max: 130 (marquee: 250)   Bedrooms: 37

The hotel is set on the banks of the River Stour, and has an island garden.
Catering: In house

SERVICES:
- Marriage Licence

Price Guide: Prices on application.

Catering (sit down): from £10.95pp
Catering (buffet): from £3.95pp

Buckland-Tout-Saints Hotel, Kingsbridge
T: 01548 853055
F: 01548 856261
Contact: Julie Hudson
Party Max: 150 (marquee: 200)   Bedrooms: 14

This Queen Anne mansion is set in 4.5 acres of grounds featuring fountains, gardens and a terrace, where a jazz band can play by arrangement.
Catering: In house

SERVICES:
- Marriage Licence

Price Guide: Prices on application.
Catering (sit down): from £20.00pp
Catering (buffet): from £15.00pp

Budock Vean Hotel, Falmouth
T: 01326 250288
F: 01326 250892
Contact: Tamara Ferguson
Party Max: 200   Bedrooms: 73

This golf and country house hotel is set in 65 acres of gardens and woodlands with its own foreshore to the Helford River. Guests can arrive and depart by boat, dependant upon the tide. Helicopters and hot air balloons can also land on site.
Catering: In house

FACILITIES:
- Helipad
- Hot Air Balloons

SERVICES:
- Marriage Licence

Price Guide: Prices on application.
Catering (sit down): from £12.00pp

Burgh Island Hotel, Bigbury on Sea
T: 01548 810514
F: 01548 810243
Contact: Tony Porter
Party Max: 80 (marquee: 80)   Bedrooms: 15

Burgh Island Hotel is an Art Deco building, built in 1929, set on its own 26 acre tidal island. It can be reached across the sands when the tide is out (6 hours a day), or via the hotel's own sea tractor when the tide is in. The hotel also has its own smugglers' pub on the island (built 1336), as well as a helipad. (An exclusive-use 2-day package for 36 people, including meals is £8,528). One of its claims to fame is that Edward and Mrs Simpson apparently retreated to the hotel to escape the press.
Catering: In house

FACILITIES:
- Helipad

SERVICES:
- Exclusive Use
- Marriage Licence

Price Guide: Prices on application.
Catering (sit down): from £32.00pp (including canapes, coffee + petits fours)

WEST COUNTRY

Burton Farm, Kingsbridge
T: 01548 561210   F: 01548 561210
Contact: Anne Rossiter
Party Max: 18

Originally owned by the Duke of Devonshire, Burton Farm is a 325 acre farm with a dairy herd and two flocks of pedigree sheep. The Farmhouse dates from the 15th Century. Parties can be catered for in the Garden Room. Guests can stay in the farmhouse (catered) on on cottages on the estate.
Catering: Self catering

SERVICES:
• Exclusive Use
Price Guide: Prices on application.

Cadbury House Country Club, Bristol
T: 01934 844343   F: 01934 834390
E: info@cadbury-house.co.uk   W: www.cadbury-house.co.uk
Contact: Sarah Finn
Party Max: 360 (marquee: unlimited)

This is an 18th Century country house set in 14 acres of private parkland, and approached by a tree-lined driveway.
Catering: In house

SERVICES:
• Marriage Licence
Price Guide: Prices on application.
Catering (sit down): from £18.70pp

Carlyon Bay Hotel, St Austell
T: 01726 812304   F: 01726 814938
Contact: Mr P J Brennan
Party Max: 120   Bedrooms: 73

Dramatically located on craggy cliffs above the Bay, this venue enjoys spectacular sea views. In addition, the hotel is set in 250 acres of grounds, including championship golf course and pool.
Catering: In house

SERVICES:
• Marriage Licence
Price Guide: Prices on application.
Catering (sit down): from £14.00pp

Carnarvon Arms Hotel, Dulverton
T: 01398 323302   F: 01398 324022
Contact: Kate Howells
Party Max: 120 (marquee: 80)   Bedrooms: 25

The hotel is a Victorian building set in 50 acres. Its features include lounges with log fires and a billiard room.
Catering: In house

SERVICES:
• Marriage Licence
Price Guide: Prices on application.
Catering (sit down): Catering from £10.50pp

Charlton House & The Mulberry Restaurant, Nr Bath
T: 01749 342008   F: 01749 346362
E: enquiry@charltonhouse.com   W: www.charltonhouse.com
Contact: Vanessa Willetts, Special Events Manager
Party Max: 80 (marquee: 150)   Bedrooms: 16

Situated 18 miles from Bath, Charlton House is owned by the founders of the famous Mulberry label. Their place in the country has become a luxurious hotel and restaurant and has been restored and refurbished using the Mulberry Home Collection. Charlton House offers numerous facilities inlcuding saunas and fishing.
Catering: In house

FACILITIES:
• Helipad   • Indoor Pool   • Gym
• Hot Air Balloons   • Tennis   • Saunas
• Fishing
SERVICES:
• Exclusive Use   • Flowers   • Piped Music
• Valet Parking
Price Guide: £3000 - £4000 per day.
Catering (sit down): from £30pp
Catering (buffet): from £25pp

Chine Hotel, Bournemouth
T: 01202 396234   F: 01202 391737
E: reservations@chinehotel.co.uk
W: www.chinehotel.co.uk
Contact: Manuel J Ortega
Party Max: 200   Bedrooms: 92

The Chine Hotel has direct access to the beach through three acres of landscaped gardens.
Catering: In house

SERVICES:
• Marriage Licence
Price Guide: Prices on application.
Catering (sit down): from £18.50pp
Catering (buffet): from £7.50pp

Chiseldon House Hotel, Chiseldon
T: 01793 741010   F: 01793 741059
Contact: Edna Reeves
Party Max: 130 (marquee: 250)   Bedrooms: 21

This Grade II listed building has hosted themed events in the past such as medieval weddings and Caribbean weddings featuring a steel band around the hotel's swimming pool. Some of the bedrooms feature four poster beds.
Catering: In house

FACILITIES:
• Outdoor Pool
SERVICES:
• Marriage Licence
Price Guide: Prices on application.
Catering (sit down): from £12.50pp

Cockington Court, Torquay
T: 01803 606035   F: 01803 690391
E: countrysidetrust@free4all.co.uk
W: www.countryside-trust.org.uk

WEST COUNTRY

Contact: Amanda Sherwin, Marketing & Business Development Manager

Party Max: 70 (marquee: unlimited)

Cockington Court is home to a thriving craft centre where visitors can watch craftspeople at work. The court is set in 450 acres of beautiful parkland which includes a Norman Church, organic and rose gardens, lakes and woodland. The Court is a short walk from the idyllic thatched village of Cockington; also a short ride by horse and carriage. There is a licensed cafe on the site.
Catering: In house

FACILITIES:
- Riding

SERVICES:
- Marriage Licence

Price Guide: Prices on application.

Combe Grove Manor Hotel, Bath
T: 01225 834644   F: 01225 834961
E: heather.brown@combegrovemanor.com
W: www.combegrovemanor
Contact: Functions Manager

Party Max: 100   Bedrooms: 40

This elegant manor house, set in 82 acres of gardens and woodland, was built in 1698 and is now a hotel and country club.
Catering: In house

SERVICES:
- Marriage Licence

Price Guide: Prices on application.
Catering (sit down): from £25.00pp

Coppleridge Inn, Shaftesbury
T: 01747 851980   F: 01747 851858
Contact: Chris Gudinge or Simon Lane

Party Max: 120 (marquee: 250)   Bedrooms: 10

The Inn is a converted 17th Century farm set in 15 acres of meadow and woodland. The Inn's function room is an oak timbered former barn.
Catering: In house

SERVICES:
- Marriage Licence

Price Guide: Prices on application.
Catering (sit down): £5.00 - £20.00pp

Cotehele, Saltash
T: 01579 351346   F: 01579 351346
E: cctlce@smtp.ntrust.org.uk
Contact: Lewis Eynon, Property Manager

Party Max: 80

Cotehele estate, formerly owned by the Edgcumbe family, is now looked after by the National Trust. The ancient house, surrounded by a magnificent gardens with woodland, provides the backdrop to 2 venues, a Grade I 15th Century barn in the garden, and a former inn (Grade II listed), which is now a tearoom at Cotehele Quay on the bank of the River Tamar.
Catering: In house

SERVICES:
- Flowers

Price Guide: from £150
Catering (sit down): from £21.50pp
Catering (buffet): from £18.50pp

The Council House, Bristol
T: 0117 922 2366   F: 0117 922 3383
E: conference-office@bristol-city-gov.uk
Contact: Peter Ochmann, Sarah Thompson, Libby Deekes, Lettings & Functions Team

Party Max: 500

This Grade II listed building, opened by the Queen in 1956, features a marble recepton hall and walnut panelled Mayor's Reception Room. The Council House is located bordering College Green and adjacent to Bristol's 12th Century cathedral.
Catering: In house

SERVICES:
- Exclusive Use
- Cake
- Marriage Licence
- Disco/Dance
- Flowers
- Photography

Price Guide: £88 - £!27 per hour + vat. The Committee Room hire is 25% of the appropriate conference hall rate. Discounts are available for block bookings.
For wedding receptions prices start at £530 for half a day to £1500 for a full day (12 hours).
Catering (sit down): from £9.15pp
Catering (buffet): from £3.60pp

Cricklade Hotel & Country Club, Cricklade
T: 01793 750751   F: 01793 751767
Contact: Paul Judge

Party Max: 120   Bedrooms: 46

This Cotswold manor house, set in its own grounds, features a nine hole golf course.
Catering: In house

FACILITIES:
- Golf

SERVICES:
- Marriage Licence

Price Guide: Prices on application.
Catering (sit down): from £23.00pp

Cross Tree House, Lopen
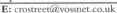
T: 01460 240476   E: crostreet@vossnet.co.uk
W: www.crosstree.co.uk
Contact: John Milner, Owner

Party Max: 50

Cross Tree House is a beautiful Grade II listed 17th Century thatched farmhouse with many original features including flagstone floors, beamed ceilings, inglenook fireplaces, etc. The rooms are comfortable with robust antique furniture and Turkish rugs. It has a private walled garden with croquet lawn and paddock and is surrounded by lovely countryside with a profusion of historic houses, abbeys and gardens. To the south are the rolling hills of Dorset and to the north the fascinating levels and moors.

WEST COUNTRY

Catering: Contract (any)/Self catering

FACILITIES:
- Llama Trekking
- Cycling
- Paragliding
- Croquet

SERVICES:
- Exclusive Use

Price Guide: £560 - £2800
Catering (sit down): from £13pp
Catering (buffet): from £10pp

Crossmead, Exeter
T: 01392 263585 **F:** 01392 263587
E: crossmead@exeter.ac.uk or k.m.pollock2exeter.ac.uk
W: www.ex.ac.uk/EAD/Dsd.hospson.htm
Contact: Catherine Bridgeman, Manager

Party Max: 200 (marquee: 400)   Bedrooms: 82

Crossmead, 1 mile from the centre of Exeter, is an attractive Victorian merchant's house set in 5 acres of landscaped grounds, and offering a choice of rooms for functions. Bed and breakfast is available in standard or en suite rooms. This venue is run by the University of Exeter.

Catering: In house

FACILITIES:
- University Sports Facilities

SERVICES:
- Exclusive Use
- Marriage Licence
- Flowers
- Disco/Dance
- Valet Parking

Price Guide: Prices on application.
Catering (sit down): from £11.50pp
Catering (buffet): from £6pp

Crownhill Fort, Plymouth
T: 01752 793754 **F:** 01752 770065
E: ltcfort@aol.com **W:** www.crownhillfort.co.uk
Contact: James Breslin, Fort Administrator

Party Max: 1000 (marquee: 1000)

Built in the 1860s, the Fort is the largest and best preserved on Plymouth's great Victorian fortifications. Now restored to its former glory, the fort offers a unique environment for functions and meetings. Fireworks by arrangement only.

Catering: Contract approved list

SERVICES:
- Exclusive Use
- Flowers
- Cake
- Performance Area

Price Guide: Prices on application
Catering (sit down): POA
Catering (buffet): POA

Crudwell Court Hotel, Crudwell
T: 01666 577194 **F:** 01666 577853
Contact: Derek & Karen Woods

Party Max: 50 (marquee: 140)   Bedrooms: 15

This 17th Century rectory, which changed hands in April 2000, is situated in three acres of garden and features a heated outdoor swimming pool for use during the summer. The new owners have plans to refurbish the hotel, so we suggest party organisers contact the hotel for an update on facilities and prices.

Catering: In house

FACILITIES:
- Outdoor Pool

SERVICES:
- Marriage Licence

Price Guide: Prices on application.
Catering (sit down): from £23.00pp

Cumberwell Park, Bradford-on-Avon
T: 01225 863322 **F:** 01225 868160
E: party@cumberwellpark.co.uk
W: www.cumberwellpark.co.uk
Contact: Ceri Powell, Events Coordinator

Party Max: 240

This striking Wiltshire barn style venue, characterised by timber beams, offers panoramic country views and operates as a golf club and function venue. Various sized function rooms are available, catering for up to 240 guest, while there is parking for 200 cars. Excellent food and service is offered within a friendly, welcoming environment. There is a choice of extensive buffet and dining menus and a comprehensive wine list. This venue is situated on the A363 between Bath and Bradford-on-Avon.

Catering: In house

FACILITIES:
- Helipad
- Golf
- Shooting
- Paint Ball
- Hot Air Balloons
- Quad Bikes/Off Road
- Archery

SERVICES:
- Exclusive Use
- Marriage Licence
- Disco/Dance
- Performance Area

Price Guide: Charges are made per head, depending on catering required. Room hire rates only are available on application.
Catering (sit down): from £15.50pp
Catering (buffet): from £9pp

Curdon Mill, Williton
T: 01984 656522 **F:** 01984 656197
E: curdonmill@compuserve.com
Contact: Mr & Mrs Criddle, Owners

Party Max: 85   Bedrooms: 6

Curdon Mill, a sandstone watermill, is a pretty 2-star country hotel set amidst acres of farmland at the foot of the Quantocks. In the summer this venue offers a fully lined marquee for functions, while in the winter months larger parties, luncheons, weddings, etc, can take place in the Pavilion which can be festively decorated. The restaurant here holds 1 rosette.

Catering: In house

SERVICES:
- Exclusive Use
- Marriage Licence
- Flowers

Price Guide: £600 - £800 per day.
Catering (sit down): from £20pp
Catering (buffet): from £5.25pp

WEST COUNTRY

De Vere Royal Bath Hotel, Bournemouth
T: 01202 555555   F: 01202 292421
E: michele.whitwam@devere-hotels.com
W: www.devereonline.co.uk
Contact: Michelle Whitwam
Party Max: 400 (marquee: unlimited)   Bedrooms: 140

The Royal Bath Hotel is the only 5-star hotel in Bournemouth and is located in the centre of this seaside resort. It is set in its own grounds with views across the bay. The hotel has a choice of 8 function rooms, ranging in capacity from 20 t0 400.
Catering: In house

SERVICES:
• Marriage Licence
Price Guide: Prices on application.
Catering (sit down): from £55.00pp
Catering (buffet): from £8.50pp

Deer Park Hotel, Honiton
T: 01404 41266   F: 011404 46598
Contact: Janet Gwynn, Hospitality
Party Max: 120 (marquee: 250)   Bedrooms: 88

This Georgian mansion (built 1720) is set in 35 acres of parkland, where helicopters and hot air balloons may land.
Catering: In house

FACILITIES:
• Helipad
SERVICES:
• Marriage Licence
Price Guide: Prices on application.
Catering (sit down): from £14.50pp

Dillington House, Ilminster
T: 01460 52427   F: 01460 52433
E: ccrocker@somerset.gov.uk   W: www.dillington.co.uk
Contact: Carol Crocker
Party Max: 147 (marquee: 300)   Bedrooms: 32

This Grade II listed house was once the home of Lord North, Prime Minister to George III. Somerset County Council took responsibility for Dillington in 1949. The grounds feature a croquet lawn and putting green, while the back terrace looks out across the rose garden to parkland.
Catering: In house

FACILITIES:
• Croquet   • Putting
SERVICES:
• Marriage Licence
Price Guide: Prices on application.
Catering (sit down): from £20.00pp

Dorchester Municipal Buildings, Dorchester
T: 01305 265840   F: 01305 266085
E: cornexchange@dorchester-tc.gov.uk
W: www.dorchestercornexchnage.co.uk
Contact: Miss Louise Harding, Administrative Assistant
Party Max: 300

The Grade II municipal buildings, a distinctive feature of the town centre, are owned by the Town Council and have 4 rooms with capacities of 20, 40, 120 and 300. The Town Hall and the Council Chamber both hold a Civil Wedding Licence. A bar, full kitchen facilities for outside catering, limited parking and a stair climber, are available at no extra cost, together with the services of the on-site caretaker.
Catering: Self catering

SERVICES:
• Exclusive Use   • Marriage Licence   • Disco/Dance
• Performance Area
Price Guide: £56.50 + vat - £71 + vat per session. Hourly rates start at £24.

The Dower House, Padstow
T: 01841 532317   F: 01841 532667
Contact: Paul & Patricia Brocklebank
Party Max: 40 (marquee: 60)   Bedrooms: 6

This Grade II listed building is now a small hotel on the edge of Padstow town. The terrace overlooks the Camel estuary and the distant hills of Bodmin moor.
Catering: In house

SERVICES:
• Marriage Licence
Price Guide: Prices on application.
Catering (sit down): from £15.00pp
Catering (buffet): from £12.00pp

Durrant House Hotel, Northam
T: 01237 472361   F: 01237 421709
Contact: Maria or Mark Borg
Party Max: 300 (marquee: unlimited)   Bedrooms: 125

This old Georgian mansion set in three acres, has its own swimming pool, sauna and solarium, and is developing a leisure complex.
Catering: In house

FACILITIES:
• Swimming Pool   • Sauna   • Solarium
SERVICES:
• Marriage Licence
Price Guide: Prices on application.
Catering (sit down): from £14.00pp
Catering (buffet): from £11.50pp

East Close Country Hotel, Nr Christchurch
T: 01425 672404   F: 01425 674315
Contact: Malcolm R Davies
Party Max: 100 (marquee: 500+)   Bedrooms: 16

This hotel features walled gardens, both ornamental and working.
Catering: In house

SERVICES:
• Marriage Licence
Price Guide: Prices on application.
Catering (sit down): from £13.95pp
Catering (buffet): from £7.95pp

WEST COUNTRY

Eggesford Barton, Chulmleigh
T: 01769 580255 **F:** 01769 580256
E: heyeseggesfordb@compuserve.com
Contact: P N Heyes
Party Max: 120 (marquee: unlimited)   Bedrooms: 9

This is a listed period building, set in 100 acres, with a riverside setting.
Catering: In house

SERVICES:
- Marriage Licence

Price Guide: Prices on application.
Catering (sit down): from £20.00pp
Catering (buffet): from £13.00pp

Escot House & Gardens, Ottery St Mary
T: 01404 822188 **F:** 01404 822903
E: escot@eclipse.co.uk **W:** www.escot-devon.co.uk
Contact: Mrs Lucy Kennaway, Owner
Party Max: 200 (marquee: 250)

This Grade II listed Georgian manor house is set in private parkland in rural East Devon. The property is available for exclusive useage, and provides excellent photo opportunities.
Catering: In house

SERVICES:
- Exclusive Use
- Marriage Licence
- Performance Area

Price Guide: Prices on application.
Catering (sit down): from £18pp
Catering (buffet): from £12pp

Falcon Hotel, Bude
T: 01288 352005 **F:** 01288 356359
Contact: Debbie Jones
Party Max: 150 (marquee: 300)   Bedrooms: 26

This hotel and restaurant enjoys a canalside location, yet is only two minutes' walk from the beach. The hotel claims beautiful walled gardens.
Catering: In house

SERVICES:
- Marriage Licence

Price Guide: Prices on application.
Catering (sit down): from £11.00pp
Catering (buffet): from £5.00pp

Farthings Hotel, Taunton
T: 01823 480664 **F:** 01823 481118
Contact: Hilary Murphy
Party Max: 45 (marquee: 120)   Bedrooms: 10

Farthings is a family owned Georgian country hotel set in three acres of gardens, which includes a croquet lawn.
Catering: In house

FACILITIES:
- Croquet

SERVICES:
- Marriage Licence

Price Guide: Prices on application.

Catering (sit down): from £22.00pp

Fishponds House, Honiton
T: 01404 891358 **F:** 01404 891109
E: fishpondshouse@aol.com
Contact: Anne-Marie Spalding
Party Max: 100   Bedrooms: 13

This country house hotel and restaurant is set in 45 acres of gardens and countryside. The original cottage, now part of the main bar and restaurant, was built in 1201 for the Lake Keeper who provided fish to the Cistercian monks at Dunkeswell Abbey. Year round coarse fishing is still available here.
Catering: In house

FACILITIES:
- Fishing

SERVICES:
- Marriage Licence

Price Guide: Prices on application.
Catering (sit down): from £18.50pp
Catering (buffet): from £17.50pp

Gerbestone Manor, Wellington
T: 01823 662673 **F:** 01823 663558
E: party@thebighouseco.com **W:** www.thebighouseco.com
Contact: Dee Friend, Events Manager
Party Max: 60 (marquee: 100)   Bedrooms: 10

This 700 year old manor is set in 200 acres with a 2 acre lake, with course and fly fishing, 15 acres of formal gardens, lawns and woodland. Facilities include floodlit tennis court, heated outdoor pool and sauna. Inside the 3 main reception rooms all have large open fireplaces. The house is available on a full, part-time or self catering basis. Entertainment and activities can also be arranged, such as Murder Mystery events and a Basil Fawlty impressionist.
Catering: In house / Self catering

FACILITIES:
- Helipad
- Hot Air Balloons
- Tennis
- Outdoor Pool
- Fishing
- Sauna

SERVICES:
- Exclusive Use
- Fireworks
- Murder Mystery

Price Guide: £2750 - £4950
Catering (sit down): from £39pp
Catering (buffet): from £29pp

Goldney Hall, Bristol
T: 0117 903 4873 **F:** 0117 903 4877
Contact: Ann Longney
Party Max: 150

This university hall of residence has its own listed 18th century formal gardens set in seven acres, featuring a folly and a grotto. There are 30 self-contained flats within the hall, but these are only available during vacation time; July to September.
Catering: In house

SERVICES:
- Marriage Licence

Price Guide: Prices on application.

WEST COUNTRY

Catering (sit down): POA

Grittleton House, Chippenham
T: 01249 782434   F: 01249 782669
Contact: Adrian Shipp
Party Max: 250 (marquee: 1000)

Situated in its own grounds, this Grade II listed building is available seven days a week. Reception facilities include a marquee, with a maximum capacity of 1,000.
Catering: In house

SERVICES:
- Marriage Licence

Price Guide: Prices on application.
Catering (sit down): from £15.00pp

Guyers House, Corsham
T: 01249 713399   F: 01249 712801
E: enquiries@guyershouse.com   W: www.guyershouse.com
Contact: Claire Mussell, Deputy Manager
Party Max: 150 (marquee: 300)   Bedrooms: 38

This Grade II listed building is now operating as a training and conference centre. The minimum number catered for here is 55. The ballroom features a sprung dance floor.
Catering: In house

FACILITIES:
- Croquet

SERVICES:
- Exclusive Use
- Marriage Licence
- Flowers
- Toastmaster

Price Guide: £1300 + vat for weekend exclusive use.
Catering (sit down): from £28pp
Catering (buffet): from £28pp

Haldon Belvedere, Exeter
T: 01392 833668   F: 01392 833668
Contact: Ian Turner
Party Max: 45   Bedrooms: 1

This secluded, listed building has panoramic views over Devon. The building is owned by The Devon Historic Buildings Trust, and includes an apartment which is also let, with minimum stay of 3 nights on a self-catering basis. A dinner delivery service is available locally.
Catering: Self catering/Contract (any)

SERVICES:
- Marriage Licence

Price Guide: Prices on application.
Catering (sit down): POA

Halsway Manor, Crowcombe
T: 01984 618274   F: 01984 618324
W: www.halswaymanor.com
Contact: Mrs Jenny Bowman
Party Max: 86   Bedrooms: 23

The Manor has a marriage licence for its Long Room and Hall, which is available on any day except Christmas Day.
Catering: In house

SERVICES:
- Marriage Licence

Price Guide: Prices on application.
Catering (sit down): from £25.50pp
Catering (buffet): from £6.00pp

Haven Hotel, Poole
T: 01202 707333   F: 01202 708281
E: sales@havenhotel.co.uk   W: www.havenhotel.co.uk
Contact: Rebecca Day, Lorna Winder or Christian Field
Party Max: 190   Bedrooms: 94

Haven is a 4-star hotel sited on the southernmost point of the Sandbanks peninsula, overlooking the broad sweep of Poole Bay and the Purbecks.
Catering: In house

SERVICES:
- Marriage Licence

Price Guide: Prices on application.
Catering (sit down): from £24.00pp
Catering (buffet): from £10.50pp

Headland Hotel, Newquay
T: 01636 872211   F: 01637 872212
E: office@headlandhotel.co.uk   W: www.headlandhotel.co.uk
Contact: Mrs Carolyn Armstrong
Party Max: 400 (marquee: 700)   Bedrooms: 108

This Grade II listed building is set on a Cornish headland surrounded by sea, just yards from Newquay's Fistral Beach.
Catering: In house

SERVICES:
- Marriage Licence

Price Guide: Prices on application.
Catering (sit down): from £18.00pp

Highcliffe Castle, Christchurch
T: 01425 278807   F: 01202 474438
E: m.allen@christchurch.gov.uk
W: www.christchurch.gov.uk/highcliffecastle
Contact: Mike Allen
Party Max: 95

Highcliffe Castle is an historic house, with picturesque gardens and sea views from its cliff-top position.
Catering: In house

SERVICES:
- Marriage Licence

Price Guide: Prices on application.
Catering (sit down): POA

Hornsbury Mill, Chard
T: 01460 63317   F: 01460 63317
E: hornsburymill@btclick.com
Contact: Keith and Sarah Jane Lewin
Party Max: 200 (marquee: unlimited)   Bedrooms: 5

This is a restored working corn mill and museum set in five acres of water gardens with trout lake and resident ducks.
Catering: In house

WEST COUNTRY

SERVICES:
- Marriage Licence

Price Guide: Prices on application.
Catering (sit down): from £25.00pp
Catering (buffet): from £9.50pp

Huntsham Court, Tiverton
T: 01398 361365 **F:** 01398 36146
Contact: Andrea Bolwig
Party Max: 200 (marquee: 180)   Bedrooms: 17

Huntsham Court is a Grade II listed Victorian gothic country house. British and continental style cuisine is offered here.
Catering: In house

SERVICES:
- Marriage Licence

Price Guide: Prices on application.
Catering (sit down): POA

Hurstone House, Wellington
T: 01823 662673 **F:** 01823 663558
E: party@thebighouseco.com **W:** www.thebighouseco.com
Contact: Ben Fox
Party Max: 16   Bedrooms: 7

Hurstone House, located on the edge of Exmoor, is a lovely old farmhouse dating from the 14th Century. The house was largely rebuilt in the 1920s and offers 7 bedrooms (all with TV) and 5 bathrooms. The estate runs to 50 acres and borders the meandering River Tone. Hurstone is managed by The Big House Co (see Agency Listings) who can organise catering and entertainment if required.
Catering: Self catering/In house FB

SERVICES:
- Exclusive Use

Price Guide: Weekends from £1386. Weeks from £1790.

Kingston Maurward, Dorchester
T: 01305 215023 **F:** 01305 215001
E: chris.wakefield@kmc.ac.uk
Contact: Chris Wakefield, Hospitality Services Manager
Party Max: 300   Bedrooms: 54

Kingston Maurward House was built between 1717 and 1720 for George Pitt. Approached through parkland, the house and its 35 acres of fine gardens and lawns make an adyllic setting for a party. The grand entrance hall, with its high stuccoed ceiling, central chandelier and twin marble fireplces, make an ideal room in which your guests can be greeted with reception drinks prior to your event. The elegant suite comprises 4 rooms: The Whatmoor Room, and the Wood Panelled Library can seat up to 50 guest; the Pengelly Room 80; and the Conference Hall 200.
Catering: In house

FACILITIES:
- Helipad
- Tennis
- Riding
- Pool/Snooker
- Gym

SERVICES:
- Exclusive Use
- Marriage Licence
- Flowers

Price Guide: Room hire rates start at £60 + vat for 4 hours during the week and rise to £1000 + vat for day and evening for all rooms.
Catering (sit down): from £15.95pp
Catering (buffet): from £5.95pp

Kington Manor, Chippenham
T: 01249 750655 **F:** 01249 750651
Contact: Peter Le Grys
Party Max: 400 (marquee: unlimited)

Kington Manor stands in 15 acres of parkland, featuring grounds terraced with fountains and herbaceous borders leading to a large lake.
Catering: In house

SERVICES:
- Marriage Licence

Price Guide: Prices on application.
Catering (sit down): from £20.00pp

Kitley House Hotel, Plymouth
T: 01752 881555 **F:** 01752 881667
E: sales@kitleyhousehotel.com **W:** www.kitleyhousehotel.com
Contact: Andrew Huckerby
Party Max: 140 (marquee: 250)   Bedrooms: 20

Kitley House is a Grade I listed house located in a 300 acre country estate and overlooking a lake. The house was once the home of the Bastards during the time of Elizabeth I and is still adorned with their multi-coloured coats of arms.
Catering: In house

SERVICES:
- Marriage Licence

Price Guide: Room hire £100 - £150
Catering (sit down): from £27.50pp
Catering (buffet): from £13.50pp

Langdon Court Hotel, Plymouth
T: 01752 862358 **F:** 01752 863428
E: langdon@eurobell.co.uk
Contact: Ann Cox
Party Max: 80   Bedrooms: 19

This Grade II listed Tudor manor is set alongside a formal walled garden.
Catering: In house

SERVICES:
- Marriage Licence

Price Guide: Prices on application.
Catering (sit down): POA

Langstone Cliff Hotel, Dawlish
T: 01626 868000 **F:** 01626 868006
E: Nobles@langstone-hotel.co.uk
W: www.langstone-hotel.co.uk
Contact: Geoffrey or Mark Rogers
Party Max: 400 (marquee: unlimited)   Bedrooms: 68

Langstone Cliff is a Grade II listed building set in its own grounds of 19 acres, on Devon's south coast. It has an outdoor pool and a hard tennis court.

WEST COUNTRY

Catering: In house

FACILITIES:
- Outdoor Pool
- Tennis

SERVICES:
- Marriage Licence

Price Guide: Prices on application.
Catering (sit down): from £9.00pp

Langtry Manor Hotel, Bournemouth
T: 01202 553887 F: 01202 290115
E: lillie@langtrymanor.com W: www.langtrymanor.com
Contact: Tara Howard

Party Max: 100   Bedrooms: 25

This listed building was built by Edward VII for his mistress Lillie Langtry. The Dining Room features an inglenook fireplace, minstrel's gallery, huge stained glass windows, chandeliers and 16th Century tapestries.

Catering: In house

SERVICES:
- Marriage Licence

Price Guide: Prices on application.
Catering (sit down): £14.95 - 27.00

Lanteglos Country House Hotel, Camelford
T: 01840 213551 F: 01840 212372
E: lantegloshotel@thenet.co.uk
Contact: Roger Ely

Party Max: 90 (marquee: 180)   Bedrooms: 83

This country house was designed by Augustus Pugin and built in 1847.

Catering: In house

SERVICES:
- Marriage Licence

Price Guide: Prices on application.
Catering (sit down): from £14.00pp
Catering (buffet): from £8.50pp

Larmer Tree Gardens, Salisbury
T: 01725 516228 F: 01725 516321
Contact: Miss Tracey Hartles, Events Manager

Party Max: 250 (marquee: 2000)

The Grade II listed Larmer Tree Gardens are set high on the Cranbroune Chase, providing views of the surrounding countryside. It is one of the most unusual gardens in England containing an extraordinary collection of colonial and oriental buildings, a roman temple and an open air theatre. The gardens were created in 1880 by General Pitt Riversfor 'the enjoyment and education of his estate workers and local people'. This venue is usually open to the public from April to October, 11am to 6pm.

Catering: In house

SERVICES:
- Exclusive Use
- Marriage Licence
- Performance Area

Price Guide: £2000 Saturday day rate.

Catering (sit down): from £20pp
Catering (buffet): from £20pp

Leigh Court Business & Conference Centre, Abbots Leigh
T: 01275 373393 F: 01275 374681
E: enquiry@leighcourt.co.uk W: www.leighcourt.co.uk
Contact: SallyBarker, Managing Director

Party Max: 320 (marquee: unlimited)

Leigh Court is a Grade II listed mansion house set in 25 acres of private parkland. Thre are facilities for all types of events, from balls and parties to conference and outdoor and team building activities. There are 5 interconnecting function rooms of varying sizes all decorated with 19th Century decor.

Catering: In house

FACILITIES:
- Helipad
- Shooting
- Hot Air Balloons

SERVICES:
- Marriage Licence

Price Guide: Hire fees range from £153.19 to £1753.19 + vat, depending on choice of rooms.
Catering (sit down): from £22.77 + vat
Catering (buffet): from £17.11 + vat

Leigh Park Hotel, Bradford on Avon
T: 01225 864885 F: 01225 862315
Contact: Pamela Duckett

Party Max: 150 (marquee: 200)

This Georgian country house hotel stands in five acres of grounds, with its own walled garden and vineyard.

Catering: In house

SERVICES:
- Marriage Licence

Price Guide: Prices on application.
Catering (sit down): from £28.00pp (package)

Lewtrenchard Manor, Okehampton
T: 01566 783256 F: 01566 783332
E: S&J@lewtrenchard.co.uk W: www.lewtrenchard.demon.co.uk
Contact: Mrs S Murray

Party Max: 120   Bedrooms: 8

The Manor was built in about 1600 and was once the home of the composer of 'Onward Christian Soldiers'. Internally, the house features ornate ceilings and oak panelling, carvings and open fireplaces. It is now the home of the Murray family.

Catering: In house

SERVICES:
- Marriage Licence

Price Guide: Prices on application.
Catering (sit down): from £22.50pp

Longleat, Warminster
T: 01985 844400 F: 01985 844885
E: longleat@btinternet.com W: www.longleat.co.uk
Contact: Jo Sparrow, Marketing & Events Manager

Party Max: 150 (marquee: unlimited)   Bedrooms: 8

WEST COUNTRY

Nestling within 900 acres of Capability Brown landscaped grounds, Longleat House is widely regarded as one of the most beautiful stately homes open to the public. Substantially completed in 1580, and home of the Marquess of Bath. Longleat offers several of its room for functions, including the Great Hall, the Green Library and the more modern Banqueting Suite. Longleat also specialises in outdoor events - marquee based gala dinners, corporate fun days, car launches and off-roading are just some of the activities that have taken place within the park. It also has its own famous safari park.
Catering: Contract (any)

FACILITIES:
• Quad Bikes/Off Road • Hot Air Balloons • Helipad

SERVICES:
• Marriage Licence
Price Guide: from £1500
Catering (sit down): POA
Catering (buffet): POA

Lordleaze Hotel, Chard
T: 01460 61066 **F:** 01460 66468
Contact: Functions Manager
Party Max: 200 (marquee: 100) Bedrooms: 16

This is a converted 18th Century farmhouse in a country setting. It has its own gardens and parking and is AA 3-star, and 4-crown Highly Commended as an hotel.
Catering: In house

SERVICES:
• Marriage Licence
Price Guide: Prices on application.
Catering (sit down): from £13.95pp

Lucknam Park Hotel, Colerne
T: 01225 742777 **F:** 01225 743536
E: banqueting@lucknampark.co.uk
Contact: Jenny Webb
Party Max: 60 (marquee: 100) Bedrooms: 4

This imposing Palladian mansion was built in 1720 and is set in 500 acres of grounds.
Catering: In house

SERVICES:
• Marriage Licence
Price Guide: Prices on application.
Catering (sit down): from £24.50pp

Manor Hotel, Dorchester
T: 01308 897616
F: 01308 897035
E: themanorhotel@btconnect.com
W: www.themanorhotel.com
Contact: Richard Childs
Party Max: 120 (marquee: 70) Bedrooms: 13

Mentioned in the Doomsday Book, The Manor is an ancient stone building set within 500 yards of Chesil Beach.
Catering: In house

SERVICES:
• Marriage Licence
Price Guide: Prices on application.
Catering (sit down): from £21.50pp
Catering (buffet): from £18.00pp

Manor House, Chippenham
T: 01249 782206 **F:** 01249 782159
Contact: Hannah Meager
Party Max: 125 (marquee: 200) Bedrooms: 45

This Grade II listed building is set in 26 acres of grounds, with an additional 200 acres of golf course.
Catering: In house

FACILITIES:
• Golf

SERVICES:
• Marriage Licence
Price Guide: Prices on application.
Catering (sit down): from £25.00pp

Manor House Hotel, Morehamptonstead
T: 01647 440355 **F:** 01647 440961
E: Manorhouse@principalhotels.co.uk
W: www.principalhotels.co.uk
Contact: Jill Brown
Party Max: 140 Bedrooms: 86

This hotel is set within 270 acres of private estate within the Dartmoor National Park.
Catering: In house

SERVICES:
• Marriage Licence
Price Guide: Prices on application.
Catering (sit down): from £23.50pp

Mansion House Hotel, Poole
T: 01202 685666 **F:** 01202 665709
Contact: Jackie Godden
Party Max: 120 Bedrooms: 28

This Georgian house is set in a town mews just off Poole's busy quay. It is a Grade II listed building with an elegant feature staircase.
Catering: In house

SERVICES:
• Marriage Licence
Price Guide: Prices on application.
Catering (sit down): POA

Maunsel House, Nr Bridgwater
T: 020 7352 1132 **F:** 020 7352 5697
E: sirbenslade@shirlstar.co.uk **W:** www.sirbenslade.co.uk
Contact: Carol Duddridge (at venue) or Nicky Mundie (PA to Sir B Slade)
Party Max: 150 (marquee: 150+)

This imposing 13th Century manor house is the ancestral seat of the Slade family and home of the 7th Baronet, Sir Benjamin Slade. The house can boast such visitors as Geoffrey Chaucer,

WEST COUNTRY

who apparently wrote part of the Canterbury Tales whilst staying here. The beautiful grounds and spacious rooms provide both privacy and an unique atmosphere for any special event.
Catering: Contract (any)

FACILITIES:
• Fishing
SERVICES:
• Exclusive Use
Price Guide: £100 - £1000

Milford Hall Hotel, Salisbury
T: 01722 417411   **F:** 01722 419444
E: Milfordhallhotel@cs.com
W: www.net200.co.uk/hp/milfordhall
Contact: Alison Drew

Party Max: 90 (marquee: 100)   Bedrooms: 35

This is a Grade II Georgian house which is now a family-run hotel.
Catering: In house

SERVICES:
• Marriage Licence
Price Guide: Prices on application.
Catering (sit down): from £15.50pp
Catering (buffet): from £10.00pp

Northcote Manor, Nr Exmoor
T: 01769 560501   **F:** 01769 560770
E: rest@northcotemanor.co.uk
W: www.northcotemanor.co.uk
Contact: Karen Dawson

Party Max: 80 (marquee: 200)   Bedrooms: 11

The Manor is a Grade II listed building and the former estate of the Earls of Bedford and Portsmouth. It is set in 20 acres of lawns, landscaped gardens and woodland, and features a tennis court and golf practice area. There are also horses available for riding, and there is an 18 hole golf course next door. One ceremony can take place here on any day of the year. Exclusive use of this venue costs £3000 for 1 day or £5000 for 2 days.
Catering: In house FB

FACILITIES:
• Riding   • Golf
SERVICES:
• Marriage Licence
Price Guide: Prices on application.
Catering (sit down): £20.00 - 40.00pp

Old Municipal Buildings, Taunton
T: 01823 356434
F: 01823 356329
E: omb@tauntondeane.gov.uk
Contact: Pam Kyprianou

Party Max: 150 (marquee: 1000)

The Old Municipal Hall is an ancient monument (1522) and listed building right in the centre of Taunton. Hirers are to arrange their own caterers at this venue.
Catering: Contract (any)/Self catering

SERVICES:
• Marriage Licence
Price Guide: Prices on application.

Oxenways, Axminster
T: 01404 881785   **F:** 01404 881778
E: oxenways@aol.com   **W:** www.oxenways.com
Contact: Sheila Beecham

Party Max: 50 (marquee: 120)   Bedrooms: 8+ 10

This Edwardian country house and activity centre is surrounded by 70 acres of formal gardens, pasture, lake and woodland.
Catering: In house

SERVICES:
• Marriage Licence
Price Guide: Prices on application.
Catering (sit down): from £20.00pp
Catering (buffet): from £7.50pp

Pear Tree at Purton, Swindon
T: 01793 772100   **F:** 01793 772369
Contact: Francis Young

Party Max: 70 (marquee: 150)   Bedrooms: 18

This Cotswold stone hotel, set in 7.5 acres of grounds, has achieved the RAC's highest award: The Blue Ribbon. The hotel's chef, Alan Postill, has been awarded two AA rosettes.
Catering: In house

SERVICES:
• Marriage Licence
Price Guide: Prices on application.
Catering (sit down): from £30.00pp

Penmere Manor Hotel, Falmouth
T: 01326 211411   **F:** 01326 317588
Contact: Debbie Collins

Party Max: 100   Bedrooms: 37

This Georgian manor house has five acres of secluded wooded gardens. The Head Chef here has two Rosettes. The restaurant has a menu dedicated to lobster, while the cellar has a choice of over 100 wines. The hotel has a leisure club with indoor and outdoor pools.
Catering: In house

FACILITIES:
• Indoor Pool   • Outdoor Pool   • Leisure Club
SERVICES:
• Marriage Licence
Price Guide: Prices on application.
Catering (sit down): from £10.50pp
Catering (buffet): from £6.95pp

Penventon Hotel, Redruth
T: 01209 203000   **F:** 01209 203001
E: manager@penventon.com   **W:** www.penventon.com
Contact: Functions Manager

Party Max: 300 (marquee: 200)   Bedrooms: 50

Penventon is a Georgian mansion set in its own grounds. It is a 3-star hotel which has been run by the Pascoe family since the

WEST COUNTRY

1960s. It has its own pub and leisure centre on site. The hotel has a brigade of 10 chefs and boasts an AA rosette. Special menus and themes can be created to suit. There is a grand piano in the restaurant and a brass band can be arranged. The restaurant can be themed if required.
Catering: In house

FACILITIES:
- Leisure Centre

SERVICES:
- Marriage Licence

Price Guide: Prices on application.
Catering (sit down): from £14.00pp
Catering (buffet): from £6.00pp

Plumber Manor, Sturminster Newton
T: 01258 472507
F: 01258 473370
E: book@plumbermanor.com
Contact: Mrs J Watkins, Events Manager

Party Max: 75 (marquee: 200)   Bedrooms: 16

This Jacobean manor house sits in acres of lawn in the heart of Thomas Hardy's Dorset. This peaceful country house hotel (3-star), which has been in the same family since it was built, offers 6 en-suite bedrooms in the main house, plus a further 10 bedrooms in the converted barn and courtyard in the grounds. The main bar and dining rooms have open fires, and private parties are especially catered for.
Catering: In house

FACILITIES:
- Helipad
- Tennis

SERVICES:
- Exclusive Use
- Flowers
- Disco/Dance

Price Guide: B&B rates start at £170 for 2 nights for 2 people.
Catering (sit down): from £23pp
Catering (buffet): from £20pp

Polhawn Fort, Torpoint
T: 01752 822864
F: 01752 822341
Contact: John Wicksteed

Party Max: 140 (marquee: 140)   Bedrooms: 8

This Grade II listed Napoleonic coastal fort, situated on the Rame Peninsular, is available for private and exclusive use only, and is generally hired for a full weekend period. Because the Fort is hired on an exclusive basis wedding ceremonies may be held any day of the week with no restrictions on Bank Holidays. Prices for the hire of the Fort (from £1,295 to around £4,250) include the use of all facilities (including tennis court).
Catering: Self catering/Contract (any)

FACILITIES:
- Tennis

SERVICES:
- Marriage Licence

Price Guide: Prices on application.
Catering (sit down): POA

Powderham Castle, Exeter
T: 01626 890243   **F:** 01626 890729
E: castle@powderham.co.uk   **W:** www.powderham.co.uk
Contact: Michelle Willocks, Wedding Coordinator

Party Max: 200 (marquee: unlimited)

Powderham Castle is the historic family home of the Earl of Devon. It is medieval in origin and lies in its own 200 acres deer park overlooking the estuary of the River Exe.
Catering: Contract (any)

FACILITIES:
- Helipad
- Tennis
- Shooting
- Pool/Snooker
- Hot Air Balloons

SERVICES:
- Exclusive Use
- Marriage Licence

Price Guide: Venue hire is £350 - £4000
Catering (sit down): from £12pp
Catering (buffet): from £6pp

Pump Room & Roman Baths, Bath
T: 01225 477782-477786   **F:** 01225 477476
E: historic-venuehire@bathnes.gov.uk
W: www.romanbaths.co.uk
Contact: Sharon Stewart, Anne Harris

Party Max: 200

The Grade I listed Pump Room in Bath is one of the most famous buildings in the country and is located in the centre of Bath next to Bath Abbey. This venue regrets that it cannot accept bookings for 18th or 21st birthday parties. Also avaiable for hire are the Roman Baths (see seperate entry).
Catering: Contract approved list

SERVICES:
- Exclusive Use
- Marriage Licence
- Disco/Dance
- Performance Area

Price Guide: £133 - £160 per hour.
Catering (sit down): from £26pp
Catering (buffet): from £15pp

Purbeck House Hotel, Swanage
T: 01929 422872   **F:** 01929 421194
E: purbeckhouse@easyco.uk   **Contact:** Stephane Gausseau

Party Max: 120 (marquee: 50)   Bedrooms: 18

Purbeck is a Grade II listed building, with gardens. It is in the centre of Swanage and only 300 yards from the sea front.
Catering: In house

SERVICES:
- Marriage Licence

Price Guide: Prices on application.
Catering (sit down): from £16.00pp
Evening from £9.95pp
Catering (buffet): from £17.50pp

Rose-in-Vale Hotel, St Agnes
T: 01872 552202   **F:** 01872 552700
Contact: Mrs V M Arthur

Party Max: 108 (marquee: 100)   Bedrooms: 18

This Grade II listed country house dates back to the 1760s and

WEST COUNTRY

is set in 11 acres of woods, pasture and gardens. The hotel has its own marquee sited in the grounds. This features a bar and a dancefloor. In addition, a classical pianist is available to take advantage of the hotel's own baby grand piano.
Catering: In house

SERVICES:
• Marriage Licence
Price Guide: Prices on application.
Catering (sit down): from £15.00pp

Rudloe Hall Hotel, Nr Corsham
T: 01225 810555   F: 01225 811412
Contact: Janet Fear
Party Max: 80   Bedrooms: 11

This listed Gothic building is situated in four acres of award-winning gardens and features oak panelling and high corniced ceilings.
Catering: In house

SERVICES:
• Marriage Licence
Price Guide: Prices on application.
Catering (sit down): from £22.95pp

SS Great Britain, Bristol
T: 0117 922 5737   F: 0117 930 4358
E: banquets@ss-great-britain.com
Contact: Andrea Neck
Party Max: 150 (marquee: 80)   Bedrooms: 0

The historic SS Great Britain was built in Bristol in 1843 as a liner and cargo vessel. It is now undergoing restoration, with the first class dining saloon restored in 1992 to its original 1843 condition. Accommodation is not available on board, but preferential rates have been agreed with local establishments.
Catering: In house

SERVICES:
• Marriage Licence
Price Guide: Prices on application.
Catering (sit down): from £25.00pp

Salisbury Guildhall, Salisbury
T: 01722 412144   F: 01722 434369
Contact: Anita Waddington
Party Max: 200

The Guildhall is a Georgian building with court rooms, banqueting hall, chandeliers and paintings. There is wheelchair access to the Banqueting Hall only. There is no fixed price for catering at this venue. Menus are tailored to requirements.
Catering: In house

SERVICES:
• Marriage Licence
Price Guide: Prices on application.

Scoles Manor Barns, Corfe Castle
T: 01929 480312   F: 01929 481237
E: peterandb@scoles.co.uk   W: www.scoles.co.uk
Contact: Mrs Bell
Party Max: 50

These three listed barns situated around a courtyard, are sited next to the Grade II listed Scoles Manor. The barns were converted in 1990 and now offer 4-star accommodation. The properties have views over the Purbeck countryside. The largest, the Great Barn, an easily accommodate 22 or more for meals.
Catering: Contract (any)/Self catering

SERVICES:
• Exclusive Use
Price Guide: £210 - £925 per week. Winter weekends £165 - £280.

Sconner House Inn, Torpoint
T: 01503 230276   F: 01503 230329
W: www.cornish-golf-hotels.co.uk
Contact: John de Rosa, Manager
Party Max: 200 (marquee: 300)   Bedrooms: 10 + 10

This beautiful listed Georgian manor is set in 12 acres of lush Cornish gardens and overlooks the St Germans Estuary. Now a 3-star hotel, the house offers spacious public rooms, comfortable bedrooms and good food. This venue has sister hotels nearby as well as self-catering apartments (for 25) to let, and an 18 hole golf course. Leisure facilities at these other hotels, including indoor pool and sauna, are available to Sconner House guests.
Catering: In house/Contract approved list/Self catering

FACILITIES:
• Paint Ball   • Golf
SERVICES:
• Exclusive Use   • Marriage Licence   • Flowers
• Cake   • Toastmaster   • Disco/Dance
• Live Music   • Entertainers   • Fireworks
• Photography
Price Guide: There is no facility fee here. B&B is from £30pp
Catering (sit down): from £15pp
Catering (buffet): from £5pp

Somerton Court, Somerton
T: 01458 274694   F: 01458 274693
E: owen@newopaul.freeserve.co.uk
Contact: Owen & Pauline Stephens
Party Max: 150 (marquee: yes)   Bedrooms: 6

This Grade II listed country house is set in 55 acres of parkland and gardens.
Catering: In house

SERVICES:
• Marriage Licence
Price Guide: Prices on application.
Catering (sit down): from £20.00pp
Catering (buffet): from £6.00pp

Stables Restaurant, Tiverton
T: 01884 254665/259416   F: 01884 243050/259416
Contact: Penny Woollams, Property Manager
Party Max: 60

WEST COUNTRY

This restaurant is situated in what used to be the stables and coach house to Knightshayes Court. It was designed by the Gothic revivalist architect William Burger and contains all the fairy tale character associated with his flamboyant style. This is a no smoking venue. Horse drawn canal trips take place nearby for thos looking for additional activities.
Catering: In house

SERVICES:
- Flowers
- Cake

Price Guide: Prices on application.
Catering (sit down): from £19.95pp
Catering (buffet): from £15.95pp

Stafford House, Dorchester
T: 01305 263668   F: 01305 266903
Contact: Mrs Kay Pavitt
Party Max: 75 (marquee: 200)   Bedrooms: 2

Jane Austen's Emma was recently filmed in the grounds at Stafford House (Emma was proposed to under the oak!). If that's not enough romance or glamour, Hardy apparently also wrote The Waiting Supper about the house. This is a Grade I listed private house with private riverside walks. The Library and the Drawing Room are licensed for weddings.
Catering: In house

SERVICES:
- Marriage Licence

Price Guide: Prices on application.
Catering (sit down): POA

Stonebarrow Manor, Charmouth
T: 01297 560212   F: 01297 560234
E: bomfords@hotmail.com
Contact: Sue & Mike Bomford, owners
Party Max: 40   Bedrooms: 13

The house, parts of which dates from the 16th Century, is set in around 2 acres of garden on the edge of the lovely old Dorset village of Charmouth, at the foot of Stonebarrow Hill (part of the National Trust Golden Cap Estate). The Manor is fully equipped for a group celebration.
Catering: Contract (any) / Self catering

FACILITIES:
- Pool/Snooker
- Table Tennis
- Deep Sea Fishing
- Fossil Hunts

SERVICES:
- Exclusive Use
- Cake
- Disco/Dance

Price Guide: £1600 - £3500.
Catering (sit down): POA
Catering (buffet): POA

Summer Lodge Hotel, Evershot
T: 01935 83424   F: 01935 83005
Contact: Mr Hostettler
Party Max: 60 (marquee: 200)   Bedrooms: 17

This listed building has a four acre walled garden. Three rooms are available for functions.
Catering: In house

SERVICES:
- Marriage Licence

Price Guide: Prices on application.
Catering (sit down): from £21.00pp

Symondsbury Manor, Bridport
T: 01308 456288   F: 01308 456525
E: peter@symondsbury.com   W: www.symondsbury.com
Contact: Peter W Hitchin, Owner
Party Max: 150 (marquee: 200)

This 16th Century listed manor house is set in its own grounds near the sea in an area of outstanding natural beauty. The house has a very private 2 acre garden and is near an attractive village with a good pub. Bridport is 1.5 miles away.
Catering: In house / Self catering / Contract approved list

SERVICES:
- Exclusive Use
- Toastmaster
- Entertainers
- Flowers
- Disco/Dance
- Photography
- Cake
- Live Music
- Performance Area

Price Guide: £500 - £2995
Catering (sit down): from £22pp
Catering (buffet): from £12pp

Ta Mill, Launceston
T: 01840 261797   F: 01840 261381
E: helen@tamill.co.uk
W: www.tamill.co.uk
Contact: Helen Harvey, Owner
Party Max: 25

Ta Mill is a secluded rural hideaway in North Cornwall between Bodmin Moor and the coast. It is surrounded by countryside in a tranquil valley with 15 acres of meadow, woodland and a fishing lake. Accommodation is is traditional stone and slate cottages, houses and lodges. The main farmhouse sleeps up to 10 people. If all the properties were taken, 54 people could be accommodated.
Catering: Self catering

Price Guide: from £180/week. Christmas and New Year from £850/week.

Taunton School, Taunton
T: 01823 349244
F: 01823 349244
E: enterprises@tauntonschool.co.uk
W: www.tauntonschool.co.uk/enterprises
Contact: Kathryn Howard, Events Manager
Party Max: 500 (marquee: 1000+)

This private school on the outskirts of the town is suitable for small informal dinners to large banquets. Six suites are available for marriage ceremonies and there is a chapel on site, which may be used for blessings.
Catering: In house

FACILITIES:
- Helipad
- Gym
- Outdoor Pool
- Indoor Pool
- Tennis
- Pool/Snooker
- Shooting
- Watersports
- Table Tennis

WEST COUNTRY

SERVICES:
- Exclusive Use
- Toastmaster
- Piped Music
- Performance Area
- Valet Parking

Price Guide: £250 - £500/day. Easter weekend from £2000.
Catering (sit down): from £16pp
Catering (buffet): from £7pp

Tiverton Castle, Tiverton
T: 01884 253200 **F:** 01884 254200
E: tiverton.castle@ufl.net
Contact: Mrs Alison Gordon, Owner

Party Max: 130 (marquee: 200)

Few buildings evoke such an immediate feeling of history as Tiverton Castle. Once home of the powerful medieval Earls of Devon, and later captured by Fairfax during the Civil War, the furnishings and displays reflect the Castle's history. Romantic ruins within the beautiful walled gardens make the Castle an atmospheric and picturesque venue for all kinds of occasions. It is privately owned and managed, and personal service and flexibility for any occasion can be offered. Seven miles from Tiverton and 14 from Exeter, there is easy motoring access to many local attractions and sporting facilities.
Catering: Contract approved list

FACILITIES:
- Fishing

SERVICES:
- Exclusive Use
- Marriage Licence

Price Guide: Prices on application.
Catering (sit down): POA
Catering (buffet): POA

Tone Dale House, Wellington
T: 01823 662673 **F:** 01823 663558
E: party@thebighouseco.com
W: www.thebighouseco.com
Contact: Ben Fox

Party Max: 50   Bedrooms: 11

Tone Dale is an impressive, Georgian Palladian villa set in 4 acres of landscaped grounds, centring on the mill stream which supplied the once thriving woollen mill. The house and gardens have been carefully restored by the current owner. There are 10 bedrooms in the main house and an 11th (a large room with minstrel's gallery and own bathroom) in the ivy clad Old Laundry. This property is marketed by The Big House Company - see Agency Listings - which can also organise catering if required. Table tennis and pool are available on site. Murder Mystery events and a Basil Fawlty impressionist can be arranged for your entertainment.
Catering: In house/Self catering/Contract approved list

FACILITIES:
- Helipad
- Hot Air Balloons
- Pool/Snooker
- Table Tennis

SERVICES:
- Exclusive Use
- Fireworks
- Entertainers

Price Guide: £2750 - £4850
Catering (sit down): from £39pp
Catering (buffet): from £29pp

Trevigue, Bude
T: 0140 230418 **F:** 01840 230418
Contact: Gayle Crocker

Party Max: 30   Bedrooms: 4

This National Trust owned farmhouse is built around a cobbled courtyard. Catering is in-house and, although the farmhouse holds a liquor licence, this does not extend to a late night licence. Trevigue prides itself on the use of top quality produce enhanced by the subtle use of sauces, herbs and seasonings. The venue has hosted live music in the past, such as classical string quartets. In addition to the three bedrooms situated in the farmhouse, a further two rooms are located in the Mediterranean-style annex a few hundred yards from the main building.
Catering: In house

SERVICES:
- Marriage Licence

Price Guide: Prices on application.
Catering (sit down): from £20.00pp

Wellisford Farm House, Wellington
T: 01823 662673 **F:** 01823 663558
E: party@thebighouseco.com **W:** www.thebighouseco.com
Contact: Dee Friend, Events manager

Party Max: 30

Peacefully situated in a charming valley, this spacious house stands in its own open-plan country gardens, just 200 yards from the River Tone, which is available for fishing. There is also an on-site riding school. The house is surrounded by farmland with a 2 mile river frontage within an arable working farm (the owners' home is a discreet distance away). The house has been refurbished and features inglenook open fires and stripped wooden floors throughout. This property is managed by The Big House Co (see Agency Listings), who can also arrange catering if required. Murder Mystery weekends have been popular here.
Catering: Self catering/Contract approved list

FACILITIES:
- Helipad
- Hot Air Balloons

SERVICES:
- Exclusive Use
- Fireworks
- Entertainers

Price Guide: £1900 - £3290
Catering (sit down): from £39pp
Catering (buffet): from £29pp

Whitwell Farm Cottages, Colyton
T: 0800 09 20 419/01297 553803/
F: 01297 552911
E: 100755.66@compuserve.com
W: www.a5star.co.uk
Contact: Mike Williams

Party Max: 10

These are 2 award winning 5-star self-catering 4 & 5 bedroom Grade II cottages (The Stable - for 8 and The Granary - for 10) set in a quiet rural corner of East Devon. The cottages are spacious and well-equipped with wood burner, 4-poster beds, ensuite bathrooms and an enclosed garden. Outside caterers

WEST COUNTRY

can be arranged.
Catering: Self catering

SERVICES:
- Exclusive Use

Price Guide: The Stable - £370 - £995/week The Granary - £560 - £1270/week

Wilton House, Salisbury
T: 01722 746720 **F:** 01722 744447
E: tourism@wiltonhouse.com **W:** www.wiltonhouse.com
Contact: Mrs Sally Salmon, Tourism Administrator

Party Max: 200 (marquee: 300)

Wilton House is a beautiful stately home and home to the 17th Earl of Pembroke and his family. Enjoy this stunning house to celebrate a very special occasion, dine in the magnificent Double Cube Room, dance the night away in the atmospheric setting of the Visitor Centre, hold your conference meeting in a room of your choice or hold your summer ball in a marquee on the lawns by the river with the House as a stunning backdrop and enjoy free car parking and experienced caterers on site.
Catering: In house

FACILITIES:
- Shooting
- Go Karting
- Quad Bikes/Off Road

SERVICES:
- Exclusive Use
- Flowers
- Cake
- Toastmaster
- Disco/Dance
- Photography
- Performance Area

Price Guide: Prices for dining, conference and wedding functions are priced per head and include a facility fee for the premises. Full details on request.
Catering (sit down): from £25pp
Catering (buffet): from £15pp

Winter Gardens Pavilion, Weston-Super-Mare
T: 01934 417117 **F:** 01934 612323
Contact: Mrs V Thomson

Party Max: 600

The Winter Gardens is an elegant 1920s building with a seafront location. It is owned by North Somerset Council and has a wedding licence for four suites, including the circular Pavilion Ballroom. Capacities range from 60 to 700.
Catering: In house

SERVICES:
- Marriage Licence

Price Guide: Prices on application.
Catering (sit down): from £15.00pp
Catering (buffet): from £5.00pp

Yarlington House, Wincanton
T: 01747 838910 **F:** 01747 838684
E: b.desalis@btinternet.com
Contact: Monica de Salis, Organiser

Party Max: 80 (marquee: 300)

This Grade II listed private house is a red brick Georgian building set in parkland. It overlooks fields all round and has landscaped gardens featuring a rose and wisteria arbour in the sunken garden, and an apple pergola which looks down to the laburnham walk. The house is used for smaller functions, while a marquee can be used for larger gatherings.
Catering: Contract approved list

FACILITIES:
- Helipad
- Tennis
- Outdoor Pool

SERVICES:
- Exclusive Use
- Marriage Licence

Price Guide: Day rate from £1100. Christmas and New Year from £2000.
Catering (sit down): from £28pp
Catering (buffet): from £22pp

Yenton Hotel, Bournemouth
T: 01202 556334 **F:** 01202 298935
Contact: Mr M C McIntosh

Party Max: 200 (marquee: 200) Bedrooms: 22

The Yenton is set in an acre of gardens on a tree lined avenue. The Tudor Restaurant and Brodies Restaurant are both licensed for civil ceremonies.
Catering: In house FB

SERVICES:
- Marriage Licence

Price Guide: Prices on application.
Catering (sit down): £5.00 - £25.00pp

EAST OF ENGLAND

Angel Hotel, Bury St Edmunds
T: 01284 753926 F: 01284 750092
Contact: Karen Gough or Natasha Lyfon
Party Max: 200   Bedrooms: 42

This 14th century, creeper-clad listed building, was immortalised by Dickens as the hostelry where Mr Pickwick enjoyed an evening meal.
Catering: In house

SERVICES:
• Marriage Licence
Price Guide: Prices on application.
Catering (sit down): from £7.50pp

Barley Town House, Royston
T: 01763 848997
Contact: PW Smith, Chairman of Management Committee
Party Max: 150

This 450 year old building is Barley's village hall. The Grade II listed timberframe building is on 2 floors and comprises a large hall, a small hall, committee room, 2 kitchens, modern toilets (including disabled) and a car park.
Catering: Contract (any)

SERVICES:
• Exclusive Use   • Marriage Licence
Price Guide: Prices on application.

Barns Hotel, Bedford
T: 01234 270044 F: 01234 273102
W: www.corushotels.com
Contact: Sharon Marchelewicz
Party Max: 120 (marquee: unlimited)   Bedrooms: 48

This riverside hotel comprises a 13th Century tithe barn and a 16th Century manor house.
Catering: In house

SERVICES:
• Marriage Licence
Price Guide: Prices on application.
Catering (sit down): Wedding package from £48.50pp

Beadlow Manor Golf & Country Club, Nr Shefford
T: 01525 860800 F: 01525 861345
Contact: Neil Coupland
Party Max: 300 (marquee: 500)   Bedrooms: 33

The Club is set in 300 acres of rural Bedfordshire and features two 18-hole golf courses and lakes. The original building dates from the mid-19th century, but there have been modern additions over the years. Italian food is a speciality. In the past, the Club has hosted Medieval and Gothic style weddings (all in black), has organised fireworks and allowed helicopters to land in the grounds. Guests staying overnight have full complimentary use of the health centre which includes sauna and Jacuzzi.
Catering: In house

FACILITIES:
• Golf   • Helipad   • Health Centre

SERVICES:
• Marriage Licence   • Fireworks
Price Guide: Prices on application.
Catering (sit down): from £19.70pp
Catering (buffet): from £7.35pp

Belvoir Castle, Grantham
T: 01476 870262 F: 01476 870443
E: info@belvoircastle.com W: www.belvoircastle.com
Contact: Andrew Norman, Castle & Park Comptroller
Party Max: 600 (marquee: unlimited)

This is a stunning 19th Century castle standing on the edge of a ridge with commanding views over the surrounding countryside. The Castle offers spacious rooms, suitable for a variety of uses. The park surrounding the castle is also available for events.
Catering: Contract approved list

FACILITIES:
• Helipad   • Shooting   • Go Karting
• Hot Air Balloons   • Tennis   • Quad Bikes/Off Road
• Classic CArs   • Truck Driving   • Hovercraft
• Falconry

SERVICES:
• Flowers   • Cake   • Performance Area
Price Guide: from £400 + vat
Catering (sit down): from £30pp + vat
Catering (buffet): from £18.50pp + vat

Bolding Way Holiday Cottages, Holt
T: 01263 588666/0800 05 60 996
F: 01263 588666
E: holiday@boldingway.co.uk
W: www.boldingway.co.uk
Contact: Charlie Harrison, owner
Party Max: 20

There are three cottages on this site set in communal gardens with croquet, badminton and a barbecue area. Two of the cottages are linked via an interconnecting door. The venue is regulary used for private and corporate parties. The cottages are a 10 minute walk from the sea in the heart of the North Norfolk coatline. This venue can also arrange corporate training and adventure days for all ages. Extra accommodation can also be organised. This venue can arrange all kinds of activities, including tank driving. Various equipment is also available for hire including deck chairs, picnic baskets, bicycles, etc. There is also an on-site store which has a video library and games.
Catering: Self catering/Contract (any)

FACILITIES:
• Tank Driving   • Video Library   • Pool/Snooker
• Croquet   • Badminton

SERVICES:
• Exclusive Use   • Valet Parking
Price Guide: 2 or 3 cottages together cost from £510 (2 properties) to £2150 for 3 properties over New Year for one week. Short Breaks are also available ranging from £420 to £640 for all 3 properties.
Catering (sit down): from £8pp
Catering (buffet): from £8pp

EAST OF ENGLAND

Brackenborough Arms Hotel, Louth
T: 01507 609169 **F:** 01507 609413
Contact: Ashley
Party Max: 150 (marquee: unlimited)   Bedrooms: 24

The hotel is situated in the heart of the Lincolnshire Wolds in its own landscaped grounds.
Catering: In house

SERVICES:
- Marriage Licence

Price Guide: Prices on application.
Catering (sit down): from £14.00pp

Briggens House Hotel, Stanstead Abbots
T: 01279 829955 **F:** 01279 793685
Contact: Georgian Young
Party Max: 160 (marquee: 220)   Bedrooms: 54

Briggens House Hotel is a Grade II listed, 17th century, building set in 80 acres of parkland.
Catering: In house

SERVICES:
- Marriage Licence

Price Guide: Prices on application.
Catering (sit down): from £32.50pp
Catering (buffet): from £15.00pp

Broom Hall Country Hotel, Thetford
T: 01953 882125 **F:** 01953 882125
E: enquiries@broomhallhotel.co.uk
W: www.broomhallhotel.co.uk
Contact: Simon Rowling
Party Max: 80   Bedrooms: 9

This privately owned 2-star Victorian country house hotel is set in an 'English country garden', and overlooking 13 acres of paddock and parkland. The hotel offers home cooked food, often using vegetables from the hotel garden. Other facilities at the hotel include an indoor swimming pool, snooker room and conservatory.
Catering: In house

FACILITIES:
- Indoor Pool
- Pool/Snooker

SERVICES:
- Marriage Licence

Price Guide: Prices on application.
Catering (sit down): from £13.50pp
Catering (buffet): from £8.50pp

Broxbourne Civic Hall, Hoddesdon
T: 01992 441931 **F:** 01992 451132
Contact: David Cooper
Party Max: 400 (marquee: 1500)

This civic building is set in 4.5 acres of grounds and features lake and tiered terrace.
Catering: Contract (any)

SERVICES:
- Marriage Licence

Price Guide: Prices on application.
Catering (sit down): POA
Catering (buffet): from £4.50pp

Channels Golf Club, Chelmsford
T: 01245 440005 **F:** 01245 442032
Contact: Tony Squire
Party Max: 200 (marquee: 1000)

The golf club boasts a 15th Century clubhouse and an 18th Century listed renovated Essex barn.
Catering: In house

FACILITIES:
- Golf

SERVICES:
- Marriage Licence

Price Guide: Prices on application.
Catering (sit down): from £21.00pp
Catering (buffet): from £7.00pp

Chenies Manor House, Rickmansworth
T: 01494 762888 **F:** 01494 762888
Contact: Mrs MacLeod Matthews
Party Max: 120

Chenies Manor just outside London, offers a converted period barn situated in its grounds.
Catering: In house/Contract approved list

Price Guide: £1000 - £1500
Catering (sit down): POA
Catering (buffet): POA

Chigwell Manor Hall, Chigwell
T: 020 8500 2432 **F:** 020 8500 9926
E: manorhall@compuserve.com **W:** www.manorhall.co.uk
Contact: Jane Meader, Banqueting Manager - Booking Office
Party Max: 120 (marquee: 50)

The Banqueting Hall of this venue is licensed to hold civil wedding ceremonies.
Catering: Contract approved list/In house

SERVICES:
- Marriage Licence
- Performance Area

Price Guide: Venue hire prices range from nothing to £500.
Catering (sit down): from £24pp
Catering (buffet): from £10pp

Chilford Hall, Linton
T: 01223 892641 **F:** 01223 894056
E: simonalper@chilfordhall.co.uk **W:** www.chilfordhall.co.uk
Contact: Rosemary Neilson
Party Max: 999 (marquee: unlimited)

Chilford Hall is a small estate of 50 acres owned by the Alper family. The estate boasts the largest vineyard in Cambridgeshire, and has a 12 acre field for any outdoor activity. One of the most unusual features of the venue is that Chilford Hall can provide its own estate bottled wine for your function. A variety of standard menus is available to simplify food selection. Special services include ribbon displays.

EAST OF ENGLAND

Catering: In house

SERVICES:
- Marriage Licence

Price Guide: Prices on application.

Clinton House, East Dereham
T: 01362 692079   F: 01362 692079
E: clintonholidays@tesco.net
W: www.gtunlimited.co./clintonhouse
Contact: John or Margaret Searle, owners

Party Max: 15   Bedrooms: 4+1

Clinton House, which has a cottage in the grounds, is an 18th Century house sleeping up to 9 + 2 cots. The single storey cottage also has its own garden and sleeps 2 (+2 on sofa bed). The house is tastefully furnished and features exposed beams, an inglenook fireplace and woodburner and a large modern conservatory. Both properties are 4-star rated.

Catering: Self catering

FACILITIES:
- Tennis
- Croquet

Price Guide: £550 - £1050

Congham Hall Hotel, King's Lynn
T: 01485 600250   F: 01485 601191
Contact: Trevor Forecast

Party Max: 100 (marquee: 180)   Bedrooms: 14

This Georgian manor house, situated only six miles from King's Lynn, stands in 30 acres of parkland and formal gardens. Head Chef, Andrew Dixon, has created several menus specially for wedding celebrations. The Hall has an attractive restaurant, the Orangery, with full length windows overlooking the lawns. Large doors open onto the terrace from here. Smaller dinner parties can be catered for in the Board Room.

Catering: In house

SERVICES:
- Marriage Licence

Price Guide: Prices on application.
Catering (sit down): £17.50 - 30.00pp

The Dacorum Pavilion, Hemel Hempstead
T: 01442 228718   F: 01442 228735
E: pavilion@dacroum.gov.uk
W: www.dacorum.gov.uk/pavilion
Contact: Claire Dolling, Marketing Officer

Party Max: 500

Situated in Hemel Hempstead town centre, The Dacorum Pavilion comprises a 1052 seat auditorium (1500 standing) for concerts, live shows, etc. Snooks Bar accommodates 125 people, while the Green Room seats 50 people. The rooms are suitable for seminars and conferences, weddings, exhibitions, etc. Live shows, comedy, rock and classical concerts regularly take place in the Main Hall.

Catering: In house

SERVICES:
- Exclusive Use
- Marriage Licence
- Piped Music

- **Performance Area**

Price Guide: £60 - £2000
Catering (sit down): from £19pp
Catering (buffet): from £8.75pp

Edgwarebury Hotel, Elstree
T: 020 8953 8227   F: 020 8207 3668
Contact: Katherine Beacom

Party Max: 120 (marquee: 100)   Bedrooms: 50

The hotel is built in the Tudor manor house style featuring big stone fireplaces and carved oak. It is set in 10 acres of grounds.

Catering: In house

SERVICES:
- Marriage Licence

Price Guide: Prices on application.
Catering (sit down): from £26.95pp
Catering (buffet): from £10.50pp

Elsham Hall Barn Theatre, Brigg,
T: 01652 688698   F: 01652 688240
Contact: Mr R Elwes

Party Max: 150 (marquee: 900)

Elsham Hall Barn Theatre is a medieval banqueting hall set in lakeside gardens.

Catering: In house

SERVICES:
- Marriage Licence

Price Guide: Prices on application.
Catering (sit down): from £16.50pp

Fanhams Hall, Ware
T: 01920 460511   F: 01920 469187
W: www.weddingguide.co.uk/fanhamshall.html
Contact: Functions Manager

Party Max: 170   Bedrooms: 85

Set in 27 acres of gardens, this listed Jacobean style building has a modern pavilion extension which has views over a small landscaped lake.

Catering: In house

SERVICES:
- Marriage Licence

Price Guide: Prices on application.
Catering (sit down): from £27.00pp

Fennes, Braintree
T: 01376 324555   F: 01376 551209
E: ned@fennesestate.co.uk   W: www.fennesestate.co.uk
Contact: Edward James Tabor

Party Max: 300 (marquee: 300)   Bedrooms: 3

Set in picturesque rural Essex, this stately Georgian country house, with beautiful air-conditioned Pavilion, can accommodate from 30 to 200.

Catering: In house

SERVICES:
- Marriage Licence

EAST OF ENGLAND

Price Guide: Prices on application.
Catering (sit down): from £27.00pp
Wines from £14.00pp

Flitwick Manor, Flitwick
T: 01525 712242   **F:** 01525 718753
Contact: Sasha Haycock
Party Max: 60   Bedrooms: 15

Flitwick Manor is set in its own grounds with a croquet lawn and tennis court.
Catering: In house

FACILITIES:
- Tennis
- Croquet

SERVICES:
- Marriage Licence

Price Guide: Prices on application.
Catering (sit down): £35.00 - 50.00pp

Friern Manor Country House Hotel, Brentwood
T: 01268 543222   **F:** 01268 419739
Contact: Mark Ansell
Party Max: 250 (marquee: 350)   Bedrooms: 5

This is a Grade II listed Georgian manor. The hotel offers a Hen Night package called 'Handbag'.
Catering: In house

SERVICES:
- Marriage Licence

Price Guide: Prices on application.
Catering (sit down): from £19.50pp

Fydell House, Boston
T: 01205 351520   **F:** 01205 358363
E: pilgrim.college@nottingham.ac.uk
W: www.nottingham.ac.uk/pilgrim
Contact: David Jones, Warden
Party Max: 30

Grade I listed Fydell House is situated in the South Square in the centre of Boston, next door to the Guildhall. It is a fine example of an 18th Century town house, with both house and garden having recently undergone a redesign to harmonise with the period of the house. The building is owned by the Boston Preservation Trust and is leased to the University of Nottingham as an Adult Education and Cultural Centre.
Catering: Contract (any)/Self catering

SERVICES:
- Exclusive Use
- Marriage Licence

Price Guide: £5 - £13 per hour There is a basic charge of £60 for wedding ceremonies.

Gardens of Easton Lodge, Great Dunmow
T: 01371 876979   **F:** 01371 876979
E: enquiries@eastonlodge.co.uk   **W:** www.eastonlodge.co.uk
Contact: Brian Creasey, Owner
Party Max: 12 (marquee: 40)

These are beautiful restored gardens set in 23 acres. The gardens, designed by Harold Peto in 1902, once belonged to the Countess of Warwick and include features such as the Italian Garden, with its balustraded sunken pool. ruined Shelley Pavilion, herringbone cobbled courtyard with fountain, tree house ruin, 'Peto' pavilion and a yew and box living sundial. The gardens are described as riveting and romantic.
Catering: Contract (any)

Price Guide: £300 - £2000
Catering (sit down): from £2.50pp

Glen Eagle Hotel, Harpenden
T: 01582 760271   **F:** 01582 460819
Contact: David Hunter
Party Max: 150   Bedrooms: 60

This country house-style hotel is set in award winning gardens.
Catering: In house

SERVICES:
- Marriage Licence

Price Guide: Prices on application.
Catering (sit down): from £23.00pp

Greshams, Cambridge
T: 01223 344012   **F:** 01223 312749
Contact: Pauline Bishop
Party Max: 100 (marquee: unlimited)

Greshams is a club based in a listed building in the centre of Cambridge. Greshams stands in its own grounds overlooking Parker's Piece and Fenners Cricket Ground. The conservatory opens out onto a private walled garden with lawns.
Catering: In house

SERVICES:
- Marriage Licence

Price Guide: Prices on application.
Catering (sit down): from £14.00pp
Catering (buffet): from £6.50pp

Hatfield House, Hatfield
T: 01707 262823   **F:** 01707 275719
Contact: Michael Pickard, Curator
Party Max: 230 (marquee: unlimited)

Seven miles from the M25 (J23), 2 miles from the A1 (J4) and opposite Hatfield railway station, this magnificent Jacobean house is home to the Marquis of Salisbury. The gardens have been created by the Marchioness is the original style influenced by John Tradescant the Elder and now managed entirely organically. Within them is the surviving wing of the Palace which was the childhood home of Elizabeth I and now used extensively for weddings and banquets. Hatfield is also home to the national collection of model soldiers, a children's play area, 5 miles of park trails, shops and a licensed restaurant.
Catering: Contract approved list

FACILITIES:
- Helipad

SERVICES:
- Exclusive Use
- Disco/Dance
- Piped Music

EAST OF ENGLAND

- Performance Area

Price Guide: Prices on application.
Catering (sit down): from £30pp
Catering (buffet): n/a

Hedingham Castle, Nr Halstead
T: 01787 463862 **F:** 01787 461473
E: hedinghamcastle@aspects.net
Contact: Mrs Diana Donoghue
Party Max: 75 (marquee: 300)

Hedingham Castle is a Grade I Norman keep, with its own banqueting hall, featuring a huge arch and minstrel's gallery. The Castle is open to the public from May to October. Adjacent to this is a privately owned Georgian family home which overlooks a lake. The Banqueting Hall in the keep, and Main Hall and Ashurst room in the house, are all licensed for marriage ceremonies.
Catering: In house

SERVICES:
- Marriage Licence

Price Guide: Prices on application.
Catering (sit down): from £35.00pp
Catering (buffet): from £25.00pp

Hertford Castle, Hertford
T: 01992 552885 **F:** 01992 505876
Contact: Events Manager
Party Max: 40

This is a Grade I listed building, dating from the 13th Century, set in tranquil riverside gardens.
Catering: In house

SERVICES:
- Marriage Licence

Price Guide: Prices on application.

Heybridge Hotel, Ingatestone
T: 01277 355355 **F:** 01277 353288
Contact: Cypriella Kyprianau
Party Max: 600   Bedrooms: 22

This Tudor building dates back to 1494. The hotel now specialises in conferences and banqueting.
Catering: In house

SERVICES:
- Marriage Licence

Price Guide: Prices on application.
Catering (sit down): from £18.00pp

Hinchingbrooke House, Huntingdon
T: 01480 375678 **F:** 01480 375698
Contact: Pauline Steel, Lettings Manager
Party Max: 200

Hinchingbrooke House is a Tudor country house built around an early 13th Century nunnery handed over to the Cromwell family at the Dissolution. In the 17th Century, the house passed to the Montagus, the Earls of Sandwich. The house shows architectural evidence from Norman times to the early 20th Century, as well as the skeletons of 2 nuns(!) and family portraits throughout the building. The house now forms the 6th form centre of a large comprehensive school.
Catering: In house/Contract (any)

SERVICES:
- Marriage Licence

Price Guide: £800 - £1000
Catering (sit down): from £18.50pp
Catering (buffet): from £4.95pp

Hintlesham Hall, Ipswich
T: 01473 652268 **F:** 01473 652463
E: reservations@hintlesham-hall.co.uk
Contact: Function Co-ordinator
Party Max: 120 (marquee: 400)   Bedrooms: 33

This Grade I listed Manor House features a Georgian façade and has Tudor origins. The Carolean Room features plasterwork ceilings dating from the end of the 17th Century. The Hall is also available for hire on an exclusive basis.
Catering: In house

SERVICES:
- Exclusive Use
- Marriage Licence

Price Guide: Prices on application.
Catering (sit down): from £27.50pp

Ipswich Guildhall, Ipswich
T: 01473 823884
Contact: Mrs J Townsend
Party Max: 200

This 15th Century Grade I listed building is situated just off Hadleigh High Street, and contains many of its original architectural features.
Catering: In house

SERVICES:
- Marriage Licence

Price Guide: Prices on application.
Catering (sit down): POA

Jarvis Comet Hotel, West Hatfield,
T: 01707 265411 **F:** 01707 264019
W: www.jarvis.co.uk
Contact: Functions Manager
Party Max: 150   Bedrooms: 101

This Grade II listed art deco building has been renovated to its former glory.
Catering: In house

SERVICES:
- Marriage Licence

Price Guide: Prices on application.
Catering (sit down): from £18.00pp
Catering (buffet): from £8.00pp

Judge's Lodgings, Lincoln
T: 01522 553343 **F:** 01522 512331
Contact: Peter Allen
Party Max: 100 (marquee: yes)   Bedrooms: 8

EAST OF ENGLAND

This historic building, located between Lincoln Castle and the Cathedral, is still used as the Judge's lodging when the Judge is sitting at the Crown Courts.
Catering: In house

SERVICES:
- Marriage Licence

Price Guide: Prices on application.
Catering (sit down): from £21.00pp

Kentwell Hall, Long Melford
T: 01787 310207   **F:** 01787 379318
W: www.kentwell.co.uk
Contact: Mrs J G Phillips, Owner
Party Max: 150 (marquee: 500+)

Kentwell House is a beautiful mellow redbrick romantic Grade I listed Tudor mansion situated in its own park and farmland. The house is surrounded by a broad moat and has many of the 16th Century service areas intact. There is a Tudor Rose brick paved mosaic maze, fine walled garden, with herb garden and potager, plus a Rare Breed farm. Kentwell can accommodate anything from a small scale private party to up over 500 if the grounds are used.
Catering: In house

FACILITIES:
- Shooting
- Tennis
- Quad Bikes/Off Road

SERVICES:
- Exclusive Use

Price Guide: Prices on application.
Catering (sit down): from £25pp
Catering (buffet): from £22.50pp

Kenwick Park Hotel & Leisure Club, Louth
T: 01507 608806   **F:** 01507 608027
W: www.kenwick-park.co.uk
Contact: Samantha Donner
Party Max: 150 (marquee: 400)   *Bedrooms: 24*

This country house is set in 500 acres of grounds.
Catering: In house

SERVICES:
- Marriage Licence

Price Guide: Prices on application.
Catering (sit down): from £15.00pp

Kimbolton Castle, Huntingdon
T: 01480 860505   **F:** 01480 861763
Contact: John McLeod, Domestic Bursar
Party Max: 200

Kimbolton Castle was the last residence of Katherine of Aragon, first wife of Henry VIII, and was rebuilt in the 18th Century by Vanbrugh, Hawksmorr and Adam. The building, now part of a school, is situated in parkland. All functions are held in the State Apartments, which vary in size and character, and contain a fine collection of Pellegrini murals. At the heart of the Castle, the Courtyard provides a splendid venue for pre-dinner drinks receptions, and memorable photographs, with an elegant 17th Century backdrop.
Catering: Contract approved list

FACILITIES:
- Indoor Pool
- Tennis
- Watersports

SERVICES:
- Performance Area

Price Guide: At the moment this venue is only available during school holidays.
Catering (sit down): from £30pp
Catering (buffet): from £15pp

King's Lynn Town Hall, King's Lynn
T: 01553 692722   **F:** 01553 691663
E: c.george@west-norfolk.gov.uk **W:** www.west-norfolk.gov.uk
Contact: Mr A Yates
Party Max: 150

The Town Hall was built in 1421 and features ornate decoration, portraits and decorative mirrors. A fixed surcharge of £31 applies to weekend hirings.
Catering: Contract (any)

SERVICES:
- Marriage Licence

Price Guide: Prices on application.
Catering (sit down): POA

Kingsford Park Hotel, Colchester
T: 01206 734301
Contact: Mr Fulvio Mussi
Party Max: 190   *Bedrooms: 10*

This is a Regency country house set in 18 acres of formal gardens and parkland. Features include sunken gardens, a Victorian walled garden and a 250 year old mulberry tree.
Catering: In house

SERVICES:
- Marriage Licence

Price Guide: Prices on application.
Catering (sit down): from £19.60pp
Catering (buffet): from £5.65pp

Knebworth Park, Old Knebworth
T: 01438 813825   **F:** 01438 813003
E: info@knebworthhouse.com
W: www.knebworthhouse.com
Contact: Natalie Hibberd, Sales Manager
Party Max: 200 (marquee: unlimited)

The Corporate Hospitality Association has awarded Knebworth Park with the Best Venue award 6 times. The venue offers 250 acres of country park (and can take 125,000 people if required), as well as the 500 year old Knebworth House itself and the 16th Century Knebworth Barns Conference & Banqueting Centre.
Catering: In house

FACILITIES:
- Shooting
- Hot Air Balloons
- Quad Bikes/Off Road

SERVICES:

EAST OF ENGLAND

- Exclusive Use
- Marriage Licence
- Flowers
- Disco/Dance
- Piped Music
- Performance Area

Price Guide: £1500 - £100,000 for house and park
Prices for barns on application (rates include food)
Catering (sit down): from £26pp
Catering (buffet): from £23pp

Lakeside Moat House, Grays
T: 01708 719988   F: 01375 390426
Contact: Functions Manager

Party Max: 150   Bedrooms: 97

This Georgian country house (formerly known as Stifford Moat House) is set in 6.5 acres of garden.
Catering: In house

SERVICES:
- Marriage Licence

Price Guide: Prices on application.
Catering (sit down): POA

The Lawn, Rochford
T: 01702 203701   F: 01702 204752
E: keddie@thelawn.co.uk   W: www.thelawnweddings.com
Contact: Mrs Keddie, Proprietor

Party Max: 140 (marquee: 250)

This Grade II listed Georgian mansion is set in 3 acres of grounds featuring rose gardens. Until recently The Lawn was a family home. Its generously proportioned rooms still contain much of the original furnishings, giving the house a warm and friendly atmosphere. Every party here has exclusive use of the house and its grounds.
Catering: In house

FACILITIES:
- Helipad
- Shooting
- Paint Ball

SERVICES:
- Exclusive Use
- Marriage Licence
- Disco/Dance
- Live Music
- Piped Music
- Performance Area

Price Guide: £250 - £750
Catering (sit down): from £18pp
Catering (buffet): from £7pp

Layer Marney Tower, Nr Colchester
T: 01206 330784
F: 01206 330784
W: www.layermarneytower.co.uk
Contact: Sheila Charrington, Owner

Party Max: 200 (marquee: unlimited)   Bedrooms: 2

This is a Grade I Tudor brick building, dating from 1520, set in formal gardens and surrounded by deer and other animals. Layer Marney is now a family home, although from April to the end of September the house and grounds are open to the public every day except Saturday 12-5pm. Function rooms available include the Long Gallery (formerly the stable and carriage block) which features a polished floor, wood panelling and a Jacobean fire place The Tea House was converted in 1999 and now offers exclusive 4-star self-catering accommodation for 4.
Catering: In house
FACILITIES:

- Helipad
- Table Tennis
- Use of 15 acre field

SERVICES:
- Exclusive Use
- Marriage Licence
- Disco/Dance
- Piped Music
- Performance Area

Price Guide: £250 - £2500
Catering (sit down): from £18pp
Catering (buffet): from £6pp

Leez Priory, Chelmsford
T: 01245 362555   F: 01245 361079
Contact: Claire Walker, Events Manager

Party Max: 250   Bedrooms: 14

Leez Priory is a listed Tudor manor house set in 40 acres of parkland, complete with lakes, lawns and a sweeping driveway. Civil marriages can take place in the Great Tower which stands adjacent to the main house. The Priory itself comprises a large oak panelled drawing room, a medieval vaulted cellar, and the Great Hall and adjoining Gate House Room.
Catering: In house

FACILITIES:
- Helipad
- Outdoor Pool
- Croquet
- Petanque

SERVICES:
- Exclusive Use
- Marriage Licence
- Flowers
- Disco/Dance
- Entertainers
- Piped Music

Price Guide: £1500 - £3950
Catering (sit down): from £32.50pp
Catering (buffet): from £12.50pp

Letchworth Hall Hotel, Letchworth
T: 01462 683747   F: 01462 481540
Contact: Mr Williams

Party Max: 180 (marquee: unlimited)   Bedrooms: 44

This listed building, features extensive gardens and two tennis courts.
Catering: In house

SERVICES:
- Marriage Licence

Price Guide: Prices on application.
Catering (sit down): from £24.50pp
Catering (buffet): from £8.95pp

Lynford Hall, Thetford
T: 01842 878351   F: 01842 878252
Contact: Louis Vella

Party Max: 500 (marquee: 500)   Bedrooms: yes

This is a Grade II listed mansion house (English Heritage), formerly the seat of the Montagu family. The grounds include Italian gardens designed by Nesfield, and an ornamental lake. The park and gardens have been featured in Country Life and on TV.
Catering: In house

SERVICES:
- Marriage Licence

Price Guide: Prices on application.
Catering (sit down): £27.00 - 49.00pp

EAST OF ENGLAND

Maison Talbooth, Colchester
T: 01206 323150 **F:** 01206 322309
E: ltreception@talbooth.co.uk **W:** www.talbooth.com
Contact: Linda Wood, PA

Party Max: 50   Bedrooms: 10

Maison Talbooth is a Victorian country hosue which enjoys a position overlooking a river valley. The hotel is licensed for civil wedding ceremonies and offers 10 spacious bedrooms. Breakfast and light meals are served at the hotel, but for lunch and dinner guests dine at the sister property, Le Talbooth restaurant, which is within walking distance or a minute by hotel courtesy car. Maison Talbooth can be hired for exclusive use conferences and 'getaways'.
Catering: In house

FACILITIES:
- Helipad

SERVICES:
- Exclusive Use
- Marriage Licence
- Disco/Dance
- Piped Music
- Performance Area

Price Guide: Daily delegate rates for the hotel and restaurant start at £35pp + vat.
Catering (sit down): from £22pp
Catering (buffet): from £15pp

Mannington Estate, Norwich
T: 01263 584175 **F:** 01263 761214
W: www.manningtongardens.co.uk
Contact: Laurel Walpole, owner

Party Max: 100 (marquee: 5000)

Mannington Gardens surround a medieval hall with moat. The Tearooms or a marquee can be made available for parties.
Catering: Contract (any)

FACILITIES:
- Pool/Snooker
- Table Tennis

SERVICES:
- Exclusive Use
- Performance Area

Price Guide: Hire prices by negotiation.
Catering (sit down): POA
Catering (buffet): POA

Marygreen Manor Hotel, Brentwood
T: 01277 225252
F: 01277 262809
E: info@marygreenmanor.co.uk
Contact: Gill Timpany

Party Max: 150   Bedrooms: 43

Marygreen Manor Hotel is a Tudor building with modern bedroom accommodation facing into an olde worlde courtyard garden.
Catering: In house

SERVICES:
- Marriage Licence

Price Guide: Prices on application.
Catering (sit down): from £20.85pp
Catering (buffet): from £13.00pp

Moore Place Hotel, Milton Keynes
T: 01908 282000 **F:** 01908 281888
Contact: Tracey Mason

Party Max: 80 (marquee: 100)   Bedrooms: 54

This Georgian mansion has 4 rooms available for functions including the Greenhouse Restaurant (80 max) and the Buckingham Suite (15 max). The restaurant is set in a courtyard overlooking a water cascade and ornamental pond.
Catering: In house

SERVICES:
- Marriage Licence

Price Guide: Prices on application.
Catering (sit down): from £22.95pp

Newland Hall, Chelmsford
T: 01245 231010 **F:** 01245 231463
E: info@newland.co.uk
W: www.newlandhall.co.uk/wedding/index.htm
Contact: Maxine Grimwade

Party Max: 264 (marquee: 300)   Bedrooms: 45

This is an outdoor events and conference centre, housed in a Grade II listed Tudor manor house set in over 100 acres of grassland, woodland and lakes.
Catering: In house

SERVICES:
- Exclusive Use
- Marriage Licence

Price Guide: Prices on application.
Catering (sit down): from £20.00pp
Catering (buffet): from £7.50pp

Newnham College, Cambridge
T: 01223 335801 **F:** 01223 335800
Contact: Mrs Heather Wynn

Party Max: 200

Founded in 1871, Newnham College is one of the only all-women colleges at Cambridge. The building is built from Victorian red brick in the Queen Anne revival style. The College offers its clients an extensive array of international wines.
Catering: In house

SERVICES:
- Marriage Licence

Price Guide: Prices on application.
Catering (sit down): £18.00 - 27.00pp

Oaklands Country House Hotel, Grimsby
T: 01472 872248 **F:** 01472 878143
Contact: Karina Ellis

Party Max: 200   Bedrooms: 45

This country house was built about 120 years ago as a small family estate. It is set in five acres of parkland and features a terrace which overlooks the lawns and water garden.
Catering: In house

SERVICES:
- Marriage Licence

Price Guide: Prices on application.

EAST OF ENGLAND

Catering (sit down): from £18.00pp
Catering (buffet): from £5.95pp

Officers' Mess Conference Centre, Duxford
T: 01223 833686
F: 01233 836959
E: mary.myers@sodexho.co.uk
W: www.iwm.org.uk
Contact: Mrs Mary Myers, Sales & Conferende Manager
Party Max: 250 (marquee: 600)

The Officers' Mess is a dedicated conference and banqueting centre: part of the Imperial War Museum Complex, but set in its own attractive grounds. Beautifully restored, the Mess is available throughout the year, with 5 rooms for hire. The full facilities of the Museum are offered here including flights in vintage aircraft and tank driving.
Catering: Contract approved list/In house

FACILITIES:
• Helipad
• Tank Driving
SERVICES:
• Exclusive Use
• Marriage Licence
• Toastmaster
• Disco/Dance
• Performance Area

Price Guide: £150 - £650 depending on menu choice and room.
Catering (sit down): from £25pp
Catering (buffet): from £15.95pp

Offley Place, Great Offley
T: 01462 768787
F: 01462 768724
W: www.offleyplace.co.uk
Contact: Louise Kozlowski
Party Max: 200 (marquee: unlimited)   Bedrooms: 23

This 17th Century country house is a listed building set in 27 acres of grounds including a rose garden and croquet lawn.
Catering: In house

FACILITIES:
• Croquet
SERVICES:
• Marriage Licence

Price Guide: Prices on application.
Catering (sit down): £25.00 - 30.00pp

Old Bridge Hotel, Huntingdon
T: 01480 424300
F: 01480 411017
Contact: Samantha Webb
Party Max: 150 (marquee: 200)   Bedrooms: 26

This Georgian, ivy covered, building sits on the banks of the River Ouse.
Catering: In house

SERVICES:
• Marriage Licence

Price Guide: Prices on application.
Catering (sit down): from £17.95pp

Old Palace, Hatfield
T: 01707 262055
F: 01707 260898
Contact: Events Manager
Party Max: 400 (marquee: unlimited)

Originally built in the late 15th century, the Old Palace was acquired by King Henry VIII in 1538 and became the childhood home of Queen Elizabeth 1st.
Catering: In house

SERVICES:
• Marriage Licence

Price Guide: Prices on application.
Catering (sit down): from £26.50pp

Old Palace Lodge Hotel, Dunstable
T: 01582 662201
F: 01582 696422
Contact: Melanie Potts
Party Max: 100   Bedrooms: 68

Old Palace Lodge is a Grade II listed Tudor building.
Catering: In house

SERVICES:
• Marriage Licence

Price Guide: Prices on application.
Catering (sit down): from £19.75pp
Catering (buffet): from £10.00pp

The Old Rectory, Ipswich
T: 01473 327200
F: 01473 730557
Contact: Richard & Pauline Wyman, owners
Party Max: 20   Bedrooms: 10

The Old Rectory is a Georgian (1823) Grade II listed building set in 2 acres in the small country village of Tattingstone. The house has a recently constructed games rooms with pool table.
Catering: Self catering

FACILITIES:
• Pool/Snooker
• Games Room
SERVICES:
• Exclusive Use

Price Guide: Prices for 2000 were from £600 - £1500 per week, depending on numbers.

Orsett Hall Hotel, Grays
T: 01375 891402
F: 01375 891135
Contact: Stephen Haynes
Party Max: 200 (marquee: 150)   Bedrooms: 22

This is a 17th listed building is set in 12 acres of grounds.
Catering: In house

SERVICES:
• Marriage Licence

Price Guide: Prices on application.
Catering (sit down): from £24.00pp

Orton Hall Hotel, Peterborough
T: 01733 391111
F: 01733 371793
E: conference@ortonhall.co.uk   **W:** www.abacushotels.co.uk
Contact: Corinne Thorpe

EAST OF ENGLAND

Party Max: 120 (marquee: yes)   Bedrooms: 65

This is a 17th Century manor house and former home of the Marquesses of Huntly. It is set in 20 acres of parkland.
Catering: In house

SERVICES:
- Marriage Licence

Price Guide: Prices on application.
Catering (sit down): from £21.00pp
Catering (buffet): from £7.00pp

Orwell Park, Ipswich
T: 01473 659140   **F:** 01473 659140
Contact: Mrs Ungate

Party Max: 150 (marquee: unlimited)

Orwell Park was originally a Georgian stately home and now acts as a preparatory school which overlooks the river Orwell and is set in 80 acres of grounds. Catering capacities vary from a waited service of 110 to 150 for a stand up buffet, while children are offered reduced catering rates. Orwell Park prides itself on the quality of its chef's cuisine.
Catering: In house

SERVICES:
- Marriage Licence

Price Guide: Prices on application.
Catering (sit down): £31.50 - 50.00pp

Parsonage Country House Hotel, Theydon Bois
T: 01992 814242   **F:** 01992 814242
Contact: Steve or Marion Dale

Party Max: 70 (marquee: 200)   Bedrooms: 6

This listed farmhouse is set in its own gardens, and features oak throughout.
Catering: In house

SERVICES:
- Marriage Licence

Price Guide: Prices on application.
Catering (sit down): from £25.00pp

Pearse House, Bishop's Stortford
T: 01279 757400   **F:** 01279 506591
E: pearse@route56.co.uk   **W:** www.pearsehouse.co.uk
Contact: Miss Julie Brook, Functions Manager

Party Max: 150   Bedrooms: 36

This is a Victorian mansion on the outskirts of Bishop's Stortford, close to the M11 and Stansted Airport. It offers an elegant restaurant with bar and an extensive wine list, as well as function rooms and 36 en-suite bedrooms.
Catering: In house

FACILITIES:
- Table Tennis

SERVICES:
- Marriage Licence   • Disco/Dance   • Piped Music

Price Guide: £50- £500

Catering (sit down): from 13.50pp
Catering (buffet): from £8.50pp

Peckover House & Garden, Wisbech
T: 01945 583463   **F:** 01945 583463
E: aprigx@smtp.ntrust.org.uk
Contact: Ian Grafton, Property Manager

Party Max: 120

This is a National Trust owned Grade II listed town house with beautiful 2 acres gardens, situated in the heart of Wisbech. A 17th Century thatched reed barn is available for functions; a full licence and public entertainment licence is held for this venue. A 2 bedroomed self-catering cottage is also available on site here.
Catering: In house

SERVICES:
- Exclusive Use   • Flowers

Price Guide: £300 - £2000
Catering (sit down): from £18pp
Catering (buffet): from £15pp

Petwood Hotel, Woodhall Spa
T: 01526 352411   **F:** 01526 353473
Contact: Linda Chalmers

Party Max: 120 (marquee: unlimited)   Bedrooms: 50

Petwood Hotel is set in 30 acres of woodland with extensive lawns and was built at the turn of the century for Lady Weigall. The house was also the war-time home of 617 Squadron, the "Dambusters", and features extensive oak panelling with a carved main staircase.
Catering: In house

SERVICES:
- Marriage Licence

Price Guide: Prices on application.
Catering (sit down): from £20.00pp

The Pier at Harwich, Harwich
T: 01255 241212   **F:** 01255 551922
E: lesley@thepieratharwich.co.uk
W: www.talbooth.com
Contact: The Manager

Party Max: 40   Bedrooms: 14

The Pier at Harwich is owned by the Milsom family who also own Maison Talbooth and Le Talbooth restaurant. The Pier is located in 2 buildings that stand on the quayside of old Harwich, overlooking the East Coast's busiest harbour. The main building, dating from the 1850s, houses 2 seafood restaurants; the Ha'penny Bistro on the ground floor and the Harbourside on the 1st floor. Most of the 7 second floor bedrooms overlook the estuary. A further 7 bedrooms are located next door building, formerly the Angel public house. This also houses the Mayflower Suite, a large comfortable sitting room which can be hired for meetings and wedding ceremonies. The Pier has recently joined with Suffolk Yacht Charters to offer a day's sailing on board a yacht followed by dinner in the Harbourside Restaurant and overnight accommodation.
Catering: In house

EAST OF ENGLAND

SERVICES:
- Exclusive Use

Price Guide: Room rates starts at £80 a night.
Catering (sit down): POA
Catering (buffet): POA

Pink Geranium, Melbourn
T: 01763 260215 **F:** 01763 262110
E: lawrence@pinkgeranium.co.uk
W: www.pinkgeranium.co.uk
Contact: Lawrence Champion, Owner

Party Max: 60 (marquee: 100)

Set in the heart of what appears to be the deepest depths of rural Cambridgeshire, the award winning Pink Geranium restaurant is only 20 minutes from Cambridge and less than an hour from London. Inglenook fireplaces, original oak beams and the calming environment set the atmosphere for complete relaxation for the ultimate wining and dining experience.
Catering: In house

SERVICES:
- Exclusive Use
- Cake
- Live Music
- Marriage Licence
- Toastmaster
- Entertainers
- Flowers
- Disco/Dance

Price Guide: Prices on application.
Catering (sit down): from £25pp
Catering (buffet): from £30pp

Ponsbourne Park Hotel, Nr Hertford
T: 01707 876191 **F:** 01707 875190
E: sutcliffe@lineone.net **Contact:** Lisa Villiers

Party Max: 180   Bedrooms: 53

This old country house, set in 170 acres of grounds, was built in 1876, and purchased by Tesco in 1987 for use as a Hotel and Management Training Centre. Ponsbourne has retained many of its original features complemented by later additions including a bedroom wing, 9-hole golf course, outdoor heated swimming pool and 5 all-weather tennis courts.
Catering: In house

FACILITIES:
- Golf
- Outdoor Pool
- Tennis

SERVICES:
- Marriage Licence

Price Guide: Prices on application.
Catering (sit down): from £30.95pp

Pontlands Park Hotel, Chelmsford
T: 01245 476444 **F:** 01245 478393
Contact: Bettina Poremba

Party Max: 250 (marquee: 200)   Bedrooms: 17

Pontlands Park is a Victorian mansion, originally built in 1879 and set in its own grounds.
Catering: In house

SERVICES:
- Marriage Licence

Price Guide: Prices on application.
Catering (sit down): from £35.00pp + 10%

Preston Priory Barn, Sudbury
T: 01787 247251 **Contact:** Mr and Mrs Adrian Thorpe

Party Max: 300

Preston Priory Barn, a renovated traditional Suffolk timber-framed barn, featured in BBC's Lovejoy. It is available for hire for a three-day period.
Catering: Contract (any)

SERVICES:
- Marriage Licence

Price Guide: Prices on application.
Catering (sit down): POA

The Priory, Ware
T: 01920 460316 **F:** 01920 484056
E: office@waretc.sagehost.co.uk **W:** www.wareonline.co.uk
Contact: Rachel Foy, PR Officer/Events Coordinator

Party Max: 100

Built as a Franciscan Friary in the late 14th Century and given to Ware in the 1920s, The Priory is now managed by Ware Town Council as Trustees of The Priory Charity. Much of the main wall structure survives from the 15th Centruy and the entrance lobby features remains of the cloister arches. Grade I listed and set in 7 acres, The Priory offers six rooms for functions, including the Conservatory, which overlooks the river.
Catering: In house

FACILITIES:
- Tennis
- Outdoor Pool

SERVICES:
- Exclusive Use
- Disco/Dance
- Piano for hire
- Marriage Licence
- Piped Music
- Cake
- Performance Area

Price Guide: Room hire fees range from £180 to £275 per function.
Catering (sit down): POA
Catering (buffet): POA

Putteridge Bury Conference Centre, Luton
T: 01582 489070/69 **F:** 01582 482689
W: www.luton.ac.uk/putteridge
Contact: Ciro Ascione, Conference & Hospitality Manager

Party Max: 500

Putteridge Bury is a neo-Elizabethan manor house, built in 1911 and situated in picturesque parkland on the Hertfordshire/Bedfordshire border. The grounds were designed by Edwin Lutyens and planted by Gertrude Jekyll. The gardens boast a refelctive pool and have massive yew hedges.
Catering: In house

FACILITIES:
- Helipad
- Shooting
- Tennis

SERVICES:
- Marriage Licence
- Disco/Dance
- Performance Area

Price Guide: Prices on application, but dependent on menu choice and numbers.
Catering (sit down): from £21pp
Catering (buffet): from £10pp

EAST OF ENGLAND

Ravenwood Hall, Bury St Edmunds
T: 01359 270345 **F:** 01359 270788
E: enquiries@ravenwoodhall.co.uk
W: www.ravenwoodhall.co.uk
Contact: Craig Jarvis, Owner

Party Max: 200 (marquee: 750)   Bedrooms: 14

Ravenwood Hall, set within 7 acres of its own lawns and woodland in the heart of Suffolk, dates from the 16th Century and retains features such as rare wall paintings and carved oak. The Hall is now a family owned 3-star hotel with its own leisure facitlites such as hard tennis court, heated swimming pool, croquet lawn and horse riding. The Hall also has its own Edwardian Pavilion (formerly a cricket pavilion), overlooking its own private garden and pond and featuring a verandah.

Catering: In house

FACILITIES:
- Helipad
- Hot Air Balloons
- Tennis
- Outdoor Pool
- Quad Bikes/Off Road

SERVICES:
- Exclusive Use
- Marriage Licence
- Flowers
- Cake
- Toastmaster
- Disco/Dance
- Live Music
- Entertainers
- Fireworks
- Photography

Price Guide: Conference room hire only ranges from £275 - £450. There is an inclusive charge for weddings.
Catering (sit down): from £19.50pp
Catering (buffet): from £10.75

Royal Cambridge Hotel, Cambridge
T: 01223 351631 **F:** 01223 352972
E: royalcambridge@zoffanyhotels.co.uk
W: www.zoffanyhotels.co.uk
Contact: Vicky Aitchison

Party Max: 140   Bedrooms: 46

The Royal Cambridge Hotel is a Georgian building located in the heart of Cambridge.
Catering: In house

SERVICES:
- Marriage Licence

Price Guide: Prices on application.
Catering (sit down): from £18.00pp
Catering (buffet): from £12.95pp

Sheene Mill Hotel, Melbourn
T: 01763 261393
F: 01763 261376
Contact: Steven & Sally Saunders

Party Max: 200 (marquee: 80)   Bedrooms: 9

This Grade II listed 17th century water mill is set on the River Mel in three acres of gardens. It was recently voted as one of the top 10 most romantic venues in the UK.
Catering: In house

SERVICES:
- Marriage Licence

Price Guide: Prices on application.
Catering (sit down): from £25.00pp

Shendish Manor, Hemel Hempstead
T: 01442 232220 **F:** 01442 230683
Contact: Tom Concannon

Party Max: 300 (marquee: unlimited)

Shendish Manor is a large stately listed building offering leisure facilities such as a golf course and health club, as well as conference facilities.
Catering: In house

SERVICES:
- Marriage Licence

Price Guide: Prices on application.
Catering (sit down): from £24.95pp

Shuttleworth, Biggleswade
T: 01767 626203 **F:** 01767 627443
E: d.spoors@shuttleworth.Org
Contact: Stephen Moorby

Party Max: 220 (marquee: unlimited)   Bedrooms: 114

This is a Grade II listed privately owned mansion dating from 1876. It is now used for events such as conferences, corporate training and country pursuits.
Catering: In house

SERVICES:
- Marriage Licence

Price Guide: Prices on application.
Catering (sit down): Packages from £42.50pp

Somerleyton Hall & Gardens, Lowestoft
T: 01502 730224 **F:** 01502 732143
E: enquiries@somerleyton.co.uk **W:** www.somerleyton.co.uk
Contact: Ian Pollard, Administrator

Party Max: 150 (marquee: 200)

Somerleyton is an early Victorian stately home with lavish architectural features. These include a conservatory style function rooms (The Loggia aand The Orangery) with their own kitchens, as well as 12 acres of gardens with an historic yew maze. There is also an additional 200 acres of parkland, with lake and woodland. The lake, Fritton Lake, is a visitor attraction in its own right and has a small golf course, putting and holiday cottages.

Catering: Contract (any)

FACILITIES:
- Helipad
- Shooting
- Tennis
- Golf
- Putting

SERVICES:
- Exclusive Use
- Marriage Licence

Price Guide: Prices on application.
Catering (sit down): POA
Catering (buffet): POA

Sopwell House Hotel, St Albans
T: 01727 864477 **F:** 01727 845636
Contact: Paul Crossey

Party Max: 500   Bedrooms: 92

This four star, Georgian country house hotel, was once the country home of Lord Mountbatten and is set in 11 acres of

EAST OF ENGLAND

gardens and grounds.
Catering: In house

SERVICES:
• Marriage Licence
Price Guide: Prices on application.
Catering (sit down): from £30.00pp

St Andrew's & Blackfriars Halls, Norwich
T: 01603 628477 **F:** 01603 762182
E: taldous.ncc.sqh@gtnet.gov.uk
Contact: Tim Aldous, Facilities Manager
Party Max: 800

This Grade I, Scheduled Ancient Monument is claimed to be 'The most complete Friary complex in the UK'. The halls will accommodate from 2 to 850 people and are both licensed for civil wedding ceremonies.
Catering: Contract approved list

SERVICES:
• Exclusive Use   • Marriage Licence   • Performance Area
Price Guide: £185 - £890
Catering (sit down): from £15.50pp
Catering (buffet): from £7.75pp

St Michael's Manor, St Albans
T: 01727 864444 **F:** 01427 848909
E: smmanor@globalnet.co.uk
W: www.stmichaelsmanor.com
Contact: Peta McKeon
Party Max: 75 (marquee: unlimited)   Bedrooms: 23

The original Manor House was built around 1512 on medieval foundations and is now a Grade II listed building set in five acres of award winning grounds.
Catering: In house

SERVICES:
• Marriage Licence
Price Guide: Prices on application.
Catering (sit down): from £27.00pp

Stoke Rochford Hall, Grantham
T: 01476 530337 **F:** 01476 530534
Contact: Conference Department
Party Max: 200   Bedrooms: 194

This Grade I listed Victorian mansion house is set in 28 acres of gardens and over 1,000 acres of parkland.
Catering: In house

SERVICES:
• Marriage Licence
Price Guide: Prices on application.
Catering (sit down): Packages from £44.50pp
Catering (buffet): from £6.95pp

Stragglethorpe Hall, Lincoln
T: 01400 272308 **F:** 01400 273816
E: stragglethorpe@compuserve.com
W: www.stragglethorpe.com

Contact: Mrs Michael Rook
Party Max: 70 (marquee: 100)   Bedrooms: yes

This former monastic building is Grade II listed and set in gardens. The Great Hall and Dining Room are both licensed for weddings which can take place here on any day except Christmas Day and Easter.
Catering: In house

SERVICES:
• Marriage Licence
Price Guide: Prices on application.
Catering (sit down): from £25.00pp

Sussex Barn, King's Lynn

T: 01485 210261/01485 210448
F: 01485 210261
Contact: Mrs Jane Thompson
Party Max: 500

Sussex Barn is located on an attractive farm in an Area of Oustanding Natural Beauty. It is a sympathetically renovated (and still working) flint and brick barn with its own well. Facilites include the main barn, a small barn, licensed bar, kitchens, parking, barbecue, dance floor and disabled facilities. The barn is also licensed for wedding ceremonies. Apart from the minimum charge of £2 per head, hirers may organise their own food and drink at this venue. The Farm also own several self-catering properties in the area sleeping from 4 to 10.
Catering: Contract (any) / Self catering

FACILITIES:
• Tennis
SERVICES:
• Exclusive Use   • Marriage Licence   • Disco/Dance
• Performance Area
Price Guide: Prices on application.

Swan Hotel, Lavenham
T: 0870 4008116
Contact: Emma Charman, Events Coordinator
Party Max: 70   Bedrooms: 51

The Swan, a Heritage hotel, is housed in a 15th Century building which has recently undergone a £2 million refurbishment.
Catering: In house

SERVICES:
• Marriage Licence
Price Guide: Prices on application.
Catering (sit down): from £26.99pp
Catering (buffet): from £10.95pp

The Swiss Garden, Biggleswade
T: 01767 626255
F: 01767 627443
Contact: Events Manager
Party Max: 200 (marquee: unlimited)

This is a listed 19th Century thatched 'Swiss' cottage, claiming romantic and intimate charm. It is described as 'perched on a grassy knoll with nine acres of historic gardens'.
Catering: Contract approved list

EAST OF ENGLAND

SERVICES:
- Marriage Licence

Price Guide: Prices on application.
Catering (sit down): POA

Le Talbooth, Colchester
T: 01206 323150 **F:** 01206 322309
E: mtreception@talbooth.co.uk **W:** www.talbooth.com
Contact: Paul Milsom, Owner
Party Max: 150 (marquee: 300)

Le Talbooth is a sister property to Maison Talbooth, a hotel. It stands on the banks of the Stour, and featured in Constable's famous painting of Dedham Vale. Gerald Milsom discovered the property in 1952 when it was a tea room and has restored and extended it over the years. It still retains the atmosphere of a 16th Century timber framed house.
Catering: In house

FACILITIES:
- Helipad

SERVICES:
- Exclusive Use
- Disco/Dance
- Piped Music
- Performance Area

Price Guide: Prices on application.
Catering (sit down): from £22pp
Catering (buffet): from £15pp

Tarantella Hotel & Restaurant, Sudbury
T: 01787 378879 **F:** 01787 378879
Contact: Mr Domenico Gargiulo
Party Max: 200   Bedrooms: 12

This is a Georgian house set in a secluded position overlooking the River Stour. The hotel is further enhanced by terrace statues and mature landscaped gardens.
Catering: In house

SERVICES:
- Marriage Licence

Price Guide: Prices on application.
Catering (sit down): from £13.25pp

Tewin Bury Farm Hotel, Nr Welwyn
T: 01438 717793
F: 01438 840440
Contact: Andrea Laver
Party Max: 200   Bedrooms: 16

This is a 17th Century listed barn, situated on the banks of the river Mimram. Functions take place in the tythe barn, stable or the farmhouse itself, with capacities varying from 20 to 200. Some of the farm's accommodation consists of two storey suites which are suitable for families and sleep four people. The 25 comfortable and individually decorated bedrooms include three four-posters.
Catering: In house

SERVICES:
- Marriage Licence

Price Guide: Prices on application.
Catering (sit down): from £30.00pp

Theobalds Park, Cheshunt
T: 01992 639771 **F:** 01992 639240
E: dpeers@initialstyle.co.uk
W: www.initialstyle.co.uk
Contact: Donna Peers, Conference Coordinator
Party Max: 250   Bedrooms: 67

Theobalds is a magnificent Georgian mansion set in 55 acres of park and woodland.
Catering: In house

FACILITIES:
- Shooting
- Hot Air Balloons
- Pool/Snooker
- Quad Bikes/Off Road
- Table Tennis

SERVICES:
- Exclusive Use
- Marriage Licence
- Disco/Dance
- Performance Area

Price Guide: from £48pp + vat
Catering (sit down): from £32.50pp
Catering (buffet): from £32.50pp

Thurning Hall, East Dereham
T: 01263 587200
Contact: Pauline Harrold
Party Max: 80 (marquee: 200)

This private house is a remote mid 18th Century Georgian hall, set in woodland and approached via a tree-canopied drive. It was recently used for the filming of Mill on the Floss. There are two walled gardens for marquees, and excellent settings for photographs.
Catering: In house

SERVICES:
- Marriage Licence

Price Guide: Prices on application.
Catering (sit down): POA

Tuddenham Mill Country Inn, Newmarket
T: 01638 713552
F: 01638 715406
W: www.ravenwoodhall.co.uk
Contact: Richard Clayfield, Manager
Party Max: 150 (marquee: 250)

Tuddenham Mill is set in 12 acres of Riverside walks and mature gardens. The Grade II listed building, which is mentioned in the Domesday Book, is steeped in 1000 years of history and is complete with working water wheel. 3 rooms are available for functions; The Meal Room - with water wheel(15), The Loft - with balcony over pond (50) and the Stone Room - beams and views (100).
Catering: In house

SERVICES:
- Marriage Licence
- Toastmaster
- Disco/Dance
- Live Music
- Entertainers
- Fireworks
- Performance Area
- Valet Parking

Price Guide: Conference hire: Meal Room - £25 Loft Room - £75 Stone Room - £175 Otherwise venue hire is included in meal prices.
Catering (sit down): from £9.95pp
Catering (buffet): from £15.95pp

EAST OF ENGLAND

Vaulty Manor, Maldon
T: 01621 855628 F: 01621 841105
E: info@vaulty-manor.co.uk
W: www.vaulty-manor.co.uk
Contact: Jason

Party Max: 200 | Bedrooms: 10

Vaulty Manor is a collection of Grade II listed buildings which are used as a restaurant and holiday cottages. The buildings are set in 12 acres of grounds with a lake.
Catering: In house/Self catering

SERVICES:
- Marriage Licence

Price Guide: Prices on application.
Catering (sit down): from £30.00pp
Catering (buffet): from £10.00pp

Wadenhoe House Conference & Training Centre, Peterborough
T: 01832 720777
F: 01832 720410
W: www.wadenhoe.com
Contact: Carron McMillan, General Manager

Party Max: 120 | Bedrooms: 27

Wadenhoe House is a Jacobean manor house set in 7 acres of landscaped grounds. The house has a colourful history, in the 19th Century gaining prominence when the houe was extended to provide a weekend retreat for Disraeli and the cabinet. In 1996 the house was converted into a residential training centre. It was most recently refurbished in 1990.
Catering: In house

FACILITIES:
- Helipad
- Golf
- Shooting
- Gym
- Croquet
- Bowls

SERVICES:
- Exclusive Use
- Marriage Licence
- Piped Music

Price Guide: Exclusive use of Wadenhoe is £3700 + vat for 24 hours. Residential day rates start at £135pp + vat. Lunches and dinners start at £15pp + vat.
Catering (sit down): £75 - £80pp
Catering (buffet): £75 - £80pp

The Watermill Hotel, Hemel Hempstead
T: 01442 349955
E: watermill@sarova.co.uk
W: www.sarova.com
Contact: Lara Mitchard

Party Max: 120 | Bedrooms: 75

This hotel is set in a riverside location and built around an old flour mill. It has 10 acres of grounds and a riverside decking area.
Catering: In house

SERVICES:
- Marriage Licence

Price Guide: Prices on application.
Catering (sit down): from £25.50pp
Catering (buffet): from £10.00pp

Wensum Lodge Hotel, Fakenham
T: 01328 862100 F: 01328 863365
W: www.scoot.co.uk/wensum-lodge-hotel
Contact: Miranda Bishop

Party Max: 250 | Bedrooms: 17

The hotel is a former grain store which stands on the banks of the River Wensum by the original mill house.
Catering: In house

SERVICES:
- Marriage Licence

Price Guide: Prices on application.
Catering (sit down): POA

White Hart Hotel, Lincoln
T: 0870 4008117
F: 01522 531798/514265
E: heritgehotels_lincoln.white_hart@forte-hotels.com
Contact: Amelia Wilson

Party Max: 200

The hotel is located in a 14th century building adjacent to Lincoln Cathedral and across the square from Lincoln's medieval castle.
Catering: In house

SERVICES:
- Marriage Licence

Price Guide: Prices on application.
Catering (sit down): from £22.00pp
Catering (buffet): from £22.00pp

Whitehall Hotel, Broxted
T: 01279 850603
F: 01279 850385
Contact: Jonathon Beck

Party Max: 150 (marquee: 250) | Bedrooms: 25

The family owned Whitehall Hotel is an Elizabethan manor house set in a walled garden. The hotel is conveniently situated for Stansted Airport.
Catering: In house

SERVICES:
- Marriage Licence

Price Guide: Prices on application.
Catering (sit down): from £20.00pp

Wivenhoe House Hotel, Colchester
T: 01206 863666
F: 01206 868532
Contact: Functions Manager

Party Max: 120 (marquee: 200) | Bedrooms: 47

Wivenhoe House is a Georgian mansion, which now operates as a hotel and conference centre.
Catering: In house

SERVICES:
- Marriage Licence

Price Guide: Prices on application.
Catering (sit down): from £20.20pp

EAST OF ENGLAND

Woburn Abbey, Woburn
T: 01525 290666 **F:** 01525 296549
E: catering@sculpturegallery.co.uk
W: www.sculpturegallery.co.uk
Contact: Nigel Robinson, Catering Manager

Party Max: 270

Woburn Abbey, set in a landscaped 3000 acre deer park, has been the main home of the Dukes of Bedford for over 400 years. The Sculpture Gallery was built as an Orangery in 1789 for the 5th Duke. In 1818 it was enlarged to house the 6th Duke's collection of marble statuary and reliefs. In 1968 the present, 13th Duke, moved many of the sculptures from the Gallery, enabling it to be restored, making it a magnificent setting for functions. The Gallery overlooks the private gardens and a lake filled with carp, and home to ornamental ducks.
Catering: *In house*

SERVICES:
- Marriage Licence
- Toastmaster
- Disco/Dance
- Piped Music

Price Guide: Hire prices on application.
Catering (sit down): from £39pp
Catering (buffet): from £39pp

Wolterton Park, Norwich
T: 01263 768444 **F:** 01263 761214
W: www.manningtongardens.co.uk
Contact: Laurel Walpole (Lady Walpole), owner

Party Max: 100

Wolterton Park surrounds an 18th Century mansion house. The park features a lake and landscaped grounds.
Catering: *In house/Contract (any)*

FACILITIES:
- Pool/Snooker
- Table Tennis

SERVICES:
- Exclusive Use
- Performance Area

Price Guide: Prices by negotiation

Woodlands Manor Hotel, Bedford
T: 01234 363281 **F:** 01234 272390
E: www.grandheritage.com/hotels
Contact: Emma White

Party Max: 120 (marquee: 60)   *Bedrooms: 33*

This is a secluded period manor house set in four acres of wooded and landscaped grounds. It is only two miles from the centre of Bedford.
Catering: *In house*

SERVICES:
- Marriage Licence

Price Guide: Prices on application.
Catering (sit down): from £27.50pp
Catering (buffet): from £22.00pp

HEART OF ENGLAND

Abbey Hotel, Great Malvern
T: 01684 892332
F: 01684 892662
Contact: Sharon Haw

Party Max: 300 (marquee: 0) Bedrooms: 105

Set in the centre of Malvern, The Abbey adjoins the old Bendictine Priory and enjoys beautiful views over the Severn Valley.
Catering: In house

SERVICES:
• Marriage Licence

Price Guide: Prices on application.
Catering (sit down): from £16.50pp
Catering (buffet): from £13.95pp

Albrighton Hall Hotel, Shrewsbury
T: 01939 291000 F: 01939 291123
Contact: Jan Deeming, Conference & Events Manager

Party Max: 200 (marquee: n/a) Bedrooms: 39

Albrighton Hall, a Macdonald hotel, is a listed building, built in 1630. It is set in 14 acres of grounds that include an ornamental lake and a croquet lawn.
Catering: In house

SERVICES:
• Marriage Licence

Price Guide: Prices on application.
Catering (sit down): POA

Allt Yr Ynys Country House Hotel, Walterstone
T: 01873 890307 F: 01873 890539
E: allhotel@compuserve.com
W: www.allhotel.co.uk
Contact: Howard Williams, Proprietor

Party Max: 120 (marquee: 150) Bedrooms: 19

Allt Yr Ynys is a Grade II listed building located in the Brecon Beacons National Park. It has a riverside location, and features a knot garden. The hotel boasts an award winning restaurant. Helicopters and hot air balloons may use the grounds.
Catering: In house

FACILITIES:
• Helipad

SERVICES:
• Marriage Licence

Price Guide: Prices on application.
Catering (sit down): from £19.50pp
Catering (buffet): from £12pp

Alveston Manor, Stratford-upon-Avon
T: 0870 4008181 F: 01789 414095
Contact: Claire McCarthy

Party Max: 120 (marquee: 200) Bedrooms: 106

This is a riverside hotel and restaurant. The grounds are suitable for a marquee with a capacity for accommodating up to 200 people.
Catering: In house

SERVICES:
• Marriage Licence

Price Guide: Prices on application.
Catering (sit down): from £27.00pp

Ansty Hall Hotel, Coventry
T: 01203 612222
F: 01203 602155
E: info@anstyhall.macdonald-hotels.co.uk
W: www.macdonaldhotels.co.uk
Contact: Sarah Stanley, Conference and Banqueting Manager

Party Max: 160 (marquee: 150) Bedrooms: 60

Ansty Hall is a Grade II listed Georgian house, set in eight acres of private gardens and located near a canal and the golf course. Helicopters can land on site, and the nearby canal is navigable. Numerous services can be organised or recommended including fireworks.
Catering: In house

SERVICES:
• Marriage Licence • Fireworks

Price Guide: Prices on application.
Catering (sit down): from £45.00pp (package)
Catering (buffet): from £12.15pp

Ardencote Manor Hotel, Claverdon
T: 01926 843111
F: 01926 842646
E: hotel@ardencote.co
W: www.ardencote.com
Contact: Mrs D Sale

Party Max: 150 (marquee: 0) Bedrooms: 77

This hotel and country club, originally a Victorian manor house residence, is set in 40 acres of grounds, gardens and lakes. Several rooms are available for functions including the Palms Conservatory, which overlooks the gardens, fountain and maze; the Henley Suite; and the Oak Room, which is a classical dining room with oak panelling and has a capacity of 46.
Catering: In house

SERVICES:
• Marriage Licence

Price Guide: Prices on application.
Catering (sit down): from £47.50pp (wedding package)

The Ashe, Ross-on-Wye
T: 01989 563336
F: 01989 563336
Contact: Mrs MR Ball, Owner

Party Max: 21

This venue comprises a Granary, Mill, Stable and Orchard Cottage, situated in quiet countryside. Guests have free use of the on-site 18 hole par 3 golf course, tennis court and fishing lakes. The dining area in the Mill is suitable for larger groups.
Catering: Self catering

FACILITIES:
• Golf • Tennis • Fishing

Price Guide: Prices on application.

HEART OF ENGLAND

Avoncroft Museum Of Historic Buildings, Bromsgrove
T: 01527 831363-831886 **F:** 01527 876934
E: avoncroftenterprises@compuserve.com
W: www.avoncroft.org.uk
Contact: Laura Wiles
Party Max: 200 (marquee: unlimited)

The Museum of Historic Buildings, Guesten Hall, has a medieval roof set within a modern, specially designed building. Helicopters and hot air balloons may use the grounds.
Catering: In house

FACILITIES:
- Helipad

SERVICES:
- Marriage Licence

Price Guide: Prices on application.
Catering (sit down): from £20.00pp
Catering (buffet): from £6.00pp

Aylestone Court Hotel, Hereford
T: 01432 341891 **F:** 01432 267691
E: aylshotel@aol.com
Contact: Mr C A Chapman
Party Max: 60 (marquee: 10000) Bedrooms: 9

This Georgian hotel is set in one acre of gardens.
Catering: In house

SERVICES:
- Marriage Licence

Price Guide: Prices on application.
Catering (sit down): from £16.95pp
Catering (buffet): from £18.50pp

Barnsdale Country Club, Exton
T: 01572 757901 **F:** 01572 756235
Contact: Jane Downs (T: 01572 722209)
Party Max: 200 Bedrooms: 34

This Best Western hotel and restaurant is also a club and time share site. The Club is set in a 60 acre estate of gardens and woodland on the shores of Rutland Water. Wheelchair access is limited.
Catering: In house

SERVICES:
- Marriage Licence

Price Guide: price comment
Catering (sit down): from £13.50pp

Bass Museum, Burton on Trent
T: 01283 511000
F: 01283 513509
E: enquiries@bass-museum.com
W: www.bass-museum.com
Contact: Mrs S Stokes
Party Max: 170 (marquee: 0)

The Bass Museum of Brewing is housed in brewery buildings dating from 1835. Shire horse stables are also on the site.
Catering: In house

SERVICES:
- Marriage Licence

Price Guide: Prices on application.
Catering (sit down): POA

Bear Of Rodborough Hotel, Stroud
T: 01453 878522 **F:** 01453 872523
Contact: Mr C Ashby
Party Max: 100 (marquee: 0) Bedrooms: 47

This 17th Century building is surrounded by 500 acres of National Trust land. The restaurant serves traditional English cuisine.
Catering: In house

SERVICES:
- Marriage Licence

Price Guide: Prices on application.
Catering (sit down): from £14.00pp

Beaumanor Hall, Loughborough
T: 01509 890119 **F:** 01509 891021
Contact: Liz Funnell
Party Max: 160 (marquee: 0)

The Hall was originally built in the 1840s for a wealthy landowner. It was purchased by Leicestershire County Council in 1974 as a training and conference centre for council employees. Features include ornate ceilings, wood carvings and elaborate stone and plaster work. There is also a galleried central hall with sweeping staircase and stained glass windows.
Catering: In house

SERVICES:
- Marriage Licence

Price Guide: Prices on application.
Catering (sit down): from £15.50pp
Catering (buffet): from £4.70pp

Billesley Manor Hotel, Alcester
T: 01789 279955 **F:** 01789 764145
E: revmgr@billesleymanor.co.uk
W: www.billesleymanor.co.uk
Contact: Functions Manager
Party Max: 125 (marquee: 250) Bedrooms: 41

This is a 16th century manor house set in 11 acres of parkland.
Catering: In house

SERVICES:
- Marriage Licence

Price Guide: Prices on application.
Catering (sit down): from £26.00pp
Catering (buffet): from £8.50pp

The Birches, Nr Worcester
T: 01886 812251
Contact: Alyson Cox
Party Max: 150 (marquee: 150)

The Birches is a timbered converted barn in a private location overlooking a trout lake.
Catering: In house

HEART OF ENGLAND

SERVICES:
- Marriage Licence

Price Guide: Prices on application.
Catering (sit down): from £20.00pp
Catering (buffet): from £10.50pp

Birmingham Botanical Gardens, Birmingham

T: 0121 456 2244 **F:** 0121 450 4620
E: bbg.conferences@redcliffe.com
W: www.redcliffe.com
Contact: Sue Stanley, Wedding Coordinator

Party Max: 700

Three suites are available for functions at the Birmingham Botanical Gardens. These are Victorian landscaped formal gardens originally created by John Claudius Loudon, the Scottish landscape architect. The gardens feature lawns, a fountain, rock and alpine gardens, a shrubbery of rhododendrons and a pinetum. There was once a resident alligator here 'Miss Issi', but we understand she is now gone and left no decendants. This venue is used for both private and corporate functions.
Catering: In house

SERVICES:
- Marriage Licence   • Piped Music   • Performance Area

Price Guide: Rates vary depending on time and function. As a guide, however, room hire is only charged for Wedding Receptions that continue after 6pm and these range from £200 for the smallest suite to £250 for the largest.

Blotts Hotel & Country Club, Nottingham

T: 0115 933 5656 **F:** 0115 933 4696
Contact: Sandra Heathcote

Party Max: 600 (marquee: 700)   Bedrooms: 6

This banqueting venue is set in five acres of open parkland with car parking for 200 cars. Many celebrity weddings have apparently been held at this hotel.
Catering: In house

SERVICES:
- Marriage Licence

Price Guide: Prices on application.
Catering (sit down): from £16.50pp
Catering (buffet): from £7.50pp

Bourton Manor, Nr Much Wenlock

T: 01746 785531 **F:** 01746 785683
Contact: Chris Stewart

Party Max: 80 (marquee: 180)   Bedrooms: 8

Bourton Manor is set in its own grounds and is a listed country house dating from the 16th Century. Internal features include oak panelling and a Queen Anne staircase.
Catering: In house

SERVICES:
- Marriage Licence

Price Guide: Prices on application.
Catering (sit down): 12.00 - 25.00pp

Brandon Hall Hotel, Brandon

T: 01203 542571 **F:** 01203 545771
Contact: Functions Manager

Party Max: 110 (marquee: 0)   Bedrooms: 60

This is a county house hotel set in 17 acres of gardens and woodland.
Catering: In house

SERVICES:
- Marriage Licence

Price Guide: Prices on application.
Catering (sit down): from £18.75pp
Catering (buffet): from £8.00pp

Burford House, Nr Tenbury Wells

T: 01584 810777 **F:** 01584 810673
E: treasures@burford.co.uk
Contact: Nicholas English

Party Max: 40 (marquee: 500)

The House's panelled entrance hall leads to the Burford House Gardens, a plantsman's paradise set in the picturesque valleys of the River Teme and Ledwych Brook and home to the National Clematis Collection. Reception facilities are not available in the House itself, although a marquee is available with a capacity from 60+ seated up to 500.
Catering: In house

SERVICES:
- Marriage Licence

Price Guide: Prices on application.
Catering (sit down): POA

Calcot Manor, Nr Tetbury

T: 0870 2411693 **F:** 01666 890394
E: reception@calcotmanor.co.uk **W:** www.calcotmanor.co.uk
Contact: Rachel Sadler, Conference & Banqueting Manager

Party Max: 120   Bedrooms: 28

This country house hotel was originally a farm house and features beautiful stone barns and stables, including a 14th Century tithe barn built by Cistercian monks who farmed the land here in the 14th Century. Set in peaceful, leafy gardens, the hotel claims a good reputation for its Conservatory Restaurant, and also offers informal dining in its Gumstool Inn.
Catering: In house

FACILITIES:
- Helipad   • Tennis   • Outdoor Pool
- Croquet

SERVICES:
- Exclusive Use   • Marriage Licence

Price Guide: There is no facility fee for this venue.
Catering (sit down): from £23pp
Catering (buffet): from £22pp

Castle Ashby, Northampton

T: 01604 696696 **F:** 01604 696516
E: anreafowkes@castleashby.co.uk **W:** www.castleashby.co.uk
Contact: Andrea Fowkes, Director of Sales & Marketing

Party Max: 300 (marquee: 1500)   Bedrooms: 26

HEART OF ENGLAND

Built in 1574 to entertain Queen Elizabeth I, Castle Ashby is the ancestral home of the Compton family. The Grade I listed house is nestled amidst 200 acres of parkland designed by Capability Brown, and is not open to the public, but is available for private and corporate entertaining. It offers 26 ensuite bedrooms and elegant reception rooms adorned with fine paintings, rich tapestries and beautiful antiques. Mod cons include a heated swimming pool, well-equipped gym and all weather tennis court. Castle Ashby can also arrange a wide variety of country pursuits for guests.

Catering: In house

FACILITIES:
- Helipad
- Go Karting
- Tennis
- Croquet
- Indoor Pool
- Gym
- Pool/Snooker
- Boules
- Shooting
- Hot Air Balloons
- Quad Bikes/Off Road

SERVICES:
- Exclusive Use
- Marriage Licence

Price Guide: Prices range from £180 to £10,180 + vat. Wedding package prices are available on request.
Catering (sit down): from £42pp + vat
Catering (buffet): from £42pp + vat

Castle Hotel, Kirby Muxloe
T: 0116 239 5337   F: 0116 238 7868
Contact: Mr T Doblander
Party Max: 140 (marquee: 150)   Bedrooms: 32

The Castle Hotel is set in a quiet village, just four miles from Leicester city centre. At the back of the hotel is the remains of a 14th Century castle, with wooden bridge. The hotel also has large award-winning gardens. Helicopters and hot air balloons may use the grounds. Cuisine at the hotel is described as 'English/Continental'.

Catering: In house

SERVICES:
- Marriage Licence

Price Guide: Prices on application.
Catering (sit down): from £19.50pp

Charingworth Manor, Chipping Camden
T: 01386 593555   F: 01386 593353
Contact: Functions Manager
Party Max: 50 (marquee: 150)   Bedrooms: 26

This historic country house is set on a private estate in the rolling Cotswold countryside.

Catering: In house

SERVICES:
- Marriage Licence

Price Guide: Prices on application.
Catering (sit down): from £35.00pp
Catering (buffet): from £30.00pp

Chatsworth, Bakewell
T: 01246 582204   F: 01246 583536
Contact: John Oliver
Party Max: 70

Chatsworth is home to the Dukes of Devonshire. It was built in 1552 but was largely remodelled in the 17th Century. The house is set in a 105 acre garden featuring a 200 metre Cascade, the Willow Tree Fountain, glasshouses, rose, cottage and kitchen gardens. Several rooms are available for conferences and private functions. Private tours are available.

Catering: In house

Price Guide: Prices on application.

Cheltenham Racecourse, Cheltenham
T: 01242 570150   F: 01242 579356
Contact: Functions Manager
Party Max: 350 (marquee: 10000)

As one might expect from a venue used to dealing with large crowds, Cheltenham Racecourse emphasises the flexibility of its catering services. It is excellently equipped to deal with groups from 10 to 350.

Catering: In house

SERVICES:
- Marriage Licence

Price Guide: Prices on application.
Catering (sit down): from £18.00pp

Clarendon Suites, Edgbaston
T: 0121 454 2918   F: 0121 455 0859
E: info@clarendon-suites.co.uk
W: www.clarendon-suites.co.uk
Contact: Maureen Hadley, Stuart Parry or Martin Robinson, Conference & Banqueting Managers
Party Max: 800 (marquee: n/a)

Situated within its own grounds, with car parking for 300 cars, this conference and banqueting venue is within minutes of Birmingham city centre and New Street railway station. It is also located conveniently close to motorways. This venue offers numerous suites.

Catering: In house

SERVICES:
- Marriage Licence
- Performance Area

Price Guide: Prices range from £20 per hour for the Committee Room to £750 for a 9am to 5pm event in the main Clarendon Suite (Ballroom and Dining Room).
Catering (sit down): from £12pp
Catering (buffet): from £4.50pp

Clearwell Castle, Forest of Dean
T: 01594 832320   F: 01594 835523
E: clearwell@mainline.co.uk
W: www.brideshead.co.uk
Contact: Sharon Lake, General Manager
Party Max: 300

Clearwell Castle is a magnificent Grade I listed Gothic Mansion set in the heart of the beautiful Forest of Dean. The castle offers exclusive use for family parties of all kinds, with the Ballroom capable of seating 160, and the vaulted medieval servants hall with a capacity for 300.

Catering: In house

HEART OF ENGLAND

FACILITIES:
- Croquet

SERVICES:
- Exclusive Use
- Disco/Dance
- Performance Area
- Marriage Licence
- Entertainers
- Toastmaster
- Piped Music

Price Guide: £1250 - £3500
Catering (sit down): from 32.50pp
Catering (buffet): from £12.50pp

Combermere Abbey, Nr Whitchurch
T: 01948 662876   **F:** 01948 660920
E: cottages@combermereabbey.co.uk
W: www.combermereabbey.co.uk
Contact: Melanie Allen

Party Max: 150 (marquee: 150)   Bedrooms: 75

This is a Grade I listed Abbey on the Combermere estate, overlooking the 160 acre lake. Marquees for dinner/dance and larger functions take place in the restored Walled Garden. Accommodation for up to 50 can be provided in designer-decorated cottages in the award-winning converted stables.
Catering: Contract approved list

SERVICES:
- Exclusive Use
- Marriage Licence

Price Guide: Prices on application.
Catering (sit down): from £25.00pp

The Commandery, Worcester
T: 01905 361821   **F:** 01905 361822
Contact: Amanda Lunt

Party Max: 100

The Commandery is a Grade I listed building dating from around the 15th Century. It offers a variety of historic rooms for private evening functions, including the Great Hall.
Catering: Contract (any)

SERVICES:
- Exclusive Use

Price Guide: £17.50 - £180
Catering (sit down): POA

Coombe Abbey Hotel, Binley
T: 01203 450450   **F:** 01203 452035
Contact: Sales Office

Party Max: 120 (marquee: 0)   Bedrooms: 63

This 12th Century Abbey, which is set in 550 acres of grounds, has been tastefully restored into a luxury hotel, which has medieval, 18th Century and Victorian features. Three rooms are licensed to hold ceremonies: the De-Canville room, which has a capacity of 23 guests; the Centre Court which can take 100; and the Abbeygate room, which accommodates 146. The hotel prides itself as being "no ordinary hotel" and consequently plans "no ordinary weddings".
Catering: In house

SERVICES:
- Marriage Licence

Price Guide: Prices on application.

Catering (sit down): from £31.50pp

Corse Lawn House Hotel, Corse Lawn
T: 01452 780771   **F:** 01452 780840
E: hotel@corselawnhouse.u-net.com
W: www.corselawnhousehotel.co.uk
Contact: Giles Hine

Party Max: 80 (marquee: 0)   Bedrooms: 19

The hotel is housed in a Grade II listed building with a large ornamental pond at the front. The hotel claims to be in all the major food guides. Helicopters and hot air balloons may use the grounds here.
Catering: In house

SERVICES:
- Marriage Licence

Price Guide: Prices on application.
Catering (sit down): from £18.00pp
Catering (buffet): from £18.00pp

Cotgrave Place, Stragglethorpe
T: 0115 9333344   **F:** 0115 9334567
Contact: Vincent Toussaint, Food & Beverage Manager

Party Max: 250 (marquee: 0)

This golf and country club is set in 250 acres of parkland.
Catering: In house

SERVICES:
- Marriage Licence

Price Guide: Prices on application.
Catering (buffet): from £7.25pp

Coventry City FC, Coventry
T: 02476 234000   **F:** 02476 630318
Contact: Raj Athwal

Party Max: 200 (marquee: 10000)

The club has a total of 30 hospitality and conference rooms which are capable of catering for as few as two to up to 24,000 people. There are six rooms licensed to hold ceremonies, one of which is the restaurant, which actually overlooks the pitch. Ceremonies are available seven days a week, including match days, and are available without reception facilities, if required. Outdoor photography includes the use of the pitch.
Catering: In house

SERVICES:
- Marriage Licence

Price Guide: Prices on application.
Catering (sit down): POA

Cressbrook Hall & Cottages, Buxton
T: 01298 871289/0800 358 3003 **F:** 01298 871845
E: cressbrook-hall@connectfree.co.uk
W: www.smoothhound.co.uk/a01538.html
Contact: Mrs B Bailey

Party Max: 80   Bedrooms: 5 + 7

Cressbrook Hall is a William (1830-35) house, set in 20 acres of spectacular countryside with views of a limestone gorge. In the Hall itself the Sitting/Drawing Room is currently used for

Top and Above: Phyllis Court Club, Henley-on-Thames See p53

a good party's all in the planning,
and then some planning and oh, a bit more planning.

planning tools When it comes to organising a party there's an awful lot to remember. So to stop you stressing, confetti have introduced a range of personalised planning tools, including a checklist, a guest manager, gift list and your own web pages. So you don't forget a thing.

And if you register with us you could also win some great prizes to make your party go with a bang.

There now, feeling better?

confetti.co.uk
weddings and special occasions

Top Left: Lennoxlove House, Scotland. See p160 **Top Right:** Eastnor Castle. Ledbury. See p98
Above: Longleat, Warminster. See p68

Top Left & Right: Cross Tree House, Lopen. See p62 **Above:** One Great George Street, London. See p21

Top: Cumberwell Park, Bradford on Avon. See p63 **Above:** The Old Rectory, Cheltenham. See p106

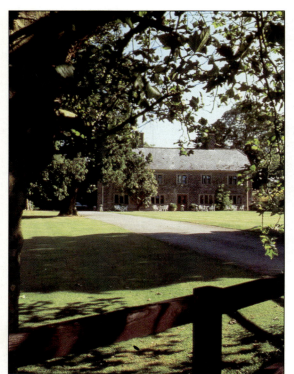

Top Left: Plumber Manor, Sturminster Newton. See p71 **Top Right:** National Railway Museum, York. See p131
Above: Flagstone Farm, Stow-on-the-Wold. See p99

Top Left & Right: Cromlix House. Scotland See p157   **Above:** The Lawn, Rochford. See p82

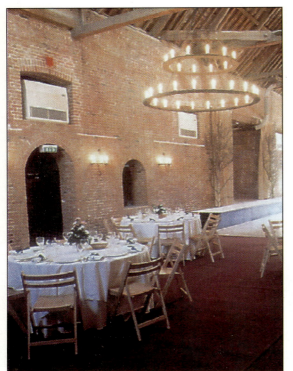

Top Left & Right: Sussex Barn, King's Lynn. See p88 **Above:** Combermere Abbey, Whitchurch. See p96

Top Left & Right: Amadeus Centre, London. See p9   **Above:** Newick Park, Newick. See p38

Top Left: Salomons, Tunbridge Wells. See p41 **Top Right:** Kingston Maurward, Dorcheser. See p67
Above: Bolding Way Holiday Cottages, Holt. See p76

NOBLE'S PARTY VENUES GUIDE 1ST EDITION

Top Left & Right: Glynhir Mansion, Wales. See p150   **Above:** Sparkles Hotel, Blackpool. See p122

Top Left: Haldon Belvedere, Exeter. See p66 **Top Right:** Beth Ruach, St David's. See p147
Above: Davenport House, Bridgnorth. See p97

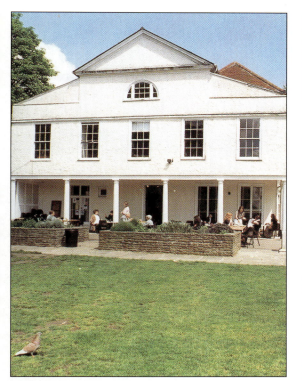

Top Left: Lauderdale House, London. See p19   **Top Right:** Tone Dale House, Wellington. See p74
Above: Clearwell Castle, Forest of Dean. See p95

Above: Polhawn Fort, Cornwall. See p71

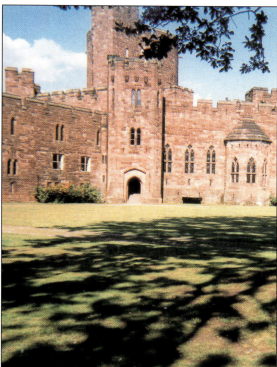

Top Left: Coppermines & Coniston Cottages, Coniston. See p136 **Top Right:** Peckforton Castle, Peckforton. See p120 **Above:** Silchester House, Silchester. See p54

Top Left & Right: Le Gothique, London. See p19 **Above Left:** The Roof Gardens, London. See p23
Above Right: Sutton House, London. See p25

HEART OF ENGLAND

functions, although the Orangery is currently undergoing restoration, and will be available from May 2001. Accommodation for up to 50 is available in the Hall (5 bedrooms), as well as in 7 self-catering cottages the Hall grounds. The venue is said to be suitable for team building and management training groups as well as for family celebrations and evening dinners.
Catering: In house

SERVICES:
- Exclusive Use

Price Guide: Prices on application.
Catering (sit down): POA

Dales & Peaks Hotel, Matlock
T: 01629 733775 **Contact:** Mr Banks
Party Max: 36 (marquee: 110)   Bedrooms: 6

The hotel is housed in a Victorian building with a 3/4 acre walled garden. The Red House Stables, adjacent to the hotel, house a vintage car and carriage museum, the exhibits of which were recently used in the film of Jane Eyre. Evening functions are not possible here.
Catering: In house

SERVICES:
- Marriage Licence

Price Guide: Prices on application.
Catering (sit down): from £16.95pp (inc drinks)

Davenport House, Bridgnorth
T: 01746 716221 **F:** 01746 716021
E: murphy@davenporthouse.co.uk
W: www.davenporthouse.co.uk
Contact: Roger Murphy, Proprietor
Party Max: 124 (marquee: 300)   Bedrooms: 7

This impressive 18th Century Grade I listed country house is privately run by owners Roger and Jane Murphy who have vast and wide-ranging experience in top event management and catering. The house sits in extensive grounds at the end of a long estate drive. Only one event is ever accommodated on one day, so you have the house to yourselves. The emphasis here is on a relaxed, friendly ambience. A small number of guest bedrooms are available, if required.
Catering: In house

FACILITIES:
- Helipad
- Shooting
- Pool/Snooker

SERVICES:
- Exclusive Use
- Marriage Licence
- Flowers
- Disco/Dance
- Piped Music

Price Guide: £500 - £2000
Catering (sit down): from £35pp
Catering (buffet): from £35pp

De Vere Belfry, Wishaw
T: 01675 470301 **F:** 01675 470178
E: enquiries@thebelfry.com **W:** www.devere.com
Contact: Julie Ellis, Sales Manager
Party Max: 400 (marquee: n/a)   Bedrooms: 324

The De Vere Belfry claims to be the best located conference, golf and leisure hotel in Europe. Set in 500 acres of Warwickshire countryside, the 4-star hotel boasts 3 championship golf courses. It has been home to 3 Ryder Cup matches, with a 4th returning in 2001. Facilities include 324 bedrooms, 8 bars and 5 restaurants, as well as a nightclub.
Catering: In house

FACILITIES:
- Helipad
- Golf
- Indoor Pool
- Gym
- Tennis
- Pool/Snooker

SERVICES:
- Marriage Licence
- Flowers
- Cake

Price Guide: £300 - £7000
Catering (sit down): from £26.50pp
Catering (buffet): from £18.95pp

Delbury Hall, Craven Arms
T: 01584 841267 **F:** 01584 841441
Contact: Patrick Wrigley
Party Max: 30 (marquee: 10000)

This stately home is a Grade II listed Georgian country house (c1750), with attractive gardens. While small receptions can sometimes take place in the house, a marquee is usually erected. Catering may be either in-house or contract depending on the size of party, but there is no choice of caterer.
Catering: In house/Contract approved list

SERVICES:
- Marriage Licence

Price Guide: Prices on application.
Catering (sit down): £15.00 - 25.00pp

Dormy House Hotel, Broadway
T: 01386 852711 **F:** 01386 858636
E: reservations@dormyhouse.co.uk
Contact: Nicola Sinclair, Sales Manager
Party Max: 150 (marquee: 80)   Bedrooms: 48

This hotel, a converted 17th Century Cotswold farmhouse, has three function rooms, each with limited wheelchair access. The hotel has 2 AA rosettes and is RAC recommended. Ethnic, kosher and vegetarian food can be prepared in house.
Catering: In house

SERVICES:
- Marriage Licence

Price Guide: Prices on application.
Catering (sit down): from £30.00pp

Dovecliff Hall Hotel, Burton upon Trent
T: 01283 531818 **F:** 01283 516546
Contact: Leigh Frost
Party Max: 90 (marquee: 0)   Bedrooms: 7

This Georgian listed building set in seven acres features gardens overlooking the River Dove.
Catering: In house

SERVICES:
- Marriage Licence

HEART OF ENGLAND

Price Guide: Prices on application.
Catering (sit down): POA

Dumbleton Hall Hotel, Evesham
T: 01386 881240   **F:** 01386 881966
E: reception@dumbletonhallforce9.co.uk
W: www.dumbletonhall.force9.co.uk
Contact: Loraine Walker

Party Max: 250 (marquee: 200)   Bedrooms: 39

Dumbleton Hall dates from the early 1830s. It is built from Cotswold stone and is set in its own park with cedar-fringed duck lake. The Hall was apparently built for a cousin of Mrs Gaskell, the novelist and has many historical and literary associations.
Catering: *In house*

SERVICES:
• Marriage Licence

Price Guide: Prices on application.
Catering (sit down): from £23.00pp
Catering (buffet): from £8.95pp

East Lodge Hotel, Matlock
T: 01629 734474   **F:** 01629 733949
Contact: Mrs Mills

Party Max: 90 (marquee: 120)   Bedrooms: 15

The hotel was once the East Lodge to Haddon Hall and is set in 10 acres of grounds. It is set on the outskirts of the Derbyshire Peak District.
Catering: *In house*

SERVICES:
• Marriage Licence

Price Guide: Prices on application.
Catering (sit down): from £18.95pp

Eastnor Castle, Ledbury

T: 01531 633160   **F:** 01531 631776
E: enquiries@eastnorcastle.com
W: www.eastnorcastle.com
Contact: Simon Foster, Castle Manager

Party Max: 150 (marquee: 350)   Bedrooms: 11

This privately-owned 'fairytale' castle is set in the Malvern Hills and surrounded by a deer park and a lake. The early 19th Century historic building is now Grade I listed and offers up to 6 richly decorated state rooms for hire, including the Gothic Drawing Room, which is licensed for marriages.
Catering: *In house*

FACILITIES:
• Shooting   • Tennis   • Pool/Snooker
• Quad Bikes/Off Road   • Table Tennis
SERVICES:
• Exclusive Use   • Marriage Licence

Price Guide: Facility fee is usually £1200 - £2300 per day. Exclusive use of the castle starts at £60 per person for over 50 guests, and includes a light buffet lunch. Overnight accommodation starts at £215pp (min 8 guests) and includes dinner, b&b.
Catering (sit down): from £26.50pp
Catering (buffet): from £12pp

Edgbaston Cricket Ground, Birmingham
T: 0121 440 0747   **F:** 0121 440 0116
W: www.thebears.co.uk
Contact: Amanda Hateley, Sales Executive

Party Max: 400 (marquee: 1000+)

Many of the function rooms here overlook the internationally known cricket ground. The venue offers free car parking for guests and can cater for up to 400. Catering for all events is provided by Letherby & Christopher.
Catering: *In house*

FACILITIES:
• Helipad   • Gym   • Indoor Cricket
SERVICES:
• Exclusive Use   • Marriage Licence   • Flowers
• Disco/Dance   • Entertainers   • Piped Music
• Performance Area

Price Guide: Venue hire is £200 - £600.
Catering (sit down): from £18.50pp
Catering (buffet): from £8.50pp

Elvaston Castle, Elvaston
T: 01332 571343   **F:** 01332 758751
Contact: Lesley Law

Party Max: 150 (marquee: 250)

This listed building is set in an historic garden and parkland estate, and now operates as a museum, with camping and a riding centre in the grounds. It is run by Derbyshire County Council. Catering is provided by Mrs Kemp's cafe on site, who can be contacted directly on 01159 231494. Flowers are usually provided at the Castle.
Catering: *Contract approved list*

FACILITIES:
• Riding
SERVICES:
• Marriage Licence   • Flowers

Price Guide: Prices on application.
Catering (sit down): POA

Eyam Hall, Hope Valley
T: 01433 631976   **F:** 01433 631603
E: nicwri@globalnet.co.uk   **W:** www.eyamhall.co.uk
Contact: Nicola Wright, Managing Partner

Party Max: 50 (marquee: 120)

Eyam Hall is a Grade II listed, 17th Century manor house in the historic 'plague village' of Eyam. It has been the home of the Wright family for over 300 years. The Dining Room can be booked for private dinner parties and the Hall for reception. Larger groups can be accommodated in the 17th Century function room or in a marquee in the historic garden. The farm buildings here have been converted into craft units.
Catering: *In house*

SERVICES:
• Exclusive Use   • Marriage Licence

Price Guide: Rooms in house from £250/day. Garden from £750/day.
Catering (sit down): from £15pp
Catering (buffet): from £8.50pp

HEART OF ENGLAND

Fairlawns at Aldridge, Walsall
T: 01922 455122 **F:** 01922 743210
E: welcome@fairlwans.co.uk **W:** www.fairlawns.co.uk
Contact: John Pette

Party Max: 150 (marquee: 0)   Bedrooms: 50

This is an extended Victorian house with restaurant, and health club, set in 9 acres of landscaped grounds.
Catering: In house

FACILITIES:
- Health Club

SERVICES:
- Marriage Licence

Price Guide: Prices on application.
Catering (sit down): from £22.50pp
Catering (buffet): from £18.50pp

Fawsley Hall, Nr Daventry
T: 01327 892000 **F:** 01327 892001
E: fawsley@compuserve.com **W:** www.fawsleyhall.com
Contact: Stephanie Pinto, Sales Manager

Party Max: 150   Bedrooms: 30

This Tudor manor house, with Georgian and Victorian wings, is surrounded by rolling parkland and has now become a 4-star hotel. Features of the house include a restored vaulted roof in the great hall, and beautifully decorated spacious bedrooms and bathrooms. Several rooms are available for functions, from meeting rooms for 12-18 to suites for 120.
Catering: In house

FACILITIES:
- Helipad
- Tennis

SERVICES:
- Exclusive Use
- Performance Area

Price Guide: 7 different meeting room rates are available on request.
Catering (sit down): from £30pp
Catering (buffet): from £25pp

Fischer's Baslow Hall, Baslow
T: 01246 583259 **F:** 01264 583818
Contact: Susan Fischer

Party Max: 40 (marquee: 0)   Bedrooms: 6

This is a small, privately run Derbyshire Manor House on the edge of the Chatsworth estate.
Catering: In house

SERVICES:
- Marriage Licence

Price Guide: Prices on application.
Catering (sit down): from £27.00pp

Flagstone Farm, Stow-on-the-Wold
T: 01451 832215 **F:** 01451 832215
E: awhitney@btclick.com
W: www.cotswoldfarmhouse.com
Contact: Ann Whitney, Manager

Party Max: 35   Bedrooms: 20

Flagstone Farm offers 6 spacious converted Cotswold stone barns, sited in an area of Outstanding Nautral Beauty. This is a non-working farm of about 14 acres, incuding 4 acres of woodland. The converted barns sleep between 2 and 14 people and feature beamed ceilings, exposed stone walls and stone fireplaces. Facilities on site include shared use of the grounds, childrens play area, hard tennis court, games room with snooker and table tennis and an open games barn with badminton, cricket, skating, pitch & putt, croquet and archery.
Catering: Contract (any)/Self catering

FACILITIES:
- Helipad
- Pool/Snooker
- Archery
- Golf
- Table Tennis
- Putting
- Tennis
- Croquet
- Playground

SERVICES:
- Exclusive Use
- Flowers
- Fireworks

Price Guide: £560 - £1650 for 14 people

Fossebridge Inn, Cheltenham
T: 01285 720721 **F:** 01285 720793
Contact: Tim or Caroline Bevan

Party Max: 60 (marquee: 120)   Bedrooms: 11

This is a Grade II listed Tudor building housing a pub and set in gardens with a lake. The pub holds an AA Rosette for its food.
Catering: In house

SERVICES:
- Marriage Licence

Price Guide: Prices on application.
Catering (sit down): from £12.95pp

Frogmill Inn, Cheltenham
T: 01242 852237 **F:** 01242 820237
Contact: John Griffith

Party Max: 200   Bedrooms: 16

Frogmill Inn dates from the Domesday Book and is set in five acres. There are two dining areas, one for up to 60, one for up to 200.
Catering: In house

SERVICES:
- Marriage Licence

Price Guide: Prices on application.
Catering (sit down): from £15.00pp

Grafton Manor, Bromsgrove
T: 01527 579007 **F:** 01527 575221
W: www.graftonmanorhotel.co.uk
Contact: Stephen Morris

Party Max: 300 (marquee: 300)   Bedrooms: 20

The Manor dates from 1567, but was substantially rebuilt in the early 18th Century. The Manor is available on an exclusive use basis.
Catering: In house

SERVICES:
- Exclusive Use
- Marriage Licence

Price Guide: Prices on application.
Catering (sit down): from £33.75pp

HEART OF ENGLAND

Grange Hall, Southam
T: 01926 813933 F: 01926 811414
Contact: Mrs Carole Gwillam, Administrator
Party Max: 250

Grange Hall is set in its own gardens and has a fully licensed bar, stage and kitchen, as well as syndicate rooms.
Catering: Contract (any)/Self catering

SERVICES:
- Exclusive Use
- Performance Area

Price Guide: £40 - £200 per day

Great Occasions at Broad Marston Manor, Stratford on Avon
T: 01789 720252 F: 01789 720252
Contact: Elizabeth Smalley and Michael Smalley, Owners
Party Max: 50 (marquee: 100+)   Bedrooms: 10-12

This is an historic Grade II listed 10 bedroomed Cotswold stone manor house featuring mullioned windows and 4-poster beds. Surrounded by paddocks, ponds and semi-formal gardens, the manor enjoys seclusion within its grounds, yet is handy for some of the Cotswolds most beautiful towns and villages. A listed medieval barn and dovecot are also on site here. The barn will be available for functions shortly.

A large beamed dining room seating up to 25 can adequately cope with the most ambitous catering requirements. This venue offers a special party package, which can include full or part catering, maid service and various leisure options.
Catering: In house

FACILITIES:
- Pool/Snooker
- Archery

SERVICES:
- Exclusive Use
- Flowers
- Toastmaster
- Cake
- Magician

Price Guide: £1250 - £3250
Catering (sit down): from £18pp
Catering (buffet): from £10pp

Great Tythe Barn, Tetbury
T: 01666 502475 F: 01666 502358
E: info@gtb.co.uk W: www.gtb.co.uk
Contact: Julian Benton, Owner
Party Max: 300 (marquee: 600)   Bedrooms: 4 + cottages

The Great Tythe Barn is situated in the south Cotswold Hills. The 17th Century barn is a Grade II listed building which dominates a spacious courtyard where exotic chickens and ducks roam freely. Bordered by gardens and 11 Cotswold stone cottages, the atmosphere is relaxed and tranquil.
Catering: In house

FACILITIES:
- Tennis

SERVICES:
- Exclusive Use
- Marriage Licence
- Flowers
- Cake
- Toastmaster
- Disco/Dance
- Live Music
- Entertainers
- Fireworks
- Photography

Price Guide: £530 - £1100 + vat for first 5 hours.

Catering (sit down): from £20pp
Catering (buffet): from £12.50pp

Hagley Hall, Stourbridge
T: 01562 882408 F: 01562 882632
Contact: Lesley Haynes, Events Manager
Party Max: 300 (marquee: 1000)

The last of the Grand Palladian houses, designed by Sanderson Miller and completed in 1760, Hagley Hall contains the finest examples of Rococo plasterwork by Francesco Vassali and a unique collection of 18th Century furniture and family portraits, including works by Van Dyck, Reynolds and Lely. Within easy reach of the M6, M42 and M40, this venue is open to the public for guided tours in January and February and on Bank Holidays. It also specialises in corporate entertaining, conferences and weddings.
Catering: In house

FACILITIES:
- Helipad
- Shooting
- Quad Bikes/Off Road

SERVICES:
- Exclusive Use
- Marriage Licence
- Flowers

Price Guide: Facility fee £1300 + Vat (corporate rate), £1600 + vat for weddings.
Catering (sit down): from £28pp + vat
Catering (buffet): from £28pp + vat

Hambleton Hall, Rutland
T: 01572 756991 F: 01572 724721
E: hotel@hambletonhall.com W: www.hambletonhall.com
Contact: Graeme Matheson, Restaurant Director
Party Max: 64   Bedrooms: 17

Hambleton is one of the UK's leading country house hotels offering luxurious accommodation and Michelin star cuisine. It was originally built in 1881 as a hunting box, and has views over Rutland Water. It claims friendly and well-trained staff; experts at organising very special occasions for both individuals and larger parties.
Catering: In house

FACILITIES:
- Helipad
- Tennis
- Watersports
- Outdoor Pool

SERVICES:
- Exclusive Use
- Marriage Licence
- Flowers
- Valet Parking

Price Guide: £8,000 - £12,500
Catering (sit down): from £24pp

Hanbury Hall, Droitwich
T: 01527 821214 F: 01527 821251
E: hanbury@smtp.ntrust.org.uk
Contact: Grace Elford
Party Max: 100 (marquee: 130)

This National Trust property offers its Drawing Room, Hall and Library for functions. These are available at any time from November to March, but from April to October the Hall (with sweeping staircase and log fire) is available mornings only from Sunday to Wednesday. Exclusive use is provided of all ground

HEART OF ENGLAND

floor rooms and the 20 acre garden. There are restrictions for indoor photography.
Catering: Contract (any)

SERVICES:
• Marriage Licence
Price Guide: price comment
Catering (sit down): POA

Harthill Hall, Nr Bakewell
T: 01629 636190   **F:** 01629 636190
E: Nicola@harthillhall.co.uk   **W:** www.harthillhall.co.uk
Contact: Nicola Bunting
Party Max: 40   Bedrooms: 18

The Hall dates from the 12th Century and features a cobbled courtyard surrounded by listed building. It is now used as Country house cottages.
Catering: In house

SERVICES:
• Marriage Licence
Price Guide: Prices on application.
Catering (sit down): from £17.00pp
Catering (buffet): from £10.00pp

Hatherly Manor Hotel, Down Hatherly
T: 01452 730217   **F:** 01452 731032
Contact: Maria Heap
Party Max: 250 (marquee: 150)   Bedrooms: 51

This 17th Century manor house, set in 37 acres, is available for functions in one of five suites. The Manor House has an AA Rosette for its food.
Catering: In house

SERVICES:
• Marriage Licence
Price Guide: Prices on application.
Catering (sit down): from £18.95pp

Hatton Court Hotel, Upton St Leonards
T: 01452 617412   **F:** 01452 612945
E: Res@hatton-court.co.uk   **W:** www.hatton-hotels.co.uk
Contact: Functions Manager
Party Max: 80 (marquee: 0)   Bedrooms: 7

Hatton Court is a 17th Century Cotswold manor house, set in seven acres of gardens and 30 acres of pasture. Its position at 600 ft above sea level provides excellent views over the Severn Valley.
Catering: In house

SERVICES:
• Marriage Licence
Price Guide: Prices on application.
Catering (sit down): from £35.00pp

Highbury, Moseley
T: 0121 449 6549   **F:** 0121 442 4782
Contact: Mrs J Tanner
Party Max: 150 (marquee: 150)   Bedrooms: 7

Highbury enjoys a secluded parkland setting three miles from Birmingham city centre. Originally built as the home of Joseph Chamberlain MP in 1878, it features a central Hall with a first floor Minstrel's Gallery. The Drawing Room looks out over the house's south-facing terrace, grounds and surrounding parkland. Highbury's seven bedrooms are only available to guests by prior arrangement.
Catering: In house

SERVICES:
• Marriage Licence
Price Guide: Prices on application.
Catering (sit down): from £17.00pp

Hilton Puckrup Hall Hotel, Tewkesbury
T: 01684 296200   **F:** 01684 850788
Contact: Functions Manager
Party Max: 200 (marquee: 100)   Bedrooms: 84

This Regency mansion is set in over 140 acres of parkland, and has its own 18 hole golf course. Two rooms are available for functions; the Gloucester Suite and the Ballroom. The hotel has its own helipad.
Catering: In house

SERVICES:
• Marriage Licence
Price Guide: Prices on application.
Catering (sit down): from £25.00pp
Catering (buffet): from £9.25pp

Holme Pierrepont Hall, Nr Nottingham
T: 0115 933 2371
Contact: Robert Brackenbury, Business Manager
Party Max: 100 (marquee: 200)

HolmePierrepont is a stately home, built in 1500, set in a rural setting, 5 miles from the centre of Nottingham. The house is surrounded by 30 acres of park and gardens and is available on an exclusive basis for a variety of events from wedding receptions and private parties to seminars and conferences. The Long Gallery (75' x 20') can seat up to 100 for dinner. The Ball Room (22' x 20') and Drawing Room (26' x 19' are ideal for seminars and conferences. All 3 rooms can be used to complement each other. Customers can bring in quad bikes, archery, etc, to use in the grounds.
Catering: Contract approved list

FACILITIES:
• Helipad
Price Guide: Prices on application.
Catering (sit down): POA

Holt Castle, Worcester
T: 01905 621806   **F:** 01905 621586
E: enquiries@holtcastle.co.uk   **W:** www.hotlcastle.co.uk
Contact: Mrs Debbie Fox, Manager
Party Max: 130 (marquee: 130)   Bedrooms: 1

Holt Castle is a privately owned Grade I listed building, comprising a 14th Century tower (overlooking the river Severn), which is attached to a 15th Century manor house. Within the

HEART OF ENGLAND

grounds is a formal rose garden. Four rooms are licensed for wedding ceremonies with varying capacities from 25 to 100, and these are available any day of the year. A bridal suite is also available here.
Catering: Contract approved list

FACILITIES:
- Pool/Snooker

SERVICES:
- Exclusive Use
- Marriage Licence
- Piped Music
- Valet Parking

Price Guide: £250 - £3000

Hopton Court, Kidderminster
T: 01299 270734/0411731896 **F:** 01299 271132
E: chris@hoptoncourt.fsnet.co.uk
Contact: Christopher or Sarah Woodward
Party Max: 60 (marquee: unlimited)

Hopton Court is an English Heritage Grade II listed building with a Grade II★ refurbished conservatory and refurbished stable block. The house and stables date from 1776 and are set in parkland and 1800 acres of countryside. Facilities are available for parties and corporate entertainment.
Catering: In house

FACILITIES:
- Helipad
- Shooting
- Paint Ball
- Hot Air Balloons
- Quad Bikes/Off Road

SERVICES:
- Exclusive Use
- Marriage Licence
- Disco/Dance
- Live Music
- Entertainers
- Fireworks
- Piped Music
- Performance Area

Price Guide: Hire fees range from £350 - £500.
Catering (sit down): from £31.50pp
Catering (buffet): from £15pp

Ireley Grounds, Cheltenham
T: 01242 603736 **F:** 01242 603736
Contact: Make and Pauline Wright
Party Max: 150 (marquee: 500)   Bedrooms: 4

This is a private house and banqueting suite set in six acres of grounds, with three acres of gardens, ponds and views of the Cotswolds. Pig roasts, medieval banquets, barbeques and ethnic cuisine are all available.
Catering: In house

SERVICES:
- Marriage Licence
- Pig Roasts
- Themeing

Price Guide: Prices on application.
Catering (sit down): from £18.00pp
Catering (buffet): from £15.00pp

Jarvis Bowden Hall, Upton St Leonards
T: 01452 614121 **F:** 01452 611885
W: www.jarvis.co.uk/weddings
Contact: Rachel Perry
Party Max: 200 (marquee: 200)   Bedrooms: 72

This is a Grade II listed Regency building with private grounds and lawns leading to a lake. A recent wedding here included a casino evening for guests.
Catering: In house

SERVICES:
- Marriage Licence

Price Guide: Prices on application.
Catering (sit down): from £25.00pp
Catering (buffet): from £28.00pp

Keele Conference Park, Keele
T: 01782 584025 **F:** 01782 713058
Contact: Anne Nicholls
Party Max: 600 (marquee: 10000)   Bedrooms: 67

This Grade II listed building featuring lakes and Italian gardens, was originally owned by the Sneyd family.
Catering: In house

SERVICES:
- Marriage Licence

Price Guide: Prices on application.
Catering (sit down): POA

Kelham Hall, Newark
T: 01636 655951 **F:** 01636 655952
E: kelham.hall@initial-catering.co.uk
Contact: John Underwood, Catering Manager
Party Max: 500 (marquee: n/a)

Kelham Hall is a very large Victorian Gothic mansion, which includes the later addition of a Byzantine style chapel which is now used as a conference centre. The building is set in 42 acres of gardens and parkland adjacent to the River Trent. The property is now owned by Newark and Sherwood District Council and the Hall is used as its headquarters. It is close to the A1 and Newark.
Catering: Contract approved list/In house

FACILITIES:
- Helipad
- Tennis

SERVICES:
- Exclusive Use
- Marriage Licence
- Piped Music
- Performance Area

Price Guide: Prices on application.
Catering (sit down): from £20pp
Catering (buffet): from £7pp

Kingfisher Barn, Abingdon
T: 01235 537538 **F:** 01235 537538
E: liz@kingfisherbarn.demon.co.uk
Contact: Liz Beaumont
Party Max: 34   Bedrooms: 10

Kingfisher Barn is a renovated 17th Century barn, with its own licensed bar, and converted stable buildings providing overnight accommodation. The Barn is surrounded by countryside and a short distance from the River Thames. It is possible to hire the whole site on an exclusive use basis with staff at the Barn able to help organise your stay. Items such as sports equipment can be arranged and artists can be brought in such as musicians and painters. All staff here are Social Services cleared to work with children under the age of 8. Caterers and

HEART OF ENGLAND

staff can be recommended.
Catering: In house

SERVICES:
- Exclusive Use

Price Guide: Barn only Saturday night £800 (including bar and staff and furniture). All accommodation, one night, £550.

Langar Hall, Langar
T: 01949 860559 **F:** 01949 861045
E: langarhall-hotel@ndirect.co.uk **W:** www.langarhall.com
Contact: Reception

Party Max: 40 (marquee: 120)   Bedrooms: 10

Langar Hall Hotel and Restaurant, situated in the Vale of Belvoir, is suited to small private parties. This 3-star hotel stands in quiet seclusion beside an Early English church, overlooking gardens and sheep grazing amongst ancient trees in the park. This venue is licensed for civil wedding ceremonies.
Catering: In house

FACILITIES:
- Helipad
- Hot Air Balloons

SERVICES:
- Exclusive Use
- Marriage Licence
- Flowers
- Piped Music

Price Guide: Prices on application.
Catering (sit down): from £25pp
Catering (buffet): from £30pp

Lea Marston Hotel, Lea Marston
T: 01675 470468 **F:** 01675 470871
Contact: Sharon Smith

Party Max: 180   Bedrooms: 49

The hotel is set in 20 acres of grounds and features a nine hole golf course.
Catering: In house

FACILITIES:
- Golf

SERVICES:
- Marriage Licence

Price Guide: Room hire from £195.
Catering (sit down): from £19.95pp
Catering (buffet): from £6.95pp

Locko Park, Nr Derby
T: 01332 662785
F: 01332 281942
Contact: Miss G C Phillipson

Party Max: 100

This Grade II listed private house is set in formal gardens and surrounded by parkland. All catering is managed in-house, and is arranged on an individual basis, hence no price guides. No evening receptions.
Catering: In house

SERVICES:
- Marriage Licence

Price Guide: Prices on application.

Longmynd Hotel, Church Stretton
T: 01694 722244 **F:** 01694 722718
E: reservations@longmynd.co.uk **W:** www.longmynd.co.uk
Contact: Max Chapman

Party Max: 110   Bedrooms: 50

Longmynd is a Regency style building, with more recent additions, set in 15 acres of private landscaped grounds, and is set against the backdrop of the South Shropshire Hills. The hotel has two restaurants and its own leisure club including outdoor swimming pool.
Catering: In house

FACILITIES:
- Outdoor Pool
- Leisure Club

SERVICES:
- Marriage Licence

Price Guide: Prices on application.
Catering (sit down): 19.95 - 30.50pp

Lords of the Manor, Cheltenham
T: 01451 820243 **F:** 01451 820696
Contact: Iain Shelton

Party Max: 120   Bedrooms: 27

This former rectory dates from the 17th Century, and is set in eight acres of parkland. The award-winning restaurant offers reception facilities for a maximum of 50. Accolades include a Michelin star.
Catering: In house

SERVICES:
- Marriage Licence

Price Guide: Prices on application.
Catering (sit down): from £26.00pp

Lygon Arms, Broadway
T: 01386 852255 **F:** 01386 858611
E: info@the-lygon-arms.co.uk **W:** www.savoy-group.co.uk
Contact: Mrs Simone Hancox, Revenue Manager

Party Max: 90   Bedrooms: 65

This 16th Century coaching inn, set in the heart of the village, is situated at the foot of the Cotswolds and features antique furniture and log fires. It is owned by the Savoy Group.
Catering: In house

FACILITIES:
- Indoor Pool
- Gym
- Tennis
- Pool/Snooker

SERVICES:
- Exclusive Use
- Marriage Licence

Price Guide: Room hire rates are £200 - £650
Pianist hire from £200
Catering (sit down): from £24pp

Makeney Hall, Milford
T: 01332 842999 **F:** 01332 842777
Contact: Maureen Keating

Party Max: 180   Bedrooms: 45

A Victorian country house hotel, Makeney Hall is set in six acres of gardens on the edge of the Derwent Valley. Helicopters

HEART OF ENGLAND

can land on site.
Catering: In house

FACILITIES:
- Helipad

SERVICES:
- Marriage Licence

Price Guide: Prices on application.
Catering (sit down): from £22.25pp
Catering (buffet): from £10.50pp

Manor House Hotel, Moreton-in-Marsh
T: 01608 650501   F: 01608 651481
Contact: Miss Meriel Neighbour
Party Max: 100   Bedrooms: 39

This listed building dates back to 1545. It has links with the Creswyke family and has its own resident ghost, and a priest hole. The AA Rosetted restaurant can prepare vegan and vegetarian dishes on request.
Catering: In house

SERVICES:
- Marriage Licence

Price Guide: Prices on application.
Catering (sit down): from £21.00pp
Catering (buffet): from £19.95pp

Manor House Hotel, Leamington Spa
T: 01926 423251   F: 01926 425933
Contact: Jan Deeming
Party Max: 200   Bedrooms: 53

Said to be home of the first Lawn Tennis Club, this listed building features smooth landscaped lawns and was opened in 1847. The hotel offers special overnight rates to guests including a traditional English breakfast.
Catering: In house

SERVICES:
- Marriage Licence

Price Guide: Prices on application.
Catering (sit down): from £12.90pp
Drinks packages from £5.55pp

Manor School of Fine Cuisine, Nottingham
T: 01949 81371   F: 01949 81371
Contact: Claire Tuttey, Owner
Party Max: 65 (marquee: 450)   Bedrooms: 6

This school is housed in a Georgian Grade A manor house set in its own ground with a duck pond. The venue calims luxurious reception rooms and sole use of the facilities.
Catering: In house/Self catering

FACILITIES:
- Helipad
- Hot Air Balloons
- Riding
- Shooting

SERVICES:
- Exclusive Use
- Cake
- Marriage Licence
- Toastmaster
- Flowers
- Disco/Dance
- Live Music
- Entertainers
- Fireworks
- Photography

Price Guide: There is no facility fee for this venue.
Catering (sit down): from £14pp
Catering (buffet): from £5pp

Marston Farm Hotel, Sutton Coldfield
T: 01827 872133   F: 01827 875043
Contact: Katie Humphries
Party Max: 150 (marquee: 120)   Bedrooms: 37

This is a modernised 17th Century farmhouse next to the Birmingham Fazeley canal, and was once owned by Robert Peel, Prime Minister during 19th Century and founder of the police force. It is set in 9 acres of grounds. Marston Farm has its own moorings on the canal, while helicopters and hot air balloons may use the grounds.
Catering: In house

FACILITIES:
- Helipad

SERVICES:
- Marriage Licence

Price Guide: Prices on application.
Catering (sit down): from £46.00pp
Catering (buffet): from £8.95pp

Maynard Arms Hotel, Grindleford
T: 01433 630321   F: 01433 630445
Contact: Jonathan and Joanne Tindall
Party Max: 180   Bedrooms: 10

Built in 1898, this is a traditional coaching inn with views over its landscaped gardens and the Hope Valley.
Catering: In house

SERVICES:
- Marriage Licence

Price Guide: Prices on application.
Catering (sit down): from £19.00pp
Catering (buffet): from £8.75pp

Middleton Hall Trust, Tamworth
T: 01827 283095
F: 01827 285717
E: weddings@middleton-hall.co.uk
W: www.middleton-hall.co.uk
Contact: David Chadwick
Party Max: 150 (marquee: 250)

This is a Grade II listed building that was formerly the home of naturalist Francis Willoughby, the world famous naturalist. It is now cared for by a private charitable trust. The Hall, set in 40 acres of conservation parkland, has a Tudor barn, and walled gardens. The earliest buildings date from the 13th Century with additions from the 16th and 19th Centuries. The Hall itself dates from the 17th Century. The whole Hall is available on an exclusive basis. It is available everyday of the week except Sundays from April to September. Middleton Hall Catering has no standard menu and will tailor meals to your requirements. They will also stock favourites wines, etc.
Catering: In house

HEART OF ENGLAND

SERVICES:
- Exclusive Use
- Marriage Licence

Price Guide: Prices on application.
Catering (sit down): from £18.00pp
Catering (buffet): from £9.00pp

Munstone House, Hereford
T: 01432 267122   **F:** 01432 267122
Contact: Yvonne Hodges
Party Max: 600   Bedrooms: 29

Munstone House is set in 2 acres of landscaped gardens overlooking open countryside. It is 2 miles from Hereford town centre.
Catering: In house

SERVICES:
- Marriage Licence

Price Guide: Prices on application.
Catering (sit down): from £12.50pp
Catering (buffet): from £5.50pp

Nailcote Hall Hotel, Coventry
T: 01203 466174   **F:** 01203 470720
Contact: Karen Bentley
Party Max: 150 (marquee: 150)   Bedrooms: 38

This 17th Century country house hotel is a Grade I listed building set in 15 acres.
Catering: In house

SERVICES:
- Marriage Licence

Price Guide: Prices on application.
Catering (sit down): packages from £35.50pp

The Nash, Kempsey
T: 01905 821397   **F:** 01905 821397
Contact: Brenda Bennett
Party Max: 120 (marquee: 300)   Bedrooms: 10+

The Nash is a Grade II listed Tudor manor house set in 47 acres of parkland and woods with 11 acres of formal gardens. The interior retains oak panelling and Italian plasterwork, while the building itself features towering brick chimneys and stone mullioned windows.
Catering: In house

SERVICES:
- Marriage Licence

Price Guide: Prices on application.
Catering (sit down): from £22.50pp
Catering (buffet): from £9.00pp

New Priory Hotel, Hereford
T: 01432 760264
F: 01432 761809
Contact: K J Benjamin
Party Max: 150 (marquee: unlimited)   Bedrooms: 8

This former historical monastery, now an hotel and restaurant, is set in over 3 acres of grounds.
Catering: In house

SERVICES:
- Marriage Licence

Price Guide: Prices on application.
Catering (sit down): from £8.50pp
Catering (buffet): from £5.00pp

Newstead Abbey, Ravenshead
T: 01623 793557   **F:** 01623 797136
Contact: Brian Ayers
Party Max: 100

This Grade I listed monument was originally a 12th Century monastery, which later became the country residence of Lord Byron. The Abbey is set in 320 acres of parkland, with 28 acres of Japanese, Rose and French gardens. Nottinghamshire City Council took over ownership of the Abbey in 1939. The Abbey features a separate restaurant, the White Lady Restaurant, which is run by an independent caterer. For further information please contact Mrs Crisp on 01623 797392.
Catering: Contract approved list

SERVICES:
- Marriage Licence

Price Guide: Prices on application.
Catering (sit down): POA

Normanton Park Hotel, Oakham
T: 01780 720315   **F:** 01780 721086
Contact: Functions Manager
Party Max: 180 (marquee: 200)   Bedrooms: 34

The hotel was originally the stable block to the Georgian Normanton Manor House. It is only 50 yards from the edge of Rutland Water and set in five acres of parkland. A late night drinking licence can be applied for and catering arrangements are flexible.
Catering: In house

SERVICES:
- Marriage Licence

Price Guide: Prices on application.
Catering (sit down): from £15.00pp

Norwood Park, Southwell
T: 01636 815649   **F:** 01636 815702
E: sarah@norwoodpark.org.uk
W: ww.norwoodpark.org.uk
Contact: Sarah Dodds, Events Manager
Party Max: 150 (marquee: 200+)

This is a unique stables and fruit store conversion with an open courtyard, perfect for parties and dinner/dances. The venue is adjacent to a country house in grounds of medieval parkland.
Catering: Contract approved list

FACILITIES:
- Helipad
- Go Karting
- Golf
- Hot Air Balloons
- Paint Ball
- Quad Bikes/Off Road

SERVICES:
- Exclusive Use
- Disco/Dance
- Marriage Licence
- Performance Area
- Flowers
- Valet Parking

Price Guide: £1000 - £1500+

HEART OF ENGLAND

Noseley Hall, Billesdon
T: 0116 259 6487 **F:** 0116 259 6989
E: arthur@noseley.demon.co.uk **W:** noseleyhall.co.uk
Contact: Mr Arthur G Hazlerigg, Owner

Party Max: 150 (marquee: 500)

Grade II listed Noseley Hall is a small private stately home that has been in the same family since 1419. It is now open to the public.
Catering: Contract approved list

FACILITIES:
- Helipad
- Shooting
- Hot Air Balloons
- Pool/Snooker
- Quad Bikes/Off Road

SERVICES:
- Exclusive Use
- Marriage Licence
- Flowers

Price Guide: £1500 - £2500
Catering (sit down): from £35pp + vat
Catering (buffet): from £20pp + vat

Old Colehurst Manor, Market Drayton
T: 01630 638833 **F:** 01630 638647
E: bjorn@colehurst.co.uk **W:** www.colehurst.co.uk
Contact: Lord Bjorn Teksnes, Owner

Party Max: 150   Bedrooms: 10

Old Colehurst Manor is a unique Grade I listed Elizabethan manor. Lovingly restored by Lord and Lady Teksnes, but with mods cons such as underfloor heating, baths, showers and comfortable beds. The house is devoted to providing the full-on 17th Century experience; not just wining and dining, but sleeping (the ghosts are all friendly we are assured), and even getting married. Lord and Lady Teksnes clearly enjoy playing host and do so with style.
Catering: In house

SERVICES:
- Exclusive Use
- Cake

Price Guide: £75pp - £500 for 2 days over Christmas and New Year.
Catering (sit down): from £30pp evening
Catering (buffet): from £12pp

The Old Rectory, Cheltenham
T: 01242 673766 **F:** 01242 676011
E: fesey@aol.com **W:** www.theoldrectory.com
Contact: Karen and Mike Fesemeyer, Proprietors

Party Max: 100   Bedrooms: 10 + 7

This 19th century former rectory offers views across the Severn Valley to the Malvern Hills. It is set in 2 acres of gardens in an Area of Outstanding Natural Beauty. The house offers 2 large reception rooms, a conservatory with a snooker table and a residents' bar. Parties have exclusive use of the house for the whole day. Wheelchair access is limited. As well as ten bedrooms (two with hand-carved 4-posters), the venue offers 8 cottages (4-crown rating).
Catering: In house

FACILITIES:
- Outdoor Pool
- Pool/Snooker

SERVICES:
- Exclusive Use
- Marriage Licence
- Toastmaster

- Piped Music

Price Guide: £300 - £1000 per day
Catering (sit down): from £21.95pp
Catering (buffet): from £12.95pp

The Old Vicarage, Nr Bridgenorth
T: 01746 716497
F: 01746 716552
E: admin@the-old-vicarage.demon.co.uk
W: www.oldvicarageworfield.com
Contact: Peter Iles, Owner

Party Max: 42   Bedrooms: 14

This Edwardian 3-star country house hotel stands in 2 acres of mature gardens and offers 14 spacious bedrooms and 4 coach house rooms. The award winning menus use fresh and organic produce locally sourced.
Catering: In house

SERVICES:
- Exclusive Use
- Marriage Licence
- Flowers
- Cake
- Piped Music
- Valet Parking

Price Guide: Prices range from £75 - £175 per room per night for accommodation.
Catering (sit down): POA

The Orangery, Towcester
T: 01327 858092
F: 01327 858009
Contact: Mrs Carol Sargeant, Owner

Party Max: 200 (marquee: 700)   Bedrooms: 120

New for 2001, and on the West Park private estate, is The Orangery, overlooking a private cricket ground and set in rolling private parkland which was once part of the royal hunting forest of Whittlewood.
Catering: In house

FACILITIES:
- Helipad
- Golf
- Indoor Pool
- Shooting
- Paint Ball
- Go Karting
- Gym
- Quad Bikes/Off Road
- Table Tennis

SERVICES:
- Exclusive Use
- Disco/Dance
- Performance Area

Price Guide: from £500
Catering (sit down): from £21pp
Catering (buffet): from £26pp

Painswick Hotel, Stroud
T: 01452 812160
F: 01452 814059
Contact: Helen Pugh

Party Max: 120 (marquee: 100)   Bedrooms: 19

This Grade II listed Palladian style stone building was formerly a rectory. It is set in its own gardens featuring a croquet lawn.
Catering: In house

SERVICES:
- Marriage Licence

Price Guide: Prices on application.
Catering (sit down): from £20.00pp

HEART OF ENGLAND

Pengethley Manor Hotel, Ross on Wye
T: 01989 730211   **F:** 01989 730238
Contact: Diana Thompson
Party Max: 85   Bedrooms: 25

This listed Georgian country house is set in 15 acres of gardens. The hotel boasts chef Ferdinand Van Der Knaap. An unusual event hosted here recently was on the theme of a Victorian Tea Party.
Catering: In house

SERVICES:
• Marriage Licence
Price Guide: Prices on application.
Catering (sit down): from £20.00pp

Penrhos Court Hotel, Hereford
T: 01544 230720   **F:** 01544 230754
E: daphne@penhos.co.uk   **W:** www.penrhos.co.uk
Contact: Daphne Lambert
Party Max: 120 (marquee: 100)   Bedrooms: 19

Dating back to 1280, there are three periods to the main house, including the great medieval Cruck Hall and an Elizabethan wing with oak beams. Penrhos prides itself on its organic produce which is grown in the Court's own garden. The Court has 19 bedrooms, two of which have four poster beds.
Catering: In house

SERVICES:
• Marriage Licence
Price Guide: Prices on application.
Catering (sit down): from £28.00pp

Pittville Pump Room, Cheltenham
T: 01242 523852   **F:** 01242 526563
E: jayneb@cheltenham.gov.uk
Contact: Jayne Bradley
Party Max: 300 (marquee: 75)

This neo-classical Grade I listed building is managed by Cheltenham Borough Council and houses the Cheltenham Spa waters. There are several rooms available. The Pump Room offers flexible menus, allowing guests to choose between courses on the day.
Catering: In house

SERVICES:
• Marriage Licence
Price Guide: Prices on application.
Catering (sit down): from £15.00pp

Polo Club Marquee, Westonbirt
T: 01666 890391   **F:** 01666 890519
E: catering@calcotmanor.co.uk
W: www.calcotmanor.co.uk/cateringhtm
Contact: Andrew Cole, Operations Manager
Party Max: 60 (marquee: 500)

Located between Royal Highgrove and Westonbirt Arboretum, the Polo Club Marquee can provide the perfect location for entertaining. This new function venue is a framed marquee, adjoining the clubhouse, with wooden floor, heating if required, and a view over the polo ground, where matches can be arranged. The marquee is available for hire throughout the summer. Food is prepared in a dedicated catering kitchen of Calcot Manor under the supervision of Chef Director, Michael Croft.
Catering: Contract approved list

FACILITIES:
• Helipad
SERVICES:
• Exclusive Use
Price Guide: £1500 - £2000
Catering (sit down): from £17pp
Catering (buffet): from £15.50pp

Prestbury House Hotel & Restaurant, Cheltenham
T: 01242 529533   **F:** 01242 227076
Contact: Jacqueline Whitbourn
Party Max: 70 (marquee: 100)   Bedrooms: 17

This 300 year old country manor house is Grade II listed and set in four acres of grounds.
Catering: In house

SERVICES:
• Marriage Licence
Price Guide: Prices on application.
Catering (sit down): POA

Prestwold Hall, Loughborough
T: 01509 880236   **F:** 01509 889060
E: henryweldon@hotmail.com   **W:** prestwold-hall.com
Contact: Henry Weldon, Events & General Manager
Party Max: 200 (marquee: 1000)

Prestwold Hall is a privately owned stately home available for private or corporate hire. The house itself, largely remodelled in 1843 and now Grade I listed, contains a lot of marble, Italian plaster work, fine 18th Century English and European furniture and a large collection of family portraits. The grounds, gardens and airfield can also be used and are suitable for clay pigeon shooting, motor sports and activity days.
Catering: In house

FACILITIES:
• Helipad   • Riding   • Shooting
• Go Karting   • Hot Air Balloons   • Outdoor Pool
• Quad Bikes/Off Road • Motorsports   • Archery
• Indoor Games   • Airfield
SERVICES:
• Exclusive Use   • Marriage Licence   • Disco/Dance
• Performance Area
Price Guide: £350 - £1600 per day
Catering (sit down): from £26pp
Catering (buffet): from £20pp

Queen's Hotel, Burton upon Trent
T: 01283 564993   **F:** 01283 517556
E: aardvark@bigfoot.com   **Contact:** Colin Roberts
Party Max: 150   Bedrooms: 38

This is a traditional 16th Century coaching inn in the town

HEART OF ENGLAND

centre. It has a 3-star RAC comfort award and is Grade II listed.
Catering: In house

SERVICES:
- Marriage Licence

Price Guide: Prices on application.
Catering (sit down): from £18.95pp
Catering (buffet): from £7.95pp

Renishaw Hall, Nr Sheffield
T: 01246 432310   **F:** 01246 430760
E: info@renishawhall.free-online.co.uk
W: www.sitwell.co.uk
Contact: Mr Peter William McGilben
Party Max: 120 (marquee: 200)

Renishaw Hall has been the family residence of the Sitwell family since the mid 17th Century. The grounds include an Italianate garden, which was laid out at the turn of the 20th Century and includes carp filled ornamental features, a Gothic temple and hidden gardens. There is also a lake, woodlands and caves. Functions take place in the Stable Block or a marquee.
Catering: In house

SERVICES:
- Marriage Licence

Price Guide: Prices on application.
Catering (sit down): from £15.00pp
Catering (buffet): from £10.00pp

Riber Hall, Matlock
T: 01629 582795   **F:** 01629 580475
E: info@riber-hall.co.uk
Contact: Pat Needham
Party Max: 70

Riber Hall is one of Derbyshire's old country houses, dating from the 15th Century. Features include a walled garden and orchard and it has been nominated by the AA as one of the most romantic hotels in Britain.
Catering: In house

SERVICES:
- Marriage Licence

Price Guide: Prices on application.
Catering (sit down): from £20.00pp

Ringwood Hall Hotel, Chesterfield
T: 01246 280077   **F:** 01246 472241
Contact: Joanne Cutt
Party Max: 150 (marquee: 400)   *Bedrooms: 24*

Ringwood Hall is set in 28 acres of gardens. Helicopters and hot air balloons can use the Hall grounds, which have also been host to firework displays.
Catering: In house

SERVICES:
- Marriage Licence

Price Guide: Prices on application.
Catering (sit down): from £15.95pp
Catering (buffet): from £6.95pp

Risley Hall Hotel, Risley
T: 0115 939 9000   **F:** 0115 939 7766
Contact: Functions Manager
Party Max: 160 (marquee: 200)   *Bedrooms: 16*

This 16th century Grade II listed building is set in five acres of gardens. The Baronial Hall, where wedding ceremonies can take place, was once the Prince of Wales' hunting lodge.
Catering: In house

SERVICES:
- Marriage Licence

Price Guide: Prices on application.
Catering (sit down): from £23.50pp

Rowton Castle Hotel, Shrewsbury
T: 01743 884044   **F:** 01743 884949
E: post@rowtoncastle.co.uk **W:** www.rowtoncastle.co.uk
Contact: Lynda Jardine, Events Manager
Party Max: 150   *Bedrooms: 19*

Rowton Castle is a Grade II listed building set in 17 acres of grounds. A castle has stood in the grounds at Rowton for nearly 800 years. It is now a 3-star country hotel, as well as a family home, and is luxuriously furnished. This impressive castle features rising turrets and a grand facade, plus a magnificent drive way which is guarded by an splendid Cedar of Lebanon. The building is romantically floodlit at night.
Catering: In house

FACILITIES:
- Helipad
- Hot Air Balloons

SERVICES:
- Exclusive Use
- Marriage Licence
- Toastmaster
- Disco/Dance
- Entertainers

Price Guide: £3000 - £3500 exclusive use (including 19 bedrooms and breakfast for 43 guests). Usual accommodation rates here are from £59 - £159 per room per night including breakfast.
Catering (sit down): from £20pp
Catering (buffet): from £12pp

Salford Hall Hotel, Evesham
T: 01386 871300   **F:** 01386 871301
E: reception@salfordhall.co.uk **W:** www.salfordhall.co.uk
Contact: Sally Pearce
Party Max: 100 (marquee: 150)   *Bedrooms: 34*

This Tudor manor is a Grade I listed building, restored 10 years ago. The hotel has two AA Rosettes for its cuisine. It is possible to take over the whole hotel, with a minimum of 34 bedrooms.
Catering: In house

SERVICES:
- Exclusive Use
- Marriage Licence

Price Guide: Prices on application.
Catering (sit down): from £30.00pp

Shakespeare Houses, Stratford-upon-Avon
T: 01789 201808   **F:** 01789 263138
E: tourism@shakespeare.org.uk **W:** www.shakespeare.org.uk
Contact: Norma Sweeney, Special Units Organiser
Party Max: 250

HEART OF ENGLAND

As well as the world famous Shakespeare's Birthplace and Anne Hathaway's Cottage in Stratford the Trust looks after Hall's Croft and Nash's House, both just a short walk from the RST, and also Mary Arden's House nearby. Each of the houses has its own distinctive character and appeal, and offers a unique setting for special events, which can include after-hours house and garden tours. Hire fees and catering arrangements vary with each property, but information is available on application.
Catering: In house

SERVICES:
- Exclusive Use
- Performance Area

Price Guide: Prices vary according to site - details on application

Sheriff's Lodge, Nottingham
T: 0115 924 0088 **F:** 0115 911 2225
W: www.sheriffslodge.co.uk
Contact: Sheila Harrod, Director/Owner
Party Max: 250 (marquee: 500)

This is a Victorian school which was refurbished 10 years ago to create a medieval style banqueting hall. Parking is available here for up to 50 cars.
Catering: In house

SERVICES:
- Exclusive Use
- Cake
- Live Music
- Performance Area
- Marriage Licence
- Toastmaster
- Entertainers
- Flowers
- Disco/Dance
- Piped Music

Price Guide: £150 - £1000
Catering (sit down): from £10pp
Catering (buffet): from £5pp

Shrewsbury Castle, Shrewsbury
T: 01743 361196 **F:** 01743 358411
E: museums@shrewsbury-atcham.gov.uk
Contact: Lynn Ford, Finance & Administration Officer
Party Max: 36

Originally built in the 11th Century of timber, Shrewsbury Castle holds a commmanding position on the only land approach to the town. It has been a private residence since the time of Elizabeth I and the restoration in the late 1700s was supervised by the young Thomas Telford. Many of the interior architectural features date from that time.
Catering: Contract (any)

SERVICES:
- Exclusive Use
- Marriage Licence
- Flowers

Price Guide: Weddings from £100. Other private hire by arrangement.
Catering (sit down): POA

Shugborough Estate, Nr Stafford
T: 01889 881388 **F:** 01889 881323
E: shugborough.promotions@staffordshire.gov.uk
W: www.staffordshire.gov.uk
Contact: Anne Wood, Sales & Events Manager
Party Max: 80 (marquee: 300)

The Shugborough Estate is the 900 acre home to the Earls of Lichfield, the present Earl being Patrick Lichfield; famous photographer and cousin of the queen. Shugborough is the ideal venue for conferences, meetings, corporate activities and activity days.
Catering: Contract approved list

FACILITIES:
- Helipad
- Hot Air Balloons
- Shooting
- Watersports
- Go Karting
- Quad Bikes/Off Road

SERVICES:
- Marriage Licence
- Piped Music

Price Guide: Lichfield Suite £11- £22.50 + vat + catering. Hire of Salon in evening from £750 + vat + catering. Major special events from £1000 + vat per day.
Catering (sit down): from £15pp
Catering (buffet): from £7pp

Silverstone Circuit, Towcester
T: 01327 320298 **F:** 01327 858268
E: nicola.Thompson@silverstone-circuit.co.uk
W: www.silverstone-circuit.co.uk
Contact: Nicola Thompson, Events Coordinator
Party Max: 300

Formula 1 motor racing is one of the most popular sports in the world and has made Silverstone a globally renowned venue. The Jimmy Brown Centre, where Grand Prix winners face the world's media is the main indoor facility at Silverstone and can accommodate up to 300 people. Place above the pit lane, the Jimmy Brown Centre looks out over the start line of the Grand Prix circuit creating an unique atmosphere. The venue also offers the British Racing Drivers' Clubhouse with a main reception area for up to 120.
Catering: Contract approved list/In house

FACILITIES:
- Helipad
- Hot Air Balloons
- Shooting
- Quad Bikes/Off Road
- Go Karting

SERVICES:
- Marriage Licence
- Performance Area
- Flowers
- Live Music

Price Guide: Event management for the day delegate package starts at £45pp. Day hire for the Jimmy Brown Centre starts at £2000, and £2500 for the Clubhouse.
Catering (buffet): from £15.25pp

Slade House Farm, Nr Ashbourne
T: 01538 308123
F: 01538 308777
E: AlanPhilp@sladehousefarm.co.uk
W: www.sladehousefarm.co.uk
Contact: Pat Philp
Party Max: 14

Slade House Farm, left unoccupied for over a quarter of a century, has been carefully restored and renovated, while still retaining the original character, to provide quality accommodation in three separate properties, each within its own garden set in 7 acres of farmland and an idyllic peaceful location.
Catering: Self catering

FACILITIES:
- Table Tennis

HEART OF ENGLAND

SERVICES:
- Exclusive Use
- Flowers

Price Guide: £350 - £2000

Stapleford Park, Nr Melton Mowbray
T: 01572 787522 **F:** 01572 787651
E: ae-events@stapleford.co.uk **W:** www.stapleford.co.uk
Contact: Lucy Swift, Special Events Coordinator

Party Max: 150 | Bedrooms: 51

This well-known Grade II listed building, now a 4-star hotel, is set in grounds designed by Capability Brown. The Orangery (max 150) and the Morning Room (max 26) are available for wedding ceremonies on any day of the year except Christmas, New Year, Easter and Bank Holidays. Numerous other rooms are available for functions, including The Grand Hall (300) and the Mews (12). The Old Kitchen is perhaps one of the most interesting rooms and seats 26 for dinner. Stapleford has its own Clarins Spa, with other facilities inlcuding shooting, falconry, riding and Jonathan Palmer's Motorsport Experience. More unusual activities offered include Sumo Wrestling, Carriage Riding, Giant Scalexttric and Pork Pie Making!

Catering: In house

FACILITIES:
- Helipad
- Indoor Pool
- Tennis
- Croquet
- Fishing
- Golf
- Shooting
- Cycling
- Petanque
- Falconry
- Riding
- Gym
- Pork Pie Making!
- Horseshoes
- Spa

SERVICES:
- Exclusive Use
- Cake
- Valet Parking
- Marriage Licence
- Disco/Dance
- Flowers
- Piped Music

Price Guide: £100 - £2000 + vat
Exclusive hire costs from £13,500 to £18,500 + vat
Catering (sit down): from £28pp
Catering (buffet): from £28pp

Stratton House Hotel, Cirencester
T: 01285 651761
Contact: Claire Mallen

Party Max: 140 | Bedrooms: 41

This country house hotel is set in its own grounds near Cirencester.

Catering: In house

SERVICES:
- Marriage Licence

Price Guide: Prices on application.
Catering (sit down): POA

Sudeley Castle, Nr Cheltenham
T: 01242 602308 **F:** 01242 602959
E: marketing@sudeley.org.uk
Contact: Erica Jones, Marketing Officer

Party Max: 200 (marquee: 1000) | Bedrooms: 29

Located in the heart of the Cotswolds and set in gardens an 80 acres of parkland, Sudeley Castle is home to Lord and Lady Ashcombe, has royal connections going back over 1000 years and was once the palace of Queen Katherine Parr. The Castle offers several function rooms including the Banqueting Hall, with high ceilings, exposed beams and open fire, and the Chandos Hall, a converted Georgian smithy. The Library is also available for a limited number of special occasions each year. The Castle also offers 14 self-catering cottages.

Catering: In house

FACILITIES:
- Helipad
- Go Karting
- Shooting
- Hot Air Balloons
- Paint Ball
- Quad Bikes/Off Road

SERVICES:
- Exclusive Use
- Valet Parking
- Flowers
- Cake

Price Guide: £250 - £1000+
Catering (sit down): from £30.20pp
Catering (buffet): from £11.50pp

Sweeney Hall Hotel, Oswestry
T: 01691 652 450 **F:** 01691 652 805
Contact: Sean Evans

Party Max: 130 | Bedrooms: 9

This is a Grade II listed Georgian country house set in its own grounds and parkland.

Catering: In house

SERVICES:
- Marriage Licence

Price Guide: Prices on application.
Catering (sit down): from £14.25pp
Catering (buffet): from £6.00pp

Swinfen Hall Hotel, Nr Lichfield
T: 01543 481494 **F:** 01543 480341
E: swinfen.hall@virgin.net
Contact: Neil Atkinson, General Manager

Party Max: 120 | Bedrooms: 19

Swinfen Hall is a beautiful Georgian manor house set in quiet Staffordshire countryside, 2 miles south of Lichfield.

Catering: In house

FACILITIES:
- Tennis

SERVICES:
- Marriage Licence
- Valet Parking
- Piped Music
- Performance Area

Price Guide: £45 - £1000+
Catering (sit down): from £27.50pp
Catering (buffet): from £14pp

Talbot House, Glossop
T: 01457 852006
F: 01457 852006
Contact: Annette Beever

Party Max: 120 (marquee: yes)

This characterful Victorian House set in grounds with woodland and a terraced garden and pond, is located close to the town centre.

Catering: In house

HEART OF ENGLAND

SERVICES:
- Marriage Licence

Price Guide: Prices on application.
Catering (sit down): from £11.00pp
Catering (buffet): from £4.50pp

Tewkesbury Park Hotel, Tewkesbury
T: 01684 295405 **F:** 01684 292386
Contact: Jodie Smith or Sarah Nockton
Party Max: 200 (marquee: 200)   Bedrooms: 78

This a Golf and Country Club set in 176 acres of parkland. Numerous services can be organised including fireworks, cars and helicopters.
Catering: In house

FACILITIES:
- Helipad
- Golf

SERVICES:
- Marriage Licence
- Fireworks

Price Guide: Prices on application.
Catering (sit down): from £18.50pp
Catering (buffet): from £15.00pp

Thornbury Castle, Thornbury
T: 01454 281182 **F:** 01454 416188
Contact: Wendy Patterson
Party Max: 65 (marquee: 250)   Bedrooms: 18

This former Tudor castle is now run as an award-winning hotel and restaurant. It still retains a vineyard and walled gardens within its 15 acres. The restaurant has two, baronial style, dining rooms. The top catering package here includes 8-course banquets.
Catering: In house

SERVICES:
- Marriage Licence

Price Guide: Prices on application.
Catering (sit down): £23.00 - 58.75pp

Thornescroft Restaurant, Wolverhampton
T: 01902 700253
F: 01902 700853
Contact: Thomas Clarke, Director and Head Chef
Party Max: 150 (marquee: 200)

Seven miles from Wolverhampton and set in landscaped gardens, this Georgian farmhouse, built in around 1750, is now converted to an a la carte restaurant serving traditional and more modern continental cuisine. Other than catering, there is no additional hire fee for this venue, although exclusive use is by agreement only.
Catering: In house

FACILITIES:
- Helipad

SERVICES:
- Exclusive Use
- Marriage Licence
- Toastmaster
- Disco/Dance
- Piped Music
- Performance Area

Price Guide: No venue hire fee.
Catering (sit down): from £16.95pp
Catering (buffet): from £9.95pp

Towcester Racecourse, Towcester
T: 01327 353414 **F:** 01327 358534
E: towcester-races.demon.co.uk
Contact: Maria Billingham
Party Max: 250 (marquee: unlimited)

Towcester boasts a building of outstanding architectural excellence overlooking one of Britain's most picturesque racecourses. Helicopters can land on site here.
Catering: In house

FACILITIES:
- Helipad

SERVICES:
- Marriage Licence

Price Guide: Prices on application.
Catering (sit down): from £25.00pp

Trentham Gardens, Stoke on Trent
T: 01782 657341 **F:** 01782 644536
Contact: Karen Nixon
Party Max: 1000 (marquee: 1000)

This conference and leisure centre is set in a 750 acres estate featuring Italian gardens. Three rooms are available (from 50 to 1000 guests), on any day of the year.
Catering: In house

SERVICES:
- Marriage Licence

Price Guide: Prices on application.
Catering (sit down): from £15.00pp
Catering (buffet): from £6.00pp

The Tunnel House, Cirencester
T: 01285 770280 **F:** 01285 770120
Contact: Pam Glazier,
Party Max: 130

The Tunnel House Inn and Barn is set in 4 acres of land beside the Thames Severn Canal in an area of outstanding natural beauty.
Catering: In house

SERVICES:
- Marriage Licence

Price Guide: Prices on application.
Catering (sit down): from £20.00pp
Catering (buffet): from £10.00pp

Uttoxeter Racecourse, Uttoxeter
T: 01889 562561 **F:** 01889 562786
E: info@uttoxeterracecourse.co.uk
W: www.uttoxeterracecourse.co.uk
Contact: Lisa Needham, Commercial Executive
Party Max: 400 (marquee: unlimited)

Uttoxeter has been voted regional racecourse of the year for the last 10 years. It is set in 60 acres in the picturesque Dove Valley, with facilities including an exhibition hall, two large restaurants and 50 other rooms of varying sizes. Packages can include private box with closed circuit television, free bar and club admission badges, while services can include behind the scenes tours.
Catering: Contract approved list/In house

HEART OF ENGLAND

FACILITIES:
- Helipad

SERVICES:
- Marriage Licence

Price Guide: £200 - £2000 per day.
Catering (sit down): from £25pp
Catering (buffet): from £15pp

Warwick Castle, Warwick
T: 01926 495421 F: 01926 406611
W: www.warwick-castle.co.uk
Contact: Sales Department
Party Max: 200 (marquee: 2000)

Warwick Castle stands above the banks of the River Avon and was first fortified by William the Conqueror in 1068. The Castle spans 9 centuries of war and peace, with different parts of the castle echoing different periods in history from Medieval to Victorian times. You may hire the vaulted undercorft for a vibrant medieval feast for example, the 18th Stables or State Dining Room, the 14th Century Great Hall, or you may learn about Victorian life at a Royal Weekend Party. Alternatively you may use the 60 acres of grounds landscaped by Capability Brown. Warwick also offers a full corporate hospitality and event management service.
Catering: Contract approved list

FACILITIES:
- Helipad

SERVICES:
- Exclusive Use   • Flowers   • Cake
- Toastmaster   • Disco/Dance   • Live Music
- Entertainers   • Fireworks   • Piped Music
- Performance Area

Price Guide: Prices vary depend on function. Medieval feasts start at £49.50pp with a facility fee of £1200. Formal dinners in the Great Hall start at £39.50pp plus a £4500 facility fee.
Catering (sit down): from £39.50pp
Catering (buffet): from £39.50pp

West Park House, Towcester
T: 01327 857336
F: 01327 857336
Contact: Mrs Carol Sargeant, Owner
Party Max: 000 (marquee: 200)   Bedrooms: 120

This country house and gardens and set in rolling parkland which was once part of the royal hunting Forest of Whittlewood. It is available for exclusive hire.
Catering: In house

FACILITIES:
- Helipad   • Golf   • Indoor Pool
- Shooting   • Paint Ball   • Go Karting
- Gym   • Quad Bikes/Off Road

SERVICES:
- Exclusive Use   • Marriage Licence • Disco/Dance
- Performance Area

Price Guide: from £500.
Catering (sit down): from £21.95
Catering (buffet): from £26.75

Weston Park, Nr Shifnal
T: 01952 852100 F: 01952 850430
E: enquiries@weston-park.com
W: www.weston-park.com
Contact: Alison Robbins, Sales & Marketing Manager
Party Max: 150 (marquee: unlimited)   Bedrooms: 28

Weston Park, seat of the Earls of Bradford, is a 17th Century building set in 2000 acres of parkland, with landscaped grounds designed by Capability Brown in the 18th Century. The house has had many noted visitors, and was chosen by the Prime Minister, Tony Blair for the Retreat Day of the G8 Summit in 1998. Now held in trust for the nation by The Weston park Foundation, the venue is only available on an exclusive use basis. All accommodation is based on taking a minimum of 12 rooms.
Catering: In house

FACILITIES:
- Helipad   • Shooting   • Hot Air Balloons
- Quad Bikes/Off Road

SERVICES:
- Exclusive Use   • Marriage Licence • Flowers
- Toastmaster   • Valet Parking

Price Guide: Residential conference rates start at £185pp. Without accommodation rates start at £800 (facility fee) for private dining in The Orangery.
Catering (sit down): from £45pp
Catering (buffet): from £25pp

Wood Norton Hall, Evesham
T: 01386 420007
F: 01386 420679
E: woodnortonhall.info@bbc.co.uk
W: www.woodnortonhall.co.uk
Contact: Susie Sedgwick, Event Coordinator
Party Max: 55 (marquee: 150)   Bedrooms: 45

This Grade II listed country house is set in 170 acres of Worcestershire countryside, 2 miles north west of Evesham on the edge of the Cotswolds. Le Duc's restaurant has 2AA rosettes for fine food and there are 45 indivudualy decorated double bedrooms. The Hall has extensive original oak panelling and fabulous decor, winning the Heart of England Tourist Board Hotel of the Year Award 2000. The accommodation here includes a disabled suite.
Wood Norton offers several packages including hot air ballooning, helicopter breaks and even 'television presenter for a day' breaks.
Catering: In house

FACILITIES:
- Helipad   • Shooting   • Paint Ball
- Gym   • Hot Air Balloons • Tennis
- Outdoor Pool   • Pool/Snooker   • Quad Bikes/Off Road

SERVICES:
- Exclusive Use   • Marriage Licence • Cake
- Disco/Dance   • Valet Parking

Price Guide: £150 - £2000 room hire. Conference packages start at £40 per delegate for the Day Conference package.
Catering (sit down): from £19.50
Catering (buffet): from £19.50

HEART OF ENGLAND

Woodend Farm, Tewkesbury

T: 01684 299749 **F:** 01684 291554
E: cotswoldfarm@woodendfarm
Contact: Philip Workman, Owner

Party Max: 45

Woodend Farm is situated in a secluded position affording specatacular views across the Avon Valley and Cotswolds. All the properties for rent at the farm are Grade II listed and full of 16th and 17th Century character.

Catering: Contract (any)/Self catering/In house

FACILITIES:
- Hot Air Balloons
- Outdoor Pool
- Pool/Snooker
- Table Tennis

SERVICES:
- Exclusive Use

Price Guide: £100 - £2000.
Catering (sit down): from £13.50pp
Catering (buffet): from £16.50pp

NORTH WEST

Albert Halls, Bolton
T: 01204 334433   F: 01204 523945
E: sue.wilkinson@bolton.gov.uk
Contact: Sue Wilkinson, Customer Service Manager
Party Max: 300

This is a Grade I listed building set in the heart of Bolton, and offers a magnificent blend of Victorian architecture with good catering and technical facilities. The Albert can accommodate from 20-300 guests for banqueting, parties and wedding receptions, offering a variety of rooms.
Catering: In house

SERVICES:
- Exclusive Use
- Disco/Dance
- Piped Music
- Marriage Licence
- Live Music
- Performance Area
- Toastmaster
- Entertainers

Price Guide: There is no room hire fee for catered events. Otherwise, price depends on room used but starts at £30/hr (valid until 03/01).
Catering (sit down): from £15.70pp
Catering (buffet): from £6pp

Alderley Edge Hotel, Alderley Edge
T: 01625 583033   F: 01625 586343
Contact: Gaynor Holland, Function Co-ordinator
Party Max: 100   Bedrooms: 46

Originally a mill owner's private residence (1850), this country house hotel is set in its own grounds with views over the surrounding countryside. The hotel holds two AA rosettes for its food and has its own bakery.
Catering: In house

SERVICES:
- Marriage Licence

Price Guide: Prices on application.
Catering (sit down): from £22pp
Catering (buffet): from £10.95pp

Arley Hall & Gardens, Nr Northwich
T: 01565 777353   F: 01565 777465
E: arley@info-guest.com   W: www.arleyestate.zuunet.co.uk
Contact: Eric Ransome, Event Coordinator
Party Max: 100 (marquee: 200)

Arley Hall is the ancestral home and estate (over 2,000 acres) of Viscount Ashbrook. It is a mock Jacobean house, built in the 1840s, and features a Grade II listed hall, distinctive ceilings and wood panelling, and famous gardens.
Catering: In house

SERVICES:
- Marriage Licence

Price Guide: Prices on application.
Catering (sit down): POA

Ashton Memorial, Lancaster
T: 01524 33318   F: 01524 33318
Contact: Elaine Charlton, General Manager
Party Max: 120

The Ashton Memorial, a Grade I listed building, sits within the landscaped gardens of Williamson Park, on the hill overlooking Lancaster.
Catering: Contract approved list

SERVICES:
- Marriage Licence

Price Guide: Hire of the hall is from £400.
Catering (buffet): from £7pp

Astley Bank Hotel, Darwen With Blackburn
T: 01254 777700   F: 01254 777707
Contact: Nigel Ainscow
Party Max: 120 (marquee: 200)   Bedrooms: 37

The hotel is in a period house, built in about 1800, set in formal gardens and woodland extending to six acres. Live modern music is not permitted here, although a disco is possible.
Catering: In house

SERVICES:
- Marriage Licence

Price Guide: Prices on application.
Catering (sit down): from £20pp
Catering (buffet): from £18pp

Bartle Hall Country Hotel, Nr Preston
T: 01772 690506   F: 01772 690841
Contact: General Manager
Party Max: 500 (marquee: 200)   Bedrooms: 12

Bartle Hall is a Grade II listed building set in 16 acres of landscaped gardens and woodland.
Catering: In house

SERVICES:
- Marriage Licence

Price Guide: Prices on application.
Catering (sit down): £8 - £30pp

Belmore Hotel, Trafford
T: 0161 973 2538   F: 0161 973 2665
Contact: Carol Deaville
Party Max: 120   Bedrooms: 23

This privately-owned Victorian hotel, built in 1875, is set in mature gardens. The hotel has recently benefited from an extensive refurbishment and is now credited as a 4-star, 2 rosette establishment.
Catering: In house

SERVICES:
- Marriage Licence

Price Guide: Prices on application.
Catering (sit down): from £30.00pp
Catering (buffet): from £15.00pp

Blackpool Tower Ballroom, Blackpool
T: 01253 622242
Contact: Julie Fetterman
Party Max: 500

A major landmark, Blackpool Tower is a Grade I listed building. In keeping with the ambience of the building, an organist can be provided if required.

NORTH WEST

Catering: In house
SERVICES:
• Marriage Licence
Price Guide: Prices on application.
Catering (sit down): POA

Bolholt Country Park Hotel, Bury
T: 0161 764 3888 **F:** 0161 763 1789
Contact: Tracey Whaley, Conference Co-ordinator
Party Max: 400 (marquee: unlimited)   Bedrooms: 170

Set in its own private estate of approximately 50 acres, just two miles from Bury, one of the claims to fame for this listed building is that it is the birthplace of the first Dean of Harvard University. The original building has been extended with the addition of a leisure centre and tennis courts completed in 1996.
Catering: In house

FACILITIES:
• Tennis   • Leisure Centre
SERVICES:
• Marriage Licence
Price Guide: Prices on application.
Catering (sit down): from £23pp

Bowler Hat Hotel, Birkenhead
T: 0151 652 4931   **F:** 0151 653 8127
Contact: Greg Ballasty, General Manager
Party Max: 280   Bedrooms: 32

The hotel is a Grade II listed building and is set in 1.5 acres of gardens. The hotel is AA recommended.
Catering: In house

SERVICES:
• Marriage Licence
Price Guide: Prices on application.
Catering (sit down): from £16.95pp
Catering (buffet): from £9.45pp

Bramall Hall, Stockport
T: 0161 485 3708   **F:** 0161 486 6959
Contact: Events Coordinator
Party Max: 60 (marquee: 200)

This is a Grade I listed Tudor building. While there are in-house catering facilities, other caterers are also permitted.
Catering: In house/Contract (any)

SERVICES:
• Marriage Licence
Price Guide: Prices on application.
Catering (sit down): from £25pp

Brereton Hall, Sandbach
T: 01477 535516
F: 01477 533093
Contact: Ian Bell, Operations Manager
Party Max: 250

This Grade I private house, completed in 1585, is claimed to be the first brick built mansion in Cheshire. The ground floor is now reserved for functions.

Catering: In house
SERVICES:
• Marriage Licence
Price Guide: Prices on application.
Catering (sit down): £20 - £40pp

Bury Town Hall, Bury
T: 0161 253 6026
Contact: Graeme Ramsden
Party Max: 50

This is a 1937 Art Deco civic building with many original features. The Town Hall has four function suites on the first floor, which can cater for parties of up to 400: the catering for which is operated by Bury Contract Catering. In addition to standard fare, they are able to provide vegetarian and kosher dishes.
Catering: Contract approved

SERVICES:
• Marriage Licence
Price Guide: Prices on application.
Catering (sit down): POA

Capesthorne Hall, Macclesfield
T: 01625 861955 - 861221   **F:** 01625 861619
Contact: Gwyneth Jones, Hall Manager
Party Max: 150 (marquee: 600)

This privately owned house, with extensive lakeside gardens and woodlands, is affiliated to the Historic Houses Association and English Heritage. Availability is limited.
Catering: In house

SERVICES:
• Marriage Licence
Price Guide: Prices on application.
Catering (sit down): from £25pp
Catering (buffet): from £20pp

Chester Racecourse, Chester
T: 01244 323170   **F:** 01244 344971
E: kpaddock@chester-races.com   **W:** www.chester-races.co.uk
Contact: Kirsty Paddock, Events Manager
Party Max: 500 (marquee: 250)

Overlooked by the Medieval walls of the ancient fortress town of Chester, the racecourse hosts racing on 11 days of the year, but is available as a flexible venue on all other days.
Catering: In house

FACILITIES:
• Helipad
SERVICES:
• Marriage Licence   • Disco/Dance
Price Guide: £85 - £2600

Crabwall Manor, Chester
T: 01244 851666   **F:** 01244 851400
E: sales@crabwall.com   **W:** www.crabwall.com
Contact: Sarah Bolton, Banqueting Manager
Party Max: 80

Crabwall Manor is a country house hotel set in its own private

NORTH WEST

grounds. The 4-star hotel has won numerous awards every year since it opened in 1987, including 3 rosettes for its cuisine. Facilities include 17m indoor swimming pool, conference rooms and 4-poster suites.
Catering: In house

FACILITIES:
- Helipad
- Gym
- Indoor Pool
- Pool/Snooker
- Shooting

SERVICES:
- Marriage Licence
- Piped Music

Price Guide: Room hire starts at around £275. Overnight accommodation is from £90 for a double room.
Catering (sit down): from £27pp
Catering (buffet): from £18pp

Craxton Wood Hotel, Puddington
T: 0151 347 4000 **F:** 0151 347 4040
E: info@craxton.macdonald-hotels.co.uk
W: www.macdonald-hotels.co.uk
Contact: Emma Clarke, Conference Office Supervisor
Party Max: 400 (marquee: yes)   Bedrooms: 73

Craxton Wood is a period building set in 27 acres of woodland. It is part of the Macdonald Hotels group of hotels. The hotel has a 2 rosette restaurant, and barbecues on the lawn are popular here.
Catering: In house

SERVICES:
- Marriage Licence

Price Guide: Prices on application.
Catering (sit down): from £25pp
Catering (buffet): from £12pp

Crazy Horse Saloon, West Morecambe Bay
T: 01524 410024 **F:** 01524 831399
Contact: Sharon Leeson, Marketing Manager
Party Max: 300

The Crazy Horse Saloon is a western style saloon bar sited in an American theme park. In keeping with the theme, outdoor barbecues are a speciality at the Saloon. The venue can also provide themed characters such as cowboys and Indians.
Catering: In house

SERVICES:
- Marriage Licence

Price Guide: Prices on application.
Catering (sit down): from £10pp
Catering (buffet): from £5pp

Crewe Hall, Crewe
T: 01270 253333 **F:** 01270 253322
E: sales@crewehall.com **W:** www.crewehall.com
Contact: Kieran Parker, Sales Manager
Party Max: 350   Bedrooms: 25

This 17th Century Grade I listed mansion was owned by the Queen until 1998. Crewe Hall offers a variety of dining rooms in a period setting. Menus can be tailored to requirements. There are several highly decorated rooms including the Great Library, Carved Parlour and Drawing Room which are available for functions. This venue now offers 4-star accommodation.
Catering: In house

FACILITIES:
- Helipad
- Hot Air Balloons
- Shooting
- Tennis
- Go Karting
- Quad Bikes/Off Road

SERVICES:
- Marriage Licence
- Toastmaster
- Entertainers
- Piped Music
- Flowers
- Disco/Dance
- Fireworks
- Cake
- Live Music
- Photography

Price Guide: Prices on application.
Catering (sit down): from £12.95pp
Catering (buffet): from £12.50pp

Crown Hotel, Nantwich
T: 01270 625283 **F:** 01270 628047
Contact: Phillip J Martin
Party Max: 150   Bedrooms: 18

This Grade I listed building, built in 1583, is situated in the town centre. The Minstrels' Gallery and Royal Cavalier Room hold licences for wedding ceremonies.
Catering: In house

SERVICES:
- Marriage Licence

Price Guide: price comment
Catering (sit down): POA

Devonshire House Hotel, Liverpool
T: 0151 264 6600 **F:** 0151 263 2109
Contact: Jenny Moore, Conference & Banqueting Co-ordinator
Party Max: 350   Bedrooms: 54

Devonshire House is a Grade II listed building set in 1.5 acres of landscaped gardens. Devonshire House was Merseyside Hotel of the Year in 1997, NWTB Best Small Hotel 1998 and holds a four crown, highly commended, rating.
Catering: In house

SERVICES:
- Marriage Licence

Price Guide: Prices on application.
Catering (sit down): from £15.00pp
Catering (buffet): from £6.55pp

East Lancashire Masonic Hall, Manchester
T: 0161 832 6256 **F:** 0161 839 3775
Contact: Hans Riedlsperger, General Manager
Party Max: 200

Located in the centre of Manchester, the Masonic Hall, now a listed building, was completed in 1929. It features marble pillars and Spanish galleries. Two main suites are available for afternoon and evening receptions, while 6 smaller suites can accommodate fewer numbers of guests.
Catering: In house

SERVICES:
- Marriage Licence

Price Guide: Prices on application.

NORTH WEST

Catering (sit down): from £14.55pp

Flixton House, Flixton
T: 0161 912 3004   **F:** 0161 912 3040
Contact: Lettings Office
Party Max: 100 (marquee: yes)

Flixton House is set in parkland with its own Victorian walled garden. Kosher, Caribbean and Halal cuisine can all be provided. Unusual events here have included a Gothic themed wedding.
Catering: In house

SERVICES:
- Marriage Licence

Price Guide: Prices on application.
Catering (sit down): from £12.95pp
Catering (buffet): from £4.95pp

Garstang Country Hotel, Garstang
T: 01995 600100   **F:** 01995 600950
Contact: Karen Marsh
Party Max: 300 (marquee: 200)   Bedrooms: 32

This family-owned hotel and golf club is set in a quiet location. Various services can be arranged for you, including fireworks.
Catering: In house

SERVICES:
- Marriage Licence   • Fireworks

Price Guide: price comment
Catering (sit down): from £16.75pp

Gibbon Bridge Hotel, Preston
T: 01995 61456   **F:** 01995 61277
E: wedding@gibbon-bridge.co.uk
W: www.gibbon-bridge.co.uk
Contact: Janet Simpson, Managing Director
Party Max: 300 (marquee: 400)   Bedrooms: 30

The Gibbon Bridge Hotel is set in award-winning grounds overlooking the Longridge Fells in the heart of the Forest of Bowland.
Catering: In house

SERVICES:
- Marriage Licence

Price Guide: price comment
Catering (sit down): from £24.50pp

Granada Studio Tours, Manchester
T: 0161 832 9090   **F:** 0161 834 3684
Contact: Jenny Smith (0161 828 5444)
Party Max: 500

Functions can take place on the Baker Street set (from Sherlock Holmes), in the Rover's Return and Stables Restaurant, in the Baronial Hall, or the Starlight Theatre - (sadly not in the mock up of the House of Commons).
Catering: In house

SERVICES:
- Marriage Licence

Price Guide: Prices on application.
Catering (sit down): from £26.25pp package

Haigh Hall, Wigan
T: 01942 832895   **F:** 01942 831081
Contact: Ms Stazicker, Manager
Party Max: 400 (marquee: unlimited)

This is a Georgian house overlooking a golf course and the valley of the River Douglas. It is possible for hot air balloons and helicopters to use the grounds, upon discussion. Guests can arrive and depart by boat from the Leeds Liverpool Canal.
Catering: Contract approved list

FACILITIES:
- Helipad

SERVICES:
- Marriage Licence

Price Guide: price comment
Catering (sit down): from £11.40pp
Catering (buffet): from £5.60pp

Hartford Hall, Northwich
T: 01606 75711   **F:** 01606 782285
Contact: Lawrence Thompson, Manager
Party Max: 150   Bedrooms: 20

This former nunnery and manor house, which dates from the 16th Century, still retains many period features, and is set in its own grounds. In addition to more formal receptions, the venue offers informal midweek champagne specials (from £9.95pp) which are held in the garden, weather permitting.
Catering: In house

SERVICES:
- Marriage Licence

Price Guide: Prices on application.
Catering (sit down): from £20pp
Catering (buffet): from £15pp

Hulme Hall, Wirral
T: 0151 644 8797
Contact: Mr P Mortimer, Proprietor
Party Max: 550

This Grade I listed building is home to a banqueting hall which is available for functions.
Catering: In house

SERVICES:
- Marriage Licence

Price Guide: Prices on application.
Catering (sit down): from £14pp

Kilhey Court Hotel, Wigan
T: 01257 472100   **F:** 01257 422401
Contact: Catherine Briely
Party Max: 300 (marquee: 300)   Bedrooms: 61

The original part of this hotel is Victorian (1884), but it has since been extended. The hotel is set in its own grounds of around 10 acres.
Catering: In house

SERVICES:
- Marriage Licence

NOBLE'S PARTY VENUES GUIDE 1ST EDITION

NORTH WEST

Price Guide: Prices on application.
Catering (sit down): from £21.00pp

Knowsley Hall, Prescot

T: 0151 489 4827   **F:** 0151 480 5580
E: events@knowsley.com
Contact: Annie Hall, Event Manager

Party Max: 325   Bedrooms: 11

Knowsley has been the home of the Earls of Derby since 1380. This stately home, and apparently Europe's largest safari park, is now let on an exclusive basis. Catering here is by the One Michelin Star, 5-star hotel The Chester Grosvenor. The house can be let complete with butlers, maids and housekeepers.
Catering: In house

SERVICES:
- Marriage Licence

Price Guide: Prices on application.
Catering (sit down): from £32.00pp
Catering (buffet): from £26.00pp

Lancashire County Cricket Club, Manchester

T: 0161 282 4020   **F:** 0161 282 4030
E: sales.lccc@ecb.co.uk   **W:** www.lccc.co.uk
Contact: May Byrom, Senior Sales Co-ordinator

Party Max: 140   Bedrooms: 68

This world famous club, which was refurbished in 1997, and is located a few minutes from Manchester's city centre. Nearly all the rooms have a good view of the cricket pitch. Opened in 1999, the Old Trafford Lodge now provides 68 rooms; 34 of which overlook the ground. House wines start at £10.45 a bottle.
Catering: In house

SERVICES:
- Marriage Licence

Price Guide: Prices on application.
Catering (sit down): from £14.50pp
Catering (buffet): from £9.50pp

Leasowe Castle Hotel, Wirral

T: 0151 606 9191   **F:** 0151 678 5551
Contact: Mr Harding, Owner

Party Max: 200 (marquee: 400)   Bedrooms: 50

This listed building is 400 years old and set in five acres of land.
Catering: In house

SERVICES:
- Marriage Licence

Price Guide: Prices on application.
Catering (sit down): from £16.50pp
Catering (buffet): from £19.00pp

Leighton Hall, Carnforth

T: 01524 734474   **F:** 01524 720357
E: leightonhall@yahoo.co.uk   **W:** www.leightonhall.co.uk
Contact: Mrs C S Reynolds, Owner

Party Max: 100 (marquee: 200)

Exclusive use is available for this historic house on the edge of the Lake District. The earliest records of Leighton start in 1246, although the current house dates from 1763. Much of the house is in the neo-Gothick style of the early 19th Century. The house is set in traditional gardens featuring roses, herbaceous borders and a shrubbery walk.
Catering: Contract approved list

FACILITIES:
- Helipad
- Tennis
- Shooting
- Quad Bikes/Off Road
- Paint Ball

SERVICES:
- Exclusive Use
- Flowers

Price Guide: £800 - £1500 per day.
Catering (sit down): from £20pp
Catering (buffet): from £15pp

Mains Hall, Poulton-le-Fylde

T: 01253 885130   **F:** 01253 894132
E: enquiries@mainshall.co.uk
W: www.mainshall.co.uk
Contact: Reception

Party Max: 150 (marquee: 200)   Bedrooms: 12

This Grade II listed 16th Century manor house is set in 5 acres on the banks of the River Wyre, close to Blackpool and the Lake District. The Hall has a separate function room with dance floor, is is said to be ideal for house parties.
Catering: In house

FACILITIES:
- Helipad
- Shooting

SERVICES:
- Exclusive Use
- Disco/Dance
- Performance Area
- Marriage Licence
- Entertainers
- Cake
- Piped Music

Price Guide: Prices on application.
Catering (sit down): from £30pp
Catering (buffet): from £15pp

Manchester Town Hall, Manchester

T: 0161 234 3039
F: 0161 234 3242
Contact: Steve Lewis

Party Max: 500

This Grade I listed civic building offers several function rooms ranging from the smaller committee rooms (for 50 people) to the Lord Mayor's Parlour, Banqueting Room, Reception Room and Conference Hall (all for 150 people), and The Great Hall (for 500 people). The Great Hall features a 70 foot high ceiling bearing the arms of the principal countries and towns with which Manchester has traded. The walls are adorned with murals by Ford Maddox Brown. All catering requests can be provided apart from Kosher cuisine.
Catering: In house

SERVICES:
- Marriage Licence

Price Guide: Prices on application.
Catering (sit down): from £10.95pp

NORTH WEST

Marine Hall, Fleetwood
T: 01253 771141 **F:** 01253 771141
Contact: Michael Brook
Party Max: 400 (marquee: unlimited)

The Marine Hall is a 1930's period civic building, set right by the sea and with its own gardens.
Catering: Contract approved list

SERVICES:
- Marriage Licence

Price Guide: Prices on application.
Catering (sit down): from £12.00pp
Catering (buffet): from £6.00pp

Middle Flass Lodge, Nr Clitheroe
T: 01200 447259 **F:** 01200 447300
W: http://mflodge.freeservers.com
Contact: Joan Simpson & Nigel Quayle, Proprietors
Party Max: 30 *Bedrooms: 5*

Formerly a barn and cow byre, this building was converted to a restaurant and 4-diamond guest house in 1996. The Lodge is situated in the Ribble Valley in the heart of the Forest of Bowland; good walking country. The owners, one a former Head Chef, boast personal and professional attention.
Catering: In house

SERVICES:
- Exclusive Use

Price Guide: from £22pp per night b&b
Catering (sit down): from £18pp

Mill at Croston, Croston
T: 01772 600110 **F:** 01772 601623
Contact: Max Pierce
Party Max: 250 *Bedrooms: 46*

The Mill was originally a farm building that has now been converted to a 46 bedroom hotel with restaurant, bar and banqueting complex.
Catering: In house

SERVICES:
- Marriage Licence

Price Guide: Prices on application.
Catering (sit down): from £14.95pp

Mollington Banastre Hotel, Chester
T: 01244 851471 **F:** 01244 851165
Contact: Banqueting Manager
Party Max: 200 (marquee: 100) *Bedrooms: 63*

This country house dating from 1857 is set in over eight acres, which includes formal gardens, croquet lawns and tennis. Specialities of the house include a pig roast barbecue. The hotel has also arranged fireworks for wedding parties.
Catering: In house

FACILITIES:
- Tennis
- Croquet

SERVICES:
- Marriage Licence
- Fireworks
- Pig Roasts

Price Guide: Prices on application.
Catering (sit down): from £19.50pp

Mottram Hall Hotel, Mottram St Andrew
T: 01625 822135 **F:** 01625 828950
Contact: Helen Ventisei
Party Max: 220 (marquee: 600) *Bedrooms: 132*

This Georgian hotel is set in 270 acres.
Catering: In house

SERVICES:
- Marriage Licence

Price Guide: Prices on application.
Catering (sit down): from £27pp

Ness Botanic Gardens, South Wirral
T: 0151 353 0123 **F:** 0151 353 1004
E: ejs@liverpool.ac.uk
Contact: Dr Joanna Sharples, Business Administrator
Party Max: 160 (marquee: 200)

A late night liquor licence can be applied for if required at this venue. While no accommodation is available on the premises, a list of local accommodation can be provided.
Catering: Contract approved list

SERVICES:
- Marriage Licence

Price Guide: Prices on application.
Catering (sit down): from £18pp

Northcote Manor, Langho
T: 01254 240555 **F:** 01254 246568
E: admin@northcotemanor.com
W: www.northcotemanor.com
Contact: Craig J Bancroft, Owner
Party Max: 150

Northcote Manor is a country house set in its own grounds which provides a totally private setting for a special celebration. The Manor can accommodate 95 guests in the main restaurant, 40 guests in the Birtwistle Suite, Northcote's private dining room, with adjacent drawing room for pre-celebration drinks. Northcote Manor may be hired as a total takeover, including the 14 bedrooms. In 2000 Northcote was voted Independent Hotel of the Year by Caterer & Hotelkeeper magazine.
Catering: In house/Contract (any)

FACILITIES:
- Helipad

SERVICES:
- Marriage Licence
- Disco/Dance
- Piped Music

Price Guide: For exclusive use of the manor, a minimum spend of £5,500, excluding bar and bedrooms, would be expected.
Catering (sit down): from £27.50pp
Catering (buffet): from £22pp

Nunsmere Hall, Nr Chester
T: 01606 889100 **F:** 01606 889055
E: reservations@nunsmere.co.uk
W: www.nunsmere.co.uk

NORTH WEST

Contact: Malcolm McHardy, Director
Party Max: 70 (marquee: 250)   Bedrooms: 36

This historic hall is surrounded on three sides by a 60 acre lake. The room hire fee includes flowers and harpist.
Catering: *In house*

SERVICES:
- Marriage Licence

Price Guide: Room hire from £500.
Catering (sit down): from £26.50pp

Old Hall Hotel, Sandbach
T: 01270 761221   **F:** 01270 762551
Contact: C P J Reysenn, Director
Party Max: 120

This Grade I listed building features an original Elizabethan facade. The Tudor room is licensed for wedding ceremonies.
Catering: *In house*

SERVICES:
- Marriage Licence

Price Guide: Prices on application.
Catering (sit down): from £12.00pp
Catering (buffet): from £4.25pp

Olde England Kiosk, Darwen
T: 01254 701530
E: oldeenglandkiosk@btinternet.com
Contact: Mr B Winder, Owner
Party Max: 120

This curiously named venue is a listed building built in the mock Tudor style. It is situated in 75 acres of woodland with ornamental lakes and waterfalls.
Catering: *In house*

SERVICES:
- Marriage Licence

Price Guide: Prices on application.
Catering (sit down): from £12.95pp
Catering (buffet): from £4.75pp

The Orwell, Wigan
T: 01942 323034   **F:** 01942 242456
E: orwell@gofree.co.uk   **W:** wiganpier.co.uk
Contact: Dean McDonald, Director
Party Max: 400

The Orwell, a converted Victorian cotton warehouse situated on the canalside, is now a freehouse public house and function venue specialising in real ales and good food. It has two large function suites, late bars and full public entertainment licences.
Catering: *In house*

FACILITIES:
- Pool/Snooker
- 10-Pin Bowling
- LaserQuest

SERVICES:
- Exclusive Use
- Marriage Licence
- Disco/Dance
- Entertainers
- Piped Music
- Performance Area

Price Guide: A £100 room hire fee is charged for Saturday bookings between June and September. The resident DJ here charges £120 per function.

Catering (sit down): from £9.99pp
Catering (buffet): from £2.99pp

Park Hall Hotel, Chorley
T: 01257 452090
F: 01257 451838
Contact: Alison Wilcock, Wedding Co-ordinator
Party Max: 450 (marquee: unlimited)   Bedrooms: 140

Park Hall is set in 137 acres of grounds featuring a scenic lake and medieval banqueting hall. Helicopters and hot air balloons may use the hotel grounds. For those looking for a period feeling, however, the hotel can offer a medieval banquet with full entertainment.
Catering: *In house*

FACILITIES:
- Helipad

SERVICES:
- Marriage Licence

Price Guide: Prices on application.
Catering (sit down): from £14.95pp
Catering (buffet): from £9.95pp

Peckforton Castle, Peckforton
T: 01829 260930
F: 01829 261230
E: peckfortoncastle@peckfortonfs.net.co.uk
Contact: Mrs E Graybill, Owner
Party Max: 275 (marquee: 2000)   Bedrooms: 45

Peckforton claims to be the only intact Medieval-style castle in Britain. It was actually built during the Victorian era and is now Grade I listed and was used for the filming of Robin Hood. As well as medieval banquets, this secluded Castle can also arrange a barn dance or a concert harpist, or a professional disco.
Catering: *Contract approved list*

FACILITIES:
- Helipad

SERVICES:
- Exclusive Use
- Marriage Licence
- Disco/Dance
- Piped Music
- Performance Area
- Themeing

Price Guide: £750 - £2500+
Catering (sit down): from £22.95pp
Catering (buffet): from 2.95pp

Pickering Park Country House, Preston
T: 01995 600999
F: 01995 602100
E: hotel@pickeringpark.demon.co.uk
Contact: David Bush
Party Max: 150 (marquee: 100)   Bedrooms: 16

This country house is set in two acres of rural Lancashire parkland.
Catering: *In house*

SERVICES:
- Marriage Licence

Price Guide: Prices on application.
Catering (sit down): from £23.00pp
Catering (buffet): from £11.50pp

NORTH WEST

Quaffers Theatre Restaurant, Stockport
T: 0161 494 0234   **F:** 0161 406 6372
Contact: Norma Levy
Party Max: 1150 (marquee: 150)

This well known Northern venue has its own hydraulic stage system, which presents the most unusual and dramatic opportunities for the imaginative.
Catering: In house

SERVICES:
- Marriage Licence

Price Guide: Prices on application.
Catering (buffet): from £5.75pp

Queen Elizabeth Hall, Oldham
T: 0161 911 4071   **F:** 0161 911 3094
E: els.qeh.arts@oldham.gov.uk   **W:** www.oldham.gov.uk
Contact: Shelagh Malley, Systems and Administration Manager
Party Max: 1000

Situated at the foot of the Pennines, 5 minutes from the M62 (J20) and 20 minutes from Manchester city centre, this multi-purpose building offers flexibility and value for money. The Hall itself and two suites are available for hire.
Catering: Contract (any)

SERVICES:
- Exclusive Use
- Marriage Licence

Price Guide: Fees range from £40 - £88 for minimum 4 hours hire per suite to £165 for 8 hours hire of the Chadderton Suite when the Council's in-house bar and catering facilites are used. Modest additional charges are made for extra staff, hire of eqiupment and even Box Office ticket sales.
Catering (sit down): from £14pp
Catering (buffet): from £3.50pp

Raby House Hotel, Willaston
T: 0151 327 1900   **F:** 0151 327 1900
Contact: Sean McKenna, Events Manager
Party Max: 180 (marquee: 500)   Bedrooms: 10

This is a country house hotel, built in 1867, with lakeside views, fountains, waterfalls and gardens. Raby House has hosted 16th and 17th Century themed weddings.
Catering: In house

SERVICES:
- Marriage Licence

Price Guide: Prices on application.
Catering (sit down): from £15.00pp

Reaseheath College, Nantwich
T: 01270 613210   **F:** 01270 613286
E: carolp@reaseheath.ac.uk
Contact: Mrs Caroline Platt, Conference Co-ordinator
Party Max: 120 (marquee: unlimited)   Bedrooms: 18+

Dating from the 18th Century, Reaseheath Hall is now a further education college set in 12.5 acres of landscaped gardens featuring an ornamental lake. One of the main features of the interior of the college building is its panelled hall with sweeping staircase. In addition to the 18 bedrooms, student rooms can provide extra guest accommodation out of term time.
Catering: In house

SERVICES:
- Marriage Licence

Price Guide: from £100
Catering (sit down): from £15.00pp
Catering (buffet): from £15.00pp

Rosehill House Hotel, Burnley
T: 01282 453931   **F:** 01282 455628
Contact: Jacky Doherty
Party Max: 150 (marquee: 200)   Bedrooms: 25

This listed stone mansion features ornate architecture, including highly decorative ceilings.
Catering: In house

SERVICES:
- Marriage Licence

Price Guide: Prices on application.
Catering (sit down): from £19.50pp
Catering (buffet): from £7.50pp

Rowton Hall Hotel, Rowton
T: 01244 335262   **F:** 01244 335464
Contact: Mr P Parry, General Manager
Party Max: 180 (marquee: 400)   Bedrooms: 42

This country manor house, built in 1779, stands in 8 acres of award winning gardens. Helicopters and hot air balloons can make use of the grounds.
Catering: In house

FACILITIES:
- Helipad

SERVICES:
- Marriage Licence

Price Guide: Prices on application.
Catering (sit down): from £19.70pp
Catering (buffet): from £13.35pp

Royal Northern College of Music, Manchester
T: 0161 907 5289
F: 0161 273 7611
E: Allan.taylor@rncm.ac.uk
Contact: Allan Taylor, Events Manager
Party Max: 600

This arts centre and college of music has a licence for its main concert hall and can provide use of a Steinway grand piano and organ. Choir balconies and orchestral seating can also be made available.
Catering: In house

FACILITIES:
- Piano

SERVICES:
- Marriage Licence

Price Guide: Room hire from £500
Catering (buffet): from £7pp

NORTH WEST

Saddleworth Hotel, Oldham
T: 01457 871888 **F:** 01457 871889
Contact: Anthony
Party Max: 150   Bedrooms: 8

The Saddleworth Hotel was originally built in 1800 as a pack horse station. It is set in nine acres which includes woodlands and landscaped gardens.
Catering: In house

SERVICES:
• Marriage Licence
Price Guide: Prices on application.
Catering (sit down): £550 for 15 people

Sandhole Farm, Congleton
T: 01260 224419   **F:** 01260 224766
Contact: Veronica Worth, Proprietor
Party Max: 40 (marquee: unlimited)   Bedrooms: 17

This is a privately owned farmhouse, with a former stable block converted into 15 en-suite bedrooms. You can bring in your own caterer to Sandhole Farm, so we are unable to provide a price guide. A liquor licence can be applied for as required.
Catering: Contract (any)

SERVICES:
• Marriage Licence
Price Guide: from £225

Scaitcliffe Hall Hotel, Todmorden
T: 01706 818888   **F:** 01706 818825
Contact: Manager
Party Max: 250 (marquee: 300)   Bedrooms: 30

This 17th century listed country house is set in 16 acres of landscaped grounds. Brass bands are a speciality at the Scaitcliffe Hall Hotel, which also offers what it claims to be 'the best of modern British cuisine'.
Catering: In house

SERVICES:
• Marriage Licence
Price Guide: Prices on application.
Catering (sit down): from £16.95pp
Catering (buffet): from £4.95pp

Shaw Hill Hotel, Chorley
T: 01257 269221
F: 01257 261223
Contact: Mrs B Welding, Conference & Banqueting Co-ordinator
Party Max: 300   Bedrooms: 30

This is a Georgian mansion set in 92 acres of parkland. Function rooms include the Vice-President's Lounge and the Penina Suite.
Catering: In house

SERVICES:
• Marriage Licence
Price Guide: Prices on application.
Catering (sit down): from £18.25pp
Catering (buffet): from £7.00pp

Shireburn Arms Hotel, Nr Clitheroe
T: 01254 826518
F: 01254 826208
W: www.smoothhound.co.uk/hotels/shirebur.html
Contact: Steven Alcock
Party Max: 250   Bedrooms: yes

The Shireburn Arms is a Grade I listed building dating from the 16th Century, and claims unrivalled views over the Ribble Valley.
Catering: In house

SERVICES:
• Marriage Licence
Price Guide: Prices on application.
Catering (sit down): from £13.95pp
Drinks packages start at £5.45pp
Catering (buffet): from £6.50pp

Smithills Coaching House, Bolton
T: 01204 840377
F: 01204 844442
Contact: Mrs Fairclough, Office Manager
Party Max: 150

This Grade I listed building was originally the stables of the nearby Smithills Hall which dates back to the early 17th Century. Smithills provides a comprehensive brochure on the venue, including visuals of possible room layouts.
Catering: In house

SERVICES:
• Marriage Licence
Price Guide: Prices on application.
Catering (sit down): from £10.95pp
Catering (buffet): from £7.95pp

Sparkles Hotel, Blackpool
T: 01253 343200
F: 01253 345104
W: www.sparkles.co.uk
Contact: Mrs Sparkle, Owner (aka Su Ryan)
Party Max: 100   Bedrooms: 16

Sparkles is described by its owner as a 'giant Victorian doll' house', where each room (reception rooms and bedrooms) is decorated to a fairytale or fantasy theme. Rooms vary from The Chocoholic Room to luxury Teddy Bears' Picnic Suite or the Barbie Room. Not surprisingly, this venue is fast becoming known as the most unusual celebration hotel in the North West, with corporate parties, family celebrations and children's parties just some of the events that have been hosted here. The hotel can be hired exclusively, with a party designed around your requirements. The hotel has no alcohol licence, but guests may supply their own. The hotel is close to all Blackpool's major attractions.
Catering: Contract approved list / In house

SERVICES:
• Exclusive Use   • Flowers   • Disco/Dance
Price Guide: £90 - £3000+
Catering (sit down): from £25pp
Catering (buffet): from £16.50pp

NORTH WEST

Sparth House Hotel, Accrington
T: 01254 872263   **F:** 01254 872263
Contact: Shirley Tattersall
Party Max: 250 (marquee: 150)   *Bedrooms: 16*

The Sparth House is a listed building (1740) featuring period interiors and gardens.
Catering: In house

SERVICES:
- Marriage Licence

Price Guide: Prices on application.
Catering (sit down): from £17.00pp
Catering (buffet): from £7.00pp

Springfield House Hotel, Nr Preston
T: 01253 790301   **F:** 01253 790907
Contact: Mrs M E Cookson, Proprietor
Party Max: 150 (marquee: 200)   *Bedrooms: 8*

This is a Grade II listed Georgian building set within walled gardens.
Catering: In house

SERVICES:
- Marriage Licence

Price Guide: Prices on application.
Catering (sit down): from £19.00pp

St Mary's Chambers, Rossendale
T: 01706 223222 (venue) 01706 211368 (holding co)
F: 01706 231113 (venue) 01706 831818 (holding co)
E: boys@stmaryschambers.com or boys.holdings@virgin.net
W: www.stmaryschambers.com
Contact: Hilary Proud, Conference & Functions Manager
Party Max: 140

Nestling in the Rossendale Valley, yet only minutes away from the M66, St Mary's Chambers occupies an imposing position overlooking the Pennine Moors. This Grade II listed building has been lovingly restored to offer state-of-the-art facilities, providing the finest Conference & Banqueting Centre in East Lancashire.
Catering: Self catering/Contract approved list

SERVICES:
- Disco/Dance
- Performance Area

Price Guide: £15 - £19.50pp per day
Catering (sit down): from £13.75pp
Catering (buffet): from £5.95pp

Statham Lodge Hotel, Lymm
T: 01925 752204
F: 01925 757406
Contact: Reception
Party Max: 250 (marquee: unlimited)   *Bedrooms: 38*

This Georgian manor house is set in its own landscaped grounds featuring an 8-hole pitch and putt course. In the past the hotel has hosted medieval banquets, Caribbean weddings and Indian weddings. A discount is offered to guests who wish to stay overnight at the hotel.
Catering: In house

FACILITIES:
- Pitch & Putt

SERVICES:
- Marriage Licence

Price Guide: Prices on application.
Catering (sit down): from £17.00pp
Catering (buffet): from £5.50pp

Stirk House Hotel, Nr Clitheroe
T: 01200 445581   **F:** 01200 445744
Contact: Mr M Weaving
Party Max: 300   *Bedrooms: 50*

Originally a 16th Century manor house, Stirk House has landscaped gardens to the front.
Catering: In house

SERVICES:
- Marriage Licence

Price Guide: Prices on application.
Catering (sit down): £12.50 - 31.00pp

Sutton Hall, Macclesfield
T: 01260 253211   **F:** 01260 252538
Contact: R Bradshaw, Proprietor
Party Max: 100 (marquee: 150)   *Bedrooms: 10*

Sutton Hall is a listed, 16th Century, part timber framed building by the canal.
Catering: In house

SERVICES:
- Marriage Licence

Price Guide: Prices on application.
Catering (sit down): from £25.00pp

Tabley House, Knutsford
T: 01565 750151   **F:** 01565 653230
Contact: Peter Startup, Administrator
Party Max: 50 (marquee: unlimited)

Tabley claims to be the finest Palladian mansion in the North West. It was built in the 1760s and is st in a 4,000 acre estate which include parkland, marquee and events sites and 2 lakes. The house is now owned by The Victoria University of Manchester and contains the first collection of English paintings ever made, period furniture and Leicester family memorabilia. Rooms available for functions, such as meetings, concerts, lectures, weddings, etc include The Gallery, the 16th Century chapel and the Tea Room. The house is open to the public (Thurs - Sun + Bank hols) between April and October.
Catering: Self catering

SERVICES:
- Exclusive Use
- Marriage Licence

Price Guide: Prices on application.

Tatton Park, Knutsford
T: 01625 534400 - 534406   **F:** 01625 534403
E: tatton@cheshire.gov.uk   **W:** www.tattonpark.org.uk
Contact: Oliver Knapp, Events Manager
Party Max: 400

NORTH WEST

Tatton Park is one of England's most complete estates. It is managed by the National Trust and financed by Cheshire County Council. Its 2 historic houses are set in 1000 acres of rolling parkland with lakes, tree-lined avenues and herds of red and fallow deer. It also has award-winning gardens, a working farm, speciality shops and a programme of special events.
Catering: Contract approved list

FACILITIES:
- Riding

SERVICES:
- Marriage Licence

Price Guide: Prices on application
Catering (sit down): POA

Tree Tops Country House Hotel, Formby
T: 01704 879651   **F:** 01704 879651
Contact: Ann Marie Jackson
Party Max: 150 (marquee: 150)   Bedrooms: 100

This listed building was the former dower house to Formby Hall and is set in three acres of woodland. The hotel boasts a speciality in French and traditional English cuisine.
Catering: In house

SERVICES:
- Marriage Licence

Price Guide: Prices on application.
Catering (sit down): from £25.00pp

Warmingham Grange, Sandbach
T: 01270 526276 - 256257   **F:** 01270 256413
W: www.warminghamgrange.com
Contact: Christopher Wright, Proprietor
Party Max: 200 (marquee: 850)

Built by Lord Crewe, this Grade II listed Georgian house has its own gardens and views over the Cheshire countryside. Functions are held in Lancelots Garden Suite, with exclusive use of the main entrance and Georgian portico. This suite includes the Drawing Room, Conservatory and Champagne Terrace. The venue also offers the Brasserie on the Hill and Galahads Stately Barn.
Catering: In house

FACILITIES:
- Helipad
- Shooting
- Hot Air Balloons

SERVICES:
- Exclusive Use
- Marriage Licence
- Toastmaster
- Disco/Dance
- Live Music
- Entertainers
- Fireworks
- Piped Music
- Performance Area
- Valet Parking

Price Guide: No room hire fee if 50 diners in day in 100 in evening.
Catering (sit down): from £15.95pp
Catering (buffet): from £6.95pp

West Tower Country Hotel, Ormskirk
T: 01695 423328   **F:** 01695 424821
Contact: Mrs Brenda Williams
Party Max: 175   Bedrooms: 10

Once the home of a Liverpool shipping magnate, and built in 1785, West Tower has recently been fully restored.

Catering: In house

SERVICES:
- Marriage Licence

Price Guide: Prices on application.
Catering (sit down): from £17.0pp
Catering (buffet): from £9.95pp

White Lion Inn, Crewe
T: 01270 500303   **F:** 01270 500303
Contact: Mrs AJ Davies
Party Max: 65   Bedrooms: 16

Originally a Tudor farmhouse, the Inn has now been extended to offer a hotel, restaurant and bars; the heavily beamed lounge bar is in the original part of the building. Outside there are gardens and a bowling green.
Catering: In house

FACILITIES:
- Bowls

SERVICES:
- Marriage Licence

Price Guide: Prices on application.
Catering (sit down): from £17.00pp

Willington Hall Hotel, Tarporley
T: 01829 752321   **F:** 01829 752596
Contact: Mr R Pigot, Owner
Party Max: 75   Bedrooms: 10

This neo-Elizabethan manor house was actually built in 1825, and was converted to a hotel by the owning family nearly 20 years ago. The house is set in its own park with a lake. Sadly evening parties are not possible here.
Catering: In house

SERVICES:
- Marriage Licence

Price Guide: Prices on application.
Catering (sit down): from £18.00pp

Wincham Hall Hotel, Wincham
T: 01606 43453   **F:** 01606 40128
Contact: Sarah Psaila, Hotel Manager
Party Max: 160 (marquee: 800)   Bedrooms: 10

This period country residence is set in six acres of landscaped grounds with a walled garden and a lily pond.
Catering: In house

SERVICES:
- Marriage Licence

Price Guide: Prices on application.
Catering (sit down): POA

Winnington Hall, Northwich
T: 01606 784171   **F:** 01606 74873
E: bookings@winnall.dempn.co.uk
W: www.winnall.demon.co.uk
Contact: Susan Golden, Manager
Party Max: 200

NORTH WEST

This listed building is both a restaurant and conference centre. Winnington Hall claims to specialise in first rate food, and can provide balloons for parties.
Catering: *In house*

SERVICES:
- Marriage Licence

Price Guide: Prices on application.
Catering (sit down): from £40.00pp

Wythenshawe Hall, Wythenshawe
T: 0161 234 7780   **F:** 0161 234 7142
Contact: Rosemary Hamer, Sales Manager

Party Max: 120 (marquee: 300)

The Library and The Grandfather Room are available at this venue. While there is no accommodation on the premises, this venue has preferential rates with local establishments.
Catering: *In house*

SERVICES:
- Marriage Licence

Price Guide: Prices on application.
Catering (sit down): from £10.00pp
Catering (buffet): from £7.95pp

YORKSHIRE

Alder House Hotel, Batley
T: 01924 444777   **F:** 01924 442644
E: info@alderhouse.co.uk   **W:** www.alderhouse.co.uk
Contact: Clive Sowler, General Manager
Party Max: 100 (marquee: 100)   Bedrooms: 20
This is a privately-owned Georgian house hotel, set in over 2 acres.
Catering: In house

SERVICES:
- Marriage Licence   *Price Guide: Prices on application.*
Catering (sit down): from £15.95pp
Catering (buffet): from £6.95pp

Aldwark Manor Golf Club, York
T: 01347 838146   **F:** 01347 838867
Contact: Martyn Burns
Party Max: 120 (marquee: 150)   Bedrooms: 28
This Club is housed in a listed building, dating back to 1865. The Club offers traditional English fayre, and has a range of complete packages on offer.
Catering: In house

SERVICES:
- Marriage Licence
Price Guide: Prices on application.
Catering (sit down): from £32.00pp

Allerton Castle, Nr Knaresborough
T: 01423 331123   **F:** 01423 331125
E: garritts@aol.com   **W:** www.allertoncastle.co.uk
Contact: Helen Garritt, CoordinatorAdministrator
Party Max: 700 (marquee: unlimited)
This Grade I listed Gothic revival stately home, set in 200 acres of parkland, is only hired out on an exclusive-use basis. Lawned terraces and a reflection pool provide photo opportunities.
Catering: Contract approved list

SERVICES:
- Marriage Licence
Price Guide: Prices on application.
Catering (sit down): from £35.00pp + vat

Aske Hall, Richmond
T: 01748 823222
F: 01748 823252
E: mhairiMercer@aske.co.uk
Contact: Mhairi Mercer, Administrator
Party Max: 130 (marquee: 750)
Aske Hall is described as a Georgian gem, with chapel, follies, terraced gardens and a lake in Capability Brown parkland. A 13th Century Pele Tower and a remodelled Jacobean tower remain an integral part of the house. Aske is available for corporate entertainment, functions, artistic performances, as a film location, for outdoor pursuits, etc.
Catering: Contract approved list

FACILITIES:
- Helipad
- Shooting
- Paint Ball
- Hot Air Balloons
- Tennis
- Quad Bikes/Off Road

SERVICES:
- Exclusive Use
- Flowers
- Fireworks
Price Guide: £1500 (day) - £10,000 (week)
Catering (sit down): from £38pp   Catering (buffet): from £28pp

Bagden Hall Hotel, Huddersfield
T: 01484 865330   **F:** 01484 861001
Contact: Ryan Gill, General Manager
Party Max: 75 (marquee: 150)   Bedrooms: 17
This country house hotel, previously a mill owner's mansion, is set in 40 acres of parkland.
Catering: In house

SERVICES:
- Marriage Licence
Price Guide: Prices on application.
Catering (sit down): from £21.00pp

Beningbrough Hall, York
T: 01904 470666   **F:** 01904 470002
Contact: Assistant Property Manager
Party Max: 300 (marquee: 300)
This National Trust property is a Georgian hall set in 365 acres. It features many pictures on loan from the National Portrait Gallery, as well as a cantilevered staircase, fine furniture and porcelain.
Catering: In house

SERVICES:
- Marriage Licence
Price Guide: Prices on application.
Catering (sit down): from £18pp

Bertie's Banqueting Rooms, Halifax
T: 01422 371724   **F:** 01422 372830
Contact: Brett Woodward
Party Max: 250
This is a stone-built, listed and converted chapel.
Catering: In house

SERVICES:
- Marriage Licence
Price Guide: Prices on application.
Catering (sit down): POA

Bolton Castle, Leyburn
T: 01969 623981   **F:** 01969 623332
E: harry@boltoncastle.co.uk   **W:** www.boltoncastle.co.uk
Contact: Melanie Devine, Castle Administrator
Party Max: 200 (marquee: 100)
Bolton is a Medieval castle overlooking Wensleydale. It boasts superb views and its own Medieval herb and flower garden. Naturally Medieval banquets are a speciality here.
Catering: Contract (any)

SERVICES:
- Marriage Licence
Price Guide: Prices on application.
Catering (sit down): from £25.00pp
Catering (buffet): from £15.00pp

YORKSHIRE

Bretton Hall, Wakefield
T: 01924 832044   **F:** 01924 832044
Contact: Lesley Entwhistle, Events Co-ordinator
Party Max: 200 (marquee: 600)   Bedrooms: 150

Bretton Hall is a university college and 18th Century Palladian mansion. It is set in 500 acres of lakes, woods and parkland and has a marriage licence for its Music Room.
Catering: In house

SERVICES:
- Marriage Licence

Price Guide: Prices on application.
Catering (sit down): from £21.00pp
Catering (buffet): from £12.50pp

Bridge Inn Hotel, Wetherby
T: 01937 580115
F: 01937 580556
E: bridge.walshford@virgin.net
W: www.thebridgeinnhotel.co.uk
Contact: Beverley Wilks
Party Max: 175   Bedrooms: 30

This independently owned, ranch style hotel, dating from 16th Century. The Byron Room offers Rococo plasterwork and is popular room for wedding ceremonies.
Catering: In house

SERVICES:
- Marriage Licence

Price Guide: Prices on application.
Catering (sit down): from £14.50pp
Catering (buffet): from £7.95pp

Cannon Hall Museum, Barnsley
T: 01226 790270   **F:** 01226 792117
Contact: Margaret Coope, Promotions Officer
Party Max: 80 (marquee: yes)

The Museum is housed in a 17th Century house, the former home of the Spencer-Stanhope family. It is set in 70 acres of historic parkland with walled gardens dating from the 1760s.
Catering: In house

SERVICES:
- Marriage Licence

Price Guide: Prices on application.
Catering (sit down): POA

Carlton Towers, Goole
T: 01405 861662   **F:** 01405 861917
E: weddings@carltontowers.co.uk
W: www.carltontowers.co.uk
Contact: Steven Randall, Events Manager
Party Max: 200 (marquee: unlimited)

This is a Victorian gothic country house is set amidst 250 acres of parkland. Five state rooms are available for events.
Catering: In house

SERVICES:
- Marriage Licence

Price Guide: Prices on application.
Catering (sit down): from £30.00pp

Cave Castle Hotel, South Cave
T: 01430 422245   **F:** 01430 421118
Contact: Bridgitte Carter, Functions Advisor
Party Max: 250   Bedrooms: 25

This listed manor house, with castle turrets, is set in formal gardens overlooking a large lake.
Catering: In house

SERVICES:
- Marriage Licence

Price Guide: Prices on application.
Catering (sit down): from £17.00pp
Catering (buffet): from £7.50pp

Country Park Inn, Hessle
T: 01482 644336   **F:** 01482 644336
Contact: Lesley Quaker
Party Max: 400   Bedrooms: 8

The original part of the building dates back to the 1800s while the Function Suite is a modern addition. The Function Suite is actually set on the banks of the Humber, which is only a matter of inches away at high tide.
Catering: In house

SERVICES:
- Marriage Licence

Price Guide: Prices on application.
Catering (sit down): from £8.50pp

Craiglands Hotel, Ilkley
T: 01943 430001   **F:** 01943 430002
Contact: Frank Moss, General Manager
Party Max: 400 (marquee: unlimited)   Bedrooms: 60

Set amidst spectacular scenery, this Victorian building stands adjacent to the famous Ilkley Moor, set in its own 5 acres of grounds and gardens. There are 70 en-suite bedrooms, with discounts available for party guests.
Catering: In house

SERVICES:
- Marriage Licence

Price Guide: Prices on application.
Catering (sit down): from £23.50

Crathorne Hall Hotel, Yarm
T: 01642 700398   **F:** 01642 700814
W: www.arcadianhotels.com
Contact: Joanna Stokes
Party Max: 132   Bedrooms: yes

Crathorne Hall is an Edwardian building which was occupied by Lord Crathorne until 1977. It is now a luxury AA RAC 4-star hotel, part of the Arcadian Hotel Collection.
Catering: In house

SERVICES:
- Marriage Licence

YORKSHIRE

Price Guide: Prices on application.
Catering (sit down): POA

The Cutlers Hall, Sheffield
T: 0114 276 8149   **F:** 0114 279 8540
E: Brenda.andrews@sodexho.co.uk
W: www.sodexho.com
Contact: Brenda Andrews, Events Co-ordinator
Party Max: 600

Cutlers' Hall is claimed to be the finest livery hall in the north. It is a Grade II listed building in the heart of Sheffield with 7 rooms over 3 floors, decorated richly in golds, greens and reds. This venue can arrange most services. The contract caterer on site is Sodexho Prestige.
Catering: In house

SERVICES:
• Marriage Licence

Price Guide: Prices on application.
Catering (sit down): from £18.00pp
Catering (buffet): from £10.00pp

Devonshire Arms Country House Hotel, Skipton
T: 01756 710441   **F:** 01756 710564
Contact: Sarah Graham-Harrison, Sales, Conference & Banqueting Manager
Party Max: 120 (marquee: 500)   Bedrooms: 41

Originally a 17th Century coaching inn, the Devonshire Arms is now owned by the Duke and Duchess of Devonshire and enjoys a splendid setting in the Yorkshire Dales national parkland. The Devonshire Arms holds two AA rosettes for its cooking.
Catering: In house

SERVICES:
• Marriage Licence

Price Guide: Prices on application.
Catering (sit down): £25.00 - 32.00pp

Duncombe Park, York
T: 01439 770213   **F:** 01439 771114
E: sally@dumcombepark.com
Contact: Sally Potter, Wedding and Function Manager
Party Max: 600   Bedrooms: 45

Duncombe Park is a Baroque style stately home, built around 1713 and set in extensive grounds. Several richly decorated rooms are offered for events including The Salon and The Stone Hall (100 max), and the Ladies Withdrawing Room (seats 25).
Catering: In house

SERVICES:
• Marriage Licence

Price Guide: Prices on application.
Catering (sit down): from £42.00pp

Dunsley Hall Hotel, Crathorne
T: 01947 893437   **F:** 01947 893505
Contact: Steven Talbot
Party Max: 50 (marquee: 200)   Bedrooms: 17

Dunsley Hall is a country house hotel set in 4 acres of grounds.
Catering: In house

SERVICES:
• Marriage Licence

Price Guide: Prices on application.
Catering (sit down): from £12.50pp

East Riddlesden Hall, Keighley
T: 01535 607075
Contact: Liz Houseman, Assistant Property Manager
Party Max: 160

This National Trust Property is a 17th Century merchant's house. Features include embroideries, Yorkshire carved oak furniture, fine ceilings and stonework. In the grounds is an oak framed Great Barn, which has survived unchanged since the 1600s. Events here include costumed tours.
Catering: Contract approved list

SERVICES:
• Marriage Licence

Price Guide: £550 - £1600 + vat
Catering (sit down): from £20pp
Catering (buffet): from £10pp

Falcon Manor Hotel, Settle
T: 01729 823814   **F:** 01729 822087
W: www.thefalconmanor.com
Contact: Philip Atherton, Managing Director
Party Max: 100   Bedrooms: 19

The Falcon Manor is a listed building and is set in its own landscaped gardens.
Catering: In house

SERVICES:
• Marriage Licence

Price Guide: Prices on application.
Catering (sit down): POA
Catering (buffet): POA

Grange Hotel, Whitby
T: 01904 644744
F: 01904 612453
E: info@grangehotel.co.uk
W: www.grangehotel.co.uk
Contact: Shara Ross
Party Max: 100   Bedrooms: 30

The Grange is a Regency townhouse with 3 function rooms; the Green Room, the Morning Room, and the Library/Drawing Room (which does not have wheelchair access). The Library and Drawing Room with french windows, or the Green Room can be used for receptions or guests may have exclusive use of the Restaurant.
Catering: In house

SERVICES:
• Exclusive Use   • Marriage Licence

Price Guide: Prices on application.
Catering (sit down): from £10.50pp

YORKSHIRE

Haley's Hotel, Headingley
T: 0113 278 4446　　**F:** 0113 275 3342
E: info@haleys.co.uk　　**W:** www.haleys.co.uk
Contact: Pauline Cowie, Conference Co-ordinator

Party Max: 100　　*Bedrooms: 29*

Haleys Hotel claims to be a country house hotel in the city. This award winning Victorian town house boasts plush soft furnishings, fresh flowers and fine antiques and is available for exclusive use for afternoon and evening functions.

Catering: In house

SERVICES:
- Exclusive Use
- Marriage Licence

Price Guide: Prices on application.
Catering (sit down): from £24.00pp

Hazlewood Castle, Tadcaster
T: 01937 535313　　**F:** 01937 535316
E: info@hazlewood-castle.co.uk
W: www.hazlewood-castle.co.uk
Contact: Emma Davison, Assistant Business Development Manager

Party Max: 300 (marquee: 600)　　*Bedrooms: 21*

This fortified, former Knight's residence is set in 77 acres of protected woodland and parkland. The listed building now offers 3-star accommodation and boasts celebrity chef John Benson-Smith, plus a cookery school.

Catering: In house

FACILITIES:
- Helipad

SERVICES:
- Exclusive Use
- Disco/Dance
- Live Music
- Entertainers
- Piped Music
- Valet Parking

Price Guide: £700 - £3000
Catering (sit down): from £30pp
Catering (buffet): from £25pp

Heath Cottage Hotel, Dewsbury
T: 01924 465399　　**F:** 01924 459405
Contact: Mrs Williamson

Party Max: 150　　*Bedrooms: 29*

This is a privately owned and managed hotel and restaurant. It was built in 1850 and is said to be a fine example of early Victorian architecture.

Catering: In house

SERVICES:
- Marriage Licence

Price Guide: Prices on application.
Catering (sit down): from £19.00pp
Catering (buffet): from £16.00pp

Hellaby Hall Hotel, Rotherham
T: 01709 702701　　**F:** 01709 700979
E: hellabyhallreservations@paramount-hotels.co.uk
W: www.PARAMOUNT-hotels.co.uk
Contact: Paula Jennings, House Manager

Party Max: 106　　*Bedrooms: 52*

This hotel is housed in a 17th Century country house with private walled gardens.

Catering: In house

SERVICES:
- Marriage Licence

Price Guide: Prices on application.
Catering (sit down): from £22.50pp
Catering (buffet): from £7.40pp

Holdsworth House, Halifax
T: 01422 240024
F: 01422 245174
E: info@holdsworthhouse.co.uk
Contact: Claire Nicholl, Conference and Banqueting Co-ordinator

Party Max: 150 (marquee: 50)　　*Bedrooms: 40*

This 17th Century Jacobean manor house is set in its own grounds. This three star hotel features a two AA rosette restaurant.

Catering: In house

SERVICES:
- Marriage Licence

Price Guide: Prices on application.
Catering (sit down): from £25.00pp

Hoyle Court, Shipley
T: 01274 584110
Contact: Mr & Mrs D T Blair

Party Max: 100 (marquee: unlimited)

This is a Grade II Edwardian Baroque house with a south facing terrace and stone steps leading to a sunken garden. This venue claims to be one of the UK's most prestigious Masonic premises.

Catering: In house

SERVICES:
- Marriage Licence

Price Guide: Prices on application.
Catering (sit down): from £15.45pp

Imperial Crown Hotel, Halifax
T: 01422 342342
F: 01422 349866
E: imperialcrown@corushotels.com
W: www.corushotels.com
Contact: Liz Baker

Party Max: 200　　*Bedrooms: 56*

This hotel, located directly opposite Halifax train station, features an unusual mix of Edwardian garden and an American Diner with Rock Memorabilia Nightclub.

Catering: In house

SERVICES:
- Marriage Licence

Price Guide: Prices on application.
Catering (sit down): from £18.00pp
Catering (buffet): from £7.65pp

YORKSHIRE

Knavesmire Manor Hotel, York
T: 01904 702941 F: 01904 709274
Contact: Karen Smith, Manageress
Party Max: 60   Bedrooms: 21
This Georgian house (1833) was once home to the Rowntree family.
Catering: In house

SERVICES:
- Marriage Licence

Price Guide: Prices on application.
Catering (sit down): from £15.00pp

Laskill Farm Country House, Hawnby
T: 01439 798268 F: 01439 798498
E: suesmith@laskillfarm.fsnet.co.uk
Contact: Mrs Sue Smith, Owner
Party Max: 33
Laskill Farm offers several self-catering cottages, in 3 distinct groups, as well as b&b for 11 in the farmhouse itself. The Barn conversion has 4 units sleeping from 2 - 6 (16 in total), The Granary is a stand alone unit for 4-6 and the Cottages at Keldhome each sleep 4 (12 together). All the properties have oak beams, stone fireplaces and central heating.
Catering: Self catering

Price Guide: Prices on application.
Catering (sit down): POA

Linton Springs Hotel, Wetherby
T: 01937 585353 F: 01937 587579
Contact: Suzy Bower or Linsey Rowbury
Party Max: 116 (marquee: 120)   Bedrooms: 12
This hotel is set in 14 acres of park and woodland.
Catering: In house

SERVICES:
- Marriage Licence

Price Guide: Prices on application.
Catering (sit down): from £26.00pp

The Manor House, Beverley
T: 01482 881645 F: 01482 886501
E: derek@the.manor.house.co.uk
W: www.the.manor.house.co.uk
Contact: Derek & Lee Baugh, Owners
Party Max: 60   Bedrooms: 7
The Manor House is a late 19th Century house which lies in a tranquil position on a wooded flank of the Yorkshire Wolds, and on the fringe of the Beverley Westwood; the medieval pastures which overlook the town. It is set in 3 acres of grounds overlooking a horse paddock and parkland.
Catering: In house

FACILITIES:
- Helipad

SERVICES:
- Exclusive Use
- Piped Music

Price Guide: £200 - £2000/day
Catering (sit down): from £18.50pp
Catering (buffet): from £25pp

Marsden Mechanics Hall, Marsden
T: 01484 844587
Contact: Bookings Officer
Party Max: 150 (marquee: 50)
This listed building in the centre of this Pennine village is situated close to the river and the village stocks.
Catering: In house

SERVICES:
- Marriage Licence

Price Guide: Prices on application.
Catering (sit down): POA

Merchant Adventurers' Hall, York
T: 01904 654818 F: 01904 654818
E: The.Clerk@mahall-york.demon.co.uk
Contact: Mr Finlay, Clerk to the Company
Party Max: 180 (marquee: 400)
This medieval building is situated right in the centre of York, within the city walls, and has its own garden with river frontage. There is a choice of caterers. Themes may include a medieval banquet in keeping with the setting. Drinking licences can be applied for as required.
Catering: Contract approved list

SERVICES:
- Marriage Licence

Price Guide: Prices on application.
Catering (sit down): from £5pp

Monk Bar Hotel, York
T: 01904 621261 F: 01904 629175
Contact: Sharon Terry
Party Max: 200 (marquee: yes)   Bedrooms: 99
The Monk Bar Hotel is only 300 yards from the centre of York and its Minster.
Catering: In house

SERVICES:
- Marriage Licence

Price Guide: Prices on application.
Catering (sit down): from £15.00pp
Catering (buffet): from £6.95pp

Mosborough Hall Hotel, Sheffield
T: 01142 484353 F: 01142 477042
Contact: Tracy
Party Max: 150 (marquee: 200)   Bedrooms: 24
This Grade II listed building offers the Stables and the hotel restaurant. These have varying sitting and standing capacities from 75 to 150.
Catering: In house

SERVICES:
- Marriage Licence

Price Guide: Prices on application.
Catering (sit down): from £25.00pp

YORKSHIRE

National Railway Museum, York
T: 01904 626227 F: 01904 686228
E: nrmevents@nmsi.ac.uk W: www.nrm.org.uk
Contact: Rowena Pericleous, Events Executive
Party Max: 800

The National Railway Museum claims the most extensive facilities for evening entertaining in York. Stretching for 16 acres, the buildings at the Museum provide an impressive selection of venues, including the Great Hall, Balcony Galleries, The Walker Conference Suite, Gibb Lecture Theatre and South Hall. Receptions for 20 to 500 guests take place on the central platform of The Great Hall, while the Edwardian Station Hall offers a unique location for dining: guests are seated at round tables on the central platform amidst carriages and locomotives. In-house actors here canbe hired to perform short humourous and informative plays - about trains of course. Several bands also regularly play here.
Catering: In house

SERVICES:
- Exclusive Use   • Marriage Licence   • Toastmaster

Price Guide: From £600 + vat for less than 50 guests in the Station Hall. Additional hire of the Great Hall is £100 + vat. Other prices on application.
Catering (sit down): from £25.50pp
Catering (buffet): from £16pp

Oakwell Hall Country Park, Birstall
T: 01924 326240 F: 01924 326249
Contact: Barbara Angell-Baker, Administrative Officer
Party Max: 100 (marquee: unlimited)

This 17th Century Elizabethan Manor (with Brontë connections) is Grade I listed. Furnished to the year 1690, it also features a period garden. This building has a civil wedding licence, while functions usually take place in the Oakwell Barn, which is a separate building. This must be arranged separately by the hirer.
Catering: In house

SERVICES:
- Marriage Licence

Price Guide: Prices on application.
Catering (sit down): POA
Catering (buffet): POA

Old Lodge Hotel, Malton
T: 01653 690870 F: 01653 690652
Contact: N Binner
Party Max: 180 (marquee: unlimited)   Bedrooms: 9

The hotel was built as a gate house to Malton House in around 1604 and is now a listed building. Three rooms are licensed for civil marriages including the Jacobean Main Hall.
Catering: In house

SERVICES:
- Marriage Licence

Price Guide: Prices on application.
Catering (sit down): from £20pp
Catering (buffet): from £6pp

Red Lion Hotel, Skipton
T: 01756 720204 F: 01756 720292
E: redlion@daelnet.co.uk W: www.redlion.co.uk
Contact: Elizabeth Grayshon, Owner
Party Max: 60 (marquee: 100)   Bedrooms: 12

The Red Lion is a 16th Century inn set on the banks of the River Wharfe in an unspoilt Dales village. The Inn features beamed ceilings and log fires. The Red Lion boasts AA rosettes and RAC dining awards.
Catering: In house

SERVICES:
- Marriage Licence

Price Guide: Prices on application.
Catering (sit down): from £20pp
Catering (buffet): from £10pp

Rock Inn Hotel, Halifax
T: 01422 379721 F: 01422 379110
E: the.rock@dial.pipex.com W: www.rockinnhotel.com
Contact: Catherine Steele, Manager
Party Max: 300   Bedrooms: 30

Set in four acres of breathtaking Yorkshire countryside, The Rock is situated in its own serene rural valley close to Brontë country. Dating back to the 17th Century, the Rock has been extensively refurbished in recent years. A dance floor and a disco are available here.
Catering: In house

SERVICES:
- Marriage Licence

Price Guide: Prices on application.
Catering (sit down): from £16.90pp

Rogerthorpe Manor Hotel, Pontefract
T: 01977 643839 F: 01977 641571
Contact: Raeley Stenton
Party Max: 400 (marquee: 200)   Bedrooms: 24

This Jacobean Grade II listed building has been restored to create a hotel of 24 bedrooms, an oak-panelled restaurant and two large function rooms. In addition to buffets and special menus, the hotel will strive to meet the religious or dietary requirements of guests.
Catering: In house

SERVICES:
- Marriage Licence

Price Guide: Prices on application.
Catering (sit down): from £5.75pp

Rombalds Hotel, Ilkley
T: 01943 816586 F: 01943 816586
E: reception@rombalds.demon.co.uk
W: www.rombalds.co.uk
Contact: Colin R Clarkson, Proprietor
Party Max: 70   Bedrooms: 15

This is an elegant Georgian building on the edge of Ilkley Moor. The restaurant here boasts 2 AA rosettes and and ETB Silver Award. Late night liquor licences can be applied for as required.

YORKSHIRE

Catering: In house

SERVICES:
- Marriage Licence

Price Guide: Prices on application.
Catering (sit down): from £19.50pp
Catering (buffet): from £10.95pp

Rowley Manor Hotel, Little Weighton
T: 01482 848284 **F:** 01482 849900
Contact: Barbara Sims, Manager
Party Max: 150 (marquee: unlimited) *Bedrooms: 16*

This listed Georgian country house is set in 34 acres of lawns, rose gardens and parklands and was once the rectory to St Peter's Church. The rectory is said to have been built in 1621, and in 1928 the house was purchased by a shipping magnate who commissioned the pine panelling by Grinling Gibbons which now forms such a feature in the study. The Manor boasts a selection of menus, including those that allow the guests to carve meats at their own table. The Manor specialises in fresh produce and fresh fish.

Catering: In house

SERVICES:
- Marriage Licence

Price Guide: Prices on application.
Catering (sit down): from £21.50pp

Rudding Park House & Hotel, Harrogate
T: 01423 871350 **F:** 01423 844848
E: sales@rudding-park.co.uk **W:** www.rudding-park.co.uk
Contact: Joanne McBratney, Events Co-ordinator
Party Max: 250 (marquee: unlimited) *Bedrooms: 50*

Rudding Park House is a Grade I listed Regency house, set in 230 acres and designed by Wyatt in 1806. It is now an award-winning residential conference and banqueting centre, with grounds featuring woodlands and ornamental lakes and a herb garden.

Catering: In house

SERVICES:
- Marriage Licence

Price Guide: Prices on application.
Catering (sit down): £40 - £50pp

Rudstone Walk, South Cave
T: 01430 422230
F: 01430 424552
E: office@rudstone-walk.co.uk
W: www.rudstone-walk.co.uk
Contact: Laura Greenwood, General Manager
Party Max: 60 (marquee: 200) *Bedrooms: 14*

Rudstone Walk is a 400 year old farmhouse in its own secluded corner of the Yorkshire Wolds, with magnificent views. Several rooms are used for functions including the Dining Room, and Function Room, as well as the courtyard. Murder Mystery dinner parties are popular here. The farmhouse offers catered or self-catering accommodation.

Catering: In house / Self catering

FACILITIES:
- Shooting

SERVICES:
- Exclusive Use
- Disco/Dance
- Marriage Licence
- Piped Music
- Toastmaster
- Performance Area

Price Guide: £275 - £3000
Catering (sit down): from £22.50pp
Catering (buffet): from £9.50pp

Sewerby Hall and Gardens, Sewerby
T: 01262 677874 **F:** 01262 674265
E: sewerbyhall@yahoo.com
W: www.bridlington.net/sewerby
Contact: Graeme Harvey, Clerical Officer
Party Max: 80

Situated in a dramatic cliff-top position, forming the gateway to the Flamborough Heritage Coast, Sewerby Hall and Gardens, set in 50 acres of early 19th century parkland, enjoys views over Bridlington Bay. The features an Orangery, art and photographic galleries, period rooms, an Amy Johnson room displaying a collection of her awards, trophies and momentos, the History of East Yorkshire permanent display, Mayor's Parlour ad Mayoral Regalia displays, Trevor Field Trust Art Gallery and Bridlington Promenade Art Gallery. The gardens include a walled garden, pleasure gardens and a bandstand. The Hall is run by East Riding of Yorkshire Council.

Catering: In house

FACILITIES:
- Golf

SERVICES:
- Exclusive Use
- Marriage Licence

Price Guide: Venue hire is £10 - £15 per hour.
Catering (sit down): from £3.95
Catering (buffet): from £3.95

Sheffield Theatres, Sheffield
T: 0114 249 5999 **F:** 0114 201 3821
Contact: Glennys Hughes, Development Manager
Party Max: 200

Sheffield Theatres includes home to the World Snooker Championships, The Crucible. The theatres are located in the centre of Sheffield in a Grade II listed building. Special effects on stage can be created, while other services offered by the theatre include name cards, menus and seating plans, as well as table decorations.

Catering: In house

SERVICES:
- Marriage Licence

Price Guide: Prices on application.
Catering (sit down): from £22.95pp
Catering (buffet): from £13.95pp

Sheffield Wednesday FC, Sheffield
T: 0114 221 2310 **F:** 0114 221 2122
Contact: Lesley Adyer
Party Max: 250

A must for Wednesday fans, the Club has several function

YORKSHIRE

rooms, two of which overlook the pitch.
Catering: In house

Price Guide: Prices on application.
Catering (sit down): from £16.00pp
Catering (buffet): from £6.00pp

Solberge Hall, Northallerton
T: 01609 779191 **F:** 01609 780472
Contact: John Hollins, Proprietor
Party Max: 140 (marquee: 200)   Bedrooms: 24

Once a Victorian country house, Solberge Hall sits in 16 acres overlooking the moors and dales. The Hall offers two main function suites; the Garden Suite (max 100) and the Clock Tower Suite (max 120).
Catering: In house

FACILITIES:
- Helipad
- Shooting
- Hot Air Balloons

SERVICES:
- Marriage Licence
- Flowers
- Cake
- Toastmaster
- Live Music
- Entertainers
- Photography
- Piped Music

Price Guide: There is no facility fee here.
Catering (sit down): from £23pp
Catering (buffet): from £23pp

Spa Complex, Scarborough
T: 01723 376774 **F:** 01723 501322
Contact: Functions Manager
Party Max: 650

This Victorian spa complex was recently used in the filming of Little Voice. It is adjacent to the sea wall with coastal views towards the castle. Open-topped bus transport can be arranged by this venue.
Catering: In house

Price Guide: Prices on application.
Catering (sit down): from £16.50pp
Catering (buffet): from £5.50pp

Stephen Joseph Theatre, Scarborough
T: 01723 370540
F: 01723 360506
E: response@sjt.uk.com
Contact: Jaye Lewis, Events Manager
Party Max: 200

The Stephen Joseph Theatre is a 1930's Grade II listed building, with many original features, occupying a prominent position in Scarborough town. Two theatres are available for functions, as well as the Boden Room.
Catering: In house

SERVICES:
- Marriage Licence
- Cake
- Disco/Dance
- Piped Music
- Performance Area

Price Guide: £60 - £200/day
Catering (sit down): from £15pp
Catering (buffet): from £10pp

Sun Pavilion, Harrogate
T: 01423 522588 **F:** 01423 522212
E: sun-pavilion@lineone.net
Contact: Duty Manager
Party Max: 150

Set in the Grade II listed Valley Gardens and recently restored and refubished to echo the mood of its heyday, the Pavilion boasts a stained glass domed roof which creates lightness and good acoustics.
Catering: Contract approved list

SERVICES:
- Exclusive Use
- Performance Area

Price Guide: Prices on application.
Catering (sit down): POA

Treasurer's House, York
T: 01904 624247 **E:** yorkth@smtp.ntrust.org.uk
Contact: Jo Outhart, Assistant to Property Manager
Party Max: 80

This is a National Trust owned historic house in the centre of York, boasting York Minister as a backdrop to its secluded garden. Previous events here have included a wedding in full Medieval costume, with bride arriving on a white horse.
Catering: In house

SERVICES:
- Marriage Licence

Price Guide: Prices on application.
Catering (sit down): from £22pp
Catering (buffet): from £22pp

Under the Clock Tower, Wakefield
T: 01924 305121
F: 01924 305293
Contact: Simon Hartley, General Manager
Party Max: 150

'Under the Clock Tower' is actually the banqueting and restaurant complex within Wakefield Town Hall. The Victorian Town Hall was first opened in 1880 and is now a Grade I listed building. Rich wood panelling, ornate plasterwork and chandeliers make this an attractive venue.
Catering: In house

Price Guide: Prices on application.
Catering (sit down): from £14.50pp

Waterford House, Middleham
T: 01969 622090
F: 01969 624020
Contact: Everyl M Madell, Joint Proprietor
Party Max: 50 (marquee: 60)   Bedrooms: 5

This Grade II listed building, with its own walled garden, is set in Middleham, a major racehorse training centre in the Yorkshire Dales. Internally the house features period and antique furnishings and four poster beds. The hotel features in many guides, including the Good Food Guide. Guests can go on a racing stable visit during their stay if requested.
Catering: In house

YORKSHIRE

SERVICES:
- Marriage Licence

Price Guide: Prices on application.
Catering (sit down): from £25pp
Catering (buffet): from £17.50pp

Waterton Park Hotel, Wakefield
T: 01924 257911 **F:** 01924 240082
Contact: Debbie Taylor, Conference and Banqueting Manager
Party Max: 150 (marquee: 175)   Bedrooms: 42

This Georgian listed mansion is situated on an island surrounded by 26 acres of lake and is accessed by an iron bridge.
Catering: In house

SERVICES:
- Marriage Licence

Price Guide: Prices on application.
Catering (sit down): from £21.00pp

Weetwood Hall, Leeds
T: 0113 230 6000 **F:** 0113 230 6095
E: sales@weetwood.co.uk **W:** www.weetwood.co.uk
Contact: Lorraine Lollett, Conference & Reservations Manager
Party Max: 150   Bedrooms: 108

Set in 4.5 acres of wooded seclusion on the outskirts of Leeds, this purpose-built centre has been developed around a Grade II listed Jacobean manor house. Weetwood Hall provides 108 ensuite bedrooms, including 12 luxury rooms and 2 offering a four-poster honeymoon suite.
Catering: In house

SERVICES:
- Marriage Licence

Price Guide: Prices on application.
Catering (sit down): from £24.95pp

Whirlow Brook Hall, Sheffield
T: 0114 221 3003 **F:** 0114 221 3004
Contact: Michael Sharratt, Managing Director
Party Max: 150

The Hall was originally a family home and stands in 39 acres of gardens. It claims an intimate atmosphere and a warm welcome. A late night drinks licence will be applied for if required.
Catering: In house

SERVICES:
- Marriage Licence

Price Guide: Prices on application.
Catering (sit down): from £25pp
Catering (buffet): from £12pp

Whitby Pavilion, Whitby
T: 01947 820625 **F:** 01947 604487
Contact: Ann Stevenson, Manager
Party Max: 600

The Whitby Pavilion is nestled into Whitby's West Cliff, with views out over the sea, the piers and the stretch of beach to Sandsend. The Pavilion includes a Victorian proscenium arch theatre, the modern Northern Lights Suite, an Exhibition Hall and the Crystal Lounge.
Catering: In house

SERVICES:
- Marriage Licence   • Disco/Dance   • Piped Music
- Performance Area

Price Guide: Prices vary according to the area hired. Eg: Northern Lights Suite £265 - £550.
Catering (sit down): from £11pp
Catering (buffet): from £6.50pp

Whitley Hall Hotel, Sheffield
T: 0114 245 4444
Contact: Ian Davies
Party Max: 100 (marquee: 250)   Bedrooms: 18

This Elizabethan manor house is a Grade II listed building. The hotel prides itself on the quality of its traditional English cuisine.
Catering: In house

SERVICES:
- Marriage Licence

Price Guide: Prices on application.
Catering (sit down): POA

Wood Hall Hotel, Linton
T: 01937 587271 **F:** 01937 584353
Contact: Elaine Hardy
Party Max: 130 (marquee: 150)   Bedrooms: 42

Several rooms are available for functions in this Grade II listed building. A wide range of services is offered, inlcuidng reduced room rates for guests.
Catering: In house

SERVICES:
- Marriage Licence

Price Guide: Prices on application.
Catering (sit down): £27.00 - 35.00pp

Woolley Hall Conference Centre, Wakefield
T: 01226 392300 **F:** 01226 392316
Contact: Maxine Wilson, Conference Coordinator
Party Max: 136

This listed building features Italian gardens.
Catering: In house

SERVICES:
- Marriage Licence

Price Guide: Prices on application.
Catering (sit down): from £16pp
Catering (buffet): from £13pp

Wortley Hall, Sheffield
T: 0114 288 2100 **F:** 0114 283 0695
Contact: Brian Clarke, The Manager
Party Max: 250

Wortley Hall is situated in 26 acres of woodland and ornate gardens, and yet is only 2 miles from the M1. The Hall offers

YORKSHIRE

1-diamond standard b&b accommodation, mostly in twin rooms.
Catering: *In house*

FACILITIES:
- Pool/Snooker

SERVICES:
- Exclusive Use
- Toastmaster
- Disco/Dance
- Performance Area

Price Guide: Prices on application.
Catering (sit down): from £9.95pp
Catering (buffet): from £5.50pp

Wrea Head Country House, Scarborough

T: 01723 378211   **F:** 01723 371780
Contact: Mike Turner, Sales Director

Party Max: 200 (marquee: unlimited)   Bedrooms: 21

This Yorkshire country house is set in acres of grounds and gardens, which can be used by helicopters and hot air balloons. The marquee is set up permanently throughout the summer - April to November.
Catering: *In house*

SERVICES:
- Marriage Licence

Price Guide: Prices on application.
Catering (sit down): from £20pp
Catering (buffet): from £15pp

CUMBRIA

Appleby Castle, Appleby-in-Westmoreland
T: 017683 51402   **F:** 017683 51082
Contact: Tessa Wigham, Administrator
Party Max: 100 (marquee: unlimited)   Bedrooms: 15

This is an historic monument and privately owned house, set in 27 acres of riverside grounds, and is often used as a conference and training centre. The property features a 12th Century Norman keep, although much of the main building dates from 1635. The keep and the Great Hall are both licensed for ceremonies which can take place here on any day of the year. The Castle prides itself on tailoring weddings to the clients requirements, and can recommend all services from flowers to fireworks. The site is also suitable for arrival by air or water.
Catering: In house

SERVICES:
- Marriage Licence

Price Guide: Wedding ceremonies are from £160.
Catering (sit down): from £25pp
Catering (buffet): from £15pp

Armathwaithe Hall Hotel, Keswick
T: 017687 76551   **F:** 017687 76220
Contact: Joan Tomkinson, Sales Manager
Party Max: 100 (marquee: 200)   Bedrooms: 43

This 17th Century former stately home is now a family owned and run hotel, set in 400 acres of lakeside grounds. Special features include wood panelled public rooms and log fires. Three rooms are available for wedding ceremonies, which can only be conducted here if the reception is also held on the premises.
Catering: In house

SERVICES:
- Marriage Licence

Price Guide: wedding ceremony price start at £100.
Catering (sit down): from £21pp

Castle Inn Hotel, Nr Keswick
T: 017687 76401   **F:** 017687 76604
Contact: Liz Arnell, Sales Manager
Party Max: 200   Bedrooms: 14

The Castle Inn enjoys views of Bassenthwaite Lake and the highest mountains in England. Five rooms hold wedding licences, ranging in capacity from 2 to 175.
Catering: In house

SERVICES:
- Marriage Licence

Price Guide: Wedding ceremonies from £50.
Catering (sit down): from £15pp
Catering (buffet): from £6.95pp

Coot on the Tarn Restaurant, Ulverston
T: 01229 58172   **F:** 01229 588425
W: www.cootonthetarn.co.uk
Contact: Miss Louise Halliday, Wedding Coordinator/Restaurant Manager
Party Max: 300

Located on the shores of Great Urwick Tarn, The Coot Restaurant is the ideal setting for wedding receptions, civil ceremonies and private parties. The grounds of the restaurant lead down to the idyllic Tarn, with the gentle hills of Birkriee Common in the background. The venue offers a choice of 4 rooms including the Great Hall (licensed for wedding ceremonies). The venue offers complimentary flowers, and a varied choice of menu and drinks packages.
Catering: In house

SERVICES:
- Exclusive Use
- Cake
- Live Music
- Photography
- Marriage Licence
- Toastmaster
- Entertainers
- Flowers
- Disco/Dance
- Fireworks

Price Guide: Day rates start at £50 for venue hire.
Catering (sit down): from £16.50pp
Catering (buffet): from £5pp

Coppermines & Coniston Cottages, Consiton
T: 015394 41765
F: 015394 41944
E: bookings@coppermines.co.uk
W: www.coppermines.co.uk
Contact: Philip Johnston, Proprietor
Party Max: 120

The Coppermines include many old buildings, including a Victorian sawmill, which have now been restored and converted to 4 cottages sleeping 5 to 8, or interlinked to suit groups of 11 to 25. The Cottages are set in an outstanding mountain location, where hirers can take part in numerous outdoor pursuits. The owners specialise in offering weekends for groups which are offered throughout the Autumn, Winter and Spring. If you don't wish to cater for yourselves, the venue can arrange catering, from a simple breakfast to a small dinner party, or even a wedding reception. Other cottages are also available nearby. See entries for Old Stable and Old Pottery Cottage (for 12), and The Farm House (for 10) also.
Catering: Contract approved list / Self catering

FACILITIES:
- Helipad
- Outdoor Pool

SERVICES:
- Exclusive Use

Price Guide: £195 to £3000 per week.

Cragwood Country House Hotel, Windermere
T: 015394 88177   **F:** 015394 42145
Contact: Phil Hornby, Manager
Party Max: 84 (marquee: 200)   Bedrooms: 23

Cragwood is a traditional country house hotel, set in 20 acres of gardens and woodland, and is the sister venue to Merewood.
Catering: In house

SERVICES:
- Marriage Licence

Price Guide: Wedding ceremony room hire from £250.
Catering (sit down): from £22pp

CUMBRIA

Dalston Hall Hotel, Nr Carlisle
T: 01228 710271 **F:** 01228 711273
Contact: Jane Thompson, Proprietor
Party Max: 180 (marquee: 300)   Bedrooms: 12

This 15th Century mansion house set in extensive gardens was built in William the Conquerer's time. Three rooms are licensed for wedding ceremonies; The Baronial Hall, Sir John Dalston's Study, and The Library.
Catering: In house

SERVICES:
- Marriage Licence

Price Guide: Prices on application.
Catering (sit down): from £19.95pp
Catering (buffet): from £10.95pp

Ennerdales Hotel, Cleator
T: 01946 813907 **F:** 01946 815260
Contact: James Lamb, General Manager
Party Max: 200 (marquee: 160)   Bedrooms: 22

This Grade II listed building is set in landscaped gardens with fountain. The Fountain Room and Muncaster Rooms are licensed for ceremonies, which must be followed by a reception. Helicopters and hot air balloons may land here.
Catering: In house

SERVICES:
- Marriage Licence

Price Guide: Prices on application.
Catering (sit down): from £13pp
Catering (buffet): from £8pp

Farm House, Consiton
T: 015394 41765 **F:** 015394 41944
E: bookings@coppermines.co.uk **W:** www.coppermines.co.uk
Contact: Philip Johnston, Proprietor
Party Max: 12

This is a large comfortable Victorian house adjoining The Old Cottage (2-5) and has spectacular lake views, especially from the enclosed garden. The house is set in an outstanding mountain location, where hirers can take part in numerous outdoor pursuits. Other cottages are also available nearby. See entries for The Old Stable & The Old Pottery Cottage (for 25), and The Coppermines(for 25) also.
Catering: Contract approved list/Self catering

FACILITIES:
- Helipad
- Outdoor Pool

SERVICES:
- Exclusive Use

Price Guide: £185 to £1290 per week.

Greystoke Castle,, Penrith
T: 017684 83722 **F:** 017684 83072
E: douglas.Weymouth@lineone.net
Contact: Douglas Weymouth, Events Manager
Party Max: 100 (marquee: 250)

This listed building is a private house and garden with its own lake. Features include a panelled great hall and views to the Pennines.

Catering: In house

SERVICES:
- Marriage Licence

Price Guide: Prices on application.
Catering (sit down): from £22pp
Catering (buffet): from £14pp

Holbeck Ghyll, Windermere
T: 015394 32375 **F:** 015394 34743
E: accommodation@holbeck-ghyll.co.uk
W: www.holbeck-ghyll.co.uk
Contact: David Nicholson, Proprietor
Party Max: 75 (marquee: 75)   Bedrooms: 20

This 19th Century hunting lodge offers views over Lake Windermere. This venue has a Michelin star and three AA Rosettes. Three rooms are licensed for wedding ceremonies, The Lounge, The Lonsdale Room, and the Terrace Restaurant. Lawns, lakes and the Langdale mountains offer an appealing backdrop to photographs.
Catering: In house

SERVICES:
- Marriage Licence

Price Guide: Prices on application.
Catering (sit down): from £25pp
Catering (buffet): from £20pp

Holker Hall, Grange-over-Sands
T: 01539 558328 **F:** 01539 558838
E: publicopening@holker.co.uk
W: www.holkerhall.co.uk
Contact: Mrs Jillian Rouse
Party Max: 110

Two rooms of contemporary design are avaialble within the courtyard at Holker Hall. Private hire allows full use of all facilties including the courtyard area and undercover canopy. Access to Lord and Lady Cavendish' award winning gardens may be possible by prior arrangement.
Catering: In house

FACILITIES:
- Shooting

SERVICES:
- Exclusive Use
- Flowers
- Cake
- Toastmaster
- Disco/Dance
- Piped Music
- Performance Area

Price Guide: Prices on application.
Catering (sit down): from £19.95pp
Catering (buffet): from £12.95pp

Keswick Country House Hotel, Keswick
T: 017687 72020 **F:** 017687 71300
Contact: Susan Greggain, Banqueting Co-ordinator
Party Max: 160   Bedrooms: 74

This Victorian building set in four acres of award winning gardens, is now a 4-star hotel and part of the Principal Hotels group. It is only a short walk from the centre of Keswick.
Catering: In house

CUMBRIA

SERVICES:
- Marriage Licence

Price Guide: Prices on application.
Catering (sit down): from £18pp
Catering (buffet): from £8pp

Lakeside Hotel, Newby Bridge
T: 015395 31207 **F:** 015395 31699
E: weddings@lakesidehotel.co.uk **W:** www.lakesidehotel.co.uk
Contact: Jonathan Robb

Party Max: 160 Bedrooms: 80

This traditional lakeland coaching inn is set on the south shore of Lake Windermere, with its own jetties and boats. The hotel has 2 AA Rosettes and an RAC award for its food and restaurant. The price below is based on the hotel's wedding packages, which include drinks. The hotel can arrange hour long 'cocktail' cruises on the lake for up to 200 people: appropriate between day and evening receptions. Hot air balloons can also take off from behind the hotel.
Catering: In house

SERVICES:
- Marriage Licence

Price Guide: Prices on application.
Catering (sit down): from £39pp

Langdale Chase Hotel, Windermere
T: 015394 32201 **F:** 015394 32604
Contact: Mr Thomas Noblett, General Manager

Party Max: 140 (marquee: 200) Bedrooms: 30

This lakeside hotel features large gardens and views across the lake to the mountains. Party-goers can arrive or depart by boat here or make a grand entrance or exit by helicopter or balloon.
Catering: In house

FACILITIES:
- Helipad

SERVICES:
- Marriage Licence

Price Guide: Prices on application.
Catering (sit down): from £24pp
Catering (buffet): from £15pp

Leeming House Hotel, Nr Penrith
T: 017684 86622 **F:** 017684 86443
Contact: General Manager

Party Max: 80 Bedrooms: 40

This hotel is set in 27 acres on the shores of Ullswater. This busy hotel (two AA Rosettes) is not really able to cater for evening functions unless the whole hotel is taken on an exclusive use basis. However, between March and October, a steam boat (for up to 200) operates on the lake. This can be hired for dinner/dances, etc.
Catering: In house

SERVICES:
- Marriage Licence

Price Guide: Prices on application.
Catering (sit down): from £27.50pp

Linthwaite House Hotel, Windermere
T: 015394 88600 **F:** 015394 88601
E: admin@linthwaite.com **W:** www.linthwaite.com
Contact: Margaret Beath

Party Max: 64 (marquee: 500) Bedrooms: 26

This hotel is set in 14 acres of grounds with views of Lake Windermere. The hotel prides itself on its use of local produce in its modern British cuisine. Exclusive use of the entire hotel is possible.
Catering: In house

SERVICES:
- Exclusive Use
- Marriage Licence

Price Guide: Prices on application.
Catering (sit down): from £26pp
Catering (buffet): from £19pp

Low Wood Hotel, Windermere
T: 015394 33338 **F:** 015394 34072
W: www.elh.co.uk
Contact: Teresa Whiteside, Sales Manager

Party Max: 250 (marquee: 350) Bedrooms: 114

The Low Wood is situated on the shores of Lake Windermere with views across the lake to the Langdale Pikes. Helicopters and hot air balloons may use the hotel grounds.
Catering: In house

FACILITIES:
- Helipad

SERVICES:
- Marriage Licence

Price Guide: Prices on application.
Catering (sit down): from £13.95pp

Mark Close Farmhouse, Alston
T: 01434 381780
F: 01434 381780
E: jhoddy@ukonline.co.uk
Contact: Jackie Hodson, Owner

Party Max: 22 Bedrooms: 9

This farmhouse, which accommodates 22 people, is set in a large mature garden bordered by mature trees and with views over green fields and wild fells.
Catering: Self catering

SERVICES:
- Exclusive Use

Price Guide: Prices on application.

Mirage at Milton Hall, Brampton
T: 01697 741774
F: 01697 72800
Contact: The Manager

Party Max: 250

Mirage is the recently refurbished function suite at Milton Hall and is in a country setting with extensive views. Only one ceremony per day can be held at Mirage, but this must be followed by a reception at the venue.
Catering: In house/Contract (any)

CUMBRIA

FACILITIES:
- Helipad
- Paint Ball

SERVICES:
- Exclusive Use
- Marriage Licence
- Toastmaster
- Disco/Dance
- Live Music
- Entertainers
- Piped Music
- Performance Area

Price Guide: There is no venue hire fee here.
Catering (sit down): from £50pp
Catering (buffet): from £5pp

Muncaster Castle, Ravenglass

T: 01229 717614 **F:** 01229 717010
E: info@muncastercastle.co.uk **W:** www.muncastercastle.co.uk
Contact: Anne Hudson, Commercial Director

Party Max: 100   Bedrooms: 8

A beautiful stately home set in 77 acres of woodland gardens, with stunning views over the lakeland fells, Muncaster Castle is a lived in family home, furnished with exquisite antique furniture and artefacts collected over many centuries. The venue also offers a newly refurbished function rooms in the Old Laundry building situated just a few yards from the castle. Each function is individually planned and all at Muncaster are dedicated to efficient and friendly service.

Catering: In house/Contract approved list

SERVICES:
- Exclusive Use
- Marriage Licence
- Flowers
- Cake
- Disco/Dance
- Performance Area

Price Guide: All prices on application.
Catering (sit down): POA
Catering (buffet): POA

Naworth Castle, Brampton

T: 016977 3229 **F:** 016977 3679
E: office@naworth.co.uk **W:** www.naworth.co.uk
Contact: Colleen Hall, Events Manager

Party Max: 250 (marquee: 250/500)   Bedrooms: 17

Naworth Castle dates from 1335. The Old Library and the Great Hall are available for functions, with other rooms available on request. This is not an hotel, so accommodation is only available as part of a function arrangement.

Catering: In house

FACILITIES:
- Helipad
- Shooting

SERVICES:
- Exclusive Use
- Marriage Licence
- Valet Parking

Price Guide: Venue hire £2500 + vat per day.
Catering (sit down): from £25pp + vat

Netherwood Hotel, Grange Over Sands

T: 015395 32552 **F:** 015395 34121
E: blawith@aol.com
W: www.netherwood-hotel.co.uk
Contact: Messrs JD & MP Fallowfield, Resident Proprietors/Partners

Party Max: 200   Bedrooms: 28

This Grade II listed building, built for the Deakin family in 1893, claims architectural and historical interest and features oak panelling thoughout. The hotel is set in 14 acres of gardens overlooking Morecambe Bay. European, Oriental and Caribbean cuisine is offered here.

Catering: In house

SERVICES:
- Marriage Licence

Price Guide: Prices on application.
Catering (sit down): from £35pp
Catering (buffet): from £35pp

Old Stable & Old Pottery Cottages, Consiton

T: 015394 41765 **F:** 015394 41944
E: bookings@coppermines.co.uk **W:** www.coppermines.co.uk
Contact: Philip Johnston, Proprietor

Party Max: 12

These 2 cottages, nestle under the Coniston Fells in the grounds of a Georgian farmhouse, and have been converted from a stonebuilt 17th Century Bank Barn. The building has been sympathetically restored, and the 2 cottages can be joined together using an interconnecting door. The Cottages are set in an outstanding mountain location, where hirers can take part in numerous outdoor pursuits. Other cottages are also available nearby. See entries for The Coppermines (for 25), and The Farm House (for 10) also.

Catering: Contract approved list/Self catering

FACILITIES:
- Helipad
- Outdoor Pool

SERVICES:
- Exclusive Use

Price Guide: £185 to £1290 per week.

Samling at Dovenest, Windermere

T: 015394 31922 **F:** 015394 30400
Contact: Brigette Beser, Sales Manager

Party Max: 20 (marquee: 130)

Samling is apparently the Cumbrian word for 'gathering', for those of you wondering. Those gathering here would enjoy an 18th Century building, now a sophisticated private hotel available for exclusive use. The house is set in 67 acres of landscaped gardens with a pond. The Samling offers an inclusive package for 20 which includes 24 hour use of the house and grounds, with dinner, bed and breakfast and lunch, plus drinks, all for £350 per couple, or £250 per person. The overnight accommodation is in 10 suites, each with its own sitting room. The chef uses local produce wherever possible.

Catering: In house

SERVICES:
- Marriage Licence

Price Guide: Prices on application.
Catering (sit down): POA

Tufton Arms Hotel, Appleby - in -Westmoreland

T: 017683 51593 **F:** 017683 52761

NOBLE'S PARTY VENUES GUIDE 1ST EDITION

CUMBRIA

Contact: Teresa Nilsom

Party Max: 100   Bedrooms: 23

This 16th Century old coaching inn, with Victorian additions, is located in the centre of Appleby. The Tufton Arms holds an AA Rosette for its cuisine and is AA, RAC, Egon Ronay and Johanssen recommended.
Catering: In house

SERVICES:
• Marriage Licence

Price Guide: Prices on application.
Catering (sit down): from £14.50pp

Tullie House Museum & Art Gallery,
Carlisle

T: 01228 534781   **F:** 01228 810249
E: LindaI@carlisel-city.gov.uk
Contact: Linda Ivison, Catering Manager

Party Max: 370

Tullie House, an award-winning City Museum and Art Gallery, is a major visitor attraction in the North West of England. This Grade I Jacobean building, with Victorian and modern day extensions, is set in its own attractive gardens in the heart of Carlisle. The Museum tells the story of Carlisle and the Borderlands from pre-history to the present day, with special emphasis on the Roman occupation, the lawless Border Reivers and Railway history. The Museum also boasts a contemporary art gallery, gift shop, restaurant and conference facilities.
Catering: Contract approved list

FACILITIES:
• Museum Tours   • Gallery Viewing   • Croquet

SERVICES:
• Exclusive Use   • Marriage Licence   • Flowers
• Toastmaster   • Disco/Dance   • Performance Area

Price Guide: £75 - £2000.
Catering (sit down): Lunch from £8.25pp Dinner from £15pp
Catering (buffet): from £5.50pp

Ullswater Hotel, Penrith

T: 017684 82444   **F:** 017684 82303
Contact: Larry Slattery

Party Max: 150 (marquee: 500)   Bedrooms: 48

The Ullswater Hotel is set in 40 acres of private grounds on the shores of Lake Ullswater with three landing jetties, a helipad and separate children's play area.
Catering: In house

FACILITIES:
• Playground   • Helipad

SERVICES:
• Marriage Licence

Price Guide: Prices on application.
Catering (sit down): £16.50 - £30pp

NORTHUMBRIA

Alnwick Castle, Alnwick
T: 01665 510777   **F:** 01665 510876
E: enquiries@alnwickcastle.com
Contact: Event Manager
Party Max: 300

Alnwick Castle, once described as the Windsor of the North, is the main seat of the Dukes of Norhtumberland whose family, the Percys have lived here since 1309. Despite its medieval exterior, the interiors of the castle is furnished in Renaissance style and include paintings by Titian, Van Dyck and Canaletto. The Guest Hall, which is not open to castle visitors, is available for conferences and entertaining. The Castle was used for the filming of Elizabeth in 1998.
Catering: In house

Price Guide: Prices on application.
Catering (sit down): POA

Assembly Rooms, Newcastle upon Tyne
T: 0191 232 8695   **F:** 0191 261 1249
E: functions@assemblyrooms.co.uk
W: www.assemblyrooms.co.uk
Contact: Anthony Michaelides, Owner
Party Max: 400

Set in the heart of Newcastle's city centre, The Assembly Rooms is a grand Georgian building dating back to 1776. Owned and run personally by the Michaleides family, the building has been sympathetically restored. Features include a rare set of rococo chandeliers in the grand ballroom The Chandelier Room, which has two outer rooms offering full lounge bar facilities and a separate reception room. Numerous other rooms on the first floor are also available for functions, and all interlink and lead into the main ballroom. The Assembly Rooms also offer a Lower Ballroom on the ground floor, as well as syndicate rooms for small meetings. This venue has arranged discounted rooms rates with city centre hotels.
Catering: In house

SERVICES:
- Marriage Licence   • Disco/Dance   • Piped Music
- Performance Area   *Price Guide: £125 + vat to £1750 + vat.*

Catering (sit down): from £14.50pp
Catering (buffet): from £5.75pp

Auckland Castle, Bishop Auckland
T: 01388 601627   **F:** 01388 609323
E: auckland.castle@zetnet.co.uk
W: www.auckland.castle.co.uk
Contact: The Manager
Party Max: 220 (marquee: 600)

Auckland Castle, which dates back to the 12th Century, is now the home of the Bishop of Durham. A little known venue in the North East, it prides itself on exclusive and personal service. Weddings can take place in St Peter's Chapel, whilst the State Rooms provide opulence for private or corporate functions.
Catering: In house/Contract approved list

FACILITIES:
- Hot Air Balloons   •

SERVICES:
- Exclusive Use   • Toastmaster   • Disco/Dance
- Performance Area   *Price Guide: £800 - £6000*

Catering (sit down): from £20pp
Catering (buffet): from £6.50pp

Bishop Auckland Town Hall, Bishop Auckland
T: 01388 602610   **F:** 01388 604960
W: www.durham.gov.uk
Contact: Gillian Wales, Centre Manager
Party Max: 250

This is a Grade II listed civic building located in the town centre. Several rooms are available for functions.
Catering: Contract approved list

SERVICES:
- Exclusive Use   • Marriage Licence   • Disco/Dance
- Piped Music   • Performance Area   *Price Guide: Room hire fees start at £7.50 per hour rising to £23 per hour. The wedding ceremony fee is £105 withor withuot reception.*
Catering (sit down): £11 - £20pp
Catering (buffet): £1.50 - £6.95pp

Chillingham Castle, Nr Alnwick
T: 01668 215359   **F:** 01668 215463
Contact: Joanna Powel, Administrator
Party Max: 120 (marquee: unlimited)   Bedrooms: 7 appts

This Medieval fortress with Tudor additions, is a gem among the venues. The Castle is set in Italian gardens and grounds featuring a lake and views to the Cheviots. This is a popular venue for medieval themed events.
Catering: Contract (any)

SERVICES:
- Marriage Licence   *Price Guide: Prices on application.*
Catering (sit down): from £17.50pp
Catering (buffet): from £10pp

Close House Mansion, Newcastle upon Tyne
T: 01661 852255   **F:** 01661 853322
Contact: Jane Thompson
Party Max: 124 (marquee: 150)

This conference and banqueting centre is an English Heritage, Grade II listed building, set in 179 acres of wooded grounds and parkland. It features an 18-hole private golf course and helipad. Just 10 minutes from Newcastle city centre, the mansion dates back to 1779 and was once the property of a former Mayor of Newcastle. Several rooms are available for functions including the Rococo Room, decorated in the Italian Rococo style and the Bewicke Room with marble fireplace and a bay window that opens onto the east lawn.
Catering: In house

FACILITIES:
- Golf   • Helipad

SERVICES:
- Marriage Licence   *Price Guide: Prices on application.*
Catering (sit down): from £16pp

NORTHUMBRIA

De Vere Slaley Hall Hotel, Nr Newcastle-upon-Tyne
T: 01434 673350   **F:** 01434 673050
E: slaley@dircon.co.uk
Contact: Sales Co-ordinators
Party Max: 250 (marquee: unlimited)   Bedrooms: 139

A period building from the late 1800s with extensive modern additions, this impressive hotel is set amidst 1,000 acres of Northumberland forest and features a Japanese garden. A swimming pool and fully equipped gym are just two of the facilities of the hotel's health spa and leisure club.
Catering: In house

FACILITIES:
- Swimming Pool
- Gym
- Leisure Club

SERVICES:
- Marriage Licence   Price Guide: Prices on application.
Catering (sit down): from £28pp
Catering (buffet): from £28pp

Dissington Hall, Newcastle Upon Tyne
T: 01661 886063   **F:** 01661 886896
E: party@dissingtonhall.co.uk   **W:** dissingtonhall.co.uk
Contact: Michael Brown, Owner
Party Max: 240

Dissington Hall is a stunning Georgian mansion, set in 18 acres of grounds and now restored to its original splendour. The Hall has a large period banqueting room with dance floor and semi-permanent marquee, beautiful staircase and open log fires. "Great food and a friendly, off-beat approach to events mean we get very booked up." says this venue.
Catering: In house

FACILITIES:
- Helipad
- Shooting

SERVICES:
- Exclusive Use
- Marriage Licence
- Flowers
- Toastmaster
- Disco/Dance
- Live Music
- Piped Music
- Performance Area
- Valet Parking

Price Guide: £200 - £2000
Catering (sit down): from £26pp
Catering (buffet): from £16pp

Embleton Hall, Morpeth
T: 01665 570249/206   **F:** 01665 570056
Contact: Trevor Thorne, Owner/Manager
Party Max: 200 (marquee: 200)   Bedrooms: 14

Embleton Hall is an 18th Century manor house set in 5 acres of landscaped gardens. The building is now used as a 4-star hotel, with all bedrooms en suite. The dining room offers menus based on local produce and the wine list claims a good selection of labels from the New World.
Catering: In house

SERVICES:
- Exclusive Use
- Marriage Licence   *Price Guide:*

Accommodation rates are from £55 to £105 per room per nght.
Catering (sit down): from £20pp
Catering (buffet): from £20pp

Eshott Hall, Morpeth
T: 01670 787777   **F:** 01670 786000
E: eshott@btinternet.com
Contact: Margaret Sanderson
Party Max: 200 (marquee: 500)   Bedrooms: 4

Eshott is a private country house and a listed building. It boasts an exquisite ceiling in its Drawing Room. Discos or dances would take place in 'The Lost Wing', which has recently been rebuilt.
Catering: In house

SERVICES:
- Marriage Licence   Price Guide: Prices on application.
Catering (sit down): from £20pp
Catering (buffet): from £7.50pp

Espley Hall, Morpeth
T: 01670 513986
Contact: Mr J Kenworthy, owner
Party Max: 120

This Victorian merchant's house is available for hire on an exclusive basis only; thereby ensuring total privacy and personal attention. It features 15 acres of lawns and flower beds surrounded by trees.
Catering: In house

SERVICES:
- Marriage Licence
- Exclusive Use   Price Guide: Prices on application.
Catering (sit down): from £28pp

Headlam Hall Hotel, Darlington
T: 01325 730238   **F:** 01325 730790
E: admin@headlamhall.co.uk   **W:** www.headlamhall.co.uk
Contact: Jeanette Jarvis, Administration
Party Max: 200   Bedrooms: 36

This listed building is set in large formal gardens in a secluded rural location.
Catering: In house

SERVICES:
- Marriage Licence   Price Guide: Prices on application.
Catering (sit down): from £18pp
Catering (buffet): from £18pp

Horsley Hall, Bishop Auckland
T: 01388 517239   **F:** 01388 517608
Contact: Liz Curry, Proprietor
Party Max: 120 (marquee: 240)   Bedrooms: 7

This 3-storey country manor house, with views across the Dale, dates back to the 17th Century. Built as a shooting lodge for the Bishop of Durham, it was also once the home of the Hildyard family who lived in the area for nearly 500 years. An awning adjacent to the Baronial Hall can increase capacity if required.
Catering: In house

SERVICES:
- Marriage Licence

NORTHUMBRIA

Price Guide: Prices on application.
Catering (sit down): from £24pp
Catering (buffet): from £21pp

Judges Hotel, Yarm, Stockton on Tees
T: 01642 789000   **F:** 01682 782878
W: www.judgeshotel.co.uk
Contact: Shirley Downs, Front of House Manager
Party Max: 200 (marquee: 160)   Bedrooms: 21
This Victorian country house, built in 1881 is now an hotel and restaurant.
Catering: In house

SERVICES:
- Marriage Licence

Price Guide: Prices on application.
Catering (sit down): from £26pp
Catering (buffet): from £26pp

Kirkley Hall, Ponteland
T: 01661 860808   **F:** 01661 860047
Contact: Brian Glover, College Services Manager
Party Max: 110 (marquee: unlimited)   Bedrooms: 60
Kirkley Hall is the mansion house attached to a farming college. It is a listed building set in open countryside and boasts 'magnificent gardens'.
Catering: In house

SERVICES:
- Marriage Licence

Price Guide: Prices on application.
Catering (sit down): from £12pp

Langley Castle Hotel, Hexham
T: 01434 688888   **F:** 01434 684019
Contact: Anton Philips, General Manager
Party Max: 160   Bedrooms: 18
This 14th century castle is a Grade I listed building and is set in a private woodland estate. Features here include window seats set into 7 feet hick walls, richly draped 4-poster beds, an intimate restaurant and an atmospheric Drawing Room.
Catering: In house

SERVICES:
- Marriage Licence

Price Guide: Prices on application.
Catering (sit down): 120
Catering (buffet): 160

Linden Hall Hotel, Morpeth
T: 01670 500000   **F:** 01670 500001
E: stay@lindenhall.co.uk   **W:** www.lindenhall.co.uk
Contact: Lis Aransfield, Conference & Banqueting Manager
Party Max: 200 (marquee: yes)   Bedrooms: 50
Linden Hall is a Grade II listed Georgian country house hotel with gardens. Six rooms are available for parties, ranging in capacity from 4 to 200. House wines start at £12.95 per bottle, with Champagne starting at £27.50 per bottle.
Catering: In house

SERVICES:
- Marriage Licence

Price Guide: Prices on application.
Catering (sit down): Packages start at 37.50pp

Longhirst Hall, Morpeth
T: 01670 791348   **F:** 01670 791385
Contact: The Wedding Co-ordinator
Party Max: 85   Bedrooms: 75
This 19th Century building is set in 55 acres of grounds and is now used as a management training and conference centre.
Catering: In house

SERVICES:
- Marriage Licence

Price Guide: Prices on application.
Catering (sit down): from £20pp

Lord Crewe Arms Hotel, Nr Consett
T: 01434 675251   **F:** 01434 675337
Contact: Wendy Hart, Receptionist
Party Max: 65 (marquee: unlimited)   Bedrooms: 19
This scheduled ancient monument has an attractive and secluded garden. The hotel's restaurant holds an AA rosette.
Catering: In house

SERVICES:
- Marriage Licence

Price Guide: Prices on application.
Catering (sit down): from £21.75pp

Marshall Meadows Country House Hotel, Berwick Upon Tweed
T: 01289 331133   **F:** 01289 331438
Contact: Matthew Rudd, General Manager
Party Max: 200 (marquee: 200)   Bedrooms: 90
Just a quarter of a mile South of the Scottish border, this Georgian mansion was converted into a country house hotel in 1991 and is set in 15 acres of woodland and matured gardens, bordered by open farmland with sea views. The hotel states that fresh local produce plays an important part when creating its traditional home cooking. This includes fresh fish and shell fish caught daily at the nearby Scottish fishing village of Eyemouth.
Catering: In house

SERVICES:
- Marriage Licence

Price Guide: Prices on application.
Catering (buffet): from £5.20pp

Morritt Arms Hotel, Nr Barnard Castle
T: 01833 627232   **F:** 01833 627392
E: relax@themorritt.co.uk   **W:** www.themorritt.co.uk
Contact: Barbara-Anne Johnson
Party Max: 350   Bedrooms: 23
The Morritt Arms Hotel, in the hamlet of Greta Bridge, is a 17th Century listed building built on the site of a Roman settlement which is still visible today. Its Dickens bar features murals by John Gilroy.

NORTHUMBRIA

Catering: In house

SERVICES:
- Marriage Licence

Price Guide: Prices on application.
Catering (sit down): from £15.00pp

Newcastle United FC, Newcastle upon Tyne
T: 0191 201 8525   F: 0191 201 8611
Contact: Conference & Banqueting
Party Max: 600

Newcastle United FC, established over 100 years ago, now play in one of the world's most modern sporting arenas. Situated in the heart of Newcastle, St James' Park offers panoramic views over the River Tyne and the City, and has extensive parking facilities. Four rooms are available for functions.
Catering: In house

SERVICES:
- Marriage Licence

Price Guide: Prices on application.
Catering (sit down): from £9.00pp

Ormesby Hall, Ormesby
T: 01642 324188   F: 01642 300937
Contact: Deborah Osborne, PA to Estate Manager
Party Max: 80 (marquee: unlimited)

Surrounded by beautiful gardens and parkland, Ormesby Hall is an imposing and elegant mid 18th Century mansion. The tea rooms are able to accommodate receptions for up to 30, while the Victorian kitchen can seat 50. Buffets can be provided for up to 80 guests. Larger groups can be accommodated in a marquee.
Catering: In house

SERVICES:
- Marriage Licence

Price Guide: Prices on application.
Catering (sit down): from £18.50pp
Catering (buffet): from £10.50pp

Pockerley Manor, Beamish
T: 01207 231811   F: 01207 290933
E: museum@beamish.org.uk   W: www.beamish.org.uk
Contact: Helen Franklin, Interpretation Assistant
Party Max: 60

Pockerley Manor is a Georgian farmhouse which reflects the lifestyles of the 1820s. A tram can take guests to Pockerley, where a drinks reception is available, but full seating is not possible.
Catering: In house

SERVICES:
- Marriage Licence

Price Guide: Prices on application.

Ramblers Country House Restaurant, Corbridge
T: 01434 632424   F: 01434 633656
Contact: Mrs Jennifer Herrmann
Party Max: 140 (marquee: 200)

This 19th Century country house is run by husband and wife team Jennifer and Heinrich Herrmann. During the "wedding season", May to October, the restaurant cannot accept bookings for parties of less than 50 guests on Saturdays.
Catering: In house

SERVICES:
- Marriage Licence

Price Guide: Prices on application.
Catering (sit down): from £19.35pp

Ravensworth Arms Hotel, Gateshead
T: 0191 487 6023   F: 0191 482 4154
Contact: Marc and Elizabeth Birch
Party Max: 250   Bedrooms: 19

The Ravensworth Arms dates back to the 18th Century. Lewis Carol is reported to have written Alice in Wonderland here, and the mother of novelist Catherine Cookson was once an employee here. Rumour has it, the novelist was even conceived here!
Catering: In house

SERVICES:
- Marriage Licence

Price Guide: Prices on application.
Catering (sit down): from £19.50pp
Catering (buffet): from £7.95pp

Rye Hill Farm, Nr Hexham
T: 01434 673259
F: 01434 673259
E: enquireies@consult-courage.co.uk
Contact: Elizabeth Courage, owner
Party Max: 14

This is a 300 year old stone farm set in 30 acres. There is a combination of self-catering (for 9) and bed and breakfast accommodation here - and even room for the odd caravan. the accommodation is in the converted Old Byre, and the original farmhouse, where the owners live, is attached.
Catering: In house/Self catering

Price Guide: B&B is £20-£25 pp, with evening meals at £12 pp. Self catering rates vary from £350 in the low season to £650 in the high season.

Shotton Hall, Peterlee
T: 0191 5862491
F: 0191 5860370
Contact: Kay Colborn, Deputy Town Clerk
Party Max: 350

Shotton Hall, built in 1760, is set in 17.5 acres of grounds. Function facilities include a waited service with a capacity of 180 and buffet service for 280.
Catering: In house

SERVICES:
- Marriage Licence

Price Guide: Prices on application.
Catering (buffet): from £3.50pp

NORTHUMBRIA

Staincliffe Hotel, Seaton Carew
T: 01429 264301   **F:** 01429 421366
Contact: Jeff Hind, Director
Party Max: 250 (marquee: 200)   Bedrooms: 24

The Staincliffe is a pre-Victorian hotel situated on the coast with views of the sea. The hotel was recently redeveloped under the supervision of Redhouse Design, with bedroom suites individually designed by Helen Morris of the award winning Stencil Library.
Catering: In house

SERVICES:
- Marriage Licence

Price Guide: Prices on application.
Catering (sit down): from £15.95pp
Catering (buffet): from £5.25pp

Swallow Gosforth Park Hotel, Newcastle upon Tyne
T: 0191 236 4111   **F:** 0191 236 8192
Contact: Gerry Reynolds, Conference Office Manager
Party Max: 500 (marquee: 500)   Bedrooms: yes

Set in 12.5 acres of wooded parkland, this hotel overlooks Newcastle Racecourse. It offers several rooms for parties from 120 up to 600.
Catering: In house

SERVICES:
- Marriage Licence

Price Guide: Prices on application.
Catering (sit down): from £24pp
Catering (buffet): from £16pp

Theatre Royal, Newcastle Upon Tyne
T: 0191 232 0997   **F:** 0191 261 1906
Contact: Greg Miller, Press & Promotions Officer
Party Max: 100

The Theatre Royal is home to one of the most successful touring theatre companies in Britain and hosts major comapnies from around the world. A variety of catering is available in one of the corporate entertaining suites of Matchams Restaurant for pre and post performance receptions, ranging from canapes to dinner parties, buffets to banquets. For programme details call 0191 232 2061. For premium seat packages and corporate membership options call 0191 244 2518.
Catering: In house

SERVICES:
- Exclusive Use

Price Guide: Prices on application.

Tillmouth Park Hotel, Cornhill-on-Tweed
T: 01890 882255   **F:** 01890 882540
Contact: Ian G Lang, General Manager
Party Max: 270 (marquee: 200)   Bedrooms: 14

Tillmouth Park is a mansion house set in 15 acres of parkland. Now an hotel, the building features stained glass windows, open log fires, oak panelling and a minstrel's gallery from which entertainers may play.

Catering: In house

SERVICES:
- Marriage Licence

Price Guide: Prices on application.
Catering (sit down): from £17.50pp

Tuxedo Royale, Gateshead
T: 0191 477 8899   **F:** 0191 477 3297
Contact: Thelma Barnes
Party Max: 500

The Tuxedo Royale is actually a ship that has been berthed on the Tyne for approximately seven years. Catering is in-house and children can be catered for separately. Although accommodation is not available on the premises, preferential rate agreements are operated with local hotels and guest houses.
Catering: In house

SERVICES:
- Marriage Licence

Price Guide: Prices on application.
Catering (buffet): from £10.95pp

Tyne Theatre & Opera House, Newcastle upon Tyne
T: 0191 232 1551
F: 0191 230 1407
Contact: Regan Old
Party Max: 250

This Grade I listed Victorian theatre features an auditorium in the classical Victorian style based on La Scala opera house in Milan. While the venue is theoretically available seven days a week throughout the year, actual availability is dependent upon the theatre's season. It is the venue's policy to offer sole use of the premises for functions.
Catering: In house

SERVICES:
- Marriage Licence

Price Guide: Prices on application.
Catering (sit down): POA

Village Farm & Town Foot Farm, Alnwick
T: 01665 57591
F: 01665 575591
E: crissy@villagefarm.demon.co.uk
W: www.villagefarm.demon.co.uk
Contact: Mrs Christine Stoker
Party Max: 50

This venue, 3 miles from Alnwick, offers a variety of properties including a 17th Century farmhouse (sleeping 12), Scandinavian chalets and cottages, as well as on-site facilities such as indoor pool, steam room, sauna, fishing, tennis and riding.
Catering: Self catering/Contract (any)

FACILITIES:
- Indoor Pool
- Riding
- Tennis
- Sauna
- Steam Room
- Fishing

Price Guide: Prices range from £125 - £655

NORTHUMBRIA

Wallington Hall, Morpeth
T: 01670 774285   F: 01670 774420
Contact: House Manager
Party Max: 40 (marquee: 250)

This listed building, owned by the National Trust, features impressive formal gardens. Clients have use of a grand piano. Live music, discos or dancing can only take place in a marquee.
Catering: Contract (any)

SERVICES:
- Marriage Licence

Price Guide: Prices on application.
Catering (sit down): from £18.50pp

Walworth Castle Hotel, Darlington
T: 01325 485470   F: 01325 462257
Contact: Mrs R A Culley
Party Max: 120 (marquee: unlimited)   Bedrooms: 34

This 12th Century castle is set in 18 acres of gardens and woodland and offers six rooms for events.
Catering: In house

SERVICES:
- Marriage Licence

Price Guide: Prices on application.
Catering (sit down): from £14.95pp
Catering (buffet): from £5.50pp

Washington Old Hall, Washington
T: 0191 416 6879   F: 0191 419 2065
Contact: Kate Gardner or Ann Hurst, Managers
Party Max: 60

Washington Old Hall, now owned by the National Trust, is a 17th Century manor house incorporating the 12th Century remains of the home of George Washington's ancestors. The house is furnished with contemporary paintings, delftware and richly carved oak furniture. Wedding ceremonies can take place in the Great Hall.
Catering: In house

SERVICES:
- Exclusive Use
- Marriage Licence
- Piped Music

Price Guide: £250 - £650
Catering (sit down): from £16pp
Catering (buffet): from £10pp

WALES

Ashburnham Hotel, Llanelli
T: 01554 834343 **F:** 01554 834483
Contact: Susan Thomas
Party Max: 150 (marquee: unlimited)   *Bedrooms: 13*

This hotel, restaurant and public house is set in its own grounds overlooking the Ashburnham Championship Golf Links and the Gower Peninsula.
Catering: In house

SERVICES:
- Marriage Licence

Price Guide: Prices on application.
Catering (sit down): from £13.95pp

Barlings Barn, Llanbrynmair
T: 01650 521479
F: 01650 521520
E: barlbarn@zetnet.co.uk
W: www.barlbrn.zetnet.co.uk
Contact: Terry & Felicity Margolis, Proprietors
Party Max: 26

This characterful, honeysuckle clad 18th Century cottage (sleeping 10-12), plus its adjacent barn (sleeps 14-16), are set in the hills of mid Wales. The Barn and Cottage share an indoor heated swimming pool and sauna, while the Barn also has a private squash court.
Catering: Self catering/In house

FACILITIES:
- Indoor Pool
- Pool/Snooker
- Squash

SERVICES:
- Exclusive Use
- Flowers

Price Guide: Weekly rates are £430 - £2500

Baskerville Hall Hotel, Hay on Wye
T: 01497 820033
E: enquiries@baskervillehall.co.uk
W: www.baskervillehall.co.uk
Contact: Tim Northam, Events Manager
Party Max: 400   *Bedrooms: 30 + dormitories for 60*

Baskerville Hall, built in 1839, was the inspiration for Conan Doyle's Sherlock Holmes story, Hound of the Baskerville. Set in the Wye valley in its own 130 acres of Welsh countryside, the Hall overlooks the Brecon Beacons and the Black Mountains. There is usually an in house disco here every Saturday night.
Catering: In house

FACILITIES:
- Shooting
- Indoor Pool
- Paint Ball
- Go Karting
- Pool/Snooker
- Quad Bikes/Off Road
- Raft Building
- Abseiling
- Gorge Walking
- Canoeing
- Carving

SERVICES:
- Exclusive Use
- Marriage Licence
- Cake
- Disco/Dance
- Entertainers
- Performance Area
- Valet Parking

Price Guide: From £2500 per day.
Catering (buffet): from £5pp

Beth Ruach, St David's
T: 01189 266094
E: enquiries@lowermoorcottages.co.uk
W: www.lowermoorcottages.co.uk
Contact: Lillian Marlow, owner
Party Max: 20

This is a character stone and slate cottage with a log fire, in a quiet and peaceful location a few minutes walk from the coastal path and sandy beaches. The cottage is half a mile from St Davids with its Cathedral, shops, pubs and restaurants. It has enclosed private gardens, patio, barbecue and games room with table tennis and pool table.
Catering: Self catering

FACILITIES:
- Pool/Snooker
- Table Tennis

SERVICES:
- Exclusive Use

Price Guide: £250 - £1750

Bryn Boleded Libanus, Tallybont-on-Usk
T: 01874 676446 **F:** 01874 676416
E: enquiries@breconcottages.com
W: www.breconcottages.com
Contact: Elizabeth Daniel, Proprietor
Party Max: 28

This farmhouse is located on a working farm and is in two halves. The original part is 16th Century, while the later wing dates from the 18th Century. The farmhouse offers panoramic views over the Brecons with footpaths to the mountains from the farm.
Catering: Self catering

SERVICES:
- Exclusive Use

Price Guide: Price range from £490 - £950. Extra nights are charged at £80.

Brynich Farmhouse, Tallybont-on-Usk
T: 01874 676446 **F:** 01874 676416
E: liz@bcotts.idiscover.co.uk **W:** www.breconcottages.com
Contact: Elizabeth Daniel
Party Max: 17

Brynich Farmhouse is superbly situated with one of the most magnificent views across the Usk Valley to the nearby Brecon Beacons. The farmhouse, dating from the 17th Century, is well equipped and comfortable. Below the farm is the River Usk and the Brecon and Monmouth Canal.
Catering: Self catering

SERVICES:
- Exclusive Use

Price Guide: Rates vary from £500 - £1250 per week rent.

Caer Beris Manor, Builth Wells
T: 01982 552601 **F:** 01982 552586
E: caerberismanor@btinternet.com
Contact: Peter & Katharine Smith
Party Max: 200   *Bedrooms: 22*

WALES

This former home of Lord Swansea, is set in 27 acres of parkland.
Catering: In house

SERVICES:
- Marriage Licence

Price Guide: Prices on application.
Catering (sit down): from £10.95pp

Caerphilly Castle, Caerphilly
T: 029 2082 6185   **F:** 029 2082 6375
Contact: Phillip Stallard, Site Facilities Officer
Party Max: 200

This medieval castle is said to be the largest in Wales. The Great Hall here is available for functions, and wedding ceremonies. The venue provides furniture, kitchen facilities and security. The hirer is responsible for arranging all catering, insurance and licences as required.
Catering: Contract (any)

SERVICES:
- Exclusive Use
- Marriage Licence

Price Guide: Venue hire starts at £370 + vat.

Canolfan Pentre Ifan, Crymych
T: 01239 820317   **F:** 01239 820317
Contact: Steffan Jenkins
Party Max: 80 (marquee: unlimited)   Bedrooms: yes

This Tudor gatehouse, dating from 1485, is a listed building. At Canolfan Pentre Ifan you may supply your own alcohol.
Catering: In house

SERVICES:
- Marriage Licence

Price Guide: Prices on application.
Catering (sit down): £7.50 - 15.00pp

Cardiff Castle, Cardiff
T: 029 2087 8100   **F:** 029 2023 1417
E: cardiffcastle@cardiff.gov.uk
Contact: Marketing Officer
Party Max: 150

Situated in the heart of Wales's capital city, Grade I listed Cardiff Castle contains some of the most historic interiors in Britain, several of which are available for hire, including the Banqueting Hall, Library and George Thomas Suite. For an alternative celebration the castle offers a traditional Welsh banquet, complete with entertainment, in the 15th Century Medieval Hall.
Catering: In house

SERVICES:
- Marriage Licence

Price Guide: £50 - £150 per hour, depending on room.
Catering (sit down): from £17.75pp
Catering (buffet): from £7.25pp

Castle of Brecon Hotel, Brecon
T: 01874 624611   **F:** 01874 623737
W: www.breconcastle.co.uk

Contact: Duty Manager
Party Max: 200   Bedrooms: 45

The Castle of Brecon is a listed building with its own gardens and excellent views.
Catering: In house

SERVICES:
- Marriage Licence

Price Guide: Prices on application.
Catering (sit down): from £25.00pp packages

Celtic Haven Village, Lydstep
T: 01437 767600   **F:** 01437 767604
E: news-desk@activitywales.co.uk
W: www.activitywales.co.uk
Contact: Reservations
Party Max: 260 (marquee: 500)

Celtic Haven Village nestling above the beach at Lydstep and is a former 12th Century estate. This has 26 5-star cottages, with golf, tennis, gym, cinema, indoor pool and saunas all on site. The venue says that the philosphy of the staff is "The answer is Yes, now what's the question?" The Ivy Tower Village is also run by Activity Wales and sleeps 120 people.
Catering: Contract (any)/Self catering/In house

FACILITIES:
- Helipad
- Gym
- Cinema
- Golf
- Tennis
- Sauna
- Indoor Pool
- Table Tennis

SERVICES:
- Exclusive Use
- Toastmaster
- Flowers
- Valet Parking
- Cake

Price Guide: Conference centre prices start at £150 for a room for 20 people.
Catering (sit down): from £10pp
Catering (buffet): from £5pp

Cnewr Farmhouse, Brecon
T: 01874 636207   **F:** 01874 638833
Contact: Rachel Lloyd, Owner
Party Max: 14

Cnewr Farmhouse is situated on a working 12,000 acre estate in the middle of the Brecon Beacons. It has 2 separate sitting rooms - one adjoining the kitchen, which has an enormous dining table.
Catering: Self catering

FACILITIES:
- Shooting

SERVICES:
- Exclusive Use

Price Guide: £225 - £500

Coach Inn, Caernarfon
T: 01286 660212   **F:** 01286 660785
E: skypix@clara.co.uk
Contact: Stephen or Edna Williams
Party Max: 80 (marquee: 200)   Bedrooms: 8

This Inn is a Grade II listed building. Functions can take place

in its Wheelers Dining Room, which recently hosted a cowboys and indians themed wedding.
Catering: In house

SERVICES:
• Marriage Licence

Price Guide: Prices on application.
Catering (sit down): from £9.95pp
Catering (buffet): from £8.95pp

Cornist Hall, Flint
T: 01352 733241 **F:** 01352 731710
Contact: Mrs S Napier
Party Max: 180

The Cornist Hall is a Jacobean mansion set in parkland and featuring an original walled rose garden.
Catering: In house

SERVICES:
• Marriage Licence

Price Guide: Prices on application.
Catering (sit down): from £12.00pp
Catering (buffet): from £6.00pp

Court Colman Hotel, Penyfai
T: 01656 720212 **F:** 01656 724544
Contact: Vijay Bhagotra
Party Max: 150   Bedrooms: 34

Court Coleman is set in six acres of grounds, and was the seat of the Llewellyn family. Internally, the hotel features a wide sweeping staircase, oak panelled walls, and a fireplace in the hall that is a replica of one in the Doges Palace in Venice. The Ballroom is modelled on the Crystal Room in the Palace of Versailles.
Catering: In house

SERVICES:
• Marriage Licence

Price Guide: Prices on application.
Catering (sit down): from £24.50pp
Catering (buffet): from £8.95pp

Cwmwennol Country House, Saundersfoot
T: 01834 813430 **F:** 01834813430
E: cwmwennol@lineone.net
W: www.website.lineone.net/cwmwennol
Contact: Tony Smiles
Party Max: 150   Bedrooms: yes

Cwmwennol has a woodland setting, just 300 yards from the beach. The original building dates back to 1870s. The current owners took over the hotel in 1989. Recent improvements have included the refurbishment of the restaurant in Laura Ashley designs.
Catering: In house

SERVICES:
• Marriage Licence

Price Guide: Prices on application.
Catering (sit down): from £10.00pp
Catering (buffet): from £5.50pp

De Courcey's, Cardiff
T: 029 2089 2232 **F:** 029 2089 1949
Contact: Patricia and Thilo Thielmann
Party Max: 175

De Courcey's is a purpose-built restaurant and dining suite set in 3.5 acres of grounds, 15 minutes from the city centre.
Catering: In house

SERVICES:
• Marriage Licence

Price Guide: Prices on application.
Catering (sit down): from £23.00pp
Catering (buffet): from £10.95pp

Dylan Thomas Centre, Swansea
T: 01792 463980 **F:** 01792 463993
E: dylan.thomas@cableol.co.uk **W:** www.dylanthomas.org
Contact: Events Organiser
Party Max: 200

Once the Old Town Guildhall, the Dylan Thomas Centre now hosts the Dylan Thomas exhibition and also regularly hosts visual work from local artists. The Centre has a regular literature programme including the annual Dylan Thomas Celebration. The Centre offers 9 function rooms including an auditorium.
Catering: In house

Price Guide: Prices on application.
Catering (sit down): POA

Egerton Grey Hotel, Nr Barry
T: 01446 711666 **F:** 01446 711690
Contact: Anthony Pitkin
Party Max: 90   Bedrooms: 10

This former 19th Century rectory, 10 miles from Cardiff, was opened as a small luxury hotel in 1988. It is set in seven acres of gardens, with croquet lawn and tennis court, with views down to Porthkerry Park and the sea. At Egerton Grey, an alternative to the formal sit-down meal is offered: a buffet luncheon. Guests are served in the main Dining Room, but may then be seated at tables throughout the house; in the Library, the two halls, the Private Dining Room, the Drawing Room or outside.
Catering: In house

SERVICES:
• Marriage Licence

Price Guide: Prices on application.
Catering (sit down): from £17.50pp

Fairyhill, Swansea
T: 01792 390139 **F:** 01792 391358
E: postbox@fairyhill.net **W:** www.fairyhill.net
Contact: Peter & Jane Camm, Andrew Hetherington or Paul Davies, Owners
Party Max: 40 (marquee: 150)   Bedrooms: 8

This Grade II listed 18th Century former country house, now a

WALES

5-star hotel, is set in the heart of the Gower peninsula in its own 24 acres. The hotel boasts an award winning restaurant and wine list.
Catering: In house

FACILITIES:
- Helipad

SERVICES:
- Exclusive Use
- Piped Music

Price Guide: Prices start at £1120 per night B&B for all 8 rooms.
Catering (sit down): from £32pp

Fonmon Castle, Barry
T: 01446 710206   **F:** 01446 711687
E: fonmon-castle@msn.com
Contact: Ms Sophie Katzi, Castle Administrator
Party Max: 120 (marquee: 600)

This Grade I listed Norman castle, dating from around 1180, was extensively remodelled in the 12th and 18th Centuries. Features include Rococo interiors, fine collections of paintings and books, and outstanding grounds.
Catering: Contract approved list

FACILITIES:
- Shooting
- Paint Ball
- Quad Bikes/Off Road

SERVICES:
- Exclusive Use

Price Guide: Prices on application.
Catering (sit down): POA

Gliffaes Country House Hotel, Crickhowell
T: 01874 730371   **F:** 01874 730463
E: call@gliffaeshotel.com   **W:** www.gliffaeshotel.com
Contact: James Suter
Party Max: 150   *Bedrooms: 22*

Gliffaes is a Victorian, Italianate house overlooking the River Usk and set in 33 acres of parkland and gardens. The Regency style Drawing Room and the Dining Room are available for functions.
Catering: In house

SERVICES:
- Marriage Licence

Price Guide: Prices on application.
Catering (sit down): from £25.50pp

Glynhir Mansion, Llandybie
T: 01269 850438   **F:** 01269 851275
E: glynhir@glynhir.demon.co.uk
Contact: Katy Jenkins, Partner
Party Max: 75   *Bedrooms: 26*

Glynhir is a unique Grade II listed 18th Century estate in the foothills of the Black Mountains. The estate includes 6 individual cottages, flats and houses, (tastefully restored and clustered around an old farmyard), and the relaxed and informal rooms in the mansion house itself, including 7 bedrooms. Features on the estate include a dovecote and ice house, and a 30 foot waterfall in the gardens. This venue has 12 years experience in group accommodation, with the owners living on site in the main house. Use of a nearby field can usually be arranged for activities if required.
Catering: In house / Self catering

FACILITIES:
- Table Tennis

SERVICES:
- Exclusive Use
- Disco/Dance
- Fireworks
- Valet Parking
- Marriage Licence
- Live Music
- Photography
- Flowers
- Entertainers
- Performance Area

Price Guide: £19.50 - £6000 +
Wedding ceremony prices are from £250.
Catering (sit down): from £12.50pp
Catering (buffet): from £10pp

Gwydir Castle, Llanrwyst
T: 01492 641687
Contact: Judy Corbett or Peter Welford
Party Max: 80 (marquee: unlimited)   *Bedrooms: 2*

This historic, 16th Century castle is set in Grade I listed gardens.
Catering: In house

SERVICES:
- Marriage Licence

Price Guide: Prices on application.
Catering (sit down): POA

Heronston Hotel, Bridgend
T: 01656 668811   **F:** 01656 767391
E: reservations@heronston-hotel.demon.co.uk
Contact: Richard Watson, Conference & Banqueting Coordinator
Party Max: 250   *Bedrooms: 75*

The Heronston is a modern hotel situated in the heart of Glamorgan. It offers full conference and banqueting facilities and 76 en suite bedrooms, some with French doors onto a patio area.
Catering: In house

FACILITIES:
- Indoor Pool
- Sauna
- Jacuzzi
- Solarium
- Steam Room
- Outdoor Pool

Price Guide: Prices on application.
Catering (sit down): POA
Catering (buffet): POA

Highfield Hall Hotel, Northop
T: 01352 840221   **F:** 01352 840221
Contact: Virginia Smith or Molly Millar
Party Max: 200 (marquee: unlimited)   *Bedrooms: 14*

This Georgian Grade II listed building is set in nine acres of mature gardens. The hotel was established in 1982, is family owned, and specialises in weddings.
Catering: In house

SERVICES:
- Marriage Licence

WALES

Price Guide: Prices on application.
Catering (sit down): from £16.50pp

Holly Farm, Llandridnod Wells
T: 01597 822402 **F:** 01597 822402
W: www.ukworld.net/hollyfarm
Contact: Ruth Jones, Proprietor

Party Max: 10 | Bedrooms: 5

Holly Farm is a tastefully restored Tudor farmhouse on a working farm in a peaceful location. The Farm offers 3-star b&b in ensuite bedrooms, with views over fields and woods, TV and 2 sitting rooms with log fires.
Catering: Self catering

Price Guide: £20 - £25pp b&b.

Lake Country House Hotel, Llangammarch Wells
T: 01591 620202 **F:** 01591 620457
Contact: Mr J P Mifsud

Party Max: 130 (marquee: unlimited) | Bedrooms: 19

The Lake is a Victorian Welsh country house set in 50 acres, with sweeping lawns, rhododendron lined pathways, riverside walks and a large trout lake. This is a homely sort of hotel that serves Welsh teas in front of the log fire in the drawing room every afternoon.
Catering: In house

SERVICES:
• Marriage Licence
Price Guide: Prices on application.
Catering (sit down): from £25.50pp

Lake Vyrnwy Hotel, Lake Vyrnwy
T: 01691 870692 **F:** 01691 870259
Contact: Jim Talbot

Party Max: 200 | Bedrooms: 35

This country house hotel sits overlooking the six mile long Lake Vyrnwy. The hotel holds two AA Rosettes for its restaurant.
Catering: In house

SERVICES:
• Marriage Licence
Price Guide: Prices on application.
Catering (sit down): from £17.00pp

Langland Court Hotel, Swansea
T: 01792 361545 **F:** 01792 362302
Contact: Chris Hamilton-Smith

Party Max: 220 (marquee: 300) | Bedrooms: 19

This Tudor-style house is set in award winning gardens in a quiet residential area and boasts sea views.
Catering: In house

SERVICES:
• Marriage Licence
Price Guide: Prices on application.
Catering (sit down): from £15.95pp
Catering (buffet): from £12.25pp

Llangoed Hall, Brecon
T: 01874 754525 **F:** 01874 754545
E: 101543,3211@compuserve.com
W: www.llangoedhall.com/ llangoed.html
or: www.ashley-house.com
Contact: Michelle Pepper

Party Max: 50 | Bedrooms: 23

Llangoed Hall is a listed building that sits on the banks of the river Wye and was designed by Sir Clough Williams-Ellis. The atmosphere of the house is designed to be that of your own home, and is delightfully presented in the Hall's literature. The Hall can accommodate up to 50 guests in The Orangery and a maximum of 14 in the Whistler Room. Carriages should be arranged before 6pm. Should you want to party on into the evening, it would be necessary to take the Hall on an exclusive use basis. The Hall's restaurant has three AA Rosettes and a star, and four red pavilions from Michelin.
Catering: In house

SERVICES:
• Marriage Licence   • Exclusive Use
Price Guide: Prices on application.
Catering (sit down): £17.50 - 39.00pp

Llwyndu Farmhouse, Barmouth
T: 01341 280144 **F:** 01341 281236
E: intouch@llwyndu-farmhouse.co.uk
W: www.llwyndu-farmhouse.co.uk
Contact: Mrs P. Thompson, Owner

Party Max: 14

This listed 16th Century farmhouse overlooks Cardigan Bay, with a mountain backdrop. Set in its own grounds, activities can be arranged, including climbing and gorge walking.
Catering: In house

Price Guide: Prices range from £32pp per night b&b. 7 nights accommodation with dinner in a four-poster room is £325pp.
Catering (sit down): from £14.95pp

Maerdy Cottages, Nr Llandeilo
T: 01550 777448 **F:** 01550 777067
E: danycefn@netscapeonline.co.uk
W: www.ukworld.net/maerdy.htm
Contact: Margaret Jones, Owner

Party Max: 30 (marquee: 150)

The Maerdy, 3 miles from Llandeilo, is set in quiet and secluded mature gardens. The Grade II listed 300 year old farmhouse and its original stone buildings were once the home farm of the historic Robert Peel Estate. These have now been converted into 6 cottages sleeping between 3 and 10 people. Each offers unusual comforts with traditional interiors boasting beams, panelling, antique furniture and open fires. Although these are self-catering units, servicing and catering is available and the properties are often let out to groups of up to 30
Catering: Contract (any)/Self catering

SERVICES:
• Exclusive Use
Price Guide: Prices range from £200 - £3250 per week

WALES

Catering (sit down): from £10pp
Catering (buffet): from £6pp

Margam Country Park, Port Talbot
T: 01639 881635   **F:** 01639 895897
Contact: Rosemary Lloyd
Party Max: 400 (marquee: unlimited)   Bedrooms: yes

This award-winning orangery, set in acres of ornamental gardens, was originally built in 1786 and is the biggest of its kind in Britain. Following extensive restoration work the Orangery was opened by the Queen in 1977. All catering is in-house, undertaken by the Orangery's own contract caterers.
Catering: Contract approved list

SERVICES:
- Marriage Licence

Price Guide: Prices on application.
Catering (sit down): £10.00 - 30.00pp

Memorial Hall Theatre, Barry
T: 01446 738663   **F:** 01446 741626
Contact: Mrs S Baddeley
Party Max: 350

The Memorial Hall is a period building with gardens and is a popular venue for theatre productions and concerts and wedding parties.
Catering: Contract (any)

SERVICES:
- Marriage Licence

Price Guide: Prices on application.
Catering (sit down): POA

Miskin Manor, Pontyclun
T: 01443 224204   **F:** 01443 237606
Contact: Joanna Kocker
Party Max: 150 (marquee: 500)   Bedrooms: 32

This four star hotel is housed in a Grade II listed building set in 20 acres of gardens. It has a Wales Tourist Board Five Crowns Highly Commended Award. The hotel is able to offer menus to suit your requirements, including special Welsh menus.
Catering: In house

SERVICES:
- Marriage Licence

Price Guide: Prices on application.
Catering (sit down): from £21.50pp

Museum of Welsh Life, Cardiff
T: 029 2057 3500   **F:** 029 2057 3490
Contact: Anwen Jones
Party Max: 80 (marquee: unlimited)

Functions are possible for up to 50 guests in the Main Hall at St Fagans Castle and for up to 100 in the Concert Hall at the Oakdale Institute. Hirers can contact the on-site caterers, Apple Catering on 029 2056 6985, or alternatively bring in your own caterers should you choose the Oakdale Institute or have a marquee. Limited catering is available in the Oakdale Institute.
Catering: Contract (any)/Contract approved list

SERVICES:
- Marriage Licence

Price Guide: Prices on application.
Catering (sit down): POA

Nanteos Mansion, Aberystwyth
T: 01970 624363   **F:** 01970 626332
Contact: Graham or Sue Hodgson-Jones
Party Max: 170 (marquee: 150)   Bedrooms: 7

Nanteos is a Grade II listed mansion with connections with Wagner and the Holy Grail. It is now operating as an hotel and restaurant and features a Rococo style music room, claimed to be the finest in Wales.
Catering: In house

SERVICES:
- Marriage Licence

Price Guide: Prices on application.
Catering (sit down): from £22.00pp
Catering (buffet): from £15.00pp

New House Country Hotel, Cardiff
T: 029 2052 0280   **F:** 029 2052 0324
Contact: Stephen Banks
Party Max: 200 (marquee: 300)   Bedrooms: 36

This country hotel is housed in a Grade II listed building with views of Cardiff and the Bristol Channel. The hotel has two AA Rosettes for its cuisine.
Catering: In house

SERVICES:
- Marriage Licence

Price Guide: Prices on application.
Catering (sit down): from £16.00pp

Oriel Plas Glyn-y-Weddw Gallery, Pwllheli
T: 01758 740763   **F:** 01758 740232
E: enquiry@oriel.org.uk   **W:** http://www.oriel.org.uk
Contact: David Jeffreys, Director
Party Max: 110   Bedrooms: 9

This is a leading North Wales Arts Centre offering a year round programme of exhibitions. Facilities include a restaurant, disabled access and good parking. The centre also offers a programme of art courses which are held in its residential wing.
Catering: In house/Contract (any)

SERVICES:
- Exclusive Use
- Valet Parking

Price Guide: Venue hire is from £150 - £1000.

Penrhynhalen, Bordogan
T: 01407 840253   **F:** 01407 840197
Contact: The Owner
Party Max: 18

'The Salt Merchant's House' is situated in a quiet, rural location on the island of Anglesey, and offers 7 bedrooms and 5 bathrooms and several reception rooms. The house has central heating as well as open fires. The house is not far from the Anglesey

WALES

Motor Racing School where tuition can be arranged.
Catering: Self catering

FACILITIES:
- Pool/Snooker

SERVICES:
- Exclusive Use

Price Guide: From £162 per night to £1680 for a week at Christmas and New Year.

Plas Dolguog Hotel, Machynlleth
T: 01654 702244   **F:** 01654 702530
Contact: Mrs Pritchard
Party Max: 180 (marquee: 260)   Bedrooms: 9

This is a listed 16th Century country house set in nine acres of garden and woodland.
Catering: In house

SERVICES:
- Marriage Licence

Price Guide: Prices on application.
Catering (sit down): from £12.95pp

Plas Hafod Country House Hotel, Mold
T: 01352 700177   **F:** 01352 755499
Contact: Mrs Buckley
Party Max: 150   Bedrooms: 11

Hafod Hall was built in the 1730s and features an imposing entrance and stone staircase, and a romantic garden setting of around nine acres.
Catering: In house

SERVICES:
- Marriage Licence

Price Guide: Prices on application.
Catering (sit down): from £16.95pp

Rossett Hall Hotel, Wrexham
T: 01244 571000   **F:** 01244 571505
E: reservations@rossethallhotel.co.uk
W: www.rossetthallhotel.co.uk
Contact: Debbie Pinder
Party Max: 180 (marquee: 150)   Bedrooms: 30

Rossett Hall is a Grade II listed building, built in 1750.
Catering: In house

SERVICES:
- Marriage Licence

Price Guide: Prices on application.
Catering (sit down): £16.95 - 32.00pp

Seiont Manor Hotel, Caernarfon
T: 01286 673366
F: 01286 672840
Contact: Nicola Dawson or Marianne Griffiths
Party Max: 100 (marquee: 400)   Bedrooms: 28

This is a country house hotel set in 150 acres featuring salmon river, lake and formal herb garden.
Catering: In house

SERVICES:
- Marriage Licence

Price Guide: Prices on application.
Catering (sit down): from £18.50pp
Catering (buffet): from £8.95pp

Soughton Hall Country House Hotel, Northop
T: 01352 840811
F: 01352 840382
Contact: Rosemary Rodenhurst
Party Max: 200 (marquee: 300)   Bedrooms: 14

This Georgian country house hotel is set in parkland with a half mile long, 150 year old, lime tree avenue, which can feature in wedding photographs. The house retains many original period fittings, and is full of antiques assembled for generations. Surprisingly, then, the owners of Soughton Hall welcome young children. The hotel offers a video of its wedding services.
Catering: In house

SERVICES:
- Marriage Licence

Price Guide: Prices on application.
Catering (sit down): from £23.00pp

Swallow Tree Gardens, Saundersfoot
T: 01834 812398
F: 01834 812558
E: weddings@swallowtreegardens.co.uk
W: www.swallowtreegardens.co.uk
Contact: Debbie Webber
Party Max: 60 (marquee: 100)

This restaurant is located within the Pembrokeshire National Park and has views over Carmarthen Bay.
Catering: In house

SERVICES:
- Marriage Licence

Price Guide: Prices on application.
Catering (sit down): from £16.00pp
Catering (buffet): from £6.95pp

Sychnant Pass House, Conwy
T: 01492 596868
F: 01492 596868
E: bresykes@sychnant-pass-house.co.uk
Contact: Functions Manager
Party Max: 50 (marquee: 150)   Bedrooms: 11

This is a country house hotel set in 2.5 acres with a pond and small stream.
Catering: In house/Contract (any)

FACILITIES:
- Helipad
- Hot Air Balloons

SERVICES:
- Marriage Licence
- Live Music
- Piped Music

Price Guide: Prices on application.
Catering (sit down): from £20pp
Catering (buffet): from £20pp

WALES

Tre-ysgawen Hall, Anglesey
T: 01248 750750   **F:** 01248 750035
E: enquiries@sue-rowlands-centre.org.uk
W: www.sue-rowlands-centre.org.uk
Contact: Neil Rowlands

Party Max: 200 (marquee: unlimited)   *Bedrooms: 20*

This restored country mansion dates from 1882. The Hall offers European cuisine, and is Egon Ronay recommended.
Catering: In house

SERVICES:
- Marriage Licence

Price Guide: Prices on application.
Catering (sit down): from £22.00pp
Catering (buffet): from £7.50pp

Treowen, Monmouth
T: 01600 712031   **F:** 01600 712031
E: john.wheelock@virgin.net
W: http://freespace.virginnet.co.uk/treowen
Contact: John Wheelock, Owner

Party Max: 100   *Bedrooms: 11*

Treowen is a Grade I listed Jacobean manor house surrounded by a private estate of farm and woodland in the Wye Valley. The whole house, including 11 bedrooms and private garden are let as one. The main reception rooms are the Banqueting Hall, the Dining Room, the Oak Room sitting room with open fire, and the Long Drawing Room with open fire place and grand piano.
Catering: Contract (any)/Self catering

FACILITIES:
- Table Tennis

SERVICES:
- Exclusive Use
- Marriage Licence

Price Guide: £555 - £1530 per day. Christmas and New Year £1800 - £2310.

Warpool Court Hotel, St Davids
T: 01437 720300   **F:** 01437 720676
Contact: Rupert Duffin

Party Max: 200 (marquee: 200)   *Bedrooms: 25*

The AA and RAC Three Star, two rosettes, Warpool Court Hotel enjoys sweeping views across its lawns to the coast of St Brides Bay and the off-shore islands. Inside, the hotel is embellished by 3,000 hand painted tiles decorated by the lady who lived here in the early 1900s.
Catering: In house

SERVICES:
- Marriage Licence

Price Guide: Prices on application.
Catering (sit down): from £24.00pp

West Arms Hotel, Nr Llangollen
T: 01691 600665   **F:** 01691 600622
E: gowestarms@aol.com
W: www.hotelwalesuk.com
Contact: Geoff & Gill Leigh-Ford, Proprietors

Party Max: 120 (marquee: 150)   *Bedrooms: 19*

This 16th Century hotel/shooting inn is situated at the foot of the Berwyn HIlls in the Ceiriog Valley. This is a warm cosy hotel with inglenook fireplaces, beams and slab floors.
Catering: In house

FACILITIES:
- Helipad
- Fishing
- Caving
- Cycling
- Canal Trips

SERVICES:
- Exclusive Use
- Fireworks
- Marriage Licence
- Piped Music
- Disco/Dance
- Performance Area

Price Guide: Bed and breakfast rates start at £41.50pp. Conference rates for full board start at £105pp per day.
Catering (sit down): from £15.75pp
Catering (buffet): from £7.90pp

West Usk Lighthouse, Newport
T: 01633 810126/815860   **F:** 01633 815582
E: lighthouse@tesco.net
W: smoothhound.co.uk/hotels/westusk.html
Contact: Frank & Danielle Sheahan, Owners

Party Max: 12   *Bedrooms: 6*

Built in 1812 this lighthouse is Grade II listed and has special features such as an internal well and wedge-shaped rooms. There is also a Lantern Room with 360° views over land and sea, overlooking the Severn Estuary and the Bristol Channel. This venue is available on a B&B basis only.
Catering: Self catering

Price Guide: Rates here are £400 per day B&B. Hire of the outbuilding is £50 per day.

Wolfscastle Country Hotel, Haverfordwest
T: 01437 741688/741225   **F:** 01437 741383
Contact: Function Manager

Party Max: 180   *Bedrooms: 20*

Once an old vicarage, this hotel was bought in 1976 by Andrew Stirling who now runs it with his wife Pauline. The hotel is very much a family affair.
Catering: In house

SERVICES:
- Exclusive Use
- Piped Music
- Marriage Licence
- Performance Area
- Flowers

Price Guide: £50 - £300.
Catering (sit down): from £10.75pp
Catering (buffet): from £11.50pp

Wye View Cottages, Llangurig
T: 01686 440205   **F:** 01686 440205
E: wyeview@wyeview.kitaonline.co.uk
W: www.homepages.kitaonline.co.uk/wyeview/
Contact: Stephen & Carol Clarke-Williams, Owners

Party Max: 10   *Bedrooms: 8*

Wye View Cottages, are 3 Grade 4 self-contained cottages that were converted from a 19th Century barn and sit in their own acre of ground. Together they accommodate 10 people. They are cut into the side of the 1300 feet high Foel Gurig hill, and overlook the River Wye and the Cambrian mountains. Water to the cottages is sourced from their own spring.

WALES

Catering: Self catering/In house

FACILITIES:
- Fishing
- Bowls
- Yoga
- Walking

SERVICES:
- Exclusive Use
- Flowers
- Cake
- Toastmaster

Price Guide: £140 - £299
Catering (sit down): n/a
Catering (buffet): n/a

Ystumgwern Hall Farm, Dyffryn Ardudwy

T: 01341 247249 **F:** 01341 247171
E: ynys@ystumgwern.co.uk **W:** www.ystumgwern.co.uk
Contact: Jane Williams, Owner

Party Max: 16

Ystumgwern Farm offers a 16th Century farmhouse that has been converted into two 5-dragon self-catering properties: Ynys with 3 bedrooms and Gwytheyrn with 4 bedrooms. Apartments have also been created in the nearby barn conversion. Additional facilities include landscaped lawn areas for barbecues and leisure activities.

Catering: Self catering/In house

FACILITIES:
- Pool/Snooker
- Table Tennis

SERVICES:
- Exclusive Use
- Flowers
- Cake

Price Guide: B&B is £26pp per night or £165 per week.

SCOTLAND

Achinduich Lodge, by Lairg
T: 01381 610496 **F:** 01381 610481
Contact: Wynne Bentley
Party Max: 14   Bedrooms: 5

This was one of the old fishing lodges of the Skibo estate and is situated near the Falls of Shin (apparently the best place in Scotland to see salmon leaping). The Lodge is set in large gardens with views over the surrounding hills and forests. The main house sleep 10 (self-catering), and there is a wood panelled summer annex for a further 4. There are good local facilities including the Sutherland Game and Shellfish Company supplying fresh lobsters, scallops, crab and venison. This property is managed by Large Holiday Houses - see Agency Listing. Written agreement is required for weddings or parties.
Catering: Self catering

SERVICES:
• Exclusive Use
Price Guide: House rental is from £500 - £1000 per week. Annex is extra.

Argyll's Lodging, Stirling
T: 0131 668 8686/01786 431319
F: 01786 448194
Contact: Jon MacNeil
Party Max: 120

This is claimed to be the finest and most complete example in Scotland of a 17th Century town residence. The principal rooms within the lodging have recently been restored and furnished as they would have been in 1680. Two rooms are available for functions and can be used together. The smaller room seats 26 for dinner.
Catering: In house

SERVICES:
• Exclusive Use
Price Guide: £600 - £800+
Catering (sit down): POA

Bailey Mill, Newcastleton
T: 016977 48617
F: 016977 48617
W: www.holidaycottagescumbria.co.uk
Contact: Mrs Pamela Copeland, Owner
Party Max: 40   Bedrooms: 22

This is a friendly farm holiday complex and pony trekking centre offering self-catered courtyard apartments, or B&B. Full board riding holidays are also available. All can be rented together for a large celebration.
Catering: Self catering/In house

FACILITIES:
• Riding • Pool/Snooker • Cycling
SERVICES:
• Flowers • Cake • Live Music
• Entertainers • Fireworks
Price Guide: £98 - £508
Catering (sit down): from £10pp
Catering (buffet): from £8pp

Balbirnie House, Glenrothes
T: 01592 610066 **F:** 01592 610529
E: balbirnie@breathemail.net **W:** www.balbirnie.co.uk
Contact: Rosemary Spenke, Deputy Manager/co-proprietor
Party Max: 216 (marquee: 300)   Bedrooms: 30

Balbirnie House is a Georgian mansion house dating from 1777 and set in a 416 acre country estate, with Balbirnie Park golf course surrounding the property. Now listed Grade A, Balbirnie has been caringly restored and is now a privately owned small luxury hotel. The hotel offers elegant spacious public rooms, the original Library Bar, and Orangery style restaurant and 8 different conference and dining rooms. Balbirnie's purpose-built Ballroom opened in 2000; it is Georgian in style with floor to ceiling windows and its own private garden area.
Catering: In house

FACILITIES:
• Helipad • Golf • Croquet
SERVICES:
• Exclusive Use • Flowers • Toastmaster
• Disco/Dance • Piped Music • Performance Area
• Valet Parking
Price Guide: £10,000 exclusive hire charge.
Catering (sit down): from £25pp
Catering (buffet): from £25pp

Benmore Lodge, Isle of Mull
T: 01381 610496 **F:** 01381 610481
Contact: Wynne Bentley
Party Max: 16   Bedrooms: 7

This peaceful shooting lodge is on the shores of Loch Ba and close to Ben More on the Isle of Mull and stands in its own secluded grounds. Although the lodge will sleep up to 16 people, it is most comfortably appointed for 12 adults, although those with small children could accommodate more. Facilities include a large games room with full size billiards table, darts and a piano. Fishing and a boat are included in the rental. This property is managed by Large Holiday Houses. See Agency Listing also. Written agreement is required for weddings or parties.
Catering: Self catering

FACILITIES:
• Pool/Snooker • Games Room • Fishing
• Piano
SERVICES:
• Exclusive Use
Price Guide: House rental is £1100 to £1650.

Blair Castle, Pitlochry
T: 01796 481207 **F:** 01796 481487
Contact: Geoff Crerar
Party Max: 400

Blair Castle has a colourful history and is now open to the public to show off 32 of its rooms containing a fine collection of furniture, paintings, costumes, Jacobite relics and other artefacts from 16th to 20th Century Scottish life. The Castle is home to the Duke of Atholl, who has the only remaining private army in Europe; the Atholl Highlanders. The Castle hosts public events from April to October. Three areas are available for

functions, including the Exhibition Hall for 90 and The Ballroom for 400.
Catering: Contract approved list/In house

Price Guide: Prices on application.
Catering (sit down): POA

Blairquhan Castle, Maybole
T: 01655 770239 **F:** 01655 770278
E: enquiries@blairquhan.co.uk **W:** www.blairquhan.co.uk
Contact: James Hunter Blair, Owner
Party Max: 100 (marquee: unlimited)

Blairquham is a private house and estate, which was built in 1821-24 by William Burn for the great great grandfather of the present owner. It has all its original furniture and there is a good collection of pictures, particularly of the Scottish School. The house is surrounded by its own 500 acre park with lake. Several other properties are available to let on the estate.
Catering: In house

FACILITIES:
- Helipad
- Outdoor Pool
- Pool/Snooker
- Table Tennis

SERVICES:
- Exclusive Use
- Flowers
- Disco/Dance
- Performance Area

Price Guide: Prices on application.
Catering (sit down): POA

Bowhill House, Selkirk
T: 01750 22204 **F:** 01750 22204
E: bht@buccleuch.com
Contact: Mrs P Gray
Party Max: 72

This is the home of the Duke and Duchess of Buccleuch, and is open to the public. The building dates mainly from 1812 and houses numerous works of art including works by Canaletto, Reynolds and Gainsborough. Other features at the house include a restored Victorian kitchen, a 19th Century horse drawn fire engine, plus adventure playground, nature trails and a tearoom.
Catering: In house

FACILITIES:
- Playground

Price Guide: Prices on application.

Cambo Gardens, St Andrews
T: 01333 450313 **F:** 01333 450987
E: cambohouse@compuserve.com
W: www.camboestate.com
Contact: Catherine Erskine, Owner
Party Max: 180

Home to the Erskine family since 1688, Cambo house is an imposing Victorian house set in a 1200 acre coastal estate with gardens and woodland. There are self-catering apartments in the house, as well as 4 cottages in the grounds. Its self-catering accommodation with the option of meals, along with gracious public rooms, including a spacious drawing room deocrated with paintings, Mortlake tapestries and a magnificent chandelier, allows the venue to tailor services to your requirements. Outside parties are also catered for. The gardens are open to the public.
Catering: In house/Self catering

FACILITIES:
- Golf
- Tennis
- Pool/Snooker
- Table Tennis

SERVICES:
- Exclusive Use
- Flowers
- Photography

Price Guide: Cottages prices range from £190 for the 1 bed cottage for a week to £695 for the 4 bed cottage for a week in high season. Other prices on application.

Castle Venlaw Hotel, Peebles
T: 01721 720384 **F:** 01721 724066
E: enquiries@venlaw.co.uk **W:** www.venlaw.co.uk
Contact: John Sloggie, Proprietor
Party Max: 40 *Bedrooms: 13*

Built in 1782 this castle enjoys a unique position on the slopes of Venlaw Hill overlooking Peebles, and only half and hour from Edinburgh. There are 13 fully refubished bedrooms on offer at this 4-star hotel.
Catering: In house

SERVICES:
- Exclusive Use
- Flowers
- Cake
- Toastmaster
- Disco/Dance
- Live Music
- Entertainers
- Fireworks
- Piped Music
- Performance Area

Price Guide: Prices on application.
Catering (sit down): from £20pp
Catering (buffet): from £15pp

Cawdor Castle, Nairn
T: 01667 404615 **F:** 01667 404674
E: cawdor.castle@btinternet.com
Contact: Event Manager
Party Max: 40

This romantic 14th Century castle was built as a private fortress. Later additions are mainly from the 17th Century and feature slated roofs, crow-stepped gables and mellow local stone. The house and its garden (with holly maze, paradise garden and thistle garden) are now open to the public, and the Hall is available for functions.
Catering: In house

Price Guide: Prices on application.

Cromlix House, Nr Stirling
T: 01786 822125 **F:** 01786 825450
E: reservations@cromlixhouse.com
W: www.cromlixhouse.com
Contact: David & Ailsa Assenti, Proprietors
Party Max: 60 *Bedrooms: 14*

This is an exclusive 5-star luxury country house hotel, with its own enchanting chapel as part of the house. The Victorian building, which can accommodate 6 to 50 people, is set in its

SCOTLAND

own 2000 acre working estate, and features fireplaces, panelled walls and antique furnishings. There are 2 private meeting or dining rooms, as well as numerous other reception rooms. The accommodation here includes 8 large suites with private sitting rooms. Take an 'ipix' reality tour on the award winning Cromlix web site. Falconry and archery are among the activities available here.

Catering: In house

FACILITIES:
- Helipad
- Shooting
- Hot Air Balloons
- Falconry
- Archery

SERVICES:
- Exclusive Use
- Flowers
- Cake
- Toastmaster
- Disco/Dance

Price Guide: Prices on application.
Catering (sit down): from £42pp

Dalmeny House, Edinburgh
T: 0131 331 1888   F: 0131 331 1788
E: events@dalmeny.co.uk
Contact: Event Manager

Party Max: 200

Only 7 miles from Edinburgh is Dalmeny House, family home of the Earls of Rosebery for over 300 years. The house is home to the Mentmore Rothschild collection of 18th Century furniture, as well as the 5th Earl's Napoleonic collection. Four areas are available for functions here; the smallest being the charming Library, with a capacity for 20, and the largest, The Garden Restaurant (200).

Catering: In house

FACILITIES:
- Helipad
- Shooting

Price Guide: Prices on application.

Duff House, Banff
T: 01261 818181   F: 01261 818900
Contact: The Chamberlain

Party Max: 100

Duff House is a palatial house and has had a colourful history as a hotel, sanitorium and prisoner of war camp. It is now in the hands of Historic Scotland and is open to the public. Four areas are available for functions from the North Drawing Room for 40 to the Long Gallery for 100.

Catering: In house

Price Guide: Prices on application.

Dunrobin Castle, Golspie
T: 01408 633268   F: 01408 634081
Contact: Keith Jones

Party Max: 120

This wonderfully named castle dates from the 13th Century with later additions. The building houses fine examples of furntiure, paintings, and memorabilia, while there is a Victorian museum in the grounds. The gardens, meanwhile, feature a formal parterre.

Several rooms are available in the house for functions, the largest of which will seat up to 100 for lunch, 120 theatre style. This room is also used for dances. 80 is the optimum party size. If required, marquees can be erected in the grounds, which can also be used for firework displays.

Catering: In house

Price Guide: Prices on application.

Edinburgh Castle, Edinburgh
T: 0131 668 8850   F: 0131 220 4733
Contact: Joanne MacDonald, Sales & Marketing Manager - Functions Unit

Party Max: 1000

Situated on a stunning location on the Castle Rock, with unrivalled views over the city of Edinburgh, Edinburgh Castle is probably Scotland's most famous national monument. The Jacobite Room (100 for dinner, 250 for a reception) and the Gatehouse Suite (20 for dinner, 40 for a reception), are available for private functions, or a special evening is available when the whole castle can be used for up to 1000 guests. The Jacobite Room is an 18th Century building with views over the city, while the 19th Century Gatehouse Suite has a private terraced area, offering magnificent views over the Royal Mile.

Catering: In house

SERVICES:
- Exclusive Use

Price Guide: from £450 for Gatehouse Suite to £5000+ for the whole castle.
Catering (sit down): POA

Floors Castle, Kelso
T: 01573 223333   F: 01573 226056
Contact: Phillip Massey

Party Max: 150

Home to the Duke of Roxburghe, this is claimed to be the largest inhabited castle in Scotland. The castle was designed by William Adam, with construction started in 1721. More recently the castle featured in the film Greystoke, as the home of Tarzan. The building, which houses French 17th and 18th Century furniture, tapestries and porcelain, is available for dinners, conferences, etc, with the Dining Room ad Ballroom as the function rooms. The grounds may also be used.

Catering: In house

Price Guide: Prices on application.
Catering (sit down): POA
Catering (buffet): POA

Glamis Castle, by Forfar
T: 01307 840393   F: 01307 840733
E: glamis@great-houses-scotland.co.uk
W: great-houses-scotland.co.uk/glamis
Contact: Lt Col P J Cardwell-Moore, Administrator

Party Max: 120

Situated between Aberdeen and Perth, Glamis Castle is the family home of the Earls of Strathmore and Kinghorne. It is the childhood home of The Queen Mother, the birthplace of Princess Margaret and the legendary setting of Shakespeare's

play Macbeth. Dinners here are held in the State Dining Room, with drinks served in the Great Hall. Luncheons are held in the 16th Century kitchens.
Catering: In house

FACILITIES:
- Shooting
- Archery
- Carriage Driving

SERVICES:
- Exclusive Use
- Flowers
- Cake
- Live Music
- Piped Music
- Scottish Dancing

Price Guide: Venue rental is £100 - £1000.
Catering (sit down): from £90pp
Catering (buffet): from £55pp

Glenfeochan, Kilmore
T: Large Holiday Houses - 01381 610496
Finlayson Hughes - 01738 451600
F: 01738 451900
E: mailbox@perth.ckdfh.co.uk
W: www.ckdfh.co.uk
Contact: Large Holiday Houses/Finlayson Hughes
Party Max: 18   Bedrooms: 11

Standing in 350 acres, this house faces west with views over its own land to Loch Feochan. This fine Scottish baronial house was upgraded in 1875 with a viewing turret and all main reception rooms face down to the Loch. Glenfoechan has fishing rights on the River Nell, mainly brown and sea trout, but the expert, they say, may also catch the occasional salmon. The 2nd floor bedrooms here are decorated for children. There is also a children's playroom on the first floor. Clearly geared up for large groups, the house has 2 dishwashers an even boasts and ice machine! This house is marketed by Finlayson Hughes and Large holiday Houses - see Agency Listing. Written agreement is required for weddings or parties.
Catering: Self catering

FACILITIES:
- Pool/Snooker
- Table Tennis
- Croquet
- Fishing

Price Guide: House rental is from £2100 to £3000 per week.

Hillockhead Steading, The Black Isle
T: 01381 610496   **F:** 01381 610481
Contact: Wynne Bentley
Party Max: 21

This is a traditional Scottish Highlands barn which has been converted to comprise 5 self-contained apartments. Each apartment has its own entrance and access to a communal dining room (seating up to 20), games room, kitchen and laundry room. The property is set in 160 acres on the south cost of the Black Isle, with views of the Moray Firth. Catering can be provided here if required, as can airport or railway collection car hire (self-drive or chauffered, fishing and shooting. The venue is marketed by Large Holiday Houses - see Agency Listings. Written agreement is required for wedding or parties.
Catering: Self catering/In house

FACILITIES:
- Shooting
- Fishing

SERVICES:

- Exclusive Use

Price Guide: Whole house rentalis from £1200 to £1750 per week.

Hopetoun House, Edinburgh
T: 0131 331 2451   **F:** 0131 319 1885
E: events@hopetounhouse.com
W: www.hopetounhouse.com
Contact: Lois Bayne-Jardine, Events Manager
Party Max: 400 (marquee: 2000+)

Hopetoun House, ancestral home of the Marquess of Linlithgow and claimed to be Scotland's finest stately home, is only 12 miles from Edinburgh and under an hour from Glasgow. The State apartments here are suitable for receptions and smaller dinner parties, whilst the Ballroom and Adam Stables cater for larger numbers. A variety of other rooms are also available.
Catering: In house

FACILITIES:
- Helipad
- Quad Bikes/Off Road

SERVICES:
- Flowers
- Cake
- Disco/Dance
- Performance Area
- Valet Parking

Price Guide: Exclusive use from £2000 + vat.
Catering (sit down): from £25pp + vat
Catering (buffet): from £19.50pp + vat

Isle of Erisca, Oban
T: 01631 720371   **F:** 01631 720531
E: Beppo@eriska-hotel.co.uk   **W:** www.eriska-hotel.co.uk
Contact: Mr Beppo Buchanan-Smith, Partner
Party Max: 40 (marquee: 110)   Bedrooms: 17

The Isle of Eriska is a private 300 acre island dedicated soley to the well being of its residents in the 5-star 17 bedroom main house. Reached from the mainland via the island's private vehicle bridge, Eriska is isolated, but not cut off. The house, built in 1884, features grey granite and red sandstone on the outside, and log fires and warm decor on the inside. The hotel and island offers many facilities, not least of which is the 'welly boot rack', from which guests who wish to explore the island may find the necsary footwear.
Catering: In house

FACILITIES:
- Helipad
- Golf
- Indoor Pool
- Shooting
- Gym
- Tennis
- Outdoor Pool

SERVICES:
- Exclusive Use
- Flowers
- Cake
- Toastmaster
- Live Music
- Fireworks
- Valet Parking

Price Guide: Prices on application.
Catering (sit down): from £30pp
Catering (buffet): from £30pp

Kellie Castle, Anstrudher
T: 01333 720271   **F:** 01333 720326
Contact: Michael S Ford, Property Manager
Party Max: 70 (marquee: unlimited)

Kellie Castle and garden is a fine example of domestic architec-

SCOTLAND

ture in Lowland Scotland. It dates from the 14th Century and was sympathetically restored by the Lorimer family in the 19th Century. The castle contains magnificent plaster ceilings, a mural by Phoebe Anna Traquair, painted panelling, and fine furniture designed by Sir Robert Lorimer. The garden has a collection of old fashioned roses and herbaceous plants which are cultivated organically.

Catering: Contract approved list

SERVICES:
• Exclusive Use

Price Guide: £200 for 2 hours, the remainder by negotiation.
Catering (sit down): POA
Catering (buffet): POA

Kintradwell Lodge, Brora
T: 01381 610496   F: 01381 610481
Contact: Wynne Bentley
Party Max: 12   Bedrooms: 6

This is a fine country house on an 8000 acre estate. The house overlooks the Moray Firth and is a short walk from a privately owned beach. There is also a pretty walled garden and an enclosed tennis court. About 1 mile from the house is stone bothy which is ideal for barbecues and picnics and cn be reached on foot or by vehicle. Inside there is a large drawing room with snooker table and a cosier 'snug'. A housekeeper (2 hours a day and fishing are included in the rental. A cook can be provided on request. This house is marketed by Large Holiday Houses - see Agency Listing. Wedding and parties by written agreement only.

Catering: Self catering

FACILITIES:
• Shooting   • Pool/Snooker   • Fishing

SERVICES:
• Exclusive Use

Price Guide: House rental is from £1050 to £1400 per week.

Kirkton House, Cardross
T: 01389 841951
F: 01389 841868
E: noble@kirktonhouse.co.uk
W: www.kirktonhouse.co.uk
Contact: Stewart & Gillian Macdonald, P{artners
Party Max: 30   Bedrooms: 6

This is an old converted farmstead hotel in tranquil countryside, with panoramic views of the River Clyde. The venue offers a cosy relaxed ambience for small parties, with the personal attention of your hosts. There is a broad choice of home-cooked dinners (recommended by a Taste of Scotland), which can be served at an oil lamplit table or tables. Stabling and a paddock can be made available for horses.

Catering: In house

SERVICES:
• Exclusive Use   • Flowers   • Valet Parking

Price Guide: B&B rates start at £29.50 per room.
Catering (sit down): from £19.50pp
Catering (buffet): from £15pp

Lennoxlove House, Haddington
T: 01620 823720   F: 01620 825112
E: info@lennoxlove.org   W: www.lennoxlove.org
Contact: Fay Angus, House Administrator
Party Max: 120 (marquee: 350)

Lennoxlove, which dates from the 14th Century, is home to the Duke of Hamilton. It is set in 600 acres of private estate 21 miles south east of Edinburgh. The house is now home to the former Hamilton Palace collection of furniture and paintings and a collection of Mary Queen of Scots' mementoes. Principle rooms for hire include the centuries old Great Hall for formal occasions, plus the interconnecting Oak Room, Dining Room and Entrance Hall. Any combination of these rooms can be tailored to suit individual requirements. The chapel here is regularly used for weddings and concerts, while the grounds can accommodate marquees for larger events. Catering here is by 'Fat Lady' Clarissa Dickson Wright.

Catering: In house

FACILITIES:
• Quad Bikes/Off Road   • Highland Games

SERVICES:
• Exclusive Use

Price Guide: £500 - £1100
Catering (sit down): from £36pp
Catering (buffet): from £25pp

Manderston, Duns
T: 01361 883450   F: 01361 882450
E: palmer@manderston.demon.co.uk
W: www.manderston.co.uk
Contact: Lord Palmer, Owner
Party Max: 60   Bedrooms: 10

Manderston is a stately home, privately owned, and set in 56 acres of beautiful gardens. The house is richly furnished with sumptuous apartments, marble floors and a silver staircase. It is located 35 miles from Edinburgh, 12 miles from the A1 at Berwick-upon-Tweed. Clay pigeon shooting, and residential and non-residential house parties are regular events at this venue, but any activity can be arranged on request.

Catering: In house/Contract (any)

FACILITIES:
• Shooting   • Tennis   • Pool/Snooker

SERVICES:
• Flowers   • Disco/Dance   • Performance Area

Price Guide: Fees are £600 perday for the house, + £150 per person per night + £5 service charge per person, per night.
Catering (sit down): POA

New Lanark Mill Hotel, Lanark
T: 01555 667200   F: 01555 667222
E: hotel@newlanark.org   W: www.newlanark.org
Contact: Stephen Owen, General Manager
Party Max: 150   Bedrooms: 38 + 14

Surrounded by native woodlands and close to the famous Falls of Clyde, this cotton mill village was founded in 1785 and became famous as the site of Robert Owen's radical reforms. Now restored as a living community and attraction, the history

SCOTLAND

of the village (nominated as a World Heritage Site) is interpreted in an award-winning Visitor Centre. The hotel offers 4-star accommodation in a Grade A listed building, and Waterhouses self-catering cottages are also available.
Catering: In house/Self catering

SERVICES:
- Flowers
- Cake
- Toastmaster
- Disco/Dance
- Live Music
- Entertainers
- Fireworks
- Photography
- Piped Music
- Performance Area

Price Guide: £500 - £3000
Catering (sit down): POA

Scone Place, Perth
T: 01738 552300 **F:** 01738 552588
E: visits@scone-place.co.uk **W:** www.scone-place.co.uk
Contact: R Nurick, The Administrator
Party Max: 200 (marquee: 1000)

This is an unique historic house and one-time crowning place of Kings of Scotland. It is set in woodland grounds and lawns. The venue is available for private functions and corporate events indoors and outside at any time of the year (indoors only from 7pm in April to October).
Catering: In house

FACILITIES:
- Helipad
- Hot Air Balloons

SERVICES:
- Flowers
- Gift Sales

Price Guide: £1050 facility fee, plus catering and drinks.
Catering (sit down): from £50pp
Catering (buffet): from £30pp

Skirinish House & Cottage, Isle of Skye
T: 01381 610496 **F:** 01381 610481
E: largeholidayhouses@cali.co.uk
Contact: The Owner
Party Max: 14   Bedrooms: 5 + 2

Skirinish stands in its own grounds in the middle of a sheep farm, with the shore about 300 metres away. The house is a traditional farmhouse on three floors, dating from the late 1700s, and accommodates 10 comfortably. The Cottage at the side of the house can accommodate a further 4, and can be taken separately or in conjunction with the house.
Catering: Self catering

SERVICES:
- Exclusive Use

Price Guide: House rental is from £600 - £950 per week, while the cottage is from £300 - £400 per week.

Stirling Castle, Stirling
T: 0131 668 8686/01786 450000 **F:** 01786 464678
Contact: Jon MacNeil
Party Max: 800

Stirling Castle is considered by many to be one of the grandest of all Scottish castles. The castle has links with Mary Queen of Scots, William Wallace and Robert the Bruce and was the favourite royal residence of successive Scottish kings. Several rooms are available for functions here (for exclusive hire only) including the Great Hall (400) and the King's Presence Chamber (80). The whole castle can also be hired, accommodating 800 for a reception. The Great Hall has recently been restored to its 16th Century splendour and features stained glass windows, huge fireplaces, minstrel's gallery and a magnificent oak roof.
Catering: In house

SERVICES:
- Exclusive Use

Price Guide: £1600 to £5500+
Catering (sit down): POA
Catering (buffet): POA

Strathfillan Lodge, Crianlarich
T: 01381 610496 **F:** 01381 610481
Contact: Wynne Bentley
Party Max: 18   Bedrooms: 9

This is a spacious, warm and well equipped family house set in large and well maintained gardens. All bedrooms have en-suite bathrooms, television and tea and coffee making facilities. The wood panelled Hall and Dining Room, with magnificent views of Ben More, can seat up to 18. A daily housekeeper is included in the rental, and a cook can be arranged if required. This property is marketed by Large Holiday Houses - see Agency Listing. Written agreement is required for weddings or parties.
Catering: Self catering

Price Guide: House rental is from £1450 to £2200 per week.

Strathtay House, by Pitlochry
T: 01738 860842 **F:** 01738 860843
Contact: Michael Macphail, Owner
Party Max: 35   Bedrooms: 6

This is a spacious 2-storey, sun-lit house in a delightful Perthshire village with nearby upmarket grocer's shop. The house is split-level, has a spacious south-facing balcony and en-suite master bedroom with dressing room. Close by is a famous 'white water' part of the River Tay where rafting and canoeing competitions take place. Overlooking the River Tay, just 5 minutes walk from the house, is a new restaurant with a pub nearby. A 9-hole golf course is a short walk from the house and the resort of Pitlochry, with its famous 'Theatre is the Hills' is just a 20 minute drive away.
Catering: Self catering

Price Guide: From £350 - £950 per week.

Thirlstane Castle, Lauder
T: 01578 722430 **F:** 01578 722761
E: admin@thirlstanecastle.co.uk **W:** www.thirlstanecastle.co.uk
Contact: Peter Jarvis, Castle Administrator
Party Max: 150 (marquee: unlimited)

One of 7 'Great Houses of Scotland', Grade I listed Thirlstane Castle lies 28 miles south of Edinburgh, off the A68 by Lauder. It stands in beautiful Borders countryside. Thirlstane is open to the public, but private and corporate functions can often be

SCOTLAND

enjoyed in the state rooms which feature exquisite 17th Century ceilings. Non-destructive events can be held in the grounds, with or without marquees.
Catering: *Contract approved list*

FACILITIES:
- **Highland Games**
- **Falconry Displays**
- **Whisky Tasting**

Price Guide: From £1000 per day.
Catering (sit down): from £35pp
Catering (buffet): from £10pp

IRELAND

Ballycumber House, Co Offaly
T: 00 353 902 30106 **F:** 00 353 902 30106
Contact: Constance Hanniffy
Party Max: 16   Bedrooms: 7

This is a 4-star approved country mansion, originally built as a castle and converted to a dwelling in 1748. It is set in its own mature woodlands, with private access to the River Brosna. Private fishing is available on the estate. A maid service is optional.
Catering: Self catering

SERVICES:
- Exclusive Use

Price Guide: Prices start at £240 for 2 nights and rise to £600 for a week.

Carbury House, Co Sligo
T: 00 353 71 43378 **F:** 00 353 71 47433
E: carbury@indigo.ie
Contact: Peter & Martha Davey, Owners
Party Max: 20   Bedrooms: 6

This is a luxurious spacious home on the N15. All rooms are en suite with TVs, etc.
Catering: In house FB

Price Guide: B&B here is £19pp.
Catering (sit down): from £12pp

Croaghross, Co Donegal
T: 00 353 74 59548 **F:** 00 353 74 59548
E: jkdeane@iol.ie **W:** www.croaghross.com
Contact: John and Kay Deane, owners
Party Max: 10

This is a guest house sleeping 10.
Catering: In house

Price Guide: Prices on application.

Glendine House, Co Wexford
T: 00 353 51 389258 **E:** glendinehouse@eircom.net
Contact: Annie Crosbie, Owner
Party Max: 16

This Georgian house, built in 1830, overlooks the Barrow estuary in the village of Arthurstown. The houses is located beside the 4-star Dunbrody Country House Hotel, and has several award winning restaurants nearby.
Catering: Self catering

SERVICES:
- Exclusive Use

Price Guide: B&B starts at £25pp. Self-catering is £200 - £300 per week. For room hire (seating 20), rental is £50 per hour.
Catering (sit down): POA

Harbour Masters House, Co Offaly
T: 00353 509 51532/51480 **E:** gkirwan@iol.ie
Contact: Grainne Kirwan, Owner
Party Max: 10

This beautiful restored listed Georgian residence is situated on the banks of the Grand Canal in the heart of the Irish Midlands. The house features a roof top balcony, private enclosed yard and a landscaped garden. Pubs, shops and a post office are all within 50 metres. Fishing is popular from this venue which will provide angling advice, and even offer a bait fridge for your use!
Catering: Self catering/In house B&B

FACILITIES:
- Fishing

Price Guide: From £200 per day. From £1750 for a week, and from £500 for a weekend.

Springfort Hall Hotel, Co Cork
T: 00 353 22 21278 **F:** 00 353 22 21557
E: stay@springfort-hall.com **W:** www.springfort-hall.com
Contact: Paul Walsh, General Manager
Party Max: 300   Bedrooms: 49

Tucked away amid tranquil woodlands and landscaped gardens, is the 3-star Springfort Hall Hotel. This estate dates back to the Norman invasion of Ireland in 1169 and for centuries has remained the property of the landed gentry. The building itself is Georgian and listed Grade A.
Catering: In house/Contract approved list

FACILITIES:
- Helipad

SERVICES:
- Exclusive Use
- Disco/Dance
- Live Music
- Entertainers
- Piped Music
- Performance Area

Price Guide: B&B starts at £90 for a double standard room.
Catering (sit down): from £40pp
Catering (buffet): from £30pp

Wellpark House, Co Galway
T: 0039 0564 412672 **E:** ghlubran@gol.grosseto.it
Contact: Geraldine Hynes, Owner
Party Max: 11

Wellpark is a Georgian country house and grounds situated in the region of Connemara. It has an acre of grounds which includes mature gardens, lawns and an orchard. The house is 5 minutes from Lake Corrib, facing the river Owenriff where, in May each year, you can see the salmon leaping upstream. The house is rated 4-star by the Irish Tourist Board.
Catering: Self catering

Price Guide: From £950 for a week over Christmas and New Year.

NOBLE'S PARTY VENUES GUIDE 1ST EDITION   163

INDEX

A
41 Portland Place ...9
Abbey Hotel ... 92
Abbots Barton ... 28
Achinduich Lodge ... 156
Albert Halls ... 114
Albrighton Hall ... 92
Alder House Hotel ... 126
Alderley Edge Hotel ... 114
Aldwark Manor Golf Club ... 126
Alexander House Hotel ... 28
Alexandra Palace ...9
Alexandra Suite ... 28
All Yr Ynys Country House ... 92
Allerton Castle ... 126
Alnwick Castle ... 141
Alton House Hotel ... 45
Alverbank Country House ... 45
Alverton Manor ... 58
Alveston Manor ... 92
Amadeus Centre ... 9, ix
Amberley Castle ... 28
Angel Hotel ... 76
Anne of Cleves House ... 28
Ansty Hall Hotel ... 92
Appleby Castle ... 136
Apsley House ... 9
Arched House ... 58
Ardencote Manor Hotel ... 92
Argyll's Lodging ... 156
Arley Hall ... 114
Armathwaite Hall ... 136
Armourers' & Brasiers' Hall ... 9
Arts Club ... 28
Ashburnham Hotel ... 147
Ashdown Park Hotel ... 28
Ashe, The ... 92
Ashton Court Mansion ... 58
Ashton Memorial ... 114
Aske Hall ... 126
Assembly Rooms ... 58
Assembly Rooms ... 141
Astley Bank Hotel ... 114
Auckland Castle ... 141
Aurora Garden Hotel ... 45
Avington Park ... 45
Avoncroft Museum ... 93
Aylestone Court ... 93

B
BAFTA ... 9
Bailey Mill ... 156
Bailiffscourt Hotel ... 29
Balbirnie House ... 156
Ballycumber House ... 163
Banks of England Sports Centre... 10
Banqueting House ... 10
Barbican Centre ... 10
Barley Town House ... 76
Barlings Barn ... 147
Barn Hotel ... 10
Barns Hotel ... 76
Barnsdale Country Club ... 93
Barnsgate Manor Vineyard... 29
Bartle Hall ... 114
Bartley Lodge Hotel ... 45
Barton Hall ... 58
Baskerville Hall hotel ... 147
Bass Museum ... 93
Bassetsbury Manor ... 45
Bath Guildhall ... 58
Bath Spa Hotel ... 59
Beadlow Manor ... 76
Bear of Rodborough ... 93
Beaumanor Hall ... 93
Beauport Park Hotel ... 29
Beech House ... 45
Beeches, The ... 59
Begden Hall Hotel ... 126
Belmore Hotel ... 114
Belvedere Restaurant ... 10
Belvoir Castle ... 76
Beningbrough Hall ... 126
Benmore Lodge ... 156
Bentley Wildfowl & Motor Museum ... 29
Berkeley Hotel ... 10
Bertie's Banqueting Rooms ... 126
Beth Ruach ... 147, xii
Billesley Manor Hotel ... 93
Bindon Country House Hotel ... 59
Birches, The ... 93
Birmingham Botanical Gardens ... 94
Bishop Auckland Town Hall ... 141
Bishopstrow House ... 59
Bitton House ... 59
Blackheath Halls ... 10
Blackpool Tower Ballroom ... 114
Blair Castle ... 156
Blairquhan Castle ... 157
Blenheim Palace ... 46
Blotts Hotel ... 94
Bluebell Railway ... 29
Bolding Way ... 76, x
Bolholt Country Park ... 115
Bolton Castle ... 126
Bookham Grange Hotel ... 29
Boringdonhall ... 59
Bosinver Farmhouse ... 59
Botleigh Grange Hotel ... 46
Boughton Monchelsea Place ... 29
Bourne Hall ... 30
Bourton Manor ... 94
Boutler's Lock Hotel ... 46
Bowhill House ... 157
Bowler Hat Hotel ... 115
Bowood Golf & Country Club ... 60
Brackenborough Arms ... 77
Braddon Cottages ... 60
Bramah Museum ... 10
Bramall Hall ... 115
Brandon Hall ... 94
Brandshatch Place Hotel ... 30
Brereton Hall ... 115
Bretton Hall ... 127
Brewery, The ... 11
Brickwall House ... 30
Bridge House Hotel ... 60
Bridge Inn Hotel ... 127
Briggens House ... 77
Brighton Dome ... 30
Brighton Museum & Art Gallery ... 30
Brighton Racecourse ... 30
British Musuem ... 12
Broad Marston Manor ... 100
Broom Hall ... 77
Broome Park ... 30
Broxbourne Civic Hall ... 77
Bryn Boleded Libanus ... 147
Brynich Farmhouse ... 147
Buckland-Tout-Saints ... 60
Budock Vean ... 60
Burford House ... 94
Burgh House ... 12
Burgh Island ... 60
Burley Manor ... 46
Burnham Beeches Hotel ... 46
Burton Farm ... 61
Bury Town Hall ... 115
Buxted Park ... 31

C
Cadbury House ... 61
Caer Beris Manor ... 147
Caerphilly Castle ... 148
Cafe de Paris ... 12
Calcot Manor 94
Cambo Gardens ... 157
Cambridge Cottage ... 1
Canning House ... 11
Cannizaro House .. 11
Cannon Hall Museum ... 127
Canolfan Pentre Ifan ... 148
Canonbury Academy... 11
Cantley House Hotel ... 46
Capesthorne Hall ... 115
Carbury House ... 163
Cardiff Castle ... 148
Carey's Manor Hotel ...46
Carlton Towers ... 127
Carlyon Bay ... 61
Carnarvon Arms ... 61
Castle Ashby ... 94
Castle Hotel ... 95
Castle Inn Hotel ... 136
Castle of Brecon ... 148
Castle Venlaw Hotel ... 157
Cave Castle Hotel ... 127
Cawdor Castle ... 157
Celtic Haven Village ... 148
Channels Golf Club .. 77
Channels Golf Club ... 77
Charingworth manor ... 95
Charlton House ... 61
Chartridge Conference Centre ... 46
Chatsworth ... 95
Chaucer Hotel ... 31
Chelsea Old Town Hall ... 12
Cheltenham Racecourse ... 95
Chenies Manor House ... 77
Chester Racecourse ... 115
Chewton Glen Hotel ... 47
Chiddingstone Castle ... 31
Chigwell Manor Hall .. 77
Chilford Hall ... 77
Chillingham Castle ... 141
Chilston Park Hotel ... 31
Chilworth Manor ... 47
Chine Hotel ... 61
Chiseldon House ... 61
Chiswick House ... 12
Churchill Intercontinental ... 12
City of London Club ... 12
Clandon Park ... 31
Clarendon Suites ... 95
Claridge's Hotel ... 12
Clearwell Castle ... 95, xiii
Clinton House ... 78
Cliveden ... 47
Close House Mansion ... 141
Cnewr Farmhouse ... 148
Coach Inn ... 148
Cobham Hall ... 31
Cockington Court ... 61
Combe Grove Manor ... 62
Combermere Abbey ... 96, viii
Commandery, The ... 96
Commonwealth Insititue ... 13
Compleat Angler Hotel ... 47
Congham Hall ... 78
Cooling Castle Barn ... 32
Coombe Abbey Hotel ... 96
Coot in the Tarn ... 136
Coppermines ... 136, xv
Coppleridge Inn ... 62
Corn Exchange ... 47
Cornist Hall ... 149
Corse Lawn House Hotel ... 96
Cotehele ... 62
Cotgrave Place ... 96
Cotton's Atrium ... 13
Council House ... 62
Country Park Inn ... 127
Court Colman Hotel ... 149
Court Room ... 32
Courtauld Gallery ... 13

INDEX

Coventry City FC ... 96
Crabwall Manor ... 115
Cragwood Country House ... 136
Craiglands Hotel ... 127
Crathorne Hall Hotel ... 127
Craxton Wood Hotel ... 116
Crazy Horse Saloon ... 116
Cressbrook Hall ... 96
Crewe Hall ... 116
Cricklade Hotel .. 62
Croaghross ... 163
Cromlix House ... 157, vii
Cross Tree House ... 62, iv
Crossmead ... 63
Crown Hotel ... 116
Crownhill Fort ... 63
Crudwell Court ... 63
Cumberwell Park ... 63, v
Curdon Mill ... 63
Cutlers Hall, The ... 128
Cwmwennol Country House ... 149

D

Dacorum Pavilion ... 78
Dairy, The ... 47
Dales & Peaks Hotel ... 97
Dalmeny House ... 158
Dalston Hall ... 137
Darnley Arms ... 32
Dartmouth House ... 13
Davenport House ... 97, xii
De Courcey's ... 149
De La Warr Pavilion ... 32
De Vere Belfry ... 97
De Vere Royal Bath ... 64
De Vere Slaley hall ... 142
Deer Park Hotel ... 64
Delbury Hall ... 97
Design Museum ... 13
Devonshire Arms Country House Hotel ... 128
Devonshire House Hotel ... 116
Dicken's House Museum ... 13
Dillington House ... 64
Dimbola Lodge ... 48
Dissington Hall ... 142
Dorchester Hotel ... 13
Dorchester Municipa; Buildings ... 64
Dormy House Hotel ... 97
Dorney court ... 48
Dorton House ... 48
Dovecliff Hall ... 97
Dower House ... 64
Duff House ... 158
Duke of York's Headquarters ... 14
Duke's Hotel ... 14
Dulwich College ... 14
Dumbleton Hall ... 98
Duncombe Park ... 128
Duncton Mill ... 32
Dunrobin Castle ... 158
Dunsley Hall Hotel ... 128
Durrant House ... 64
Dylan Thomas Centre ... 149

E

East Close Country Hotel ... 64
East Court ... 32
East Lancashire Masonic Hall ... 116
East Lodge Hotel ... 98
East Riddlesden Hall ... 128
Easthampstead Park ... 48
Eastnor Castle ... 98, iii
Eastwell Manor ... 33
Edgbaston Cricker Ground ... 98
Edgwarebury Hotel ... 78
Edinburgh Castle ... 158
Egerton Grey Hotel ... 149
Eggesford Barton ... 65
Elmers Court ... 48
Elsham Hall Barn Theatre ... 78
Eltham Palace ... 14
Elvaston Castle ... 98
Embleton Hall ... 142
Ennerdales Hotel ... 137
Escot House ... 65
Eshott Hall ... 142
Espley Hall ... 142
Essebourne Manor ... 48
Eyam Hall ... 98

F

Fairfield Halls ... 14
Fairlawns ... 99
Fairyhill ... 149
Falcon Hotel ... 65
Falcon Manor Hotel ... 128
Falgstone Farm ... 99
Fanhams Hall ... 78
Farm House ... 137
Farthings Hotel ... 65
Fawsley hall ... 99
Fennes ... 78
Finchcocks ... 33
Fischer's Baslow ... 99
Fishponds House ... 65
Flagstone Farm ... 99, vi
Flitwick Manor ... 79
Flixton House ... 117
Floors Castle ... 158
Fonmon Castle ... 150
Foreign Press Association ... 14
Forest Park Hotel ... 49
Fort Brockhurst ... 49
Fossebridge Inn ... 99
Fountain Court Hotel ... 49
Four Seasons Hotel ... 14
Fredericks Restaurant ... 15
Frensham Heights ... 33
Friern Manor ... 79
Frogmill Inn ... 99
Fulham House ... 15
Fulham Town Hall ... 15
Fydell House ... 79

G

Garden Hotel ... 33
Gardens of Easton Lodge ... 79
Garstang Country Hotel ... 117
Gerbestone Manor ... 65
Gibbon Bridge Hotel ... 117
Gilbert Collection ... 15
Glamis Castle ... 158
Glazier's Hall ... 15
Glen Eagle Hotel ... 79
Glendine House ... 163
Glenfeochan ... 159
Gliffaes Country House Hotel ... 150
Glynhir Mansion ... 150, xi
Golden Hinde Sailing Ship ... 15
Goldney Hall ... 65
Goodwood House ... 33
Goodwood Racecourse ... 33
Goring Hotel ... 16
Grafton Manor ... 99
Granada Studio Tours ... 117
Grand Hotel ... 34
Grange Hall .. 100
Grange Hotel ... 128
Great Ballard School ... 34
Great Conservaotry ... 16
Great Fosters ... 34
Great Tythe Barn ... 100
Greshams ... 79
Greystoke Castle ... 137
Grittleton House ... 66
Grosvenor House Hotel ... 16
Grovefield Hotel ... 49
Guard's Polo club ... 49
Guyer's House ... 66
Gwydir Castle ... 150

H

Hagley Hall ... 100
Haigh Hall ... 117
Haldon Belvedere... 66, xii
Haley's Hotel ... 129
Halsway Manor ... 66
Ham House ...16
Hambleton Hall ... 100
Hammersmith Town Hall ... 16
Hampton Court Palace ... 34
Hanbury Hall ... 100
Harbour Master's House ... 163
Hartford Hall ... 117
Harthill Hall ... 101
Hatfield House ... 79
Hatherly Manor Hotel ... 101
Hatton Court Hotel ... 49
Hatton Court Hotel ... 101
Haven Hotel ... 66
Hawkwell House Hotel ... 50
Hayes Galleria ... 16
Hazlewood Castle ... 129
Headlam Hall ... 142
Headland Hotel ... 66
Heath Cottage Hotel ... 129
Heath Cottage Hotel ... 129
Hedingham Castle ... 80
Hellaby Hall Hotel ... 129
Hendon Hall Hotel ... 16
Heronston Hotel ... 150
Herstmonceux Castle ... 34
Hertford Castle ... 80
Heybridge Hotel ... 80
Highbury ... 101
Highclere Castle ... 50
Highcliffe Castle ... 66
Highfield Hall Hotel ... 150
Highgate School ... 17
Hillockhead Steading ... 159
Hilton Puckrup Hall ... 101
Hilton St Ermin's ... 17
Hinchingbroke House ... 80
Hintlesham Hall ... 80
HMS Warrior ... 50
Holbeck Ghyll ... 137
Holdsworth House ... 129
Holker Hall ... 137
Holly Farm ... 151
Holme Pierrepont ... 101
Holt Castle ... 101
Honeyclub ... 34
Hook House Hotel ... 50
Hop Farm Country Park ... 34
Hopetoun House ... 159
Hopton Court ... 102
Hornsbury Mill ... 66
Horsley Hall ... 142
Horsted Place ... 35
Howard, The ... 17
Hoyle Court ... 129
Hulme Hall ... 117
Huntsham Court ... 67
Hurlingham Club ... 17
Hurstone House ... 67
Hyatt Carlton Tower ... 17
Hythe Imperial ... 35

I

Imperial Crown Hotel ... 129
Imperial War Museum ... 17
Inn on the Lake ... 35
Institute of Directors ... 17
Ipswich Guildhall ... 80
Ireley Grounds .. 102

INDEX

Ironmongers' Hall ... 18
Isle of Erisca ... 159

J

Jarvis Bowden Hall ... 102
Jarvis Comet Hotel ... 80
Jarvis Great Danes Hotel ... 35
John Rennie ... 50
Judge's Lodgings ... 80
Judges Hotel ... 143

K

Keele Conference Park ... 102
Kelham Hall ... 102
Kellie Castle ... 159
Kensington Palace ... 18
Kensington Town Hall ... 18
Kentwell Hall ... 81
Kenwick Park ... 81
Kenwood House ... 18
Keswick Country House ... 137
Kilhey Court Hotel ... 117
Kimbolton Castle ... 81
King's Lynn Town Hall ... 81
Kingfisher Barn ... 102
Kingsford Park Hotel ... 81
Kingston Maurward ... 67, x
Kingswood House Centre ... 18
Kington manor ... 67
Kintradwell Lodge ... 160
Kirkley Hall ... 143
Kirkton House ... 160
Kitley House ... 67
Knavesmire Manor Hotel ... 130
Knebworth Park ... 81
Knowle Restaurant ... 35
Knowsley Hall ... 118
Komedia ... 35

L

Lains Barn ... 50
Lainston House ... 50
Lake Country House Hotel ... 151
Lakeside Hotel ... 138
Lake Vyrnwy Hotel ... 151
Lakeside Moat House ... 82
Lancashire County Cricket Club ... 118
Landmark London Hotel ... 18
Lanesborough Hotel ... 19
Langar Hall ... 103
Langdale Chase Hotel ... 138
Langdon Court ... 67
Langland Court Hotel ... 151
Langley Castle ... 143
Langrish House ... 51
Langshott Manor ... 35
Langstone Cliff ... 67
Langtry Manor ... 68
Lanham Hilton ... 19

Lanteglos Country House Hotel ... 68
Larmer Tree Gardens ... 68
Laskill Farm ... 130
Lauderdale House ... 19, xiii
Lawn, The ... 82, vii
Layer Marney Tower ... 82
Le Gothique ... 19, xvi
Le Manoir Aux Quat'Saisons ... 51
Le Talbooth ... 89
Lea Marston Hotel ... 103
Leasowe Castle Hotel ... 118
Leeds Castle ... 36
Leeming House Hotel ... 138
Leez Priory ... 83
Leigh Court ... 68
Leigh Park ... 68
Leith's at London Zoo ... 19
Lennoxlove House ... 160, iii
Letchworth Hall Hotel ... 82
Lewtrenchard Manor ... 68
Linden Hall ... 143
Lingfield Park ... 51
Linthwaite House Hotel ... 138
Linton Springs ... 130
Little Thakeham ... 36
Llangoed hall ... 151
Llwyndu Farmhouse ... 151
Locko Park ... 103
London Palladium ... 19
London Planetarium ... 20
London Scottish Reg. HQ ... 20
Long Hall ... 36
Long Hall ... 51
Longhirst Hall ... 143
Longleat ... 68, iii
Longmynd Hotel ... 103
Lord Crewe Arms ... 143
Lordleaze Hotel ... 69
Lords of the Manor ... 103
Loseley Park ... 36
Low Wood Hotel ... 138
Luckanm park ... 69
Lygon Arms ... 103
Lyndhurst Park ... 52
Lynford Hall ... 82
Lythe Hill Hotel ... 36

M

Machin Conservatory ... 20
Madame Tussauds ... 20
Maerdy Cottages ... 151
Mains Hall ... 118
Maison Talbooth ... 83
Makeney Hall ... 103
Manchester Town Hall ... 118
Mandarin Oriental Hyde Park ... 20
Manderston ... 160
Mannington Estate ... 83
Manor Barn ... 36

Manor Hotel ... 69
Manor House ... 51
Manor House ... 69
Manor House Hotel (Leam'ton) ... 104
Manor House Hotel (Moreton) ... 104
Manor House Hotel ... 69
Manor House, The ... 130
Manor School of Fine Cuisine ... 104
Manor, The ... 37
Mansion House ... 37
Mansion House Hotel ... 69
Margam Country Park ... 152
Marine Hall ... 119
Mark Close Farmhouse ... 138
Market House ... 37
Marle Place ... 37
Marriot Goodwood Park ... 37
Marsden Mechanics Hall ... 130
Marshall Meadows ... 143
Marston Farm Hotel ... 104
Marwell Hotel ... 52
Marygreen Manor Hotel ... 83
Maunsel House ... 69
May Fair Intercontinental ... 20
Mayfair Club ... 20
Maynard Arms Hotel ... 104
Memorial Hall Theatre ... 152
Merchant Adventurers' Hall ... 130
Middle Flas Lodge ... 119
Middleton Hall Trust ... 104
Milford Hall ... 70
Mill at Croston ... 119
Mill House Hotel ... 52
Mirage at Milton Hall ... 138
Miskin Manor ... 152
Missenden Abbey ... 52
Mollington Banastre Hotel ... 119
Monk Bar Hotel ... 130
Monkey Island ... 52
Morritt Arms Hotel ... 143
Mosborough Hall Hotel ... 130
Mottisfont Abbey ... 52
Mottram Hall Hotel ... 119
Mount Ephraim Gardens ... 37
Muncaster Castle ... 139
Munstone House ... 105
Museum of Welsh Life ... 152

N

Nailcote Hall Hotel ... 105
Nanteos Mansion ... 152
Nash, The ... 105
National Maritime Museum ... 20
National Portrait Gallery ... 21
National Railway Museum ... 131, vi
Natural History Museum ... 21
Naworth Castle ... 139
Ness Botanic Gardens ... 119
Netherfield Place ... 37

Netherwood Hotel ... 139
New Connaught Rooms ... 21
New House Country Hotel ... 152
New Lanark Mill ... 160
New Mill Restaurant ... 52
New Place Management Centre ... 52
New Priory Hotel ... 105
Newcastle United FC ... 144
Newick Park ... 38, ix
Newland Hall ... 83
Newnham College ... 83
Newstead Abbey ... 105
Nizel's golf Club ... 38
Normanton Park Hotel ... 105
Northcote Manor ... 70
Northcote Manor ... 119
Northdown House ... 38
Northwood House ... 53
Norwood Park ... 105
Noseley Hall ... 106
Nunsmere Hall ... 119
Nutfield Priory ... 38

O

Oaklands Country House Hotel ... 83
Oakley court Hotel ... 53
Oakwell Hall ... 131
Oakwood House ... 39
Oatlands Park ... 38
Ockenden Manor ... 39
Officer's Mess ... 84
Offley Place ... 84
Old Bridge Hotel ... 84
Old Colehurst Manor ... 106
Old Hall Hotel ... 120
Old Lodge Hotel ... 131
Old Market ... 39
Old Mill, The ... 53
Old Municioal Buildings ... 70
Old Palace Lodge ... 84
Old Rectory ... 106, v
Old Rectory, The ... 84
Old Ship Hotel ... 39
Old Stable ... 139
Old Vicarage ... 106
Olde England Kiosk ... 120
One Gt George Street ... 21, iv
One Whitehall Place ... 21
Orangery at the Mill ... 39
Orangery, The ... 106
Oriel Plas Glyn-y-Weddw Gallery ... 152
Ormesby Hall ... 144
Orsett Hall Hotel ... 84
Orton Hall Hotel ... 84
Orwell Park ... 85
Orwell, The ... 120
Osterley Park ... 21
Oxenways ... 70

INDEX

P
Painshill Landscape Garden ... 39
Painswick Hotel ... 106
Painted Hall ... 22
Palace Pier ... 39
Park Hall Hotel ... 120
Park Lane Hotel ... 22
Parsonage Country House Hotel ... 85
Pear Tree at Purton ... 70
Pearse House ... 85
Peckforton Castle ... 120, xv
Peckover House ... 85
Pekes Manor House ... 39
Pengethley Manor Hotel ... 107
Penmere Manor ... 70
Penrhos Court Hotel ... 107
Penrhynhalen ... 152
Penshurst Place ... 40
Penventon Hotel ... 70
Petwood Hotel ... 85
Pewsey Vale Charter Cruises ... 53
Philpots Manor ... 40
Phyllis Court Club ... 53, i
Pickering Park ... 120
Pier at Harwich ... 85
Pink Geranium ... 86
Pittville Pump Room ... 107
Plas Dolguog Hotel ... 153
Plas Hafod ... 153
Plumber Manor ... 71, vi
Pockerley Manor .. 144
Polhawn Fort ... 71, xiv
Polo Club Marquee ... 107
Ponsbourne Park ... 86
Pontlands Park ... 86
Potter's Heron Hotel ... 53
Powder Mills Hotel ... 40
Powderham Castle ... 71
Prestbury House Hotel. ... 107
Prestwold Hall ... 107
Priory, The ... 86
Prston Priory Barn ... 86
Pump House ... 22
Pump Room & Roman Baths ... 71
Purbeck House Hotel ... 71
Putteridge Bury Conf Centre ... 86

Q
Quaffers Theatre Restaurant .. 121
Queen Elizabeth Hall ... 121
Queen's Hall ... 40
Queen's Hotel ... 107
Queen's House ... 22
Quex House ... 40

R
Raby House Hotel ... 121
Ramblers Country House Rest ...144
Ranger's House ... 22
Raven's Ait Island ... 22
Ravenswood ... 40
Ravensworth Arms Hotel ... 144
Ravenwood Hall ... 86
Read's Restaurant ... 41
Reaseheath College ... 121
Red Lion Hotel ... 131
Regent Banqueting Suite ... 23
Rembrandt Hotel ... 23
Renishaw Hall ... 108
Rhinefield House ... 53
Riber Hall ... 108
Richmond Gate Hotel ... 23
Richmond Hill Hotel ... 23
Richmond Theatre ... 23
Ringwood Hall Hotel ... 108
Risley Hall Hotel ... 108
Ritz Hotel ... 23
Rock Inn Hotel ... 131
Rogerthorpe Manor ... 131
Rombalds Hotel ... 131
Romney, Hythe & Dymchurch
 Railway ... 41
Roof Gardens ... 23, xvi
Rose-in-Vale Hotel ... 71
Rosehill House Hotel ... 121
Rossett Hall ... 153
Rowhill Grange ... 41
Rowley Manor Hotel ... 132
Rowton Castle ... 108
Rowton Hall Hotel ... 121
Royal Academy of Arts ... 23
Royal Armouries ... 54
Royal Berkshire ... 54
Royal Cambridge Hotel ... 87
Royal College of Art ... 24
Royal Geographical Society ... 24
Royal Northern College of
 Music ... 121
Royal Observatory ... 24
Royal Opera House ... 24
Royal Pavilion ... 41
Royal Society of Arts ... 24
Royal United Services Institute ... 24
Rudding Park House ... 132
Rudloe hall Hotel ... 72
Rudstone Walk ... 132
Runnymede Hotel ... 41
Rye Hill Farm ... 144

S
Saddleworth Hotel ... 122
Salde House Farm ... 109
Salford Hall Hotel ... 108
Salisbury Guildhall ... 72
Salomons ... 41, x
Samling at Dovenest ... 139
Sandhole Farm ... 122
Sandown Park ... 42
Saville Court ... 42
Scaitcliffe Hall Hotel ... 122
Scoles Manor Barns ... 72
Scone Place ... 161
Sconner House Inn ... 72
Searcy's ... 25
Seiont Manor ... 153
Sewerby Hall ... 132
Shakespeare's Houses ... 108
Shaw Hill Hotel ... 122
Sheen Mill Hotel ... 87
Sheffield Theatres ... 132
Sheffield Wednesday ... 132
Shendish Manor ... 87
Sheriff's Lodge ... 109
Shireburn Arms Hotel ... 122
Shotton Hall ... 144
Shrewsbury Castle ... 109
Shugborough Estate ... 109
Shursted Court ... 42
Shuttleworth ... 87
Silchester House ... 54, xv
Silvertone Circuit ... 109
Sir Christopher Wren's House ... 54
Skinner's Hall ... 25
Skirnish House ... 161
Smithills Coaching House ... 122
Soho House ... 25
Solberge Hall ... 133
Solent Hotel ... 54
Somerley ... 54
Somerleyton Hall ... 87
Somerton Court ... 72
Sopwell House ... 87
Soughton Hall ... 153
Spa Complex ... 133
Sparkles Hotel ... 122, xi
Sparth House Hotel ... 123
Spencer House ... 25
Spread Eagle Hotel ... 42
Springfield House Hotel ... 123
Springfoot Hall Hotel ... 163
Squerryes Court ... 42
SS Great Britain ... 72
St Augustine's ... 42
St Mary's Chambers ... 123
St Michael's Manor ... 88
St Nadrew's & Blackfriars Halls ... 88
Stables Restaurant ... 72
Stafford House ... 73
Staincliffe Hotel ... 144
Stanhill Court Hotel ... 42
Stansted Park ... 55
Stanwell House ... 55
Stapleford Park ... 110
Statham Lodge Hotel ... 123
Stationer's Hall ... 25
Stephen Joseph Theatre ... 133
Stirk House Hotel ... 123
Stirling Castle ... 161
Stoke Park ... 55
Stoke Rochford Hall ... 88
Stonebarrow Manor ... 73
Stonor Arms ... 55
Stowe House ... 55
Stragglethrope ... 88
Strathfillan Lodge ... 161
Strathtay House ... 161
Stratton House Hotel ... 110
Studley Priory ... 55
Sudbury House Hotel ... 56
Sudeley Castle ... 110
Summer Lodge Hotel ... 73
Sun Pavilion ... 133
Sussex Barn ... 88, viii
Sutton Hall ... 123
Sutton House ... 25, xvi
Swainston manor ... 56
Swallow Gosforth Park ... 145
Swallow Tree Gardens ... 153
Swallows Oast ... 43
Swan ... 88
Swarling Manor ... 43
Sweeney Hall Hotel ... 110
Swinfen Hall Hotel ... 110
Swiss Garden ... 88
Sychnant Pass House ... 153
Symondsbury Manor ... 73
Syon Park ... 26

T
Ta Mill ... 73
Tabley House ... 123
Talbot House ... 110
Tarantella Hotel ... 89
Tatton Park ... 123
Taunton School ... 73
Templeton ... 26
Tenterden Town Hall ... 43
Tewkesbury Park Hotel ... 111
Theatre Royal ... 145
Theobalds park ... 89
Thirlstane Castle ... 161
Thornbury Castle ... 111
Thornescroft Restaurant ... 111
Thurning Hall ... 89
Tillmouth Park Hotel ... 145
Tiverton Castle ... 74
Tone Dale House ... 74, xiii
Tottington Manor ... 43
Towcester Racecourse ... 111
Trafalgar Tavern ... 26
Tre-ysgawen Hall ... 154
Treasurer's House ... 133
Tree Tops Country House Hotel ... 124
Trentham Gardens ... 111
Treowen ... 154
Trevigue ... 74

INDEX

TS Queen Mary ... 26
Tuddenham Mill ... 89
Tufton Arms ... 139
Tullie House Museum ... 140
Tunnel House, The ... 111
Turkey Court ... 43
TuTu L'Auberge ... 43
Tuxedo Royale ... 145
Twein Bury Farm ... 89
Tylney Hall ... 56
Tyne Theatre ... 145
Tyrells Ford ... 56
Tythrop Park ... 56

U

Ullswater Hotel ... 140
Under the Clock Tower ... 133
Uttoxeter Racecourse ... 111

V

Vaulty Manor ... 90
Victoria & Albert Museum ... 26
Village Farm ... 145
Villiers Hotel ... 56
Vineyard at Stockcross ... 56

W

Wadenhoe House ... 90
Waldorf Hotel ... 26
Wallington Hall ... 146
Waltham Court Hotel ... 44
Walworth Castle hotel ... 146
Warmingham Grange ... 124
Warpool Court Hotel ... 154
Warwick Castle ... 112
Washington Old Hall ... 146
Waterford House ... 133
Watermen's Hall ... 27
Watermill Hotel ... 90
Waterton Park Hotel ... 134
Weald & Downland Museum ... 44
Weetwood Hall ... 134
Wellisford Farm House ... 74
Wellpark House ... 163
Wensum Lodge ... 90
Wentowrth Club ... 44
West Arms Hotel ... 154
West Park House ... 112
West Tower Country Hotel ... 124
West Usk Lighthouse ... 154
Weston Park ... 112
Westover hall ... 57
Whately Hall Hotel ... 57
Whirlow Brook Hall ... 134
Whitby Pavilion ... 134
White Hart Hotel ... 90
White Lion Inn ... 124
Whitehall ... 90
Whitley Hall Hotel ... 134

Whitwell Farm Cottages ... 74
Willington Hall Hotel ... 124
Wilton House ... 75
Wincham Hall Hotel ... 124
Winchester Guildhall ... 57
Winnington Hall ... 124
Winter Gardens Pavilion ... 75
Wivenhoe House Hotel ... 90
Woburn Abbey ... 91
Wolfscastle Country Inn ... 154
Wolterton Park ... 91
Wood Hall Hotel ... 134
Wood Norton Hall ... 112
Woodend Farm .. 113
Woodlands Manor ... 91
Woodlands Park Hotel ... 44
Woodstock Town Hall ... 57
Woolley Hall Conf Centre ... 134
Wortley Hall ... 134
Wrea Head Country House ... 135
Wroxton House .. 57
Wycombe Swan ... 57
Wye View Cottages ... 154
Wythenshawe Hall ... 125

Y

Yarlington House ... 75
Yenton Hotel ... 75
York House ... 27
Ystumgwern Hall Farm ... 155